Existentialism For Dummies®

Cheat Sheet

The Existentialists

The following are the core figures of existentialism....

- **Søren Kierkegaard (1813–1855):** The Danish son of a wealthy merchant, Kierkegaard never held an academic post, but he wrote voluminously. Seen by many as the founder of existentialism, particularly Christian existentialism.

  - **Key contributions:** His analysis of religious experience, and the first developed analysis of many key existential concepts, including absurdity, anguish, authenticity, the weight of responsibility you bear for your choices, and the importance of the irrational to human life

  - **Key works:** *Either/Or* (1843), *Fear and Trembling* (1843), *Concluding Unscientific Postscript* (1846), *The Sickness Unto Death* (1849)

- **Friedrich Nietzsche (1844–1900):** The devout son of a Lutheran minister in Prussia, Nietzsche eventually broke with the church to become one of its staunchest critics and another founding father of existentialism.

  - **Key contributions:** Announcing the death of God; changing the human project from that of *finding* value and meaning to *creating* value and meaning; returning philosophy to its Greek roots and the concern for the health of the soul

  - **Key works:** *Human, All Too Human* (1878–1880), *The Gay Science* (1882–1887), *Thus Spoke Zarathustra* (1883–1891), *Beyond Good and Evil* (1886), *The Genealogy of Morals* (1887), *Ecce Homo* (1888)

- **Martin Heidegger (1889–1976):** The most thoroughly academic of the existentialists. His involvement with the Nazi party couldn't stop his magnum opus from being one of the most influential books of the 20th century.

  - **Key contributions:** Turning existentialism into the systematic study of existence, particularly of *Dasein;* developing the concepts of *being thrown* and the *situated subject*

  - **Key work:** *Being and Time* (1927)

- **Jean-Paul Sartre (1905–1980):** Heidegger's most celebrated pupil and the leading French existentialist. Philosopher, novelist, playwright, and political activist, Sartre lived the existential mantra of engagement in the world.

  - **Key contributions:** Popularizing existentialism; summarizing the existential perspective in the phrase *existence precedes essence;* developing existentialism as a philosophy of freedom

  - **Key works:** *Nausea* (1938), *Being and Nothingness* (1943), *No Exit* (1943), *Existentialism is a Humanism* (1947), *Anti-Semite and Jew* (1947)

- **Simone de Beauvoir (1908–1986):** Seen by some as a mere mouthpiece of Sartre, de Beauvoir was a brilliant thinker in her own right, and she made significant contributions to literature, feminism, and existentialism.

  - **Key contributions:** Addressing the problem of other people; the development of a sophisticated existential ethics; grounding much of modern feminism in a largely existential framework

  - **Key works:** *The Blood of Others* (1945), *The Ethics of Ambiguity* (1947), *The Second Sex* (1949), *The Mandarins* (1954)

(continued)

For Dummies: Bestselling Book Series for Beginners

Existentialism For Dummies®

The Existentialists (continued)

- **Albert Camus (1913–1960):** In many respects, Camus is the conscience of existentialism. A deeply compassionate man, his philosophy was centered on what he considered the universe's greatest injustice — death. Ironically, he died at a relatively young age.

  - **Key contributions:** Writing the greatest and most accessible of all existential novels, *The Stranger;* developing existentialism as a philosophy of absurdity; infusing existential philosophy with compassion and genuine humanity

  - **Key works:** "The Myth of Sisyphus" (1942), *The Stranger* (1942), *The Plague* (1947), *The Rebel* (1951)

Key Existential Concepts

What's existentialism all about? The following should give you some idea:

- **Absurdity:** What human beings encounter when they come into contact with the world. Absurdity is brought about because the human instinct to seek order and meaning is frustrated by the refusal of the world to be orderly or meaningful.

- **Anxiety:** Kierkegaard says, "Anxiety is the dizziness of freedom." You feel anxiety because you recognize that you and you alone are responsible for your actions. This produces the two-sided feeling of simultaneous dread and exhilaration.

- **Alienation:** The sense that you're a stranger in the world, or a stranger to yourself. Many aspects of existence can be alienating. One of the primary sources is absurdity. Ironically, the stories and systems developed by philosophy and religion to address that absurdity can be just as alienating.

- **Existence precedes essence:** Sartre's phrase to describe the existential situation humans find themselves in. It refers to the fact that when you're born, you have no meaning, no purpose, no definition. Human beings exist first, and only later define themselves.

- **The Übermensch:** The word Nietzsche uses to refer to his ideal human being. Literally "overman," the word reflects the importance in his philosophy of overcoming — overcoming traditional values, overcoming the herd mentality, and, most importantly, overcoming yourself. You overcome these things so that you might attain something greater. Nietzsche's Übermensch is an unconventional creator of values, a joyous free spirit, and one who embraces the earth instead of pining away for heaven.

- **The death of God:** The death of the notion that belief in God alone, or belief in any religious or philosophical system, is sufficient to provide human beings with the meaning, purpose, and definition they crave. It's the recognition that, because no external system can provide you with the answers, you must take responsibility for providing them yourself.

- **Subjectivity:** Your first-person perspective on the world, including the needs, desires, and emotions that accompany that perspective. The existentialists take this as a valid and important starting point for genuinely human endeavors. This can be contrasted with the scientific mindset, which always starts with objectivity — seeing people in impersonal, objective terms without emotion or appreciation for their individual point of view.

For Dummies: Bestselling Book Series for Beginners

Existentialism
FOR
DUMMIES®

by Christopher Panza
and Gregory Gale

WILEY

Wiley Publishing, Inc.

Existentialism For Dummies®

Published by
Wiley Publishing, Inc.
111 River St.
Hoboken, NJ 07030-5774
www.wiley.com

WILEY

About the Authors

Christopher Panza was born and raised in New York. After struggling unsuccessfully to figure out the meaning of his existence as a young teenager, he decided to go to the State University of New York at Purchase, where he could major in philosophy and literature and figure out all the answers. He got his degree, but no final answers to the meaning of life. After college, he spent a few more years working in business and hammering away at that meaning-of-life question. In frustration, he decided to then attend the University of Connecticut to pursue his master's and doctoral degrees (in philosophy) in order to finally get an answer. Once again, he accumulated more degrees but arrived no closer to the meaning of life. So he figured he'd at least put his degrees to work and has worked as a professor in the Philosophy and Religion Department at Drury University, in Springfield, Missouri, since 2002. He received the University's Excellence in Teaching Award in 2004, which is surprising given that he tries to infect students with the same frustrating desire to seek answers to unanswerable questions. In addition to his interests in existentialism, Chris has interests in (and teaches on) a number of other topics such as ethics, Confucianism, free will, and modern philosophy. Chris is also married and has one three-year-old daughter, Parker, with one more addition to the family on the way. Chris is hoping to infect his own children one day with the same desire to investigate life that has long invigorated him and as a result made life an interesting and mysterious experience.

Gregory Gale discovered existentialism at the tender age of 15 and has been dancing over the abyss ever since. After receiving his BA in Philosophy from the Colorado College and his MA in Philosophy from the University of Connecticut, he went wandering the earth in search of his Dasein. He has spent most of the last 15 years teaching everything from Jean-Paul Sartre to Dr. Seuss, and prides himself on making difficult material accessible to everyone. Most recently, his search for meaning, value, and a really good bourbon took him across the country in a beat-up Toyota Tercel. He wound up in Las Vegas, Nevada where he lives, works, writes, and pursues his philosophical investigations into the existential significance of Elvis Impersonators, Showgirls, and the Poker Philosophy of Doyle Brunson.

Dedication

Christopher Panza: To my wife, Christie, and my daughter, Parker, for their never ending source of love and support. Also to my mother Janice, my father Tony, and my sister Amy, all of whom have endured having a philosopher in the family for far too long.

Gregory Gale: I'd like to dedicate this book, with much love, to my father, Anthony Lloyd Gale, and my mother, Rosemary Gale. From the depth and breadth of your humanity, I learned to measure all things. I also dedicate this book to my Uncle Steve. Nietzsche said that style is a great art. You were my favorite artist.

Authors' Acknowledgments

Christopher Panza: My primary acknowledgement is to my wife, Christie, and my daughter, Parker. Both of them had to endure many months of watching me type away at a computer instead of engaging in family-oriented projects and plans. Christie has been very understanding and supportive of this project, not to mention graciously agreeing to read and edit early drafts of a few chapters. I'd also like to thank Lisa Esposito, my department head, for helping to arrange work assignments (and for taking some on herself) so that this project could be completed. Also I'd like to thank Jason Swadley, a former student, for commenting on some early chapter drafts. Lastly, I'd like to thank Charlie Ess for agreeing to serve as the technical editor for this book and providing many good and insightful comments on how to improve the draft.

Gregory Gale: There are too many people to thank, and I apologize in advance to anyone I may have forgotten. First off, thanks to the folks at Wiley Publishing for making this such a positive experience, and for all the hard work to make *Existentialism For Dummies* the best book it could be. Thanks to our project editor, Tim Gallan, for all his patience, hard work, and clear direction, which has consistently kept me on the right path. Our copy editor, Sarah Faulkner, was magnificent and often knew what I was trying to say better than I did. Our acquisitions editor, Michael Lewis, helped us distill a massive subject matter into a workable project and get it ready for prime time. Charlie Ess kept us honest by policing our content and making sure we knew what we were talking about. The book is deeper and truer for his efforts. I am deeply grateful to you all for your assistance.

I owe my involvement in this project to Adam Potthast; for getting the ball rolling I am deeply grateful. Many other friends and family members also made this possible through their support and criticism. In particular, Andrea and JJ Christensen, Tara Vazquez, David Maddow, and Lorraine Miller threw themselves into the project and were a tireless source of interest, questions, encouragement, and thoughtful criticism. Each of you has contributed to this work and I appreciate each and every one of you.

Finally, I want to thank the teachers who helped make philosophy and existentialism essential parts of my life. Fr. Richard M. Jacobs got me hooked on philosophy when he introduced me to Plato at 14, and used Theology class to open my mind rather than close it. Dr. Clark "Doc" Thayer immersed me in existentialism and postmodernism. For the former I thank you, for the latter I forgive you. Thanks also to John Riker for giving me the courage to follow my heart and live the philosophy I was studying. Finally, I must thank too many professors to name in the Philosophy Department at the University of Connecticut for pushing me harder than I've ever been pushed; for teaching me that even analytic philosophy can be done with passion, flair, love, and joy; but most of all, for your understanding when I decided it was time for me to go. Thank you.

And special thanks to my brilliant and tireless partner, Chris Panza. I could not have asked for better. Hey, Chris, I think we've almost got that boulder up the hill. . . .

Publisher's Acknowledgments

We're proud of this book; please send us your comments through our Dummies online registration form located at www.dummies.com/register/.

Some of the people who helped bring this book to market include the following:

Acquisitions, Editorial, and Media Development

Senior Project Editor: Tim Gallan

Acquisitions Editor: Michael Lewis

Senior Copy Editor: Sarah Faulkner

Editorial Program Coordinator: Erin Calligan Mooney

Technical Editor: Charles Ess, PhD

Editorial Manager: Michelle Hacker

Editorial Assistants: Joe Niesen, Jennette ElNaggar, David Lutton

Cover Photos: © Steve Bloom Images/ JupiterImages

Cartoons: Rich Tennant (www.the5thwave.com)

Art Coordinator: Alicia B. South

Composition Services

Project Coordinator: Lynsey Stanford

Layout and Graphics: Stacie Brooks, Reuben W. Davis, Melissa K. Jester, Stephanie D. Jumper, Tobin Wilkerson, Christine Williams,

Proofreaders: John Greenough, Kathy Simpson

Indexer: Galen Schroeder

Publishing and Editorial for Consumer Dummies

Diane Graves Steele, Vice President and Publisher, Consumer Dummies

Joyce Pepple, Acquisitions Director, Consumer Dummies

Kristin A. Cocks, Product Development Director, Consumer Dummies

Michael Spring, Vice President and Publisher, Travel

Kelly Regan, Editorial Director, Travel

Publishing for Technology Dummies

Andy Cummings, Vice President and Publisher, Dummies Technology/General User

Composition Services

Gerry Fahey, Vice President of Production Services

Debbie Stailey, Director of Composition Services

Contents at a Glance

Introduction 1

Part 1: Introducing Existentialism 7
Chapter 1: What Is Existentialism? 9
Chapter 2: The Big Names of Existentialism 15
Part II: The Fundamental Problem: God Is Dead 23
Chapter 3: If God Is Dead, Is Life Meaningless? 25
Chapter 4: Anxiety, Dread, and Angst in an Empty World 47

Part III: Living a Meaningful Life
in a Meaningless World 109
Chapter 5: The Challenge of Absurdity and Authenticity 73
Chapter 6: Understanding Our Unique Way of Existing in the World 111
Chapter 7: Not Tonight, Honey: Why We Need More Passion in Our Lives 131
Chapter 8: Sartre's Existentialism: Learning to Cope with Freedom 157
Chapter 9: Finding Authenticity: Facing Death, Conscience, and Time 179
Chapter 10: Kierkegaard: The Task of Being a Religious Existentialist 203
Chapter 11: Nietzsche: Mastering the Art of Individuality 235

Part IV: The Enduring Impact of Existentialism 271
Chapter 12: Fear and Loathing in Existential Politics 273
Chapter 13: Existentialism and Other Schools of Philosophical Thought ... 297
Chapter 14: Doing Psychology the Existential Way 309

Part V: Part of Tens 323
Chapter 15: Ten Great Existential Movies 325
Chapter 16: Ten Great Works of Existential Literature 341

Index 355

Table of Contents

Introduction **1**

About This Book 1

Conventions Used in This Book....................................2

Foolish Assumptions...3

How This Book Is Organized 4

    Part I: Introducing Existentialism 4

    Part II: The Fundamental Problem: God Is Dead............4

    Part III: Living a Meaningful Life in a Meaningless World 5

    Part IV: The Enduring Impact of Existentialism 5

    Part V: The Part of Tens...................................5

Icons Used in This Book 5

Where to Go from Here 6

Part I: Introducing Existentialism **7**

Chapter 1: What Is Existentialism? **9**

Existentialism Is a Philosophy 10

The Top Ten Existential Themes..................................12

Existentialism's Place in the History of Philosophy.................12

Chapter 2: The Big Names of Existentialism..................**15**

Kierkegaard Makes Philosophy Personal 16

Nietzsche Declares that God Is Dead 17

Heidegger Systematizes Existentialism 18

The French Popularize a Growing Movement......................19

Contemporary Existentialists Keep the Movement Going 21

Part II: The Fundamental Problem: God Is Dead........... **23**

Chapter 3: If God Is Dead, Is Life Meaningless?................**25**

Who Died? What the Death of God Means 26

    Just an observation, not a celebration............................27

    The death of absolute systems of thought.......................27

Killing the God Called Reason....................................30

    What reason is all about 30

    Where's the human element?..................................31

Plato: The good stuff is elsewhere..32
Kant: The world isn't knowable 35
The Death of God and Religion 37
How Christianity lost its mojo..37
Being religious isn't a "Get out of jail free" card......................39
Science Becomes Its Own Religion...40
The scientific worldview: Science as God................................41
Science can't replace God after all 42
So What Have You Lost If God Is Dead?...43
No easy answers: Rejecting all absolutes 44
The baby with the bathwater: Meaning, truth, and value 44
The danger of nihilism 45

Chapter 4: Anxiety, Dread, and Angst in an Empty World..........47
Are Emotions Key to Understanding Life?......................................48
Emotions: Not traditionally valued by philosophers 49
Emotion: A source of insight in existentialism.........................51
Recognizing the Insights That Moods Provide 54
Your moods disclose how you exist 54
Moods are the flavors of life...56
You're always tuned in to the world 58
Everyday moods and existential moods...................................59
Anxiety: The Existentialists' Favorite Mood 60
Distinguishing anxiety from fear..61
Having anxiety means you're an
individual, like it or not 63
Sensing nothingness everywhere 65
Revealing the dizziness of freedom...68
A love-hate relationship with anxiety 70

**Part III: Living a Meaningful Life
in a Meaningless World.. 109**

Chapter 5: The Challenge of Absurdity and Authenticity 73
Absurdity 101 74
Defining absurdity..74
Everyday conceptions of absurdity...75
Understanding the Irrationality
of the World..76
What makes up the world...76
Different ways of seeing order in the world 77
Like it or not, the world is entirely irrational........................79

Viewing Irrationality from a Human Perspective 80
How you can come to see accidents everywhere 81
    You're addicted to imposing order on the world 83
    The absurdity of imposing order on the disorderly 84
Authenticity 101: Striving to Be Genuine 86
    The connection between authenticity and genuineness 87
    Everybody digs authenticity 88
    Matching just the right template 89
    Understanding authenticity as representing 90
    Authentic people: In the driver's seat and in control 92
Taking Stock: Who Am I? How Can I Be Authentic? 92
    Why existentialists reject worldly authenticity 93
    Embracing existential authenticity: Seeing the
      kind of being that you are 94
    The central truth about who you
      are: Humans are absurd beings 95
    The many truths of your absurd nature 96
Authenticity 102: Living Inauthentically Means Running Away 98
    Inauthentic people take the
      path of least resistance 99
    Suicide is not the answer 100
    Covering up the truth won't save you 102
Embracing Absurdity: "The Myth of Sisyphus" 103
    Sisyphus and his punishment 103
    Rebel without a cause . . . but a smile 104

**Chapter 6: Understanding Our Unique Way of
Existing in the World 111**
Different Ways to Investigate Existence 112
Investigating the meaning of existence 112
Knowing existence means knowing you 113
    Science: Analyzing life from the outside 114
    Viewing life from the inside out 115
Living in Your Everyday World 116
    The nuts and bolts of your life 117
    Space, the final frontier of life 118
    Meaning: Life's requirement 120
    Life's a workshop, and you need tools 121
    Doing without thinking: Look, no hands! 122
Coming to Grips with Who You Are 124
    Sensing others all around you 125
    You're everyone and no one 126
    Falling away . . . from yourself 127
    Being authentic: Determining the shape of your life 129

Chapter 7: Not Tonight, Honey: Why We Need
More Passion in Our Lives **131**

Seeing Passion as a Life of Engagement.................132
    Freedom reveals the individual 133
    Cultivating a sense of passion..........................134
    It's not what you do but how you do it.........................135
Truly Passionate Life Finds a Cause.........................136
    Your cause should express your life.......................137
    You should commit to a cause worth dying for...........................138
    Choices must include mystery and risk........................140
Truth Is Passionate Living......................................142
    What is truth?..........................142
    Truth is subjective.........................143
    The paradox of living in truth 145
    Making truth yours alone........................146
    The crowd is untruth.........................148
Why Modern Life Drains You of Passion 150
    The present age is so dull.........................151
    Kierkegaard's attack on the media......................153
    The Internet: A modern passion-killer?......................155

Chapter 8: Sartre's Existentialism: Learning
to Cope with Freedom **157**

What Does It Mean to Be Free?.........................158
    Freedom means always having a choice......................159
    Free choice means free action 160
    Our most basic choice is living........................161
    What Sartre Means by "Existence Precedes Essence".................164
    A human being is not a watch 164
    Being human means being free 165
Condemned to Be Free (And Responsible) Whether
    You Like It or Not.........................167
    The inescapability of choice 169
    You bear sole responsibility for your choices.....................170
Freedom Is So Important Because It Brings Hope.....................172
    Free choice creates value and meaning........................173
    How your choices affect you.........................174
    How your choices affect the world........................176
    tFreedom is the highest good........................177

Chapter 9: Finding Authenticity: Facing Death,
Conscience, and Time **179**

Embracing Death as the Key to Life 180
    Confronting death is essential 180
    Keeping an eye on the inevitable:
        The Grim Reaper is up ahead 181
    Making choices becomes monumentalin light of death 183
    Meeting death alone: It's inevitable........................185

Conscience Nags You to Be Yourself 186
The voice of conscience is always there 187
Conscience: You talking to you about you 187
Face it: You're guilty! 188
Chin up! Face your limitations! 189
The Importance of Living in Time 191
The everyday view: You're in time 192
The existential view: Lived time 193
Pulling Yourself Together through Time 194
You always exist in the future 195
. . . And you always exist in the past 196
Joining future and past . . . in the present 200

**Chapter 10: Kierkegaard: The Task of Being a
Religious Existentialist 203**
or Not to Be Your Self 204
The self: A tension of opposites 205
The hard work of being a self: Bringing together
polar opposites 206
Being a self before God 207
Despair: Attempting toescape your true self 207
Despair: The path to sin 209
Inauthentic Life Stages: Aesthetic and Ethical 210
The aesthetic stage: Life without choices 210
The ethical stage: Finding your meaning within roles 216
Fear and Trembling: Embracing the Religious Life 222
The strange story of Abraham and Isaac 223
Why faith must be offensive 229
Why Abraham is an existential hero 231
The problem with contemporary Christians: They lack faith......231

Chapter 11: Nietzsche: Mastering the Art of Individuality 235
Investigating Who You Are 236
You can take charge of who you are 237
You're a sea of desire 238
You're biased: You can't help it; it's just you! 239
You can change: Analyzing the false
belief that you're a fixed object 239
You can be fooled by your own language 240
Understanding the Self As a Chaos Made Orderly 241
Getting a handle on your unorganized desires 241
Striving for selfhood through self-mastery 243
Being an Individual Means Being Noble 245
Nobles are in control of themselves 245
Nobles love themselves 247
Nobles have contempt for nonindividuals 248
Relishing Change As Essential to a Noble Life 249

Nobles embrace change..249
Nobles reject dogma...250
The noble life is a path, not a destination 251
Nobility Means Striving for Power..252
Life is all about power...252
True power seeks to develop internal beauty 254
Powerful nobles ignore neighbors................................255
Nobles cultivate friendships with their enemies.......................256
Nobles live dangerously..257
Being a Slave: Rejecting Individuality through Hatred 257
Coping with oppression by changing
    your interpretation of the situation...............................258
Learning to see through the eyes of hate 359
Using hatred to creatively reinterpret the world 260
Letting resentment take control of your life 261
Interpreting Christianity as just more slave talk 263
Mediocrity of the Herd: Rejecting Individuality through Conformity...264
The crowd takes away self-control................................265
The crowd represents the voice of the weak...........................266
The crowd preaches equality and mediocrity.........................267
Beyond good and evil: Breaking away from the crowd 269

Part IV: The Enduring Impact of Existentialism 271

Chapter 12: Fear and Loathing in Existential Politics 273
Are Existentialists Political?..274
Some are political; some aren't..275
Does existentialism lead to specific politics?...........................276
Does Existentialism Lead to Evil?..278
Real and Imaginary Flirtations with Nazism.................................279
Nietzsche wasn't a Nazi!..280
The Heidegger problem: A Nazi in the family............................286
Viva la Revolution! The French Left 290
The French political scene 290
Which Left is right? Sartre chooses Communism......................292
Camus rejects violence 293
Politics of liberation versus politics of life 294

Chapter 13: Existentialism and Other Schools
of Philosophical Thought 297
Existentialism's Run in the 20th Century 297
Existentialism and Modern Philosophy: A Strained Relationship.........298
Two branches of modern philosophy:
    Analytic and Continental..299

Where existentialism fits in 301
Postmodernism: Existentialism's bratty stepchild......................302
Existentialism and American philosophy................................305
Existentialism and Philosophies of the Oppressed................................306
Alienation and otherness..306
Racism as inauthenticity..307

Chapter 14: Doing Psychology the Existential Way 309

Points of Contact: Existentialism Meets Psychology...........................310
Stressing the importance of human uniqueness 310
Putting the patient's world front and center................................311
Focusing on freedom and anxiety..312
Seeing the people as goal directed..312
Finding meaning is central to your existence 313
The Existential Psychologists 314
Rollo May: Reconnecting with existence................................314
Carl Rogers: Fully functional individuals................................316
Viktor Frankl: Embracing the need for meaning...........................319

Part V: Part of Tens 323

Chapter 15: Ten Great Existential Movies 325

Ikiru (1952) 326
The Seventh Seal (1957) 327
Apocalypse Now (1979) 328
Blade Runner (1982)..330
Crimes and Misdemeanors (1989)..331
Leaving Las Vegas (1995) 332
Pleasantville (1998) 333
Fight Club (1999) 335
Stranger Than Fiction (2006) 337

Chapter 16: Ten Great Works of Existential Literature 341

Hamlet, by William Shakespeare 342
Notes from the Underground, by Feodor Dostoevsky......................343
The Death of Ivan Ilych, by Leo Tolstoy................................344
The Trial, by Franz Kafka..345
The Stranger, by Albert Camus..347
No Exit, by Jean-Paul Sartre 348
The Blood of Others, by Simone de Beauvoir.............................349
Waiting for Godot, by Samuel Beckett..350
Interview with the Vampire, by Anne Rice................................351
Run with the Hunted, by Charles Bukowski................................353

Index 355

Introduction

. . . .

*E*xistentialism is the philosophy of existence, of the nature of human existence, its value, and its meaning. Because questions about existence have very little interest when people exist as rotting corpses, existentialism is really the philosophy that studies what it is to be alive. It isn't defined so much by any unified answer to this question, but by the way in which it rejects traditional answers to questions concerning the meaning and value of human life, and the way that it insists that such questions are real and that the lack of any real answer is a problem. Existentialists, both theist and atheist, reject not only traditional religious systems that attempt to systematically provide pat answers, but also the possibility of any ultimate answers. They insist that even if a God and a heaven exist, the meaning of this life and how you should live will always be open questions, requiring decisions you must face as an individual. Because existentialism considers the questions to be important, it seeks a way of living with the fact that no answers will be forthcoming.

The French existentialist Albert Camus says the fundamental question of philosophy is that of suicide, of whether life is worth living. Although not all the existentialists approach the question from this exact vantage point, it illustrates a widely held theme — while traditional religious and ethical systems ask, "How *should* I live?" the existentialist's more fundamental question is, "How *can* I live?" If life is meaningless, if the inherited stories aren't valid, how can you even approach the question of how you should live? How can human beings hungry for meaning live and flourish without giving in to despair when no meaning is provided to them?

About This Book

Although this book is about the philosophy of existentialism and about the philosophers who developed it, it isn't a book for philosophers. It's for you.

We try to strike a balance in writing and structure. We want to meet the needs of the student who's encountering these issues in a classroom setting, as well as the needs of the interested layperson who's encountering them in real life. For both, we provide what we hope is an easy-to-read introduction in which we attempt to explain the often-complex theories of the existentialists in plain, easy-to-understand language.

Existentialism is a philosophy that attempts to be relevant to real people and real lives, and we attempt to present the material in such a way as to highlight its relevance to your own life. We expect that many of the ideas we present here will resonate with your own thoughts and concerns. Although we encourage you to dive into the rich world of existential philosophy, literature, and even movies, none of that is required. Each chapter and each section stands on its own, independent not only of the other chapters, but also of any knowledge of existentialism or philosophy in general. Everyone's welcome; come on in!

Conventions Used in This Book

Philosophy is a very precise discipline, and writing about philosophy normally requires endless caveats and multiple subclauses and clarifications that would make even a lawyer's head swim. To make a book about the existentialists readable, we have to gloss over certain distinctions, and to keep you from hunting us down and killing us, we avoid endlessly bringing up the fine print. But with that in mind, we use the following conventions throughout the book:

- **The use of the term *existentialism:*** Many people reject the notion of a unified school of thought by this name. One of the things the writers we deal with tend to have in common is that they reject the usefulness of -isms and would reject the notion that they were part of one. We feel it makes perfect sense to speak of existentialism as a school of thought, a philosophy, or even a movement as long as you understand that we aren't using the term to imply a definitive statement of what existentialism is or of what its proponents accept or believe. Rather, when we talk about existentialism, we refer to a set of overlapping themes and concerns that unite what we recognize are often, in many respects, vastly different philosophical positions.

- **The use of the term *existentialists:*** Each of the writers we deal with was fiercely independent, and many of them explicitly rejected the label. Again, we feel each of the philosophers we discuss in the book qualifies as an existentialist, by virtue of addressing a common family of concerns.

- **Phrases like "the existentialists believed" and "existentialism holds":** To the extent that existentialism exists at all, it exists at the intersection of, and in the overlapping content of, the thoughts of these various philosophers. Sometimes when presenting the big picture, however, we gloss over the differences among them. When we use phrases like these, you can be assured that a general tendency of those we call existentialists is to believe some version of the idea we ascribe to them as a group.

Be warned, however, that with just about any general statement about this group, at least one member of the group will disagree entirely; the rest likely will agree in some sense but disagree on the fine print. Never assume from statements like these that all the existentialists believe *exactly* that in *exactly* that way.

✔ **One philosopher at a time:** What the existentialists have in common are themes and concerns, such as anguish, passion, individuality, and death. In approaching these themes, we usually emphasize one philosopher at a time. For example, we focus on Nietzsche when dealing with individuality and Kierkegaard when dealing with passion. We feel this format has the advantage of focusing the discussions on these topics while giving you quality time with each philosopher. These discussions are a good way to help you get your head around the subject and understand one philosopher's point of view. Just don't assume that the philosopher we choose represents the final or definitive word of the existentialists on that topic.

✔ **The use of both past and present tense:** Like all important movements, existentialism was both of its time and timeless. It reached its zenith in the past, and its greatest thinkers lived (and died) in the past. We give you this kind of historical information in past tense, but because existentialism is still very much alive for us, we refer to its themes and the writings of the great philosophers in the present tense.

Foolish Assumptions

Philosophers are trained to avoid assumptions, but Nietzsche said to live dangerously, so we went nuts. Here are some of the things we assume about you. We assume at least one of these things is true about you; if even one is true, this book was written for you:

✔ You don't wear black all the time, and you have better things to do than spend all your time drinking coffee, chain-smoking, and cursing an impotent God (unlike your coauthors, Chris and Greg).

✔ You've heard the word *existentialism* thrown around a lot but aren't really sure what it is and what it's all about. You're curious, and you want to know more.

✔ You're a student enrolled in a class, and you need to learn about existentialism as a whole, a particular thinker, and/or a particular existential theme.

✔ You know about one or more of the existentialists, and you want to learn more about him or her and the movement he or she was part of.

✔ You're interested in art, film, literature, history, cultural studies, philosophy, psychology, European history, or one of the numerous other fields of human endeavor upon which existentialism has had an impact, and you want to go to the source to learn more about it.

✔ You've at some point questioned the meaning of your life or how to live, or you've wondered whether there's anything more.

✔ You're a Christian, Hindu, atheist, Jew, or agnostic, or you have any other belief or concern about what's ultimately true and ultimately real.

✔ You saw that Brad Pitt movie in which a bunch of guys beat one another up and want to know what the point was.

✔ You exist.

How This Book Is Organized

We arranged this book so that you can dive in at any point. Taking a class on Sartre? Start with Chapter 8. Kierkegaard? Go straight to Chapter 10. For those who want a general overview, we tried to structure the book so that it also tells a larger story. The book is broken up into five parts, each of which contains a number of chapters covering a related set of topics. You may consider reading Part I to get your feet wet and then skipping around to the subjects that interest you. Any way you feel like doing it works!

Part I: Introducing Existentialism

In this part, we give you a short historical introduction to existentialism and its major thinkers. Discover who they were and why they were so important to its development.

Part II: The Fundamental Problem: God Is Dead

In many respects existentialism is a response to a collection of problems that confront you as you try to live a fulfilling and meaningful life. The chapters in this part deal with recognizing and defining these problems. We examine Nietzsche's statement that God is dead (a statement that's about far more than just God!) as the fundamental statement of the challenges you face. We investigate how God was killed, who's to blame, and what it really means.

People feel horrible about this statement and what it means, so we discuss those feelings. Have a good cry if you want, but it isn't necessary. Finally, we discuss what kind of world you face now that God has turned up deceased and why the problem this statement represents exists not just for atheists, but for believers as well.

Part III: Living a Meaningful Life in a Meaningless World

If the existentialists just moped and cried over everything, they'd never have been invited to any parties. Much of the existentialists' work was devoted to finding ways of living, and even flourishing, in a world with the problems we describe in Part II. Part III is a collection of these methods, insights, and solutions. Consider it our description of their how-to guide to healthy and satisfying living.

Part IV: The Enduring Impact of Existentialism

In this part we examine the impact existentialism has had on philosophy and psychology. We examine why the impact on psychology has been so profound, why its impact on academic philosophy hasn't been altogether great, and what this means for its overall legacy and significance.

Part V: The Part of Tens

Every *For Dummies* book has a Part of Tens, and we wouldn't dream of leaving it out of this one. For ours, we decided to focus on what makes existentialism so accessible and relevant — namely, the way it finds its way (intentionally or unintentionally) into nonphilosophical, popular work. So we list ten terrific books and ten great films that deal with existential themes.

Icons Used in This Book

This icon alerts you to items that are particularly important for understanding what existentialism is all about. Pay close attention to these sections and keep them in mind while you read other sections. Although the text attached to this icon isn't strictly necessary for understanding other parts of the book, it often resonates with things you find elsewhere. Keeping text marked with this icon in mind can lead to a deeper, richer understanding of what the existentialists are up to.

This icon alerts you to common confusions and misconceptions about existentialism and to information that will help you avoid these pitfalls. Read these sections carefully to make sure you have the right idea about what the existentialists are saying.

This icon alerts you to direct quotes from the existentialists or other great philosophers. These quotes not only give you the philosopher's ideas straight from the horse's mouth, so to speak, but also help you get some of the color and flavor of the rich writing style many of these thinkers employ.

Existentialism is a complicated business, but it's also very personal. Many of the existentialists used personal anecdotes to bring the subject down to earth and make it more immediate. We try to do the same. Whenever we relay one of the existentialists' anecdotes or one of ours, you see this icon.

We use this icon when we want you to think about a discussion point as it relates to your own life. Or sometimes we want you to stop and really decide whether what we're discussing has merit. It's our way of saying, "Take a moment."

Sometimes understanding something difficult becomes a piece of cake when you look at it from a certain angle or think about it in a certain way. We use this icon to alert you to useful pointers that help get you oriented so you know the best way to approach this material.

Where to Go from Here

This book is arranged like an existential smorgasbord. Go where you want; take what you want! If you know nothing about existentialism at all, you may want to take a look at the first chapter. To find out who the players are and what they were doing, check out Chapter 2. Or try a sampling from Part II to see what problems existentialism is trying to tackle. Or just jump into a chapter that looks interesting. Don't be afraid; you don't need to know any of the other stuff to understand what's going on.

If you're a student, check out the Table of Contents to see what chapters deal with the thinkers or issues you're studying. Don't see what you're looking for? Need more? Check out the Index, and find out everywhere we talk about Nietzsche, anguish, or lasagna. Most of the major names have at least one chapter devoted to their thinking, but they also crop up in various other places.

So where do you go from here? As Sartre might say, you're free, so choose!

Part I
Introducing Existentialism

The 5th Wave   By Rich Tennant

"It's called that because we feel that people are entirely free and therefore responsible for what they make of themselves and for themselves. Now, do you still want the double anchovy with the fried mozzarella strips?"

In this part . . .

Many ideas past and present are described as existential, but we use "existentialism" to refer specifically to a philosophical movement that came about in Europe in the late-19th century and achieved its zenith in the early- to mid-20th century. Here we put that movement into its philosophical and historical context, and introduce the individual thinkers who developed existential philosophy. Because these thinkers were so diverse and idiosyncratic, using the term "existentialist" to describe them all is somewhat controversial. We discuss the commonalities in their thinking that link them all together, if somewhat loosely, and the individual contributions of each philosopher that make him or her so important to existentialism.

Chapter 1

What Is Existentialism?

In This Chapter

▶ Discovering what existentialism is

▶ Understanding that existentialism is a philosophy

▶ Seeing existentialism in an historical context

xistentialism is the philosophy that makes life possible.

As incomplete as this statement seems, when you understand what it means you're well on your way to understanding what existentialism is all about and what the existentialists saw themselves as doing.

But if existentialism is the philosophy that makes life possible, you may ask why you need a philosophy for that. Doesn't oxygen do a pretty good job? Yes, quite good — if all you want to do is breathe. According to the existentialists, however, you want to live a full and authentic human life, a rewarding and fulfilling life that embraces your human dignity. For that, they say, you need, at a minimum, oxygen *and* a healthy dose of existentialism. To understand why, it may help to consider that many philosophies come about as responses to a problem. Necessity is, after all, the mother of invention.

On a very general level, the problem the existentialists were concerned with was the problem of meaning. Human beings crave meaning; they crave an orderly universe that they can make sense of. When you find that the universe isn't going to cooperate, when you discover that the stories you've told yourself in an attempt to force it to have meaning have ceased to work, you feel like you're a stranger in the world.

This historical circumstance is precisely the one that the existentialists found themselves in. As the scientific and Industrial Revolutions came to a head in the 19th century, and society became increasingly secularized, the traditional social order underwent radical change in a very short time. During this period, people began to feel disconnected from the traditional belief systems that had helped them make sense of the world and of their lives. In these conditions, people may not literally commit suicide, but a kind of spiritual death — a spiritual suicide — becomes a very real danger. It occurs when people give up to resignation and surrender in the face of what they see as the pointlessness of their existence.

Existentialism is the philosophy that recognizes this problem and attempts to address it. If you want to spruce up the description we start with, you might say that existentialism is the philosophy that makes an authentically human life possible in a meaningless and absurd world.

Because the existentialists were fiercely independent and differed widely in both their precise analyses of this problem and in the details of their responses, presenting a more detailed definition — one that's both illuminating and accurate — is hard to do. What unites the existentialists, besides the problems of meaning and existence with which they all wrestled, is a series of themes and concerns that informed their discussion of these issues. We have, to a large extent, organized this book by these different themes and concerns.

Existentialism Is a Philosophy

If you've ever asked, "What does it all mean?" or "Why are we here?" or "What should I do with my life?" you've asked an existential question. Of course, these questions have been around since humans came down from the trees. Or at least since after they perfected farming, settled down, and had time for questions beyond "Where will I get my next meal?" and "Is the big toothy thing dangerous?" and "Will eating those mushrooms prevent me from living long enough to have offspring who will someday ask about the meaning of life?"

But asking a deep question doesn't make you a philosopher. What makes existentialism a *philosophy* of existence? Philosophers analyze, they pick apart, and they try to come up with reasons for their beliefs and reasoned answers for their questions. They also tend to develop systems, but as we discuss in Chapter 3, the existentialists aren't big fans of systems. In the most primitive times, human beings didn't have the time or the literacy necessary for such extended reflection and investigation. Even in today's remarkably literate society, the situation is much the same. Think of your own life. You may have asked existential questions from time to time, but between taking the kids to soccer practice, meeting your boss's or teacher's latest deadline, and doing your taxes, have you had the time to come up with much in the way of a detailed answer?

Is existentialism *really* a philosophy?

Some have argued that existentialism, especially as espoused by its earliest thinkers, can't be called a philosophy, because philosophy seeks reasons and proceeds on the basis of rational and logical arguments. An important aspect of existentialism is its *irrationalism* — its belief that rationality isn't the only or even the primary mode of human understanding and relating to the world. Further, much of the philosophy is communicated through novels, poetry, and parables. These factors have led many in the philosophical community to be dismissive of the existentialist movement as a branch of philosophy. We maintain, as many who study existentialism do, that the existentialists developed their positions and discovered much that is true through the use of careful reasoning. Does this make them hypocrites? Not at all. In *Thus Spoke Zarathustra*, Nietzsche's hero tells of meeting an ear that he only later realized was attached to the withered husk of a man. He is told that the ear-man is a great man, but Zarathustra believes he has suffered from having overdeveloped only one part of himself. The existentialists don't make this mistake; they reject the exclusive or overdevelopment of reason and embrace a broader perspective, but they don't reject their philosophical roots entirely.

Philosophy develops when a society gets to the point at which at least some of the people within it have the leisure not only to sit around asking these questions, but also to work out detailed, reasoned responses. Because of philosophy's complex and abstract nature, it also helps if you can write this stuff down. The oral tradition is great for telling historical and religious stories. These stories have great complexity, weight, and depth, and many — like the epic of Gilgamesh — are even existential in nature. The powerful themes and concepts that underlie these stories were fully abstracted from those stories only with the advent of writing. The gods' involvement in the battle of Troy over the most beautiful woman in the world is a great story to tell at the campfire over a few beers. You can hear it again and again until you know it by heart and can start telling it yourself and discussing what it means at the next campfire over a few more beers. Plato's theory of the forms? Heidegger's theory of Dasein? Sartre's explanation of the for-itself? Not so much.

By the time philosophy got up and running, then, many of these big questions already had answers that were widely accepted — even if they weren't true or very helpful. With pockets of exceptions and the stray rebel here and there, this general acceptance lasted until the end of the Middle Ages. Only then do you see the first real stirrings of modern existentialism, but even then, the philosophy is a quiet whisper in the wind for centuries: a monologue in Shakespeare, maybe a few stanzas in Milton. By the 18th century, elements of what became existentialism started cropping up regularly in literature and even philosophy; the whisper grew to a loud murmur. In the 19th century, it sprang to life as a cry in the desert, and by the 20th century, it was shouted from one side of the Atlantic to the other.

The Top Ten Existential Themes

What unifies the existentialists are the themes and concerns that tend to show up in their work. Here are the top ten themes that recur again and again in existential philosophy, as well as in art, literature, movies, and any number of other fields:

- **Absurdity:** For the existentialists, life is absurd; it makes no sense and has no meaning or ultimate purpose, but human beings need it to make sense, to have meaning and purpose.

- **Rejection of meaning-giving narratives:** It isn't enough to say that life is absurd; the existentialists repeatedly make the point that when philosophy, religion, or science tries to make sense of it, the attempts always fail.

- **Alienation:** This is the feeling that you're a stranger in your own life, a stranger in the world.

- **Anxiety:** This is the feeling of unease you get when you start to recognize that life is absurd.

- **Forlornness:** This is the feeling of loneliness you get when you realize that no one can help you make sense of your existence.

- **Responsibility:** Everyone bears responsibility. If no one is going to give you a guidebook to life, you have to bear responsibility for making your way through it and creating some kind of meaning for it.

- **Authenticity:** People want authenticity — to live in a way that's in tune with the truth of who they are as human beings and the world they live in.

- **Individuality:** An important part of developing an authentic and satisfying life is individuality. Reason, science, and systems that try to cover up the absurdity of life often take individuality from you.

- **Passion/engagement:** Being passionate or engaged is another important aspect of living an authentic life, and it's under attack from the same forces that take away your individuality.

- **Death:** This is the ultimate context for all human actions and an important source of the absurdity of life.

Why is it called existentialism?

A more technical definition of existentialism reveals the reason for its name. Existentialism is the study of *existence*. If you take existence to be everything that exists — such as chairs and tables, people and llamas — all philosophy, science, and religion would seem to have the same subject. But existentialism isn't the study of everything *that* exists; it's the study of *existence* itself — the study of what it means for

something to exist at all as opposed to not existing. It's also the study of what it means for *something*, as opposed to *nothing*, to exist at all. Of course, the primary focus of existentialism is a particular kind of existence, the kind of existence that includes existing things like you, because you're aware of your existence and capable of questioning it.

Existentialism's Place in the History of Philosophy

In the ancient world, philosophy was the study of everything there was to study. The specialization in most modern endeavors simply wasn't present. This gave philosophy a broad perspective; nothing was off limits. The place of human beings in the universe and the meaning of life were questions to which the earliest philosophers gave ample attention. Thinkers from Epicurus, who advised the pursuit of pleasure, to Aristotle, who advocated the pursuit of philosophy, tried to determine what constituted the good life and how it could be attained.

Socrates and Plato, two of the earliest and greatest of the major philosophers, were particularly concerned with how a person should live. For them, the issue was moral and spiritual. Plato saw justice as the right ordering of the soul and compared the philosopher to a doctor whose job it is to look after the health and well-being of the soul. Philosophy, then, was a highly pragmatic activity aimed at living well.

As society and philosophy developed, however, this orientation changed. Over the centuries, the overall tendency in philosophy was to become more and more specialized and more and more abstract. Indeed, after Sir Isaac Newton became everyone's paradigm for knowledge, philosophy aimed more and more at being scientific. Questions about the meaning of life and health of the soul gave way to more technical issues, well removed from the concerns of everyday life. Even ethics became a narrow discipline of separating right from wrong, as opposed to determining what makes an entire life successful.

This is where philosophy was when existentialism burst upon the scene and why existentialism was seen as such a radical departure from philosophy as it had come to be practiced. We think that in many ways existentialism represents a return to the roots of philosophy, a return to the ancients' concern with living well and even to their concern with the health of the soul. Although most of the existentialists wouldn't accept the existence of a soul in the sense that Plato gives it in his more spiritual moments, they were certainly concerned with the health of all those things traditionally associated with the soul, such as will, vitality, joy, and mental strength.

Chapter 2

The Big Names of Existentialism

In This Chapter

▶ Meeting the founders of existentialism: Kierkegaard and Nietzsche

▶ Becoming the establishment: Heidegger conquers academia

▶ Storming the realm of pop culture: Sartre, de Beauvoir, and Camus

▶ Going strong even today: Modern existentialists

*I*t's appropriate, and perhaps inevitable, that existentialism came of age in the 19th century, a period of unrest and radical social change. Science was flowering, belief in the powers of the human mind was reaching a crescendo, and the Industrial Revolution was overturning the traditional social order. Forces that had been slowly growing for centuries combined to give birth to a decidedly new way of living. The world was rushing headlong into becoming the industrial, scientific, capitalist, and mostly secular world you know today.

Born into this world were two visionary thinkers, Søren Kierkegaard and Friedrich Nietzsche, who both recognized that something was missing, something was awry in this brave new world. Caught somewhere between the stale pieties of the old and the glib fascination of the new, they demanded a new assessment of what it means to be human, what it means to live, what it means to *exist.* Both started as the pious sons of deeply religious men. From there, they each took one of the two paths that this start often leads to; Kierkegaard became a devout Christian and a man of deeply personal faith; Nietzsche became something else. Back in grad school, coauthor Greg met a fellow student who was a Christian and wanted to study Nietzsche. Why? It's always important, he said, to know your enemy.

In this chapter, we introduce you to the principal existentialists. Besides Nietzsche and Kierkegaard, we examine Martin Heidegger and the great French existentialists: Jean-Paul Sartre, Simone de Beauvoir, and Albert Camus. Heidegger was largely responsible for the development of existentialism into a systematized and (briefly) mainstream philosophy. His pupil, Sartre, became the chief exponent of existentialism in France. Although

Sartre and his circle introduced substantive and important modifications to existential philosophy, they're perhaps best known for . . . well, being the best-known existential philosophers and for making existentialism a household name. In our last section, we discuss what has become of the legacy of the great existentialists and who, if anyone, is carrying it on.

Kierkegaard Makes Philosophy Personal

Søren Kierkegaard (1813–1855) was the son of a wealthy Dutch businessman. His father was fiercely intelligent, deeply pious, and burdened by a great melancholy. It isn't entirely clear why, but Michael Kierkegaard believed that he lived under a great weight of guilt and that his life was accursed because of it. His guilt may have been related to a curse he made to heaven in his youth or the out-of-wedlock affair he seems to have had with Søren's mother before marrying her. But whatever the reason, he passed this on, along with his intelligence and piety, to his son. Themes of guilt, remorse, pain, and anguish are constant in Kierkegaard's work, which is deeply personal and often autobiographical.

The other major event that plays out repeatedly in his work is his engagement to Regina Olsen. He and Regina fell in love; the young Kierkegaard proposed, and she accepted. Just under a year after their engagement, however, Kierkegaard broke off the engagement. Only he knows why — or perhaps not even he knew for sure. In part, he seems to have thought that his melancholy made him unsuitable as a spouse, but he also seems to have magnified the decision whether or not to marry into a question of what form of life he would lead. He seems to have thought marriage was antithetical to the study and piety to which he chose to devote the rest of his life. The decision scarred him, however, and he lived the rest of his life in love with the woman he had turned away. He replayed and reexamined that decision in his writings.

Seen by many people as the founder of existentialism, Kierkegaard took his melancholy and anguish and started a path of self-discovery. What he discovered was truth not only about himself, but also about the human condition. He was one of the first to develop in an extended way (if not quite in a systematic way) central existential themes, such as the absurdity and forlornness of life, the importance and weight of choices, and the need to live passionately and authentically. He developed all these themes in a radically new kind of Christian context. He rejected the traditional pieties and systematic answers of both philosophy and the orthodox Christianity of his time. Instead, he embraced a vision of faith in which belief is considered to be a real choice and one that absolutely can't be validated or justified by reason.

More than anything, what makes him one of the two founders of existentialism is the way he made philosophy personal. The big questions have meaning only in the way they're lived individually by each person. Reasoned calculation or heavenly or church commandments can't answer questions about how to live. You must answer these concrete questions in the depths of your individual soul. You must answer questions about how to live, whether to believe, and what to do in loneliness and isolation.

Nietzsche Declares that God Is Dead

Although many people call Kierkegaard the founder of existentialism, imagining it without Friedrich Nietzsche (1844–1900) is hard. Many would give him as much if not more credit for getting the existential ball rolling. Yet he stands apart from the movement he helped to create. It's been said that calling Nietzsche an existentialist is like calling Jesus a Christian; both are the ground of everything that follows, but they transcend it at the same time. You could also say that calling Nietzsche the father of existentialism is like calling George Washington the father of Philadelphia. Nietzsche is one of the great, enigmatic thinkers of human history. Existentialism is certainly his child, but he has many, many children and a towering legacy all by himself.

Nietzsche was the son of a Lutheran pastor who was the latest in a long line of clergy in the family. Nietzsche was headed to the same life, and he embraced it with a deep piety in his youth. Nietzsche criticized religion as an insider, or former insider, as someone who knew more about Christianity and its significance than most practitioners did. Like many who lose their faith, Nietzsche spent much of his life criticizing the church for the falsehoods he felt he had been taught.

He didn't stop at the church. Nietzsche was a perceptive social critic, and little escaped his vitriol. He tore down everything he saw as false, deluded, and damaging to human flourishing. But Nietzsche wasn't simply an agent of destruction. In *The Gay Science,* he spoke of wanting to be only a yes-sayer, to find a way to affirm everything in life. Existentialism gets its fundamental optimism from Nietzsche. He had the sense that after we tear down the veil of falsehoods we've created for ourselves, we can love the world for what it really is and create a meaning that's sustaining and even joyous.

To this end, Nietzsche made his work into a literary dance of destruction, creation, and celebration. At times it's shrill, at other times poetic, but it's always playful and evades easy interpretation or systemization. Nietzsche wrote in less traditional forms than any other existentialist. He often wrote in the form of relatively short, impressionistic vignettes. In this seemingly chaotic but brilliantly orchestrated maelstrom of thought, certain themes reappear, resonate with other passages, and slowly form into more or less concrete, if somewhat slippery, ideas. Of these, we focus on those that are most important to later existentialism, particularly his belief that the world comes to you as meaningless and that creation — of values, of yourself, of the meaning of your life — is your fundamental task. It was Nietzsche who announced that God is dead, and as we explain in detail in Chapter 3, this statement, properly understood, is the start of all existentialism, even that of Kierkegaard and the Christian existentialists.

Heidegger Systematizes Existentialism

Like John the Baptist, the early existentialists had cried almost incoherently in the desert. Their writings were read by few people and understood by far fewer. Because of their playfulness, their nontraditional writing styles, and the extremely personal content of Kierkegaard's writing in particular, the existentialists were easy for mainstream philosophy to ignore, marginalize, and forget. These nuts babbling about anguish and meaning? Nonsense! Philosophy was continuing on its traditional, rationalistic path. Increasingly, that meant squaring philosophy with science, with the objective and the universal, not with the individual and the personal.

In British and American philosophy, it has stayed on that course pretty much to this day. In Europe, a growing number of people recognized that this path didn't have all the answers it was promising. What existentialism was lacking, however, was respectability. It needed the *treatment* — the philosophical development of its ideas into a great work, an expansive and systematic work that the academics could recognize as being something deserving of their attention and their respect. This happened not once, but twice — first with Martin Heidegger's magnum opus, *Being and Time,* and then with his pupil Jean-Paul Sartre's *Being and Nothingness.* (We discuss Sartre in the next section.)

Of all the existentialists, it was Heidegger (1889–1976) who was most purely an academic, most purely a philosopher. Although many of the ideas within his philosophy are radical, even revolutionary, he presents them with all the trappings of traditional, academic philosophy. Like his mentor, Edmund Husserl, Heidegger attempted to describe and analyze existence in a way that had the rigor and completeness of Newtonian physics but started from the inside, from the subjective, human point of view. But what made Heidegger's treatment different was the serious attention he gave to such existential themes as irrationalism, the importance of interpretation, living authentically, and the significance of death in defining human existence.

It was Heidegger who put the *exist* into existentialism. Heidegger was concerned not only with living, but also with what it means to *be* (as opposed to *not be*). In one sense, then, he made existentialism into a science of being. Yet, starting as it does from the subjective point of view, it's a science that never objectifies human beings. Indeed, he was at pains to avoid the kind of systematizing in which things lose their identity. An important element in his philosophy is the way people categorize their experience using words, and this process is often alienating. Perhaps, then, none of the figures we refer to as existentialists would object to the label so strenuously as Heidegger. Heidegger's work does go significantly beyond what we describe as existential concerns, and he's seen as a major figure in other movements, such as postmodernism. His elucidation of crucial existential themes and his impact upon later existentialists make him impossible to leave out, however. Sorry, Marty.

The French Popularize a Growing Movement

You aren't reading this book because of a lonely Dutchman. You aren't reading this book because of a wild-eyed, self-appointed antichrist who tried re-imagining . . . well, everything. You certainly aren't reading this book because a one-time member of the Nazi party wrote one of the most important, but also one of the densest and most indecipherable books ever written. No, you're reading this book because for a brief period in the 1940s and 1950s, nothing was cooler than existentialism. And like Bogart, Elvis, and bomber jackets, it's managed to stay cool and stay relevant. You're reading this book because a few — three, mostly — French philosophers interjected existentialism into the consciousness of Western civilization. They interjected it into art, literature, the counterculture, and the fabric of society.

Jean-Paul Sartre (1905–1980) took the traditional existential themes and injected a renewed emphasis upon the meaning and importance of human freedom. Although *Being and Nothingness* is a landmark book, even he admitted that he wrote parts of it in a sleep-deprived, caffeine-fueled, hyperkinetic daze and that those parts are at best poorly written and at worst nonsensical. What Sartre did better than any previous writer was make existentialism accessible to all people to whom it was supposedly relevant. One of the ways he did this was through the continual dialogue he engaged in with other important movements, including Christianity and Marxism. Sartre was very much a public figure involved not only in philosophy, but also in politics, the arts, and literature. Although he said he later regretted it, he also wrote the ultimate summary of the existential position — *Existentialism is a Humanism,* which is a short essay that attempts to explain the philosophy in nontechnical terms to his critics and the public at large.

Existentialists who believe in God

Atheistic existentialism has come to be seen as the dominant strain, largely because it was the orientation of Sartre and the other French existentialists who popularized it. But from the time of Kierkegaard, there has always been a persistent and important strain of existentialism that embraces the existence of God. Thinkers like the Catholic Gabriel Marcel (1889–1973) and the Jewish Martin Buber (1878–1965) have developed theologies that stress, among other things, the importance of personal relationships between people and God. Like all existentialists, they value the concrete, the personal, and the intimate over the systematized and universal. They see religion as the lived experience of individuals rather than the systematized philosophy of the church or even the Bible.

Like Kierkegaard, the original Christian existentialist, they reject the notion that faith and reason can or need to be reconciled. Reason has its place, but it shouldn't be allowed to trump the personal, the individual, and the free choice to believe, to have faith, in the absence of a complete and final rational proof. Like so much of human life, faith and the experience of the love of God are essentially irrational, and these existentialists see no reason to try to apologize for or cover up that fact. In many ways, their philosophies are a call to return to an earlier time — to a time when religion was a personal, immediate, and passionate experience, as opposed to an overly structured and overly intellectualized pursuit of the proper procedures and the proper belief with regard to some obscure point of theology.

Like Sartre, Simone de Beauvoir (1908–1986) was involved in politics and any number of public issues. Her most enduring legacy has been to define, for a generation, the feminist movement in Europe and America. Although her groundbreaking work *The Second Sex* doesn't deal with existentialism directly, her analysis of the place of women in society is erected on a largely existential structure. People may not realize it, but often when they're discussing feminism, they're discussing existentialism as well.

But perhaps what most made existentialism accessible was the fact that Sartre, de Beauvoir, and Albert Camus (1913–1960) were all authors of novels and plays as well as philosophers. Putting their ideas into fiction was putting those ideas into the language of the masses. Just as Heidegger gained academic cred for existentialism by writing a work of great technical precision and mastery, the French gave existentialism street cred with their novelizations and dramatizations, which conveyed existential themes through vivid and concrete characters in memorable and emotionally charged stories.

The greatest of these, which is still read widely today, is easily Camus's *The Stranger*. It's required reading in countless high school and college lit courses, as well as just a darned good book. Perhaps no single work by any existentialist has reached more people directly. A tale of absurdity, death, and coming to grips with the meaning of one's existence, it packs much of the philosopher's beliefs about life into a tight, easily digestible package.

Contemporary Existentialists Keep the Movement Going

Are there contemporary existentialists? Are there still romantic poets? Are there still stoic philosophers? Are there still philosophers actively developing Confucianism? Like all these important movements, existentialism was both of its time and place and timeless. There is not now, and probably will never be, another purely existential philosopher of the magnitude of Kierkegaard, Heidegger, or Sartre. Although we feel the philosophy is as relevant today as it ever was, its contribution to the human discussion has been made, and its major tenets were already developed in the classical works that fermented so much excitement in its heyday.

To some extent this means enthusiasm has lulled, but don't read too much into it. The Beatles aren't recording any new albums, either. Like the Beatles, existentialism has hardly been forgotten. Existentialism has ingrained itself in modern culture in a way that few academic philosophies have ever managed to do. Books and movies in particular continue to give voice to existential themes (for a list of some of the best, see Chapters 15 and 16). Interest in the classics of existentialism remains strong, and their influence persists not merely in philosophy, but also in today's culture, arts, and attitudes. Existentialism has always been a very personal philosophy that addresses the real human issues everyone faces. The measure of its impact isn't the number of academic philosophers developing its theories, but the number of people who are meaningfully affected by its perspective.

Are there contemporary existentialists? Yes. You and us, for a start.

Part II
The Fundamental Problem: God Is Dead

The 5th Wave   By Rich Tennant

EXISTENTIALISM
Pascal:
Nietzche:
Klerkgaard:

"Who would like to discuss the concept of free will?"

In this part . . .

Necessity is the mother of invention, and great philosophical problems are the mothers of great philosophies. For the existentialist, the mother of all problems is the death of God, which refers to more than just a religious figure and plagues even those who still believe. The death of God refers to the religious and philosophical systems of thought that human beings have created to make sense of their world. The fact that they're dead means they no longer have the clout to underwrite the sense of meaning, order, and purpose that humans desire, even need. Emotions such as angst, dread, and anxiety awaken you to the cracks in these systems, and force you to face your existence unadorned and square in the face.

Although that may sound like a bummer, it's really a good thing. Although these emotions are alerting you to a problem, they're also alerting you to the new possibilities that open up for you when you face the reality of your situation honestly. The situation you must face is the fundamental absurdity of life. Facing this situation holds the promise of living authentically, in tune with who and what you are, rather than being at odds with and alienated from yourself. The promise, in short, of living in a way that's more spiritually healthy, life-affirming, and satisfying.

Chapter 3

If God Is Dead, Is Life Meaningless?

. . . .

In This Chapter

▶ Reevaluating meaning

▶ Understanding the death of God in relation to rationalism, religion, and science

▶ Assessing what you've lost — and gained — from the death of God

. . . .

*E*instein said that a little letter called e equals mc2; Descartes said, "I think, therefore I am"; and Fred Flintstone said, "Yabba dabba doo!" Nietzsche will forever be remembered for saying, "God is dead." If you're unfamiliar with Nietzsche, and especially if you're religious, it wouldn't be surprising if you presume that his tone is mocking or gloating. Nietzsche could be quite mischievous and certainly wasn't above taking this tone with his adversaries (or his friends!), including Christians and other theists. When he speaks of the death of God, however, his tone is more somber.

> *"Where has God gone?" [the madman asked] "I shall tell you. We have killed him — you and I. We are his murderers. But how have we done this? How were we able to drink up the sea? Who gave us the sponge to wipe away the entire horizon? What did we do when we unchained the earth from its sun? Whither is it moving now? Whither are we moving now? Away from all suns? Are we not perpetually falling? Backward, sideward, forward, in all directions? Is there any up or down left? Are we not straying as through an infinite nothing?*
>
> *". . . Where is God? God is Dead. God remains dead. And we have killed him. How shall we, murderers of all murderers, console ourselves?"*
>
> —Friedrich Nietzsche, The Gay Science

So the death of God is a bloody and painful affair. But what of the question in the title of this chapter? Does his death mean life is meaningless? The answer to this question is simple. It's yes. Well, and no, actually. "God," in the various senses we describe in this chapter, has been the source and keeper of all value and meaning for the world. When you "kill God," you lose this. As Nietzsche says, you "wipe away the entire horizon." When you remove this heavenly horizon, you're left in a world without meaning. So yes, life without God is meaningless.

But God was always a bit of a hoarder. He kept all that meaning and all that value for himself — keeping it all in his heaven. So in a sense that we explain more fully in coming sections, the world as you experience it and live in it day to day was already devoid of meaning. It was allowed to borrow a certain amount to justify its existence, but it never had any of its own. This is why the death of God is so momentous for Nietzsche — and why we see it as the jumping-off point for all existentialism. Only after the death of God can you face the meaninglessness of the world and realize it's up to you to take responsibility for the direction of your own life.

And this is the very important sense in which the answer is no. Reflecting on the death of God, Nietzsche asks, "Is not the greatness of this deed too great for us? Must we not ourselves become gods simply to be worthy of it? There has never been a greater deed; and whosoever shall be born after us — for the sake of this deed he shall be part of a higher history than all history hitherto."

The world is inherently meaningless, but the essential movement of existentialism is to assert that it doesn't have to stay that way. We take over the responsibility for overseeing meaning in the world. This task isn't easy, and it's not to be taken lightly. God has done the job for well over 2,000 years; we can expect it to take us a while to get the hang of it.

The death of God means human beings no longer have a ready source of value, but it also means that whatever value we can find, or make, won't be kept at arm's length from us or from the world we live in.

In this chapter, we examine what Nietzsche really meant by the death of God, and how it's a statement about more than just that guy in the Christian and Jewish scriptures or the Koran (among other holy works). In particular, we examine how this death concerns three absolute systems of thought: rationalism, religion, and science.

Who Died? What the Death of God Means

On one level, the death of God can be taken fairly literally. God is dead, or no longer viable, as a philosophical concept. Philosophers have for eons loved to debate the existence of God. Many philosophical proofs of God's existence (we aren't saying good ones) have been made, as well as a few proofs against, the primary argument being the existence of evil (again, we aren't saying good ones). Nietzsche and the other existentialists don't involve themselves in this debate.

Just an observation, not a celebration

The death of God isn't a triumphant call of "we won the argument." Rather, it's a recognition of what's considered by these existential thinkers to be an observable, sociological fact — that God and the church aren't at the center of town anymore. More important, they aren't at the center of people's thinking and no longer have the clout to underwrite values and meaning in modern society.

So in this sense, God is that sacred being who, according to the world's major monotheistic religions, authors our existence and gives it meaning and purpose. You're valuable, in this narrative, because God loves you and has a plan for you. Further, if God created everything, then, like you, everything has a purpose — "a place for everything and everything in its place," as the old saw goes. With a living God, the universe is a very orderly place. Everything has purpose, everything has a reason, and everything is valuable because God created it with that purpose in mind and (according to most versions) loves the creation of his hands.

The death of absolute systems of thought

Although monotheism does a great job of making sense of the world and of making it an orderly place with a discernable meaning and purpose, it doesn't have a monopoly on this activity. Philosophy, science and nonmonotheistic religions all try, among other things, to develop explanatory schemes that will make sense of the world and your place in it. In doing so, they tend to get a bit carried away. They try to create systems of thought, broad theories or grand narratives that try to explain *everything*. Further, the explanations they provide tend to be top-down; the stories told by philosophy, science, and religions provide the answers to you, rather than involve you in their development in a personal way. When Nietzsche announces the death of God, he's really announcing the death of the viability of all these top-down explanatory schemes.

For simplicity, we refer to all such attempts to rationally order and make sense of the world as *absolute systems.* The philosophy of Plato and the theology of the Catholic Church are examples of absolute systems. (If you want to blur the distinctions among denominations, as Nietzsche often does, all of Christianity can be seen as an absolute system.) They can also be thought of as absolute narratives because they try to bring everything in the world into one coherent story, or set of stories, that explains everything. The explanations, or stories, that absolute systems provide attempt to give the world a meaningful context. For this reason, those explanations are often referred to as *meaning narratives*. For example, the notions of heaven and hell are part of the meaning narrative provided by many, but not all, forms of Christianity to place human action in a meaningful context by assuring us that the good are rewarded and the evil punished.

Absolute systems are absolute in two ways:

- ✔ **They explain, or at least give a context to, everything.** According to these systems of thought, nothing can't, at least in theory, be understood in terms of the system. As we write this chapter, several American preachers have come under fire for suggesting that events such as Hurricane Katrina and the attacks of 9/11 were the retribution of an angry God. Meanwhile, in the halls of academia, some biologists and evolutionary psychologists are suggesting that ethics should be understood primarily in Darwinian terms. Each absolute system tends to insist that things be understood first and foremost in *its* terms.

- ✔ **The system becomes the final arbiter of truth and reality.** Just as the Supreme Court in the United States is the final arbiter of what the Constitution says and means, the absolute system — whether it's Christianity, paganism, science, or Platonism — is the highest court of appeal for questions of ultimate reality. This is one reason why the existentialists are so touchy about being called existentialists; they don't want their thinking to be confused with an absolute system.

Another thing to remember about absolute systems is that they tend to be abstract and impersonal. In one sense, this can be a good and useful thing. The Declaration of Independence borrows from traditional, theistic, absolute systems when it states that all men are "endowed by their Creator with certain unalienable rights." If you overlook the sexist language of the times, this means — in theory, at least — that everyone gets to be treated well and have his rights respected. Resting as it so often does on the concept of "God-given rights," the concept of equal treatment before the law is very much a product of absolute systems. (Perhaps this is why existentialists haven't always been big fans of liberal democracy. For more on this subject, see Chapter 12.)

But look again at the nature of these absolute systems. Although they have their uses, one problem with absolute systems is that . . . well, they're so absolute. You always have a tension between the requirements of an absolute system and its application to individual, concrete people. Even when an absolute system provides meaning, it does so only at a distance from the individual. This meaning is often prewrapped and segregated from the human lives it's meant to sustain. As we discuss in later sections, most absolute systems historically have gone a step further and consciously removed meaning and value from human beings and the world they live in.

Although absolute systems serve a function, they aren't without their price. So although the deaths of God, of religion, and of all other absolute systems are seen as traumatic events, they also raise tremendous possibilities for humanizing your confrontation with your own existence. When the system is removed, you *must* confront that existence directly and without any false narratives intervening or comforting you. But you also *get to* confront your existence directly, honestly, and with human dignity.

You can, of course, confront your existence honestly by using perspectives garnered from reason, philosophy, religion, or science. These things aren't necessarily pernicious in and of themselves. Only when you turn them into receptacles of all meaning, and subsume yourself and your humanity to their proclamations, do you turn them into absolute systems. Human beings have a tendency to do this — to let too much of a good thing take over and become a monolithic source of direction. To understand absolute systems in more detail, read the next three sections. We examine three perspectives that at one time or another have been elevated to the status of absolute systems — rationalism, religion, and science — and explain why the existentialists see each of them as flawed and not viable as a source of an ordered understanding of the universe and our place within it.

Taking the measure of things

The Greek philosopher Protagoras famously said, "Man is the measure of all things: of things which are, that they are, and of things which are not, that they are not." Plato vilified Protagoras as a sophist — a teacher of rhetoric who taught his students to develop the most persuasive speeches without regard to logic or the pursuit of truth (sophists were one part lawyer, one part political consultant).

The statement exists only as a fragment, so assessing the exact meaning Protagoras had in mind is hard to do. If you interpret it as saying that ultimately, human beings must assess the world and its meaning, this is very close to what the existentialists have in mind. But if you tweak the statement, you can make it into a pretty fair account of the traditional view to which the existentialists are opposed: "Absolute systems are the measure of all things: of things which are meaningful, that they are, and of things which are not meaningful, that they are not." Notice the impersonal and preconditioned nature of this statement. The human element, with its passions, individual projects, and concrete existence, is completely removed. You can see, as Sartre did, the existentialists as humanists who believe that philosophy should center on the subjective human element. Existentialism, however, is also a rebellion against systems of thought that dehumanize you by removing the human element and involvement from the assessment of meaning.

Killing the God Called Reason

Reason has been the obsession of Western philosophy for well over 2,000 years. Plato, whom we discuss more later in this chapter, came to be seen by many people as the patron saint of reason. Plato's treatment of reason and of human passions is more complex and subtle than that of most of those who followed him. Indeed, existentialism in many ways harkens back to Plato's more balanced view of humanity, in which reason is seen as working in tandem with certain rightly ordered emotions. In the end, however, the emphasis in Plato's philosophy, which is magnified only in later interpretations — including those of the early Christians — is on the importance of our capacity to reason. Among other things, he extolled reason's ability to rule over and control human passions, particularly the bodily passions, which were largely seen (and still are, in many quarters) as being dangerous and destructive, without much in the way of redeeming qualities.

Any subtlety in the rationalism of Plato had pretty much evaporated by the time the existentialists were writing. Reason, in the modern sense, refers to your ability to, among other things, calculate, think logically and abstractly, weigh evidence, and process and categorize experience. In that sense, reason is often conflated in the history of Western thought with your conscience, your will, even your very self.

Western philosophy is largely rationalistic in the sense that it glorifies your ability to reason over your other traits and capacities. Rationalism is most basically a belief in the effectiveness of your reasoning and its centrality to who you are. Reason, by this way of thinking, not only allows you to plan and project ways of getting what you want, but also has the ability to determine what you should want — to determine the best form of life. Reason is the granddaddy of all absolute systems of thought, because reason — with its parsing, categorizing, and abstracting of experience — creates these systems. By creating these systems — including religious systems — human reason provides many meaning-giving narratives. So why rebel against reason?

What reason is all about

You can better understand the existentialists' problem with rationalism if you examine some of reason's characteristics:

- **Reason discovers universal truths:** Two plus two doesn't equal four for you and three for us. Mathematics is universal. Similarly, if you're on the moon and we're on Jupiter, you'll feel the effects of gravity differently from the way we do. Using his reason, however, Sir Isaac Newton was able to develop the Law of Universal Gravitation, which explains the effects of gravity in both places and everywhere else as well. Reason by its nature, then, tries to explain away difference and show how everything fits under a simple set of uniform laws.

- ✔ **Reason is abstract:** To be universal, the laws of reason must not depend upon the particulars of a situation. It doesn't matter whether you're adding two apples to two apples, two oranges to two oranges, or two apples to two oranges — the answer is always four. The particulars don't matter. Of course, *some* details do matter, but all rational thinking tries to abstract from the particulars as much as possible. For example, gravity affects a large mass differently from a small mass. This particular difference matters to the science of gravity. But does it matter whether the large mass is an elephant or a Toyota? Whether it's blue or pink? Whether it's a human being or a stone? Not at all.

- ✔ **Reason is impersonal:** In the classic scientific model, you're supposed to use reason without emotion. To some extent, this thought is the logical consequence of the first two points. They remove any possible emotional content from the objects of reason by abstracting them until they cease to be objects of any feeling. When a person becomes a number, there's nothing left to empathize with. But lack of emotional content is also, ideally, a characteristic of the rational agent doing the thinking. To think perfectly rationally is to become as computerlike as possible: a pure impartial processor of impersonal facts.

Where's the human element?

The existentialists reject the notion that the exercise of reason can be the paradigmatic exercise of your humanity, because for them, life is essentially concrete and subjective. Your humanity happens in all those places that get factored out when you try to approach things rationally. The more purely rational institutions become, then, the more abstract and distant they become. You've probably had experiences dealing with rational individuals or institutions that made you just want to scream. Sometimes, even when they're right, they're wrong. They miss the point of the question — they miss the human element.

For example, when coauthor Greg was an infant, he became very sick, and his parents took him to the hospital. While waiting in the hall for word about his condition, they asked a passing doctor, who informed them, matter-of-factly, that Greg probably wouldn't last the week and then continued walking. Ignoring the factual error, this small encounter can be seen as a metaphor for the dehumanizing element in all rationalistic systems. Although they provide some guidance, like all super-rational elements in society, they do so at a distance. You sit in the universe's waiting room hoping for some word from an absolute system that will redeem your situation — give it meaning — but it does so only on its own highly abstract and impersonal terms. Reason is dead, then, not so much because it can't find any answers, but because the answers provided by reason alone are incapable of addressing real human needs.

Plato: The good stuff is elsewhere

Christianity is Platonism for the masses.

—Friedrich Nietzsche, Beyond Good and Evil

It's been said that all philosophy is a series of footnotes to Plato. If that's true, existentialism can be seen as one long, angry footnote objecting to Plato's misplacement of the meaning of life. But Plato isn't important just to academic philosophers. Platonic ideas were taken very seriously and shaped much of the interpretation of the words of a simple carpenter from Bethlehem who also had a little impact on society. Much of existentialist criticism of Christianity (though certainly not all of it) can be traced to what many, including Nietzsche, regard as its Platonism.

Reason as the source of religion?

It may seem a contradiction to say that reason is the source of religion. Religion is about the spiritual, the mystical, and the unexplainable, right? This is true, but although the individual pieces of a religion may be mysterious and magical, when those pieces are coordinated into a belief system and the behaviors expected into a moral system, reason is at work. Reason takes a hodgepodge collection of mystical beliefs and practices and forms them into a religion. The Catholic church is the most obvious, but hardly the only, example of an institution offering an intricately ordered and thoroughly systematized belief structure. The Inquisition wasn't a product of the experience of a loving God; it was the enforcement of a certain set of rationally ordered precepts about that God which the church judged essential to being a right-thinking Christian. Similarly today, when Pat Roberson states that 9/11 or Hurricane Katrina was the product of a sinful lifestyle, as crazy as that sounds, he doesn't reference the mystery of the Holy Trinity. He tries to rationally weave events and beliefs together to form a coherent narrative. Many scientists and rationalist atheists point to examples like these to illustrate the damage they say belief in God causes. The truth, however, is that by themselves, the experiences of faith, loving God, and loving thy neighbor rarely get people into too much trouble. Only when these feelings are lost or twisted by faulty or excessive reasoning into inhumane narratives does the trouble start. This insight is the starting point of much of Christian existentialism, which attempts to strip religion of its rationalistic and oversystematized architecture and get back to a more direct experience of divinity and humanity.

A word of warning concerning the picture of both Plato and Christianity presented here: Both Platonism and Christianity are incredibly complex, broad, and rich systems of thought. Although Nietzsche often presents himself as an anti-Christian and an anti-Platonist, his thoughts and feelings about them are often conflicted. In many respects, he has a love–hate relationship with each. In what follows, we focus on the development of one strain of thought that begins as a kernel in Plato's philosophy and becomes magnified into a powerful force in Christian thinking. What Nietzsche objects to is the development of the idea that a true world exists, next to which ours is a poor copy. This notion of the true world is similarly rejected by later existentialists who stress the need to focus attention on this world — the human world.

In search of perfect forms

We don't try to explain Plato's entire complex body of work, but most of what's important for our purposes can be summed up in his theory of the *forms* — a theory in which Nietzsche interprets Plato as rationally abstracting everything good out of the world and paving the way for much of what he finds most objectionable in Christianity. The Greeks were fascinated by the relationship between the one and the many. Take *men,* for example. There are many men — tall men, short men, fat men, skinny men, brave men, cowardly men, men with one leg, men with one eye, and even men who don't have . . . well, what many of us take to be definitive of our manhood. Eunuchs are still men. As we write this chapter, the news recently announced the story of a pregnant man. No definition seems to cover all the exceptions. So what makes *this* man (suave, dashing, clean-shaven Chris) and *that* man (curmudgeonly, bearded, Danny DeVito-esque Greg) both *men?*

We can ask the same question of things like goodness, justice, and courage. Many of Plato's dialogues describe conversations in which his former mentor and full-time literary mouthpiece Socrates asks supposed experts in these subjects what the meanings of these big words are. The problem is, as with *men,* every time you come up with a definition, at least one instance doesn't seem to fit. So what's Plato's answer? The forms. Think of a form as a template, an exemplar. For every thing, for every concept, the form is the perfect example of that thing. When you say a word like *good* or *man* or *lasagna,* you're referring to this ultimate example, this perfect version of the item. All other instances of these things, like *this* man or *that* lasagna, are but imperfect copies. (Greg thinks this is pretty plausible, because every lasagna he's ever tasted except for his mother's homemade lasagna is a pale imitation. Chris thinks Greg doesn't understand Plato; read on to see why.)

So where are all these forms, and how do you know they exist, anyway? As for the second question, you know they exist not because you see them, but through the exercise of your reason, which is able to comprehend what's abstract and universal. Your senses can perceive only what's limited and particular. But your reason comprehends perfect, universal truths like those of mathematics and geometry. You can't see any perfect circles; all are marred by minor imperfections. But your reason can determine how the radius of a perfect circle would be related to its diameter, if you could find one.

Forms are good; the physical world is bad

So where are this perfect circle and the rest of the forms? In Plato's house? At the British Museum? No, forms aren't worldly. (Sorry, Mrs. Gale, your lasagna doesn't count.) In Plato's philosophy, they live in their own realm of ultimate truth and perfection. It's a perfect place, an immaterial place, a . . . heavenly place. And all the forms revolve around the one most perfect form, the form of ultimate unity and perfection — the *good*. Souls come from this place and yearn to return. And if you're very, very good, and spend a lot of time exercising your reason and ignoring your physical passions, you'll eventually go back. Until then, you're stuck here, along with everyone else — in imperfect bodies, in an imperfect world that's only a pale shadow of the true world. What Platonism represents is the introduction of *dualism,* a split or separation between the spiritual and the physical, between rational souls and irrational, passionate bodies, and (most important) between the true world and this world of shadowy appearances. The former things are good, and the latter things are bad, or at least lacking in the true perfection that lies elsewhere. Plato himself recognizes this problem and tries to rectify it by saying, among other things, that physical objects "participate" in the forms. In this way and others, he tries to unify, or at least connect, the two worlds. But concepts like participation are never fully explained. So what starts as a crack in Plato's philosophy develops into a full-grown split that, fairly or unfairly, is attributed to Plato himself by Nietzsche and others.

The existential objection

Wait, wait, wait! You start with a question essentially about the meaning of words, and now, suddenly, all truth, all meaning, all value have been taken from you and placed somewhere else. Plato creates an absolute system of thought in which the world is a miserable, debased copy of something else, something you can't see or touch or smell. He says many of your own feelings and emotions are misguided.

"Foul!" the existentialist cries. "I want my meaning. I want my value back *here!* How dare you take it from me, Plato? I want a humanity with dignity! How dare you shame me?"

But of course, Plato isn't alone. Nietzsche feels that Plato's narrative of the true world repeats itself again and again in the history of both religion and philosophy. Much of Christianity, for example, adopts this dualistic picture. God, heaven, and immortal souls are the things that are most ultimately real, good, true, and of ultimate value. The world, on the other hand, is the devil's playground. It's a fleeting place of pain, suffering, and confusion where hope rests in the belief that your soul partakes in something more, something greater than this world, and that someday, that soul may escape this mortal prison and attain that other world.

Happiness versus meaning

Nietzsche sees God's death as a problem. It's a problem many of his contemporaries also wrestle with in their increasingly secular society. The English in the 18th century developed a rationalistic, secular moral system that still influences people today. It's called *utilitarianism,* and it attempts to explain how people can act morally in a modern, scientific world devoid of superstition. They start with a simple premise: What all people really desire is happiness. From there, they proceed logically, methodically, and scientifically to show that all right action is aimed at maximizing happiness and that the right thing to do in any situation is the product of a calculus weighing all the consequences of any action upon the happiness of yourself and others.

One quick way to understand the existentialists is to look at these English philosophers and realize that what the existentialists are doing is exactly *not* that. As Nietzsche wryly notes in response to these philosophers, "Man does not desire happiness. Only the Englishman desires that." According to Nietzsche, what you actually want, what you need, is meaning. You need your life to make some kind of sense and fit into some kind of pattern. History shows repeatedly that people can suffer horribly if they believe that suffering *means* something, if they're sacrificing for something they believe in.

For Plato, the consolation is that this other world can be glimpsed here and now; it's evident through the use of reason. For true-believing Christians, especially for the Christians living in the time when the religion was most alive, the true world isn't something that can be seen in this world, but its promise is so real and so certain that it's palpable. As science progresses, however, the real world of heaven and ultimate reality are pushed farther and farther into the distance. This world becomes more and more the center of attention. But as we discuss in the following sections, that attention doesn't reverse what Plato did. The separation of the world of value from the world you live in is a persistent issue, and one that the existentialists are all committed to rejecting and correcting.

Kant: The world isn't knowable

If God wasn't dead when Kant was writing, he was on serious life support — life support that Kant's own philosophy tried to supply. Kant represents a transition between the living God of Plato and the early Christians and today's secular, scientific society in which God is no longer a defining concept. Kant lived in an age still recovering from, and in many ways still tethered to, medieval concepts of God and religion. These ideas had just started to become untenable, just started their decline as totally dominant systems of belief that determined every aspect of life and social structure. In attempting to make room for them, Kant illustrates how these narratives are failing — how people are more distant from God, heaven, and the meaning and value they conferred.

Kant created a rational philosophy that he felt would make room for religious faith in a world increasingly dominated by science and skepticism concerning the knowability of ultimate truths. To do this, he limited the scope of reason to separate a realm of scientific, rational inquiry (knowable by human reason) from the realm of faith and ultimate reality (its ultimate nature unknowable by human reason). For our purposes, his doing this has three significant effects:

✔ **It severs faith and reason.** The church's traditional attitude toward the two was that they're compatible and converge in the same ultimate truth. With the growing ascendancy of science, the church's response was similar (after certain reactionary factions within it accepted they could never burn enough heretics to make the new science go away, that is). Scientific truth is simply the revelation of the mechanics of God's creation. After Kant, however, this position became less and less philosophically tenable. Kant was himself both a spiritual man and a rationalist. For him to sever these two realms signaled that a fundamental disconnect existed between them and that the two grand writers of human narratives — reason and religion — were coming into direct conflict.

✔ **It signals a crisis in the ability of the defining systems of human society to be complete, total, and absolute definitions of reality.** Absolute systems that once held people's undivided attention and provided them with convincing narratives in which they could place total confidence and trust had begun to break down. At this point, these systems could provide answers, but they could no longer provide *the* answers.

✔ **It alienates people further from their sources of value and meaning.** For Kant, the truths of heaven still are ultimately true and ultimately real. But whereas the church says these truths are knowable by divine revelation and reinforced by the findings of science, and Plato says you can come to know them through the exercise of your reason, for Kant, their ultimate nature is *wholly unknowable*. More important, within Kant's philosophy the world as it's studied by human science is so removed from the world of ultimate truth that the earthly truths of the former can't tell us anything about the truths of the latter.

Faith in heaven is spared, but the victory is somewhat Pyrrhic. Reason and religious revelation are both crippled, and the realm that contains everything of value for human beings is put off at an even greater distance. Kant wasn't an existentialist, but it's hardly surprising that many of the existentialists were influenced heavily by him and by what they saw as his failure to ultimately save either reason or religion.

The Death of God and Religion

Although the death of God isn't *just* about God, it certainly is about God. Perhaps more accurately, it's about religion, and God is simply the focus. Religion, however, provides the answer and gives God his place and his meaning. Think of the differences between the religion of Hebrew scriptures, in which the will of God is expressed by a multiplicity of laws and rules, and the God of the Christian scriptures, in which Jesus boils these commandments down to their essentials in the love of God and the love of your neighbor. Here, you have different conceptualizations of the same God, and even of the same rules, within one broad tradition. Then you have even greater differences between the Judeo-Christian version(s) of God and the understanding of divinity in pagan and Eastern religions.

Religion puts everything, even God, in its place. It orders the universe and makes sense of it — gives it meaning. It does this by creating a narrative about God, about who he is, what he wants, and how you're related to him. Your meaning, your understanding of your place in the universe, and even your understanding of your relationship to other people is defined in terms of your relationship to God. The death of God, as it relates to religion, is saying that traditional narratives about this relationship have broken down. They no longer have what it takes to underwrite your understanding of your place in the universe.

How Christianity lost its mojo

Christianity went through two stages in which it was wildly successful, in which whatever criticism you could make against it, you'd have to acknowledge that God was alive and well. Here are those two stages:

- **Early Christianity:** Early Christians tended to keep to themselves; they lived in small, often communal, groupings. More than at any other time, perhaps, Christianity then wasn't just a set of beliefs, but a way of life. Even the Christians' Roman oppressors often remarked favorably upon their integrity and faithfulness to their beliefs. Nietzsche said people should live dangerously, and the early Christians often did. Saying you loved Jesus didn't make you an acceptable political candidate; it made you look tasty to lions. It also made you something of an outsider. Christian faith wasn't just something you inherited from the folks or took up because it was what people do. It was the product of an involved and often impassioned choice. Christian communities reinforced this choice less through sanction than through an intimately shared passion and a shared vision of life. If you walk among the Hasidic

Jews of Brooklyn or the Amish of the Dutch country in Pennsylvania today, you may wonder whether God is really dead for these people. Like the early Christians, they arrange their entire lives by the narrative of their religion.

✔ **Medieval Christianity:** Small communities can be organized and arranged in the way of early Christianity, but as the number of people in a group grows, as the followers multiply, the nature of faith changes. Humans also seem to naturally drift toward and to accept hierarchical structures. As Christianity developed, it grew from an experience into a system — a theological system with a highly organized and detailed belief structure and a political system that dispensed both knowledge and power in a hierarchical structure. Although many people consider this in itself to be the death of true religion, the church flourished as an absolute system putting everything — from God to kings to peasants — in its precise place. During the ascendancy of this system, everyone knew his place, and everyone knew what it meant to be alive. The church's narrative was (basically) universally accepted and provided the ground upon which society and everyone in it stood and lived their lives.

After the church became an absolute system, however, it became vulnerable. The problem with absolute systems is that they're so absolute. One of the reasons institutions like the church are so conservative and so hostile to any beliefs that don't fit is that the basis of the absolute system is precisely that everything *does* fit. After you start monkeying with its fundamental premises, you may be able to rework things intellectually and arrange them so that they fit with the new ideas. But you've already irrevocably contradicted the system's most fundamental premise: that the universe is an orderly place and that this system reveals that order, understands the place of everything, and can be a guide for understanding your place in that universe.

So when troublemakers like Copernicus assert that, scientifically speaking, it makes more sense to say that the earth revolves around the sun, there's some justice in the church's claim that this is heretical and will tear down all pious belief. In the long run, it did. Like a Jenga puzzle falling apart in slow motion, the slow advance of science collapsed both the perfect, all-inclusive worldview the church had created and the church's role as final arbiter of truth as author of that worldview. In many respects, what's most surprising about the church's response to thinkers like Copernicus and Galileo is that it wasn't *more* antagonistic toward them than it was.

Likewise, as its political power waned, the church became one of many competing powers and influences upon society. But an absolute system thrives on being singular. It wasn't just the church's influence and power that waned, but, as we discuss in the next section, its ability to underwrite meaning and value for its constituents. After the church became one power among many, following it became a choice to one degree or another. But that implies an *open* question. After this happens, the luster and security of absolute certainty is lost, and the hold the church has on society is broken. Without the gravitational force of this absolute certainty and the reassurance and stability that provides, people tend to drift away not only from church membership, but also from a wholehearted acceptance of the church's narrative.

Being religious isn't a "Get out of jail free" card

By the 19th century, when the first existentialists were writing, the narrative of the church had largely broken down. Much of the public piety of that age was a surface piety enforced by social convention. Churchgoers, by and large, were stuck in the same malaise and just as alienated as those who had left the church. Why? Because Christians are like samurai.

One of Greg's professors once told him in seminar, "You can't be a samurai warrior." Poor Greg was devastated. But the professor was right. Some choices aren't available to you. You could do what Forest Whitaker does in the excellent movie *Ghost Dog:* You could pick up a sword, you could pledge yourself to another person, and you could try to follow a code of honor. But being a samurai is something more. Being a samurai means being part of something larger than yourself; it means being something with a certain cultural significance. Being a samurai is part of the meaning-narrative of an entire society.

Can people be Christians today? Certainly, but they can never be Christians in the way people were Christians for hundreds of years during which the church dominated European political, intellectual, and cultural institutions. Christianity, as an absolute system providing a homogenous meaning narrative for an entire society, is dead. Being a Christian in a world in which the sun revolves around the earth, echoing in a concrete, physical way God's love and attention, is gone. Being a Christian in a world in which the teachings of the church are reflected in every physical fact, in every element of societal structure, is gone. Even if you believe in God and believe in the divinity of Jesus, *that* type of Christian is as dead as the samurai.

For the Christian existentialists, to some extent this is a good thing. The price of the church's absolute reassurance was the abdication of your individual, personal responsibility for and passionate engagement in your own faith. This, for the existentialist, is tantamount to giving up your humanity (dare we say your soul?) — a devil's bargain, to be sure.

After the church loses this privileged, absolute status, the individual must reassert himself. Christianity — real, personal, passionate Christianity — once again becomes dangerous and once again becomes possible. But it isn't something that can be taken for granted. It's *hard.* Because Christianity as a dominant system has lost its mojo, lost its ascendancy, God is as dead for the Christian as he is for the atheist. And this is attended with all the same pitfalls and turmoil.

Science Becomes Its Own Religion

Science, any good scientist will tell you, is skeptical. Its theories are always up for revision, correction, and even wholesale replacement. The scientist can't afford to be dogmatic but must always be open-minded. He's skeptical of new theories, but if they survive the rigors of scientific examination, he must accept them, no matter how they conflict with his preconceived notions, or even with established theories. Science, then, is *not* an absolute system with all the answers. It's simply a method — a collection of best practices, if you will. It's a method of searching for the truth, to which it's a humble servant.

Yeah, right. If you believe all this, we have a bridge to sell you. If science didn't kill God outright, it certainly agreed to gleefully help hammer the nails into the coffin. The traditional line of thinking about the relationship between religion and science (as told by scientists) is that science was the victim of the narrow-mindedness of the church. Scientists, according to this narrative, didn't have it out for religion; they simply wanted the freedom to explore and gain understanding. Why should the church feel so threatened? They said that they, unlike the church, were open-minded and simply wanted to use the brains God gave them to discover the truths of his creation.

There is some truth to this egalitarian view of science (just as there is some falsehood to the vilification of religion in the above narrative). But some scientists have always been willing to openly repudiate the notion of God as antithetical to a reasoned understanding of that universe. Recently, there's been a resurgence of this type of thinking. Books like *The God Delusion,* by biologist Richard Dawkins, express the notion that God is a failed hypothesis, a belief not just unprovable, but also irrational and foolish. It is, one might say, a heretical notion that must be stamped out.

Meet the new boss, same as the old boss.

The scientific worldview: Science as God

Science is always incomplete. It's always searching for truths it hasn't yet discovered. Science hasn't progressed, and probably never will progress, to the point where it can claim status as the ultimate system of knowledge by virtue of having all the answers. Instead, when science makes its claim of being the ultimate system for discovering the truths of the universe, it runs on its track record. It has a consistent record of demonstrating its ability to explain and predict more things than any other system — whether shamanism, astrology, religion, or armchair philosophizing.

What produces these results isn't the big brains of scientists or inclusion in their secret club. No, the success of science is credited to the scientific method — with the way in which scientists go about seeking the truth. Following this method has led people out of the darkness of ignorance and superstition and into the light of knowledge. Exactly what this scientific method *is,* is a question open to more debate than you may think. But here are some of its major attributes:

- ✔ **Objective rationality:** The scientist must be objective, dispassionate, and able to look at the subject matter without prejudice. That's fine for studying sturgeon, the existentialist replies, but you can't study human life this way. Come to think of it, you probably can't study sturgeon this way. Human beings simply are never disinterested observers.

- ✔ **Observation and experimentation:** This is the classic picture of the scientific method: Scientists make some observations, come up with a theory, and test that theory against the world, experimenting and making new observations. Although certainly important, it turns out this is less important, and less definitive of the activity of science, than we — and probably you — were taught in high school science class.

- ✔ **Explanatory power:** Now we're getting to the real power behind the throne. When you're comparing two theories, the stronger one is the theory that can *explain* more. Why take a theory that can explain human behavior when a competing theory explains all primate behavior?

- ✔ **Simplicity and elegance:** This is the other central pillar of scientific method. Scientists prefer less-complex theories over more-complex ones. They prefer their hypotheses to refer to as few entities as possible. Take the search for a grand unified theory, for example. Physics currently posits four forces in the universe: strong, weak, electromagnetic, and gravitational (don't sweat it; it won't be on the test, we promise!). Scientists are currently trying to find a way to show that all four forces are really the action of just one underlying force. Why? Because the observations demand it? Because they can't explain some phenomenon with these four forces? No, just because it's more simple and more elegant that way. This elegance has an aesthetic quality that scientists believe is valuable in a theory. So much for objective, dispassionate rationality.

All this is all well and good, and the existentialists don't doubt the accomplishments of thinkers like Newton. Science is certainly very effective in what it does. The problem occurs when a method for studying and learning about the *facts* of the world becomes the perspective from which you perceive and interpret the world.

For the existentialists, any set of facts is open to multiple interpretations, multiple meanings, and multiple valuations, depending on how you see the significance of those facts. But as science became the dominant world view, it started to assert the existence of only one interpretation, only one perspective: the objective, dispassionate perspective of science. Because all other worldviews have proved less effective in navigating truth and falsehood and in explaining objects and events in the universe, any *other* way of looking at the world amounts to a dangerous and retrograde superstition. At this point, science becomes more than just a useful tool for understanding the world; it becomes an absolute system proscribing our relationship to it.

Like any other absolute system, then, science assumes the mantle of final arbiter of all reality and truth. "We may not have all the answers," says the scientist, "but we possess the only valid method of getting them." At this point, science ceases to be a humble collection of best practices and becomes its own God — a new kind of ultimate, absolute system. This system doesn't provide all the answers, but it proscribes the method of searching for those answers. Certainly, this is only one way of looking at science, even among scientists. It is a perspective that was particularly ascendant at the time the existentialists were writing, however, and one that has hardly disappeared even today.

Science can't replace God after all

You may think that Nietzsche, as an avid opponent of the church, would have been thrilled with the ascendancy of science. But here's Nietzsche's description of the scientific point of view, "[God is] an idea no longer of any use . . . an idea grown useless, superfluous, *consequently* a refuted idea: let us abolish it! (Broad daylight; breakfast; return of cheerfulness and *bons sens* [good sense] . . .)"

Nietzsche isn't being sympathetic here; he's being sarcastic, even mocking. The idea that simply by ridding the world of superstition, you bring about a new, more enlightened age is ludicrous. Science simply isn't equipped to replace religion. As a purely objective inquiry into how things tick, it isn't set up to answer fundamental questions of what it means that things tick and whether or why it matters.

But science doesn't just fail to replace religion and speak to these essential human concerns. It also actually hampers your ability to address these concerns. It stands in the way because of two more characteristics of the scientific method (or perhaps we should say the scientific mindset):

- ✓ **The Donald Trump Effect:** As science continually finds more and more answers, it seeks new worlds to conquer. Overly wary of the evils of superstition and irrationality, it takes for itself more and more real estate, claiming more and more realms of the human experience and its proper subject.

- ✓ **The See No Evil/Hear No Evil/Speak No Evil Effect:** Having acquired all this real estate, science then kicks out anything that doesn't fit into the scientific worldview, anything not amenable to purely objective, rational scientific inquiry. But rather than kick it back to philosophy or religion, it debases it as mere superstition or retrograde thinking. In other words, if the scientists can't study it, no one can. If it doesn't exist as a valid object of *scientific* inquiry, it doesn't exist as a valid object of *human* inquiry and concern. Meaning? Value? They don't see it, can't hear it, and won't speak of it. If you find a way to fit it into a bar graph, let 'em know, and they'll take over from there.

Science, then, becomes another source of alienation. It not only refuses to speak to your most fundamental concerns, but also degrades and debases them, much as traditional philosophical and religious systems debased the earth.

So What Have You Lost If God Is Dead?

Existentialism is an ultimately optimistic philosophy that develops way beyond the death of God. Ultimately, the death of God is seen as a good thing. It allows you to move beyond the narratives that have sustained you to a healthier, more authentic existence. Ultimately. In the shorter term, the existentialists recognize this as a traumatic and somber event. The most obvious metaphor is funereal, seeing all humanity, existentialists included, as being in the process of mourning. This is certainly apt. The way some thinkers (particularly the French) talk about it, another apt metaphor comes to mind: that of the scorned lover. Although the existentialists don't believe in an ultimate justice, their colorful descriptions of the human situation often use the language of abandonment, betrayal, and the loss of something that was in some sense theirs. And now they're pining away for what they lost. You might take a moment — as part of the grieving process — to join them in considering what you've lost. Afterward, you can process your grief and listen to your friends console you, saying, "It's okay, you're strong, and you're better off without him."

No easy answers: Rejecting all absolutes

God and all the explanatory meaning-narratives he represents gave people answers. People like being told what to do, where to stand, where they fit, and what their function is. It's comforting, and it allows them to relax mentally and spiritually. The death of God means you've lost all absolute answers, all ultimately real and right answers to the fundamental questions of existence. This leaves you feeling like the ground has been removed from under your feet. Like a child whose training wheels are taken off without warning and feels the bicycle start to shake and wobble uncontrollably, you may be disconcerted and understandably scared.

You're like the child on the bicycle; it then falls to you to take control. When your traditional narratives fail you, you inherit a heavy burden. Perhaps no one felt this burden like Sartre. Answering charges from his critics that existentialism leaves human beings in an arbitrary universe in which the existentialist makes up morality without any ultimate, objective support, he replied that he didn't ask for it to be that way and that he was as vexed by the situation as his critics were. He said that's where humanity is, however, and you have to move forward. The only way forward is for human beings to shoulder the responsibility of providing answers for themselves. These won't be absolute, final answers, but they're the only answers you can get. You'll have to get into the habit of creating and re-creating them.

The baby with the bathwater: Meaning, truth, and value

One of the characteristics of many of the systems and meaning narratives that have always sustained people is that they placed meaning elsewhere. (See the earlier section on Plato.) One of the reasons it seems so difficult to produce meaning for yourself is that you've always been told you *can't* — that there's no meaning to be found *here*. If all value resides in, or is underwritten by, God and heaven, by forces and truths beyond the earthly realm, when you lose your sustaining faith in those otherworldly holders of value, you lose all the things they were holding as their exclusive provenance.

This is one of the reasons atheistic existentialists have been so at odds with the church. The church keeps raising eyes to heaven, and the existentialists keep lowering eyes back down. And they do bring your eyes way down. Their stories are often about ugly realities and scandalous people. They don't force you to look at these things because they want to wallow in misery or debasement. Rather, they want you to recognize that any meaning, value, truth, or beauty can be found only here, in this imperfect and often ugly world. They want you to look at it *honestly,* without varnish, without covering up its ills, without romanticizing it, and without the filter of an ultimate moral judgment upon it. They say you must learn to see it this way because your task is to find a way to accept and live in this imperfect place — the earth and the human world you're part of. You must recognize that this is the only home you have or will ever know.

The danger of nihilism

Strictly speaking, nihilism isn't something you've lost, but it may represent something you stand to lose. When something traumatic happens, when you lose someone for whatever reason, when you face a crisis that demands that you rise to the occasion, the danger always exists that you'll break, that you'll fall into hopeless despair. For the existentialists, this was the danger posed by the collapse of the traditional systems of value and belief that provided meaning to people for thousands of years.

Nihilism is the state of belief in nothing. It's the belief that nothing matters, but perhaps saying that it's the empty *feeling* that nothing matters is just as apt. Nihilism is a form of surrender or a form of despair; it's a wallowing in nothingness that the nihilist can't see beyond. Bob Dylan wrote, "When you ain't got nothin', you got nothin' to *lose.*" There's something positive and hopeful in this statement. Someone with nothing has the freedom *to.* . . . It's a freedom alive with possibility. The nihilist refuses to see this possibility. For the nihilist, when you ain't got nothin', you got nothin' to *win.* The nihilist rejects all creation and all positive projects. Like a broken record, the nihilist drones on and on, "There is nothing; there can be only nothing." Rejecting creation, the nihilist often embraces destruction. For the French, this nihilism was an underlying cause of the atrocities of the Nazis. Nihilism, then, isn't just some academic concern. It's the concern that humanity will be eaten by its own fears and anxieties and lapse into, at best, a state of stagnation and immobility and, at worst, rush headlong into a cycle of violence, murder, and self-destruction.

The existentialists were *not* nihilists. Their philosophy tries to find a way *out* of nihilism. For the existentialists, life is about creation, about creating the ground for your own meaning, creating value and making your world, and making yourself into something. It won't be easy, but they insist that although you start with nothing and must continually face the nothingness of the universe, you don't have to remain immobile there. You can assume the role of being the author of your own existence. Human beings care about and value things. The fact that there's no ultimate significance to things beyond their human significance doesn't mean that they have *no* significance. The ultimate answer to the question asked in the title of this chapter is an insistent, even defiant no. If God is dead, the existentialist proclaims, life is *not* meaningless. It has the meaning you choose to give it.

Chapter 4

Anxiety, Dread, and Angst in an Empty World

In This Chapter

▶ Analyzing the importance of feelings in existentialism

▶ Understanding how your mood helps you reach insights about life

▶ Investigating the key existential mood: Anxiety

The existentialists think that giving your emotions and feelings a place is important when you're grappling with the question of the meaning of life or of existence. For existentialists, trying to be too detached and rational when you ask such questions just won't do. Their reason makes sense: Human existence is defined by an active participation with things, by a way of coming at life.

As far as the existentialists see it, the more involved and engaged existence is, the more emotion seems to play an essential part in understanding it. Reason can be a good way to analyze things, but it promotes an understanding of things from the outside, from an observer's point of view. As a result, using reason means being detached from the things you're thinking about. Because people aren't detached from existence, favoring reason as the way to understand life is self-defeating.

As a result, existentialists think that trying to understand your life or existence requires incorporating a way of approaching it from the inside or through the very ways that people participate in existence itself. One way to do this, they think, is to pay close attention to moods. Existentialists think that moods play a primary role in providing insight into the ways your existence is structured. They emerge from your participation with life and so reveal how your existence is inherently participatory, and if you analyze them closely, they show you the basic components of that participation.

Although some moods disclose to you how you're participating right now in the world, the existentialists are also interested in the moods that have the unique ability to reveal deeper truths about yourself and your *existential* situation. Specifically, existentialists are interested in the mood of anxiety. They believe that anxiety reveals that people are individual, that a kind of nothingness lies at the heart of themselves and the world, and that they're ultimately free as a consequence.

These existential insights brought by anxiety are unsettling to most people. It's tough to think that nothingness lies at the foundation of what you are, and of what the world is, and that as a result you can find no external and firm answers about what you should do with your life. As a result, many people often try to escape from anxiety by losing themselves within the everyday participation with things in the world. They try to flee from what anxiety shows them. The existentialists, however, don't think we should do that. We need to grasp onto anxiety. It may make our lives unsettled and insecure, but it also makes our lives free.

Are Emotions Key to Understanding Life?

Everyone asks the big questions at least once or twice in their lives. Maybe you ask, "What are the meaning and significance of life?" or "Why am I here?" Although asking these questions is common enough, it's not obvious at all how to approach them. Some questions are easy. If you want to know how heavy a cup is, you know to put it on a scale. But how do you approach the *significance* of life? After all, no one has a significance meter out there to put existence into.

So where do you start? Well, at least one thing *is* clear. In today's culture, you're taught that meaningful answers to questions require that the questioner conduct her investigation from a distanced and unbiased perspective. As a result, people have long given preference to faculties like reason and the intellect in investigating important questions.

In truth, there's good reason for that; reason and the intellect do have a central place in many inquiries. But let's face it — this approach seems ill suited to the big questions about life. After all, you can't ever be detached from existence or from your life to view it from an outsider's perspective.

For the existentialist, living (or existing) is always participatory and involved. As a result, existentialism favors analysis that embraces a connection to what's being investigated. To analyze this way, existentialists think it's important to give feelings and emotions, particularly moods, a seat at the table. From their point of view, moods and emotions are good vehicles for providing insight into what they are as existing beings.

Emotions: Not traditionally valued by philosophers

Existentialism is a particular school of philosophy. Although existentialists value emotion, philosophy on the whole has had a complicated and somewhat unfriendly relationship with emotions and feelings over the course of 2,500 years. This isn't because philosophers think that humans are Vulcans (like Mr. Spock, a member of the emotionless, logical race of humanoids in *Star Trek*). They do recognize that emotions and feelings are a part of what you naturally are.

But most philosophers think that emotions and feelings don't provide you with good, accurate knowledge about the sorts of things they investigate. The conventional wisdom is that emotions don't tell you about things; they tell you how you *feel* about those things. Given that all philosophy prides itself on its search for truth and knowledge of the various aspects of reality, you're probably not surprised that philosophers are naturally interested in also investigating the best methods available for performing that search (its fancy name is *epistemology*). Emotions haven't fared well in that search!

Valuing the objective

Why did philosophers turn in this direction? Well, if you think about it, what seems like a sound way to investigate things if you want to get at the truth about something? Clearly, you want to acquire the most accurate description of the thing being investigated. And most philosophers think that to do that, you need a way of investigating that can be considered objective. Being objective traditionally means that a critical examination of a subject

- ✔ Is entirely unbiased and doesn't reflect the desires, needs, or interests of the questioner in any way.
- ✔ Is similar to the methodology of science or mathematics.

Although philosophy isn't science, it often tries to mirror the methodology of science because it's believed to be objective. Like science, most philosophy aims to carefully locate and analyze data relevant to its inquiry in an unbiased and detached way. It then seeks to use reason and the intellect to analyze this data. Many people believe that objective conclusions about the subject matter can be reached in this way.

Discounting the subjective

The central belief, one that has reigned in philosophy for thousands of years, is that using reason and the intellect allows the inquirer to perform investigations in a way that rises above prejudice and bias. Philosophers think that reason and the intellect can grasp the object being considered and look at it in a logical way that allows for detached observation.

Plato's charioteer of reason

Plato (427?–347? BC) was one of the first philosophers; he lived in ancient Greece and was a great admirer of Socrates. In his dialogue *Phaedrus* (written around 370 BC), Plato presents his analogy of a chariot for understanding the structure of the human soul. According to Plato, the soul has three parts. First is the charioteer, who plays the role of reason. The charioteer is guiding two horses, one white and one black. The white horse is spirit or drive. It doesn't cause the charioteer any trouble. The black horse, however, is unruly, and the charioteer needs to continually pull it back toward the proper direction. The black horse represents the irrational passions and feelings. Left unguided, the black horse will take off in any number of directions, depending on how it's affected by the different situations it encounters. Clearly, this undisciplined behavior on the part of the emotions disrupts the chariot as a whole (which represents *you,* in the task of living!). The job of reason (the charioteer) is to guide the passions in the right way, in accord with truth and the good — things that only reason itself can know about.

From this point of view, feelings or emotions just don't stack up very well as tools to use in critical investigations. When you allow feelings to enter into the picture, your investigation takes on a *subjective* coloring; the inquiry is inevitably affected by your personal biases because your feelings reflect your own needs and interests.

If that's right, it's thought that you wind up with a skewed investigation and an inaccurate description of things if you involve emotions or feelings. As a result, most philosophers would agree with the common claim that feelings can cause you to get too wrapped up in the situation to see things clearly.

For the most part (with a few notable exceptions), when philosophy recognizes feelings and emotions as having an important place in life, they're always subordinated to reason. For example, philosophers agree that of course it's silly to think that you shouldn't *feel* in certain ways in certain situations (because you're not a Vulcan, after all), but they always suggest that reason should guide how you understand things, the way in which you express those feelings, or how the feelings motivate and influence action. Most philosophers think that reason should always have the upper hand because it — and not the feelings themselves — provides insight into the truth about the world and about life.

Emotion: A source of insight in existentialism

Existentialism is at odds with most philosophy because it favors the use of emotions and feelings as vehicles for disclosing important insights into the nature of life. Existentialists start by claiming that people are always deeply immersed within life. As a result, trying to detach yourself from life to investigate it from a disengaged point of view is futile. Instead, a proper investigation of life or existence requires methods that acknowledge the participatory nature of that existence. A proper investigation strives to inspect existence *while* engaged within it. The central way to do this is to turn to feelings and emotions, specifically moods.

Detachment versus attachment: Lying around versus participating

Philosophers traditionally think that the best investigation of a subject is an objective and unbiased one. This view, however, requires that you adopt a very particular understanding of the relationship between the knower and the known. Think about it: To know something objectively requires you to be detached from that thing. So knowing objectively presumes that you're independent and separate from the thing you're investigating.

Detachment may be the way to go for some kinds of investigations. But the existentialists are deeply concerned with the meaning of your existence or with the significance of your life in general. Is life something that you can separate yourself from and view from an independent perspective? If the answer is no, you may want to reject a detached form of analysis as inappropriate for inquiring into the meaning of life. Instead, you may want to think about ways of gaining insights that embrace attachment and connection, as opposed to distance and detachment.

Existentialists vehemently deny the possibility of investigating life in a detached manner. So you should always remember that they strongly believe that humans are deeply immersed within life. To the existentialist, being immersed in life, or existing in the sense that you're interested in investigating, means participation.

If that's right, the existentialist seems to be arguing that things can exist in two different ways and that you can examine those types of things in two different ways. The existence you're concerned with when you ask, "What's the meaning of life?" isn't the kind of existence that you attribute to tables and chairs. The two kinds of existence are

✔ **Participatory:** Existential existence

✔ **Detached:** Lying-around existence

Tables and chairs aren't engaged with existence. Their existence is passive; they just lie about. When you say that a table exists, what you really mean is that it's there and so takes up space. Your own existence, or life, doesn't just lie about like a thing does (if you're interested in understanding more about these different ways of existing, check out Chapters 6 and 7).

As a result, when you ask about the meaning of life or existence, you surely don't mean "What does it mean to take up space?" Instead, you're asking a very different question. Really, you're asking about the nature of active, *participatory* existence. You want to know "What's the significance of *my* way of existing, which is different from the existence of a chair?" You have no way to detach from your own participation with existence, so you should approach and understand your existence through an analysis of how living itself happens or what it's like to be a participator.

Feeling emotions means being involved

Because you can't detach yourself from your existence, you need to find a way to tap *into* the deep involvement that's characteristic of your participatory way of existing. By tapping into that engagement and involvement, perhaps you can disclose worthwhile insights into the questions about life's significance. From the existential perspective, feelings or emotions or moods are the most natural candidates for tapping into the existential involvement that's characteristic of your way of existing.

Try this yourself: Thinking about life

The existentialists think that you can't abstract yourself out of your life in a way that allows you to look at life and analyze it as though you're a kind of spectator. Instead, they think that life is inherently participatory and so can be understood only through the actual process of living itself. Is this right? Try to think about your life. Typically, what you wind up doing is thinking about aspects of your life. You think of your job or about your family. But pull back farther. Try to think about *life itself,* so that you can try to see how, or in what way, it has meaning or significance. Can you do it? It seems as though no matter what you wind up thinking about, and no matter how abstract your thinking gets, you're still in the process of living *as* you do it. You never jump out of life and get the ability to say, "Aha! That's what it looks like!" This is the main point: Thinking about life is itself a way of engaging with life. There's no way out of this box! You're never able to get out of your own living to think about life like a disinterested spectator.

Ethics: Reason or feeling?

A cultural bias in today's society indicates that if you want to come to a right and accurate solution to an ethical situation, you're required to detach yourself from the situation and think about its relevant variables by using reason or the intellect. This approach was directly championed by Immanuel Kant (in a work written in 1790). He believed that reason alone, and not feeling, could allow a person to access moral truth. In modern society, this bias toward moral detachment has even led to odd gender biases about ethical capacity. Because women are typically seen as being more naturally emotional, it is held that they have a hard time removing themselves from what are taken to be irrelevant emotional variables in an ethical situation. As a result, it's believed that their way of approaching ethics is less advanced because their emotional analyses leave them with inaccurate and suspect conclusions. Men, who are thought to employ reason more naturally, and therefore would be more likely to detach from the analysis of the situation at hand, are thought to be more likely to reach accurate ethical conclusions. You're probably not surprised that feminist philosophers have attacked this bias and countered with arguments championing the role of the emotions and feeling in ethical thinking!

Why feelings and emotions and moods? Well, no other faculties are more directly immersed in life. The ways you're affected by things, or the ways your attitudes tend to dominate, structure the ways you participate with life. Feelings can be visceral. They seem to provide a nitty-gritty commentary on how people participate in the project of living, even if the insights they provide aren't necessarily intellectual.

In championing this approach to gaining awareness of insights about the human condition, some existentialists stress positive emotions such as joy and love. Others, perhaps more famously, tend to emphasize the insights that can be gleaned from looking at what at least appear to be the more negative or darker (though they need not be seen in that way) emotions, such as nausea, anxiety, boredom, and alienation.

Existentialists favor the use of emotion as a tool for gaining insight into existence, but they don't reject reason as a powerful source of knowledge. They aren't *irrationalists*. They don't *reject* reason. Instead, they believe that if you use only the intellect when you investigate big questions concerning life, you limit what you'll find. Seems reasonable, doesn't it?

Recognizing the Insights That Moods Provide

Existentialists tend to favor the analysis of mood in approaching the big questions about the meaning of life or in trying to understand at a deeper level what it means to say that a person, as an individual, exists.

One primary point that they make is that attention to your moods reveals that your existence is special and that it is best understood in terms of *how* you exist, as opposed to what your existence looks like. When you turn to these "how" questions, you discover through moods that you're always deeply immersed within the world in a way. Specifically, you're always emotionally tuned into your unique life situations in particular ways. In existing, the world of everyday objects and other people is revealed as not only intrinsically connected, but also inescapably flavored and disclosed in specific ways that correspond to the mood you're in.

Existentialists also believe that some moods are more primordial or basic to existence than others:

- **Everyday moods:** These moods reveal more about your specific relationships with beings in the world or with the things that populate the everyday aspects of life.

- **Existential moods:** These other kinds of moods bypass the everyday and disclose insights about the very structure of existence itself, or about how you're related to being in the world in general, as opposed to how you're related to specific things within the world itself.

As you see toward the end of this chapter, the existential moods, such as anxiety, are most important to the existentialists. When you face up to what anxiety shows you about how you exist, you're given the sorts of insights that you need to truly take charge of your life and become truly free.

Your moods disclose how you exist

When you bump into a person you know, it's considered polite to ask her "How are you *doing*?" or "How is it *going*?" From an existential perspective, these questions are inquiring about a very basic kind of awareness or understanding that all people have about the character of their own existence. These insights are revealed through moods.

When you hear the word *existence* thrown around, ask, "What kind of existence?" If the word is being used to refer to detached existence, the kind that applies to objects, you know that the inquiry will typically turn toward a description of the kinds of properties a thing can have when someone looks at it from the third-person, scientific point of view.

Think of a baseball. It has a detached existence. So when you wonder about its existence, you say that it's characterized by properties such as "being round" and "having a certain mass." It's detached because having those properties doesn't require any kind of inward activity on the part of the thing. The ball can just passively lie there and have those features. Because of this, you can tell what kind of properties characterize an object's existence by just looking at it from a distanced or spectator's perspective.

You, on the other hand, have a participatory existence, the kind that applies to being a subject. One way to grasp participatory existence is to think of a kind of existence that's specific to the inside looking out. To get a feel for what this means, look around. Sense the *activity* of living or existing — the sensation of actually engaging with the world that's present at every moment of your life. You don't have to be doing anything special. You can just be sitting there. But it's clear that from the inside, some kind of engagement is going on; it's a kind of existence that's different from that of the ball.

The engagement you sense is the basic dimension (not exhaustive, though) of participatory existence. If you want to know what participatory existence is like or what it's all about, descriptions such as "round" or "red" or "heavy" don't seem appropriate at all.

But you aren't like the baseball or any other kind of object; you can't talk about the kind of participatory existence subjects have by looking at them as though they're objects outside you. On the contrary, you can't describe *how* a subject exists without *being* a subject yourself. As the old saying goes, it takes one to know one. The reason is obvious: Understanding this kind of existence can't be separated from actually living in that way.

When a friend asks you how it's going, she's asking about participatory existence. She wants to know *how* you're existing right now; she wants you to characterize or describe how your participatory existence is *going* right now. Of course, most people don't consciously know that this is what they're asking. But because the questioner is a subject herself, she has a kind of implicit awareness of what she's asking about. It's the sort of thing that goes without saying. When you answer, she knows what you mean in a way that goes beyond words.

So what kind of answer should you give? Well, think about it: What kind of answers *do* you typically give? According to existentialists such as Martin Heidegger, people respond by talking about their *moods*. Instead of saying, "I'm participating roundly lately" or "I'm very circular today," you say things like "I'm sad" or "I'm pretty ecstatic!"

Mood descriptions fit only subjects and the specific participatory existence they embody. Saying that you're "in a round way today" would seem odd — just as odd as saying that a baseball is sad. Objects and subjects each have a kind of existence particular to them and a specific set of descriptions that goes along with that type of existing.

When you respond to a question about how you are, you're essentially telling the other person how you find yourself at that time. In fact, Heidegger has a German term for this; he calls it *befindlichkeit.* When you ask a person "What's up?" that's what you're asking — "How do you find yourself to exist right now?" You're saying, "Freeze-frame for a second and sense your existence. Okay, what's it like right now?"

Moods are the flavors of life

Existentialists favor the use of moods to give you insight into your own basic way of existing. But what exactly do moods tell you? According to the existentialists, when you think about mood, it turns out that it shows you that the way you exist as a subject has a complicated, though necessary, structure.

Specifically, moods tell you that:

✔ You always exist *somewhere,* and you don't have much control over the fact that your way of existing is always situated.

✔ Where you're situated matters to you or is significant to you. So you always take positions on it by being affected by the *somewhere* you exist.

✔ The position you take reveals the *way* in which you are where you are. It reveals the flavor or taste of your existence in that situation.

Your existence is always situated, whether you like it or not

This point highlights a central existential truth about the nature of life: You can't exist in a way that's separate from the concrete situations that you find yourself in. That's part of what you are; you're always engaging some worldly situation or other. Moods reveal this situation to you because they seem to point you to where you are. In a way, a mood is like a way of being connected to the specific world you find yourself in at a given time. When you're sad, *this world* is what's sad. When you're bored, *this world* is what's shown to be boring. The fact that you're always situated within a particular world isn't something you can change; it's a fundamental part of what you are.

Where you are matters to you, so you always take positions on where you are by being affected by the somewhere you exist

If this point is right, existing — or living — as a subject means always being open to the situations you're in. You're open to those situations because they always matter to you. Existing means being deeply involved in the situations you find yourself in. Unlike Switzerland, you're never neutral toward your world. You're always touched by it. This isn't surprising; those situations aren't separate from you but are a part of your very existence. This close connection, the existentialists suggest, marks the fact that your way of existing doesn't include just being somewhere or in some situation, but also means being disposed toward that situation in some way.

Your way of being disposed toward the world is characterized by the mood you're in. Because you're always somewhere, and because awareness of that somewhere comes through your mood, Heidegger suggests that you "are never free of moods." It's true, isn't it? You may be calm, annoyed, pensive, or sad, but you're always in some mood or other!

If the existentialists are right, that makes sense. Imagine that you and the situations you encounter in life are connected through an interface, and that interface is mood. Existing just means being oriented toward those situations through some interface or other. Seen in this way, moods can't be seen as something merely *in* you or as simply *outside* you. Instead, they're the medium through which you're connected to the world itself. Existing, as a result, always has a certain type of flavor. If you didn't have a mood, you wouldn't exist, because not having a mood would mean not being *somewhere* — but you can't do that!

The position you take reveals the way in which you are where you are

The last point follows the first two. If existing means being somewhere, and if being somewhere means that you're interfaced with that situation in a particular way, you're affected by the situation in a way that's colored or flavored by that mood. Basically, you're always affected. It's what you are. In a way, Descartes, who said, "I think, therefore I am," got it wrong — it's really "I'm moody, therefore I am!"

Being affected also means that your orientation toward your life gets organized in a certain way. If the world appears sad, something (you) is down. Mood reveals your way of being engaged with the situations that you can't escape from. This is important, because moods tend to structure the ways in which you think about interacting with that world. When you're down, only certain possibilities in a situation appear real to you. When you're ecstatic, a different set of possibilities appears to be real. If part of existing is interacting with what's possible, moods seem to play a central role!

These significant points show that your way of existing presupposes an inescapable connection to a world that you're always within. This point is a pretty serious one when you consider that some people think that humans can exist apart from the world! In addition, it suggests that your most basic way of being connected to the world comes from a kind of emotional or mood-based attachment, not through reason or intellect. Last, it shows that you, as an existing being, are always in a mode of active participation with the world around you.

You're always tuned in to the world

Existentialists point out that mood is an essential and basic aspect of your way of existing. If you attend to your moods, you always find yourself disposed toward the world in one sense or another. If you look closer, however, you find that because the world feels a certain way to you, the objects within it tend to *look* a certain way to you. As a result, mood tunes you in to a specific world.

Heidegger insists that in pretty much every moment of your life, you're in (or not in) the mood for this (or that). Sometimes mood leads you to be open or closed off to doing certain things because they structure what seems possible to you in that situation. Of course, the most clichéd example is sex; sometimes you're just not in the mood. As a result, certain ways of approaching situations with a spouse or lover simply don't occur to you at that time. Sometimes you're in the mood; then things look and feel different. From an existential point of view, what does this mean, though?

It says that the way in which things in the world appear to you has a feel. Things in the world aren't just "blue" or "heavy" or "textured." They're also "fearsome" or "engaging" or "interesting" or "funny" or "sexy." It's important to realize, though, that you aren't projecting these moods onto the world. It's not as though the world is moodless, and then you come along and color the world with your moods. The fact that you find yourself in the world, or in this situation or that, already includes moods. Sometimes, in fact, certain moods descend upon you, often against your will!

Moods are the flavor of your existence. Think again about being in the mood for sex. Bodies *look* appealing. They look desirable. When you're not in the mood, those same bodies look different. They look unappealing, or at least boring or uninteresting. Or think about being in a sad mood. When you're sad, the world looks like a sad place to live in. When you're in a sad mood, you tend to focus on what appears depressing to you. You turn into a glass-half-empty type of person. You can't help it; your way of being, in that moment, has *this* or *that* feel. The world *is* sad, and you're tuned in to it.

As we point out earlier in this chapter, it's a mistake to think that moods are in you and that you project them onto a neutral world, or even that a neutral world causes you to be in a mood. Instead, as Heidegger puts it, mood "comes neither from 'outside' nor from 'inside,' but arises out of Being in the world . . . "

What Heidegger means is that you don't first exist in the world and then interpret it. Instead, the fact that you exist means that your existence already *has* a mood; it already has a background that's functioning as the interpretative background for the situation you're in.

All these points come together to highlight the fact that the German word *stimmung,* which means *mood,* also means *tuning.* This connection reflects nicely what the existentialist is saying. Basically, because existing always means being in a specific mood, it also means being tuned in to the things within that world in a specific way. Your moods lead you to sense a very particular world.

Everyday moods and existential moods

Moods provide you with an important way of sensing or feeling your own existence. Moods reveal that you're always actively involved in life and that the world in which you live always matters to you; it's always significant. Your mood flavors the way in which it appears as significant. Some moods go farther, however; they allow you to sense your existence at a much deeper level, penetrating farther into what it means to exist as a subject (as opposed to an object). These moods reveal possibly disturbing insights about what lies at the core of your specific way of existing in the world as a subject.

When the existentialists talk about moods, always think "What type of mood?" The two basic kinds both refer to a different way in which your engagement with the world can be flavored. Each of those different ways of engaging with the world points to different notions of what it means to be connected to the world. There are two basic ways of thinking about *how* you can be connected to the world. Each type of connection comes with moods specific to it. Think of your basic connection to the world as having the following two worldly dimensions:

- **The everyday world:** This is the collection of individual things that you encounter in normal, everyday routine. The everyday world is composed of objects like chairs, mountains, people, and cars.

- **The existential world:** Instead of the objects in your experience, you're affected by the world of *significance* taken as a whole. This world is the collection of the ways in which the objects of your routine can appear meaningful to you.

Be careful — this point is weird and abstract, and confusing these two notions of the world is easy. Take the everyday world. When you're in a happy mood, the objects or things within your everyday, routine world are colored in terms of happiness. You've no doubt experienced this before. When you're in a good mood, you see the silver lining in everything. You become a glass-half-full person. To you, the world just *is* a happy place. You see the up side of everything around you. We call these everyday moods because they relate to your everyday, worldly experience. Your moods are focused on this or that set of things within your normal experience.

Contrast this everyday world with the existential notion of world. To see this world, don't think of what you're specifically doing right now. Instead, pull back and try to understand your engagement with the world in a much more general and abstract way. Think about how part of what you are requires being engaged with *a* world in the first place — a world of meaning. So you're not affected by a world of objects, but by systems of meaning.

Try this example: When you're in everyday moods, the way in which your workplace appears to you can be very different. It can be a place full of possibility or of a depressing, fatalistic routine that oppresses you and that you hate. But in existential moods, you begin to wonder not what your relationship is to your job, but what your relationship is to the different ways in which your job can affect you. In the existential moods, you gain a different kind of insight into your existence. You begin to gain insight into the question "How am I related to the possible set of meanings that can be used to structure my world and my experience?"

It's important to see that the existential world gets at a much deeper level of your existence. When you penetrate this deep, you're pretty much at the ground floor of your existence. In Heidegger's language, your moods are no longer focused on revealing *beings*-in-the-world (stuff lying around in your everyday world), but on revealing the mysterious phenomenon of *being*-in-the-world (what it means to *be* in the world in the first place).

Just as much as your way of engaging with everyday things in your world can be flavored by everyday moods like happiness, fear, sadness, and irritation (to name a few), your way of engaging with the existential world is flavored by mood. For the existentialists, the primary existential mood that governs this relationship is *anxiety,* which is translated in some existential works as *angst* or *dread.* Doesn't sound like an enticing mood, eh? Well, no one ever said that revealing insights about the fundamental core of your existence shouldn't be unsettling, at least just a bit!

Anxiety: The Existentialists' Favorite Mood

Anxiety is, by and large, the most important mood for existentialists. Like all moods, anxiety plays an important role in disclosing insights about your existence to you. Everyday moods tell you how you find yourself tossed into and immersed within the specific worldly situations you're always inevitably in. On the other hand, existential moods such as anxiety disclose insights about you *as* an existing thing. Anxiety reveals insights about how you're related to the world in a far more basic and fundamental way.

The fact that your basic existential situation is revealed through anxiety is revealing from the start. It implies that when you begin to become aware of your nature as an existing being, as opposed to being merely aware of your life within the everyday world of your routine, you become unsettled and uneasy. Although this is true, existentialists start by emphasizing that although anxiety is unsettling, anxiety shouldn't be confused with fear.

Anxiety shows you the following things about the meaning of your existence in a general, big-picture way:

- Anxiety affects you by making the everyday world of your routine seem insignificant and meaningless. The ways in which the world is given (or has been given) meaning and significance have no firm or necessary foundation. No possibility before you seems to address *you*.

- Anxiety also shows you that you're an individual and therefore you aren't defined by the way the world has been given meaning and significance by those around you. In fact, the ways in which you've understood your own identity in terms of the world aren't essential to what you are. So just as much of the world has no necessary structure or meaning, neither do you!

- Anxiety discloses your attraction to and repulsion from the insight that you're radically free to give your existence significance in ways of your own choosing.

In the upcoming sections, we look at the difference between anxiety and fear. From there, we turn to how anxiety shows you that the world, and you yourself, have no necessary essence or meaning (that both contain a kind of nothingness at their core). We then look at how these insights are not only disturbing — after all, they seem to leave you without a firm sense of what the world and your own self are — but also needed for you to be free.

Distinguishing anxiety from fear

If you're experiencing anxiety, you know it. You feel very unsettled and shaken. Anxiety is a nail-biting mood. But don't mistake this mood for fear, even if it does have some similarities with it. Fear and anxiety are focused on very different things.

A person who's anxious is apprehensive and uneasy. She's shaken. She feels uncomfortable and uncertain. This description sounds like fear, because when you're fearful, you're afraid of something that threatens you, and in the face of that thing, you feel unsettled and shaken. But fear and anxiety are actually different:

✔ Fear is directed at and discloses specific objects in the world; anxiety isn't about anything *in* the world at all.

✔ Fear can be resolved by attending to the objects that it points to; anxiety can't be resolved in any worldly way at all.

The next two sections explain these differences.

The direction of fear versus anxiety

Fear is always about something (or some things) *in* the world. Fear relates to your apprehension in the face of something that you can experience in your everyday life. Anxiety shares some of these characteristics; like fear, it's directed *at* something, and it makes you apprehensive. But unlike fear, anxiety isn't directly focused on anything in the world. It's as though *nothing* is the object of anxiety. The object of anxiety is just everywhere (and nowhere!), in a way.

Existentialists have different ways of explaining this. First, they think that fear has a worldly target (that dog over there with the big teeth!), whereas anxiety has your very existence as a whole as its target. Anxiety seems to be focused on the way in which you exist in the world, as opposed to any specific thing that you may be oriented toward within that world. You might say that anxiety has an existential target, and fear has a psychological target.

As an existential mood, anxiety reveals and discloses insights about what you are as an existing entity. So anxiety reveals insights into what it means to be the kind of being who must, to exist, be connected to a world in a participatory way. As a result, because anxiety is focused at your existence on this very deep level, it reveals fundamental insights about the way in which you and the world are related. So anxiety is aimed at the big picture, and fear is focused on smaller things within the picture.

The resolution of fear versus anxiety

If you're afraid of sharks, it's a good bet that when you go to the beach, you get apprehensive when you go near the water. If you're afraid of heights, you're terrified when you're in high places. Well, these things can be easily taken care of — avoid the objects that cause you fear! Move to Arkansas if you're afraid of sharks. Live in Kansas on the plains if heights bother you. Easy enough. You can actually take steps or reorganize your projects in the world in ways that allow you to deal with your fear.

Anxiety is very different. Because it's not directed at anything in the world, nothing about your routine or your worldly projects can affect it or make it go away. That doesn't mean that people don't try; people who experience existential anxiety often mistake its cause for something in the world. Many times people mistake anxiety for fear and try to avoid this or that fearful situation but find that the sense of being unsettled remains. In fact, the only way to deal with anxiety is to face it — and that means grappling, at a fundamental level, with what it means for you to exist as all. That requires a different task from deciding what specifically to do in the world itself.

Existentialists are united in agreeing that people normally don't confront their anxiety when it pops up. After all, anxiety isn't comfortable; it's a perturbed, apprehensive, unsettled mood. As a result, people often try to distract themselves with worldly projects to avoid it; they desperately start rearranging their world in an attempt to shake themselves from the clutches of its mood. However, even if you're successful temporarily, anxiety is always there, waiting for you to reexperience it. This is because anxiety is the fundamental mood that corresponds to what you are, to your very nature as an existing being.

There's no escape from anxiety; after all, hiding from yourself is like chasing your tail! Anxiety will always be there, waiting around the corner for you to lower your guard. So perhaps you should face it. After all, within anxiety lie key insights into your very being. Why not take a look?

Having anxiety means you're an individual, like it or not

One of the first things that anxiety reveals is that you're an individual. Sounds nice, right? Everyone wants to (or claims to want to) be an individual. Unfortunately, when anxiety reveals that insight, it's a little jarring, because it means a bit more than you probably think it does!

A long time ago, coauthor Chris had a very serious car wreck. For some reason, a heavy bout of existential anxiety followed it. He remembers it like it were yesterday. After the wreck, nothing in life, or in the world, seemed to have the same level of pizzazz that it had before. All the different reasons for going about his regular routine and interacting with this or that plan or project seemed equally futile and pointless. All the meanings that structured his world seemed foreign.

The world as a whole (instead of just specific things within it) can commonly become flavored or colored this way in the mood of anxiety. As Heidegger put it, in anxiety, the world of the everyday tends to fade away and leave an uncanny and unfamiliar world behind in its place. The things that compose the everyday world of your normal life just seem pointless and alien to you.

Like any mood, anxiety discloses the world in a certain way and structures your way of interacting with it. Unlike other moods, however, anxiety shows you that your typical way of living in the world — in what Kierkegaard called *immediacy* — isn't true to what you are. When you live in immediacy, you forget the question of your existence. You no longer think of yourself as a subject who must grapple with the question of how to live your life in a meaningful way.

Instead, in immediacy, you get lost in the everyday, in the world of things and the meanings that have been assigned to those things and those projects by others. Your life becomes robotic. Anxiety, on the other hand, individuates. It shows you that what you are, or your significance, isn't defined passively by the meanings you find in the world — those meanings given by others.

Anxiety does this by ripping you out of your routine and making it hard for you to reengage with it. If you've ever suddenly thought, "Whoa! Three years just went by!" you know the feeling of waking up after almost sleepwalking through your life. You get the unmistakable impression that you've been asleep for years and that you just now woke up to that realization. You were sleepwalking in a way, almost living on autopilot.

What's that like? Well, when you're on autopilot, you tend to do the things that are expected of you in your world. You pay close attention to what the world and those in the world tell you that you should do, and you follow those plans. You see yourself as a mere reflection of those exterior meanings. You don't really question anything. That's immediacy, and getting lost in its grip is easy because it's so tranquil and comfortable. Anxiety and immediacy, however, are like oil and vinegar. The mood of anxiety shatters immediacy by coloring your world in a way that shakes you and yells, "WAKE UP!"

Misunderstanding what this insight means is easy to do. The existentialists aren't saying that you aren't meant to have engagements with the world or that you should run off and join a monastery. On the contrary, part of your nature is to participate in the world — to have plans and projects. What anxiety discloses to you, however, is that you're not just an object in the world, like a chair or a ball. Objects in the world are like tools. They have significance only when it's assigned to them from the outside.

When you live in immediacy, it's as though you've accepted significance from the public or from "them" or from the crowd that dictates the meaning of the world that you find yourself immersed within. By allowing the world, and your own role as an existing subject, to be defined by "them," you allow the public world to dictate your significance, just like it dictates the significance of a tool. When you stop questioning your relationship with life or the world as a whole, you stop asking the big questions about life. You start living *like* a tool or an object, a thing that lacks that ability in the first place. The only way to rescue yourself is to grapple once more with those big questions. Anxiety puts you in the position to do that by overwhelming you in a mood that breaks you out of your immediacy and creates a space for you to once again ask those important questions.

Sensing nothingness everywhere

When the existential mood of anxiety strikes, it's never aimed at anything particular in the world. You can't point to anything as its cause. "Why are you anxious?" someone may ask. "Oh, it's nothing," you may reply. Oddly enough, you'd be right! Anxiety is a mood that senses the nothingness, or lack of foundation, at the core of the world and of yourself. One thing is for sure: Sensing nothingness isn't a comforting experience!

What is this nothing? We know what you're thinking, and no, that's not a trick question. You're thinking that nothing can't be *something,* because then it wouldn't be nothing at all! For the existentialists, however, a kind of nothing-ness does actually pervade your existence, and only mood can reveal it to you. In fact, life is shot through with nothingness from all sides. As Sartre put it, "Nothingness is coiled in the heart of Being." Strange, isn't it?

The nothing of the world

For the existentialists, part of what it means for you to exist is to always find yourself participating with the world in some way. You always find yourself there, or somewhere, in some situation. And being in a situation means being affected in certain ways. You're always in some mood or other, and as a result, the things in the world stand out to you in certain ways.

But think about this: Isn't it true that the way that a specific situation affects you, or even the mood that you fall under, is heavily dependent on the specific world into which you were born? If you'd been born in ancient Rome, a whole host of different ways of participating, interacting, and being affected by life would have been open to you. For the existentialists, that doesn't just mean that certain moods are found only in certain time periods or historical circum-stances, but also that ways in which the world (and yourself) can look to you are just as bound to the features of the world in which you live.

To use Heidegger's terminology, part of what it means to be you is to realize that you're thrown into *this* situation, into a world that has *this* past and *this* history and *this* culture surrounding it. You surely didn't put yourself there. Nonetheless, there you are! And that shows that the ways in which you can understand yourself and the world, or the ways in which you can be affected by the world, are already given to you as a part of your thrown nature. You're thrown, against your will, into the whole enchilada!

Try this yourself: Anxiety quiz

Think about the relationship you have with your own life — with the way in which you tend to come at life in a general sense. Answer the following questions about it:

✔ Have you ever entertained feelings of alienation and separation from the world of your routine?

✔ Do you ever feel as though the whole way in which the world is structured — the way in which it's understood as meaningful by others — has no foundation?

✔ Have you ever had a hard time engaging with everyday tasks because they all seem insignificant and without purpose?

✔ Have you ever felt as though the choices you make about how to live are burdensome because you recognize the importance of making choices in a way that is not robotic, that is not merely reflective of the way the people around you structure the world and give it meaning?

If you answer yes to many of these questions, you're not alone. You've sensed the nothingness at your core and at the core of the world. You feel that although the world is your home, it doesn't define you. You sense that you *can* be more than what you presently are, though you also recognize that no signs tell you which way you should go. You've experienced the mood of anxiety that underlies the whole of what you are as an existing being.

When anxiety separates you from the world by yanking you out of your routine, it brings this insight into the foreground. You begin to become aware of the accidental nature of the system of meanings you've been thrown into. You realize that you surely didn't have to be born here. You realize that the way you understand and approach things isn't necessary at all. "Hey, wait a minute," you seem to say to yourself. "I've been tricked. This is just *a* way of looking at things, not *the* way! There are other possibilities for me!"

One way to think of it is to say that anxiety reveals to you that the world (the whole system of meanings that you're thrown into) rests on *nothing* at all. The world has no reason to be structured this way, as opposed to some other way. Clearly, this isn't the way the world feels when you *aren't* anxious. When you're immersed within the everyday world (trapped within immediacy), or when you're robotically performing your regular routines, the meanings and significance of the way that the world is structured seem natural and obvious. "How could it be any other way?" you seem to think.

Anxiety reveals that all those systems of meaning are just castles built on sand. The meanings and systems of significance that structure your world have no real foundation outside themselves. As a result, the way your world is put together isn't necessary. The world, seen in this way, rests on *nothing*.

In fact, there really isn't even a convincing reason that the world as a whole has to exist in the first place! Why not total nothingness instead? In anxiety, everything around you just seems completely accidental.

The nothing that is you

It certainly isn't very comforting to think that the significance of the world, as you've been thrown into it, isn't grounded in anything final or ultimately substantial. Unfortunately, that's not the worst of it. If it's true that the meanings that make up your world are entirely accidental and groundless, where does that leave *you* as the being who exists in that world?

When anxiety pulls you out of your everyday life and shows you its lack of grounding, the mood itself makes it impossible for you to identify or understand yourself in terms of any of the meanings and significance that are given by that world. After all, those meanings don't speak to the you that anxiety reveals. They're just a set of meanings you've been thrown into. They apply to anyone but to no one individual in particular. In a very real way, you begin to sense yourself as *different* from those meanings in some way.

Think about this for a second, because it's a pretty weird result. Up until the moment of anxiety, the only way you understood yourself was in terms of the public, ungrounded world of your routine. Perhaps you understand yourself as a father or as an American. Both roles come with a whole set of meanings and ways of understanding the world and yourself. So if anxiety reveals to you that those meanings are groundless, it seems to suggest that they don't necessarily form the basis for your self-understanding. What you are is independent from those meanings in some sense. After you see this, you see that anxiety reveals that *you* (in addition to the world) are nothing as well. Nothing ultimately grounds what your identity is, or what you choose to do in life, or the plans or projects you should find important. Face it — without the world's system of pregiven meanings, you don't at the moment have any way to finally define yourself. Anxiety forces you to lose your clothes! It leaves you feeling naked and vulnerable! It's no surprise that's it's so unsettling.

So who are you? Anxiety shows you that you really are *nothing!* You don't have an essence. What a position to be in! The world is groundless and supported by nothing. Moreover, *you* have no essence either. In anxiety, you seem to have nowhere safe to turn. You're hemmed in by nothingness on all sides.

It doesn't take a rocket scientist to figure out why people tend to want to avoid anxiety. For most, even getting a glimpse of what anxiety reveals makes them freak out. In response, they run, full speed ahead, back into the immediate world of their routine, into the familiar world in which they can get lost again (we talk about this tactic more in Chapter 10). They want to forget what they've seen. They want to return to the prefabricated world of supposedly secure meanings that they can just fit themselves back into.

To think in terms of the movies, the tendency is to want to be put *back* into the matrix (immediacy, your routine) after Morpheus (the representation of anxiety, in this case) has pulled you out. For most people, if they knew what Morpheus's red pill was going to reveal to them, they'd quickly choose the blue pill and forget the whole thing! "Put me back into the matrix!" they'd yell (if you've seen the movie, some characters demand just that!).

Revealing the dizziness of freedom

The existentialists' claim that anxiety reveals the nothingness at the core of you and your world is closely linked to the claim that anxiety discloses to you that you're free.

No one starts off wanting to be nothing. We don't remember ever starting off that way. Heck, who would? Telling someone that she's nothing is usually an insult. At the very least, it's surely not comforting! Instead, you usually feel a strong desire to define yourself in terms of the meanings that the world around you provides for you, free of charge. You want to be able to say that you *are* this way or that way. You want to be able to talk as though these descriptions (whatever they are) are properties that you have (as a self), the way cups have properties like weight and color.

Those properties, you suggest, explain you to yourself and to others by pointing out your nature. Understanding yourself passively in terms of the meanings given to you explains why you do things. It basically takes the responsibility for who you are out of your hands. "That's just what I am!" you can always say. Perhaps you're a dad. As a result, you argue, you *must* do certain things, just like a cup that falls does so because it has mass. When you talk that way, however, you take away your freedom. Of course, you can always *not* do what a dad does, or you can redefine what it means to be a dad. The cup can't do that. You drop it, and its mass will hurl it down toward the ground. You're free to redefine yourself. Cups aren't. Anxiety shows you that you have the power to create yourself, because you aren't essentially any of the roles or meanings that your world assigns to you. You *are* possibility!

Nothingness means freedom

Avoiding the desire to run from anxiety into these false self-portraits of what we are, given to us by society, is important to the existentialists. You need to come face to face with what you are, and an important aspect of your nature, revealed in the insight into your own nothingness, is *possibility*. If you're *not* defined by any essence, either within yourself or one given to you by the world, you're free to direct yourself in any number of ways that are open to you by the situation you find yourself in. In short, anxiety provides an insight into nothingness that discloses to your nature as possibility, and so your freedom is made apparent to you.

Part of what you are rests in the fact that you find yourself tossed into a particular world of meanings. You don't have much choice over that. It's also true that you aren't defined by it. Together, a few points follow:

✔ You aren't free to do *anything* at all. You weren't born into ancient Rome, so seeing, experiencing, or feeling the world as an ancient Roman isn't something you can do. But your particular past, your history, and your situation do in fact open a tremendous number of possibilities for you. After you see this fact, you recognize that although you don't decide *what* system of meanings you've been thrown into, it's up to you to figure out *how* to interpret or rearrange them (we talk more about this notion, which Heidegger calls repetition, in Chapter 9).

✔ Basically, it's up to you to give meanings *to* the meanings your world provides! So your nature, revealed to you by anxiety, comes with a kind of responsibility or burden. In every second of your existence, anxiety shows you, nothing about the world forces you to choose any path at all. You're always free. That's the burden of life that you bear and that anxiety makes clear to you.

You're even free from yourself

If you're always free, you're also always free from *yourself*. How can that be, though? Think of it this way: All the actions, vows, or ways of interpreting things that are characteristic of your own past self can't guarantee that you'll do anything specific right now. After you make certain decisions or commitments, that past self becomes something that you have to give meaning and significance to in your present situation. Maybe you think your past self was nuts. Maybe not!

If that's true, you're *not* identical to your past self. You can always steer the ship in a different direction. Being a self is a continual process, a continual journey of making choices about what and who you are. At the same time, you need to be aware that the you existing *now* will *become* a past self. And this awareness makes you think about the future in a new way. Every time you make a choice or a vow, or choose a direction of life for yourself, you see that it's up to your future self to decide what the meaning of your present actions is. So you're not identical to your future self, and at the same time, you're not identical to your past self (in fact, as we show in Chapter 11, Nietzsche thinks that this project of constantly reassessing oneself in light of present experience is important to the process of living authentically).

This idea can be very unsettling. Coauthor Chris knows what this feels like because he has an acute problem with vertigo. For one thing, he hates getting on ski lifts. But why? The fear of falling isn't what unsettles him; he's unsettled by the fear that he will give in to the fear of falling and just toss himself off the lift! No matter how he tries to assure himself that it's safe and that he has nothing to worry about, he knows that his future self — the one who's terrified on the lift — is under no compulsion to see things the same way he sees them now, before he gets on the lift. Anxiety reveals that your future self may in fact do something that you're now under no power to ultimately prevent. This view of yourself can be scary.

At each moment, you must choose. Time pushes you along, and at each moment, you decide how to reinterpret the situation you're in by electing to take one path and not another. As a result, anxiety reveals a radical freedom at the core of your existence, but with it comes a heavy sense of responsibility. You're tossed into a particular *way* of being, one that must always, continuously, address the question of *how* to live. It's a great responsibility, and it's up to you to pick it up or run from it.

Of course, you *can* try to stop the anxiety, and you can try to rid yourself of these feelings. The path to do so is very clear: Just reject the insight into nothingness and grab hold of something external to you as the reason why you make the choices you do. You'll fall into some preset structure of living provided to you by the world around you. Of course, in doing this, you turn from your anxiety and fail to live in an honest way. The existentialists insist that you not do this. You *can* live in the face of your anxiety. It's hard, but no one ever said that living life to the fullest should be an easy thing to do.

A love-hate relationship with anxiety

Anxiety, freedom, and nothingness are all subjects that most people are ambivalent about. They seem to have a love-hate relationship with it all:

- ✔ On the one hand, anxiety reveals to you the awe-inspiring nature of what you are, and it opens existence to you as a great mystery that you can dive into. Yes, you *can;* you have the ability to take hold of your own existence.

- ✔ On the other hand, engaging with existence without some comforting support that you're doing things right is dreadfully nerve-wracking! Anxiety frees you, but it also takes away the illusion you previously had — and that illusion made your life neat, clean, and comfortable.

Noticing this dual nature, Kierkegaard called anxiety, specifically in its disclosure of freedom, a *sympathetic antipathy* and an *antipathetic sympathy.* That's a mouthful! What did he mean?

Try to recall an experience in which you came face to face with something dreadful and scary, but also seductively mysterious at the same time. When coauthor Chris was a little kid, that usually related to the great mysteries of the dark. The dark always contained all the things that hid behind the everyday world and lurked in the shadows, always eerily present but never actually seen.

The thing that really freaked Chris out was his dark closet, especially when it was nighttime, the comforts of daytime weren't present, and Mom and Dad were asleep. The dark closet . . . that's where *they* are! Who were "they" to the kid Chris? He didn't know! That's what freaked him out. That's why the closet was mysterious and full of possibilities. Kid Chris was pretty afraid of what hid in there. But at the same time, it induced in him what Kierkegaard might call a *sweet* fear. It was sweet, because it was as enticing as it was threatening and repulsive. No matter how much Chris feared the unknown that was in the closet, he was drawn to open the door and find out. On one hand, he was repulsed; on the other hand, he was deeply attracted to what repulsed him.

Existential existence is enticing and unnerving

What anxiety reveals works in a very similar way. If you're like most people, you're deeply attracted to the mysterious nature of your existence. At the same time, you don't *know* what it is that you can be. It's a mystery, because what it means to be free can't be entirely understood in terms of what you presently find yourself doing or in terms of the world around you. That's why it's enticing, but that's also why it's dreadfully nerve-wracking. You want to try it out, to jump into that freedom, to self-define yourself, but at the same time, you're deeply repulsed by the insecurity that this freedom brings and want it to go away.

Choosing to engage: Keeping anxiety alive

The existentialist argues that you must *choose* your mode of engagement within the world. You must take on the question of how to exist for yourself. But that means that you have to live with the unsettling nature of anxiety as part of your experience. You can't rely on false portraits of yourself that are provided by the world or even by your own past. You have to keep anxiety alive in your life. Being fully at the wheel of your life is fun and scary and definitely unsettling. You can drive where you want. You have no ultimate reasons for taking one road over another. But you may crash, too, and you have to take responsibility for that. Whatever you do, the existentialists argue, don't hand the wheel over to someone else.

Anxiety in the Garden of Eden

Kierkegaard, in his *Concept of Anxiety,* talked about his understanding of the story of the fall from grace, or the story of how Adam and Eve lost their place in the Garden of Eden. The story tells us that God commanded Adam not to eat the apples from the tree of the knowledge of good and evil, saying that if he did, he would surely die. Of course, Adam ate the apple. Typically, people explain this story by suggesting that Adam intentionally chose what was evil, so they understand the temptation that drove Adam to be *the apple* itself and the knowledge that it contained.

Kierkegaard disagreed. As far as he saw it, Adam didn't *know* what good and evil were yet; he'd have to eat from the tree to find that out. So it's odd to say that he was tempted by evil if he couldn't have any knowledge of it *until* he ate the apple. Instead, Kierkegaard wanted to understand Adam's transgression in a different way. As he saw it, the prohibition from God (which Adam also didn't totally understand, because he didn't know what death was either!) awakened *anxiety* in Adam. The anxiety was unsettling for Adam because in it, he was awakened out of his innocence (his immediacy, or his robotic routine) and into an insight of his own possibilities as a free being. Specifically, God's prohibition allowed Adam to become conscious of the fact that he could become the kind of person who doesn't do what God tells him to do. He didn't understand what being that kind of person would mean; he'd never done it before, and it was never really even possible. The prohibition made it possible. With it came the mystery of possibility, the fact that some form of existence was waiting for him to fulfill it if he wanted to, which was extremely attractive — and repulsive — to him.

Essentially, Adam sensed the possibility of being something other than what he presently was. Thus, for Kierkegaard, anxiety in the face of his own possibility is what made his own transgression possible. In eating from the tree, Adam didn't *choose* what was evil; instead, he made the choice, or rather a leap, to exist in a new way that he didn't understand. In fact, in some Jewish interpretations of the story, this very possibility — this creation of an Adam who can visualize himself as someone who can follow (through faith) or reject (through sin) God — was God's intention in the first place when he gave the prohibition to Adam!

Chapter 5

The Challenge of Absurdity and Authenticity

In This Chapter

▶ Seeing that life is absurd

▶ Understanding the importance of living authentically

▶ Living authentically by embracing absurdity

▶ Interpreting Camus's "Myth of Sisyphus"

*O*ne of the enduring appeals of existentialism is that it addresses real human issues, describing what life is like and how we as human beings should respond. When coauthor Greg was in college, his advisor asked him what he wanted to study. Being young and filled with unformed thoughts, passions, and anxieties, he said, "Philosophy that deals with important things, like life and stuff." The advisor scoffed and informed him that she had never heard of any such nonsense. She knew of no branch of philosophy that dealt with "life and stuff." Obviously, she hadn't studied much existentialism.

The existentialists consider it extremely important and worth thinking about that life is, on the whole, pretty absurd. Although all the existentialists have different ways of understanding it, for each of them it's a mad, mad world, and most people don't deal particularly well with that fact. For some reason, people really love having their salad fork in the right place, and they're really irked when things are disorderly. So you can imagine that people probably do a lot to try to avoid noticing what a crazy place the world is, but that craziness peeks through again and again.

Eventually, most people come to a point where absurdity stares them right in the face. When that point comes, you have a choice to make: stare it back in the face or walk away. The existentialists disagree about a lot of things, but they're pretty unified in thinking that staring absurdity in the face is important, because when you do that, you're living honestly and authentically. Each of them has a different way of understanding how that should be done, but they all agree on the general program that seeing that life is absurd and accepting this fact through living with absurdity in an honest, authentic way are crucial aspects of the existential worldview.

In this chapter, we give a general overview of what the existentialists mean by saying that life is absurd. After that, we offer a template for understanding authenticity and explain why the existentialists think that the best response to the absurdity of life must be an authentic one. One of the most popular essays on this topic, and a great example for understanding what the existentialists are talking about, is Albert Camus's "The Myth of Sisyphus." We help you understand what Camus thinks a hero from Greek mythology has to teach you about absurdity and authenticity and why he thinks that Sisyphus is smiling, despite the fact that he endlessly spends his days and nights moving big, heavy rocks around.

Absurdity 101

The world itself is not unreasonable, that is all that can be said. But what is absurd is the confrontation of the irrational and the wild longing for clarity whose call echoes in the human heart.

—Albert Camus, "The Myth of Sisyphus"

Saying that life is absurd can be understood as a statement about how human beings relate to the world. As many existentialists like to say, absurdity (in one sense or another) is "our situation," or the human condition. Camus himself described it as a combination of the basic "irrationality" of the world and humans' "wild longing for clarity."

As Camus puts the matter, absurdity means more than just irrationality or craziness. It isn't a statement about the world by itself. Absurdity really comes from a combination of two things: an irrational world and a person who's looking out at it and trying to make it rational. You've probably had that feeling — you know the one; you're sitting at your desk and looking at the circus around you, thinking, "I'm the only sane one here." For the existentialists, this is how human beings as a group look out onto the world. But humans don't just think that they're the sane ones; they also try to impose that sanity and order on the circus around them. The world laughs at them when they do this — and this is absurdity.

Defining absurdity

Saying that life is absurd is actually saying a couple of things. First, it says something about the world, and second, it says something about the people who face that world. Absurdity is the result of putting those two things together. Here are the three things to remember:

✔ Absurdity includes an observation about the world — its *irrationality*.

✔ Absurdity includes an observation about humans — *they long for clarity*.

✔ Life's absurdity results from connecting those two observations.

This is all absurdity really is — the juxtaposition of an irrational world with your desire that it not be that way. If you want a deeper understanding, though, take a look at the next two sections. We examine each part separately, going into a little more detail about what the world is like and what people are like. After that, we explain how the two parts together produce the absurdity of life that the existentialists are talking about.

Everyday conceptions of absurdity

Typically, you probably take absurdity to mean that something doesn't make sense in an extreme sort of way. When most people say that something is absurd, they mean that it's really, *really* unreasonable. Absurd things are pretty out there. For example, a person may say to you, "Look, the other day I saw a cow jump over the moon." You'd likely reply (well, we hope you would) that this is totally absurd. To say that it's absurd implies that it's so out of whack with what you'd expect that being forced to accept it as true would leave you dumbfounded.

Whenever you try to understand a philosophical concept or notion, start with what everyday language says about its meaning. Start with what regular people take the word or phrase to mean to get your feet on some solid ground.

Calling something absurd means that it doesn't make sense, but it doesn't mean that it's impossible. A big part of the definition is that absurdity doesn't conform to your expectations.

Here's another example: Imagine that you're watching an old cowboy movie, and you see the bad guy, the dressed-in-black gunslinger. He's giving off the impression that he's about to inflict some serious damage on someone or something. With dramatic movements, he slowly reaches for his pistol and is about to shoot down the innocent sheriff of the town. The scene is tense. As he slowly approaches the sheriff, he slips on a small toy left behind by a little kid who lives in the town. He flips upside down, breaks his neck, and dies right there. Whew! The town is saved.

More than likely, such an event would be seen as totally absurd. It's absurd not because it's impossible, but because it's totally inconsistent (like a cow jumping over the moon) with the way you normally think of the dressed-in-black bad guys from old Westerns and how they meet their ends. You'd rub your eyes and have the projectionist rewind the movie. You'd ask yourself, "Did I really just see that?" "That was absurd!" you'd scream.

Likewise, *something* about life isn't just unreasonable; it's completely out of whack with what you normally understand life to be. The existentialists also tend to agree that encountering the absurdity of human life has a very serious effect on you. Like the person who's left speechless in the theater, you're left stunned and speechless when you see a vision of why life is absurd (many people say that viewing absurdity leads to anxiety, which we discuss in Chapter 4).

Understanding the Irrationality of the World

Whenever you encounter an existentialist who calls the world irrational, you should remember that each of them means something different by that. Still, taken together, this statement usually suggests that something about the world is without logic or without pattern or reason. That seems pretty straightforward, but you can break it apart and learn a lot. For one thing, the world isn't just a place, but an entire series of objects and events. Traditionally, people have tried to find ways of understanding how those objects and events fit together. On one level, you can think of existentialism as a reaction to this way of thinking. The existentialists are saying that the order or pattern that people try to see in the world — or impose upon it — doesn't really have any ultimate grounding or foundation, because the world is without necessary structure. To acknowledge that, however, isn't an easy task!

What makes up the world

The existentialists talk a lot about the nature of the world — but what do they mean by *the world?* In common discourse, people tend to throw the term around a lot and use it differently, so we want to be clear on what existentialists mean by it. Specifically, they consider the world to be the sum of everything that has existed and that does exist, past and present: all the objects and all the ways that those objects have ever been related to one another. That's the world (in Chapter 6, we look at Heidegger's notion of the world, which is slightly different).

Try to work up to this notion of the world from your own way of using the term in everyday conversation. Typically, people tend to consider the world the collection of all the objects that currently exist. Consequently, people say things like "There's no one in the world who could make a martini like you" or "Someday, I'd like to travel the world." So when they think *world,* they think of a huge container with lots of things in it. The existentialists certainly don't disagree with this sense of the term *world,* because they think that those things are in the world too. But they want to add a bit to the notion and try to make the contents of the world somewhat bigger.

What else can you add to it? Well, the first thing you could do is let the world be a collection of things that spans time, or at least that spans time into the past. So we propose that you beef up your concept of the world and think of it as the sum of all the objects that have *ever* existed and all the objects that exist right now. Understood like this, the world is full of things like chairs; your car; Caesar, the emperor of Rome; the moon; you; me; and so on to include all past and present objects. To be sure, that's a lot of stuff.

Still, that's not *all* the world is. It's even bigger for the existentialists! The next thing to add actually does conform to some intuitions you may have about what the world is. You can detect it when you hear things like "Nothing weirder than that has ever happened in this world!" This speaker seems to be implying that events or happenings are part of the world too. So there's your mom, and then there's your living room. And there's also the fact that your mom is sitting in your living room. That's another thing (an event or happening) added to the world. So is the fact that the Boston Red Sox won the World Series. That's a part of the world too (though it's an *ugly* part of the world, according to coauthor Chris!). Seen in this way, the world is a pretty massive thing. It includes all the objects, present and past, and all history too.

Different ways of seeing order in the world

We don't know about you, but the world looks pretty orderly to us. We bet that it looks pretty orderly to you too. Think about the world as you understand it — everything that is and has ever existed, and every past and current happening and event. Now think: Isn't it hard *not* to think of it as fitting together in some way? Doesn't it look to you as though every object has a reason for existing? Doesn't it look as though everything that has happened (or is happening) did so for some reason (even if you don't know what it is)? Seeing things this way isn't hard. People may see the order in different ways, but they seem to always claim that it's out there.

Seeing order in the world can take a variety of forms. Chris remembers having a friend who very consistently cheated on his girlfriend. Chris thought that this was pretty despicable conduct, but the friend always explained it off in the same way. He said that he was *a guy,* and guys are driven to this sort of behavior by their biology. He saw the world in a certain way. He was an object in the world, and so was his girlfriend, and so was the fact that he wasn't faithful — an event. He saw himself as an object (a guy) that had certain properties (driven by biology to cheat).

Everything has a function

According to the fourth-century Greek philosopher Aristotle (384–322 BC), in the world "everything is connected." According to Aristotle, everything that exists can be given a place in a great pyramidlike structure. The pyramid works like this: All the things at one level exist because they play a role (they have a *function*) in contributing to the well-being or survival (or function) of the things at the next level up. So, for example, Aristotle put animals lower in the pyramid than humans because he thought that animals exist to do work (and provide food) for humans. Humans are then freed to perform *their* (higher) function: to be good citizens and to think about philosophy (cool deal for us, the philosophers!). According to Aristotle, everything that exists can be fit into this pyramidlike structure, giving everything a reason for existing. To think like Aristotle is to believe that everything has a place and that everything has a function.

Thus, when he cheated, his behavior made sense to him. It all came together. His behavior (an event) was logical and followed from what he was in a very rational way. It may have been a vicious rationalization, but it helped him make sense of himself and his own past behavior.

Believing in God or fate

Another way (though quite different in form) to see order or logic in the world is to believe in fate. Perhaps you think that everything has a place in God's plan. According to this way of seeing things, each thing plays a specific role in God's plan. As such, when things happen to you, they don't necessarily make sense to you in a *scientific* sense (as with Chris's cheating friend) but in a *fatalistic* sense.

Fate is creepy in a way, but it's easy to understand. You remember Oedipus, right? He was the guy from Greek mythology who was fated to marry his mother and kill his father (weird stuff, we know). Because it was fated, it didn't matter what Oedipus did to try to stop it from happening. That was his role in life, and much as he tried to avoid it, it would come to pass anyway. Weird, but Oedipus's world still makes sense; it's an orderly world, for sure.

Some people think of their own lives in this way. They think that when they meet their future wives or husbands, it's destiny or fate. We've heard people claim, when they lose their jobs, for example, that it will all work out because "everything happens for a reason." In fact, some people actually do lose their jobs and then get better ones. Usually, when this sort of thing happens, such people tend to come to see the two events as being closely and directly related. Now of course, in one sense this is true; to get a better job, you need to first lose the original one. But that's not the kind of connection these folks mean. Instead, they're implying that they lost the first job so that the better job could come to pass. That's a very different sense of fate!

Finding innate meaning or significance in events

Some existentialists, especially Friedrich Nietzsche (see Chapters 3 and 11 for more on this philosopher), noted one odd thing about seeing order and purpose in the world: that the desire for order seems to markedly increase to the degree to which it's painful to believe otherwise. If you lose your job, and it causes you distress and suffering, you want it to mean something. As Nietzsche once said, suffering isn't something that people find terribly problematic. What people do find problematic, he noted, is *meaningless* suffering. So if you can give that traumatic event meaning by placing it in a bigger picture, you're likely to do so.

You see this tendency when what appear to be senseless tragedies occur around you or in the news. To take an extreme example, you may hear about the death of a small child, especially a child who in some way touched your life, and you find yourself simply horrified to the bone by the idea that the child's death was just an accident — an event that played no larger role in the world, past, present, or future. It repulses you to think that it just happened, and that's all there is to it. Instead, you think it must have *some* larger justification that gives it meaning and significance. Maybe it's that it all works out in God's plan. Maybe it's that it happened so that tougher laws will eventually be passed that wind up saving even more children's lives. But in such cases, most people are pretty insistent that it had better be *something*.

An important part of this story about believing in the logic of the world is this: Humans don't think of themselves as being the ones who gave the world its meaning and significance. Instead, in the previous example, you seem to think that whether that small child's death is meaningful isn't something that *you* decide or create. The meaning, or significance, of all worldly objects and events is already given. It may be given by God's plan. It may be given by fate or even by science. Or maybe it's given by reason. In any case, its significance is something exterior to you; most people consider it their job to discover what that significance is (if they can).

Like it or not, the world is entirely irrational

The existentialists think that the world isn't an orderly place at all. Instead, the world is fundamentally *irrational*. It has no necessary structure, no intrinsic meaning, no innate significance, and no internal purpose whatsoever on its own. They believe that nothing is out there to discover at all.

Do you think the world is an orderly place?

Is the world really an irrational place? How do you see things? To see whether you have a similar belief system to the existentialists, ask yourself these questions:

✔ Do you think that everything that occurs happens for a reason?

✔ Do you think that you fit into a larger cosmic or divine plan?

✔ When you meet someone new, do you ever think that you were destined to meet?

✔ When a random tragedy occurs, do you insist on asking why?

✔ Do you see the troubles in life as a test or challenge that you were meant to either overcome or learn from?

Later in this chapter, you see that having an emotional pull to saying "yes" to any of these questions is part of being human. But if answering "yes" is your considered opinion, you're not particularly existential!

When they say that the world is irrational, you shouldn't take them to mean that you can't explain why particular things happen. Existentialists still think that cars get flat tires because they run out of air or that objects fall because gravity operates on them. They mean something a bit different — that there's no purpose to the world, that there's no ultimate big plan or big picture into which everything fits and gets its meaning.

This suggestion about the irrationality of the world isn't an easy one to swallow. Think about it. When you see order (or purpose or meaning) in the world, it allows you — on a very fundamental level — to feel *at home* in that world. You can feel most comfortable with yourself and with your actions when they fit into some larger schema outside you. This external framework can, in a way, be comforting because it gives you assurance that a kind of glue is holding everything together and that you can fit into the framework. The existentialists reject this idea — the senseless death of a small child, no matter how horrible you may think it is, doesn't fit into any larger, pre-established plan or logic. It just is. It just happens. It *is* senseless in the big picture because . . . well, there is *no* big picture at all!

Viewing Irrationality from a Human Perspective

Seeing the world as irrational in the existentialist sense isn't the normal way in which most people see the things around them. In fact, seeing the world as an orderly, rational place is natural. In fact, it would be pretty hard to get through the day easily if you didn't see it this way. When coauthor Greg hears a buzzer sound in the morning, he hears his alarm clock — not just a buzzer — and its function (or purpose) is to wake him. That's what it is, and that's what the sound means. He responds to the sound and gets up because he's a teacher, and he needs to be at work at 9 a.m. Teaching is his role, his function, so it makes sense that he responds to the noise coming from the little box on his bedside table and moves in predictable and understandable ways toward the shower.

Perhaps Greg decides what the buzzer means and represents; maybe it doesn't have this function independently of him. But everything in his world could be interpreted differently. If Greg is continually aware of this fact as he moves through his day, the seamless nature of his interaction with the world is threatened. Typically, our ability to effortlessly move through the world of our routines is dependent on our ability to simply respond to what we *take* things to mean. We just respond to those meanings. If every morning you asked, again, "Is that what I choose to have that buzzer mean?" and if you repeated this exercise for everything around you, it would exhaust you and cut you off from your life.

How long can you make it through your day reminding yourself that the meanings of things around you are really assigned by you and by others? Does the difficulty of keeping this kind of experiment going mean that the things in the world really *do* have intrinsic meanings, or does it point to the fact that it's hard to avoid making it look that way?

If things really do look to be so connected and chock full of meanings, if the world and events in it really appear to be fully rational and full of significance, how did the existentialists come to see the world as irrational and accidental? The problem can be extended to the rest of humanity. If you're still having problems seeing this lack of intrinsic meaning in things (or if you had a problem doing that last assignment), what can the existentialists do to help you see this? Unfortunately, it looks like they can't do anything to help you "see accidents everywhere" if you don't see them already.

How you can come to see accidents everywhere

> *There are no facts, only interpretations.*
>
> —Friedrich Nietzsche

You see the world through the filter of your experiences. Assume that you and your friend are looking at a sunset. You're both looking at *exactly* the same thing — you're having just the same sensory experiences — yet when you describe it, you both give very different explanations of what you see. You see a somber event, whereas your friend sees a happy event that signals rebirth. You don't see the world with just your physical eyes; you experience the world through the filter of your experiences, and your experiences differ from other people's experiences. A person coming from a recent breakup may see the sunset as depressing (such a person sees it as a sign of something ending), whereas someone without that experience may see it quite differently.

Because the way you see things depends on your experiences, it makes sense to say that how the world is interpreted, or what it means, depends on you. Sometimes, seeing things differently results from reading a play (many of the existentialists meant their more artistic writings to create these kinds of crisis situations within their readers, allowing them to see the world in fundamentally different ways). Sometimes, however, sudden and dramatic life events can do the trick, forcing you to recognize the fact that the meanings that the world takes on are really of your own making.

Many years ago, coauthor Chris had a very bad car accident (flipping a car over numerous times!), yet he emerged surprisingly unharmed. Afterward, Chris remembers distinctly feeling strangely alienated from his normal life and routine. All of a sudden, he became aware that working in the career he was engaged in at the time wasn't necessarily what he had to do. Before the accident, he had grown so accustomed to the job that it seemed natural and even essential to who he was. He couldn't imagine being separate from it. He had never really questioned the connection between it and his life.

Suddenly, after the accident, the same world was different; it was as though he had been long asleep and had suddenly awakened to the fact that the world around him could actually be *seen* in very different ways, that he wasn't locked into any one interpretation. On the one hand, it was an alienating experience, because Chris felt suddenly separate and isolated from the meanings the world had taken on before the accident. This experience of seeing those meanings as unnecessary, or as truly accidental, seemed to rip him out of the seamless nature of his routine (as we discuss in Chapter 4, anxiety has this very same effect). At the same time, however, it was very uplifting! Chris felt strangely not at home in his own world, but at the same time he felt invigorated, as though possibilities were multiplying for him.

Such realizations, whatever their cause, have one thing in common: You're suddenly brought face to face with the recognition that existence (your own or that of things or other people) seems indifferent to the ways that you decide to categorize it. You come face to face with the fact that the world isn't defined by any of the ways in which you choose to see and understand it (or yourself) at any point in time. As Jean-Paul Sartre put it, existence overflows the categories you try to understand it through.

en there just must be a ger! — reason

urely one lonely gunman couldn't have robbed mericans of the most powerful man in the orld, the most charismatic president in U.S. story. That wouldn't be significant enough to ke sense of the event. A few extremists with cutters couldn't have perpetrated the most astating and deadly attack on U.S. soil in ory. That would be absurd.

reason as big and power-ful as you see the event as being.

You're addicted to imposing order on the world

Human beings naturally desire order. To use Camus's phase, we "long for clarity." Think about what seems to happen when something dramatic occurs, like a near-fatal car accident or the death of a child — something that can shake your view of how you and the world fit together (or just how the world fits together itself).

After such an event, nothing makes sense; you see the world as accidental. It seems that no matter how you choose to reorganize the pieces, they could always be reorganized yet again in some different way. These endless possi-bilities reinforce your view that the world has no inherent order and no way in which it *should* be organized. Yet even in these circumstances, you can't help but organize it anyway. Even if you try to opt out and stop trying to unify the world in a way that helps make it more sensible and orderly, you just can't do it. At times, you probably even feel ridiculous, trying futilely to foist order on something that doesn't want it and didn't have it to begin with.

As the existentialists see it, people are all essentially obsessive-compulsive about their worlds being ordered. They may be sloppy, they may not clean their homes, and they may not be able to find the remote control when they want it, but they're all obsessive about the world having *some* kind of shape and meaning, and they want themselves to fit into that meaning. Your projects and plans and ambitions make sense; your actions are intelligible. Ordering the world is what you do. You can't escape it. You always evaluate and unify (through your various explanations and conceptual schemes) what's inherently unstructured, or what's inherently irrational and without logic and reason. As Nietzsche once put it, "Man first implanted values into things to maintain himself — he created the meaning of things. A human meaning! Therefore he calls himself 'man', that is, the evaluator!"

People are driven to make sense of what simply can't be made sense of. It's just who we are. You're driven to unify things, to bring things together in ways that attempt to make more and more sense of what's around you.

The absurdity of imposing order on the disorderly

Essentially, the existentialist recognition about human life is this: We're forced by our nature to be obsessive creators of meaning, and we can't help but do this in a resolute and serious way. We don't just choose values or schemes; we don't do it listlessly as though we really don't care about the way we're making sense of things.

Instead, we choose with firmness and determination. It means something to us to see the world one way and not another way; after all, the way in which we see the world is central to who we are. So we're very serious about our attempts to unify and give meaning to the world and to ourselves — even if, in the vast number of cases, we don't *consciously* recognize that we're doing it.

Instead, we seem to create the meaning and order that we see in the world and then we appear to *mistake* it as something that we found or discovered in the world itself. When you see things as they really are, you get a glimpse into not only the fact that the world has no form, but also that you've been giving it the order that it appears to have.

Although you're forced by what you are to resolutely impose order on the world around you, nothing about your project finds any justification at all, because the world itself provides no support for what you're doing. In fact, it's indifferent to us and our schemes. It's almost as though human nature is in an inevitable confrontation with the nature of the world. The world is irrational, but you nonetheless try to make sense of it.

Thus, you seem trapped in an activity that appears to have no justification or meaning. It appears *unreasonable* — not that the world is irrational or that humans are order imposers, but that you must give the world a unified character that you embrace with seriousness when in reality, no way of unifying the world has any grounding or support whatsoever. Absurdity is the fact that the two must coexist side by side.

The inkblot test: Forcing yourself to see order

Try it out yourself! What do you see in this picture? Can you force yourself to look at the picture and see nothing there? Or do you keep returning to seeing something orderly in the inkblot? According to the existentialists, you just can't help it. You're addicted! Put simply: You have an addiction to creating values or meanings that you create to make sense of the world in which you live. And you can't kick the habit!

What you learn is that your desire for order, structure, and meaning finds no happily accommodating world eager to fulfill your wants by providing answers. Just like the dressed-in-black bad guy from the Western who slips on a child's toy (check out our example of absurdity earlier in this chapter), you can imagine someone saying, "Look at that creature who can't avoid the task of continually creating meaning and unity for the world when it doesn't have any — how *absurd!*" You may even envision a comedy (though a comedy with a tragic feel!) being written about such creatures (in fact, Nietzsche's fictional work *Thus Spoke Zarathustra* is an attempt to describe a character who experiences just these sorts of insights). Think of an alien life form watching us as we furiously work at giving the world meaning, like ants scampering around making an anthill in the midst of the crashing ocean waves that keep knocking it back down again. We can imagine the spectators laughing at us, thinking, "How *futile* are its efforts! How comical this is!"

Making sense of the absurd

What's depicted in the Escher drawing is a three-dimensional impossibility. It doesn't make sense. Yet your brain and visual system can't help but try to make sense of it. This is an encounter with an interesting situation: Your longing for clarity comes into contact with what can't be made clear. Like the world, the picture rebuffs your attempts to make sense of it. Looking at it evokes the feeling of absurdity.

M.C. Escher's "Waterfall" © 2008 The M.C. Escher Company-Holland. All rights reserved. www.mcescher.com

From this perspective, do you have any question about why the existentialists think that life is absurd?

Authenticity 101: Striving to Be Genuine

For the existentialists, the only successful way to deal with the absurdity of life is through living authentically. Although not all existentialists use the specific term *authenticity* (different existentialists use different terms to express it, and they all have different ways to specifically understand how the concept works), they all agree that it's important that we struggle to acquire it in our lives.

At the simplest level, existentialists think that living authentically is important because it means living in accord with who you are or being true to who you are. As Friedrich Nietzsche once put it, the goal is to "become what you already are!" It means representing yourself in a way that can be considered genuine, which means embracing the fact that you must confront the world in your own individual way. When you look at it this way, it's hard to imagine that many people (if anyone!) would reject this goal. Most people tend to believe that living genuinely in this way is important.

It's not easy to do, though. We offer two reasons for this difficulty:

✔ Living authentically causes lots of discomfort in your life. Allowing the way in which you live to reflect a kind of conformity to the world and the pregiven meanings people present to you is always easier to do. Conforming to the crowd is easier than being your own person. But you need to be able to resist being absorbed; existentialists think that no one should hide from what he is.

✔ Living authentically is hard to do because although the existentialist notion of authenticity is similar to the common-sense notion of authenticity, the existentialist version differs in an important — but complicated — way.

The existentialists stress that being true to yourself means reflecting in your ways of living the kind of being that you are. In other words, you're living in the world in a way that reflects the fact that your eyes are wide open to your nature as an absurd being. You're living in a way that acknowledges the fact that whatever life path you pick to follow, you'll never receive any external justification for why that path was the right one for you to take.

The connection between authenticity and genuineness

A good way to start analyzing what the existentialists mean by authenticity is to first look at the way you use that term in your own common language. Almost always, the term is used to describe something that's real or genuine, and *inauthentic* is used to describe something that's artificial, counterfeit, or fake. This meaning reflects a key aspect of authenticity: An authentic thing is always true to its own nature.

As an example, suppose that you go to see the Shakespeare play *Julius Caesar*. You wouldn't say that the sword that an actor carries onstage is an authentic Roman sword, because it isn't real; after all, genuine, authentic swords aren't made of cardboard, right? It's a fake — a stage prop!

Here's another example: Maybe you've heard the term *authenticity* used on those television auction shows when a person brings in what appears to be an antique item of furniture. A very serious-minded representative on the program examines the piece, looking to see whether it's authentic. What he's checking is whether the piece is actually from the old time period that the person claims it's from. The more authentic the piece is in this case, the more it is a true and real representative of that older period.

At this point, you appear to have a pretty simple motto for living a good existential life: living in ways that are real and genuine as opposed to being fake or counterfeit. Who'd want to be a fake?

Everybody digs authenticity

One interesting thing about authentic objects, like swords and antique pieces of furniture, is that what's genuine is almost always worth more than what's counterfeit. In a general sense, being real or genuine is just understood as valuable. In the case of living authentically, of course, living in a genuine or real way doesn't mean that you're suddenly worth a lot of money. Instead, most existentialists would say that the way that you're living is more admirable (some celebrate authenticity, but still deny that it's better, whereas others are pretty clear that it should be preferred to inauthenticity).

Authenticity in popular culture

Take a stroll through a bookstore, and you quickly discover the large number of books devoted to the task of rediscovering authenticity in different aspects of human life. Some deal with rediscovering the art of authentic parenting, while others deal with how to be authentically faithful in one's romantic relationships. Some are more general, dealing with how to live an authentic life, while others are geared toward the project of making money while not losing one's authenticity. Some books even start out by recognizing that because authenticity is accorded such a high premium in society, corporations ought to learn to develop business models that focus on promoting an image of corporate authenticity. Their message: Authenticity sells. At the very least, one thing is certain: The pursuit of authenticity is selling lots of books!

Perhaps you feel differently and are saying, "Hey, stop this train and let me off — I don't really care about authenticity at all!" We'll be honest — if that's what you're saying, you're in the serious minority, at least in today's culture. Now, it may well be the case that few people *are* authentic, and it may even be true that few people truly *strive* for authenticity, but we haven't met very many people who honestly admit to not caring about it at all.

In fact, what we've noticed is the exact opposite. Most of the people we know appear to feel strongly that authenticity is a highly desirable and admirable trait. These people are always bemoaning the fact that modern life isn't terribly authentic and that people just aren't willing to be themselves. We hear it all the time — around the water cooler, at lunch, in the bar. Most people, the conversation typically goes, are fake and artificial.

And it's just not cool. Most people seem to really despise inauthenticity and tend to cringe when they feel that they've identified it in themselves or in other people around them. This is especially true the closer the person in question is to you. This isn't surprising; if caring more about people the closer they are to you is natural (and it is), and if you think that authenticity is admirable and the lack of it is dishonorable in some way, you want the people closest to you to display authenticity.

Of course, of all the people who are close to you, *you* are the most central. No one is closer to you than you. It's not surprising, then, that people have a deep desire for authenticity in their own lives and that they tend to cringe when they suspect that they've been artificial in some situation. We know that when this happens to us, we have a hard time sleeping well at night.

Matching just the right template

Knowing whether something is authentic requires first answering a crucial question: an authentic what? So you don't just ask whether something is authentic; you need an idea of what the thing in question is *claiming* to be and then you can ask whether it succeeds in that task. So if you claim to be an authentic Red Sox fan, the only way that we can verify whether you're indeed one requires that we first find out what a Red Sox fan really looks like (because he's a Yankees fan, we'll refrain from letting Chris give that description). After we have that description, we can check the alleged Red Sox fan against that information to see whether he passes the *sniff test* — to see whether that person matches the *right template* (our idea of what a real Red Sox fan looks like). This tells you that:

✔ Authenticity requires that a template or standard can be used to determine whether a given thing is real or artificial in some key respect (real Roman swords exist, or real Red Sox fans exist; you can know what they are and how they look; and you can test to see whether a thing is one of them).

> ✔ A thing is authentic when it matches the template or standard.
>
> ✔ A thing is inauthentic when it doesn't match that template or standard.

When it comes to nonhuman objects, seeing whether a particular thing is an authentic X or Y is fairly straightforward. Suppose that an actor on a stage claims that the wooden object he's holding is an authentic Roman sword from the time of Julius Caesar. The first thing you do is check the age of the object. If it's only 5 years old, it fails the sniff test, because such a sword would need to be at least 2,000 years old to be a real Roman sword of this type. Even easier, of course, you might just point out that it fails the sniff test because it's made of cardboard, and real Roman swords from that time period were never made of that (if they had been, Caesar's legions wouldn't have been terribly successful in battle).

Of course, the existentialists don't care about swords. They want to apply the notion of authenticity to a very different type of entity — to *you* (and all people). What they're claiming is that you can succeed or fail in the task of being an authentic *person*. If the understanding of authenticity as genuineness applied to people as well as to swords, you'd be able to find a template that allows you to know what an authentic person looks like. If you could acquire such knowledge, all you'd need to do is look at a particular person and see whether that person passes the sniff test. But we'll be honest — that sounds pretty odd! How can a template tell you when you're a real, genuine, or authentic person?

One thing the existentialists are adamant about is this: Unlike the case of the sword, in which the template is external to it, the question of human authenticity is determined by matching up to a standard that's *internal* to the person. If you can understand what that template is, you can check this or that person to see whether he's passing the sniff test. What this info reveals is a central facet of authentic living: Pursuing authenticity requires understanding yourself, just as it requires understanding what a sword is to know whether some object is a true, authentic sword.

Understanding authenticity as representing

All this talk about genuineness, internal and external templates, and sniff tests brings us to an essential aspect of what it means to be authentic for existentialists: It requires correct representation. To make the general point, we start with an object that we abstractly call an X. If an X is authentic in its way of existing, it exists in the world in a way that truly and accurately represents what that X truly is (that would be the template that determines what Xs really are). So X's authenticity rests on whether X, in its way of existing, is correctly represented as an X.

This way of understanding authenticity, however, presents a dilemma: If an existentialist argues that you ought to *become what you already are,* how is it possible that you're not already what you are (whatever that turns out to be)? Isn't it impossible to fail to be what you already are? How can a thing exist in a way that differs from what it really is? If this is impossible, isn't everyone authentic by default? If so, being authentic wouldn't appear to be so difficult — everyone is from beginning to end!

Continuing to look at what representing means for existentialists can provide you with some clues to solve this paradox. Things can be represented in different ways, and the differences relate to the different ways that things could be said to exist:

- ✔ Some things exist in such a way that if they can be said to represent at all, it's only insofar as something *else* does the representing for them (poor things!).

- ✔ For other types of beings, the way that they exist is very different — those things can represent *themselves* (which is a way cooler way to be, if you ask us).

Need some examples? Existentialists want you to see that two types of beings are in the world: things and people. A thing like a piece of wood is just a piece of wood (and will never be more than that) until someone else chooses to represent it as something (say, as a real sword in a play). A person, on the other hand, can choose to represent himself in the way in which he chooses to live his life. The way in which you exist is fundamentally an issue of your own choosing. The way a thing exists isn't. Things just lie around. Humans, on the other hand, choose to define themselves in the direction that they give to their lives.

These two different ways of existence help you see a very basic truth: The way that an object exists implies that objects can't misrepresent themselves (because they can't represent themselves in the first place!). But the way in which people exist opens the door to misrepresentation. As a result, it's up to you whether you choose to exist in a way that's harmonious with what you truly are (whether you live in accord with the template that reveals who you are). Given that a person can choose *not* to do this, a person can fail to be what he already is by choosing not to represent himself accurately in the way that he lives his life. Understood in this way, the paradox is solved: People can fail to be what they already are. Here are some additional examples:

- ✔ The authenticity of a *thing* depends on how some other entity represents it. So a wooden sword in a play is authentic if it's used by an actor to represent a wooden sword. If it's used to represent an antique Roman sword, it's not authentic.

- ✔ The authenticity of a *person* depends on how that person uses or represents himself through living. So if someone is by nature an individual, but he lives only by the opinions of others, he's misrepresenting what he is and failing to be authentic.

Representin'!

Represent can have many meanings — to portray, to stand for, or to be a good example of. We think that the way the existentialists use the word is close to the modern slang usage: to present, or embody in a positive way, a certain group, idea, or ideal through one's words and actions. For existentialists, representing means being accurate and uncompromisingly true. According to the Hip Hop Dictionary (www.hip hopintel.com/hiphopdictionary), *represent* means "to make a statement with your presence, words, and actions. Come strong or don't come at all type action."

If you say that you're "representin' Brooklyn!" you suggest that the way that you're living accurately *represents* the way someone from Brooklyn lives. Not surprisingly, in the vernacular, failing to properly represent oneself is seen negatively. At times, such people are seen as "going out like punks" (living cowardly), and in other cases, such a person is described as "playing himself" (treating himself as undignified by playing the fool).

Authentic people: In the driver's seat and in control

Why do people — existentialists included — seem to care so much about authenticity? What's the big deal? Why does failing to be authentic look undignified? We think that the main reason is that authentic people are in control of their own lives. They're in the driver's seat. If you're not driving the car, someone else is. If you're not authentic, you're not driving your car (yourself).

Suppose that you're an X (whatever that is). If you act in a way that portrays yourself as a Y, being an X isn't really a factor in how you're living your life. But because you're really an X, it's as though some imposter is in control of your life. You aren't in the driver's seat.

Taking Stock: Who Am I? How Can I Be Authentic?

Authenticity means living in a way that represents accurately who you are. This implies knowing the answer to a key question: Who am I? To answer, existentialists think that you have an internal template or standard for you and your way of existing, and that template forms the basis for being the kind of entity that you are. You need to figure out what that template tells you about yourself. After that's done, you can check to see whether the way that you're living passes the sniff test and is authentic.

We, in the existential sense, are the kinds of beings who are bound to the endless task of representing who we are in a world that has no intrinsic meaning (and so is ultimately meaningless). Our way of existing is absurd. You're forced to pick life directions because you exist in the world, so you take positions on how to represent (or orient) yourself within that world. However, nothing within that world ever supports one way of choosing life direction as being better or more justified than any other. The choice is always yours alone.

What this information reveals is that existential authenticity has little to do with *what* a person does and instead is concerned with *how* a person chooses the direction of his life (we explore the difference between "how" and "what" living in Chapter 7). What's important is that you reflect, in your way of approaching life, a basic set of truths that emerges from your nature as an absurd being. To embrace your absurdity through living, your choices need to reflect the fact that you exist in the world in a very unique way, that humans are passionate beings, that people are free and unique, that everyone dies, and that you aren't alone in this strange world that you live in.

Why existentialists reject worldly authenticity

When the existentialists talk about authenticity, they don't mean that a person, to be authentic, has to make this particular choice or that one. Believing that a specific set of choices is key to authenticity is to hold to *worldly authenticity* — the belief that authenticity is achieved by interacting with the specific objects in the world in certain, particular ways.

Why might a person believe that this is the path to authenticity? The most common reason is because such a person would think that the answer to who he is can be found in his character, his personality, his genetics, or perhaps even in his social role. In fact, when your friends and family talk about the loss of authenticity in the world, this is most likely the kind of authenticity that they're talking about. Thus, you may be surprised when you see your friend doing what seem to be uncharacteristic acts because they're inconsistent with his beliefs or desires.

One key fact about this notion of authenticity is that it concerns *what* the person does. If your friend is an atheist, you'll likely label him as inauthentic if he winds up praying in church because he's not being true to who he is. In this case, the way that you understand the template that tells you about a person's identity is defined by psychology or perhaps biology.

So *worldly authenticity* means that being who you are requires choosing specific life alternatives that conform to your beliefs, desires, basic psychology, or character.

The existentialists reject this notion. For the existentialist, who you are as an individual being can't be summed up by or reduced to your current beliefs, your character, or your biology. As a result, thinking of authenticity as demanding that you be consistent with these things may actually entail *inauthenticity,* because it has you conform to something that doesn't express what you really are.

Embracing existential authenticity: Seeing the kind of being that you are

Unlike worldly authenticity, existential authenticity doesn't concern itself with the specific life plans that you choose. Instead, existentialists label such life plans as inauthentic if they aren't chosen or, once chosen, lived or embodied in the right way. This being so, they concern themselves with how you approach your life. Being authentic or inauthentic is possible when you're doing just about anything. What it comes down to is how you do it.

Søren Kierkegaard, in his famous book *Fear and Trembling,* talks about the fact that his exemplary authentic person — the knight of faith (if you're interested in knowing more about this one, check out Chapter 10) — may be a tax collector or some otherwise ordinary person doing very mundane things and tasks. He warns us away from thinking that true authenticity requires a certain *type* of worldly life.

So the how matters more than the what, but what does that mean? Think of it like this: Existentialists think that if a choice is authentic, it must be true that it follows from the right procedure.

We use ourselves for this example. Greg always makes his choices by using reason. He deliberates slowly and patiently about what to do and then he chooses. Chris, on the other hand, doesn't use reason; in fact, he doesn't even deliberate. He just unthinkingly does whatever his emotions dictate at any given moment. Now, it could be the case that Greg and Chris, on some given occasion, pick exactly the same thing to do. Would you be suspicious of Chris's choices in this example? Would you be prepared to perhaps refuse to say that Chris acted authentically? If so, you think that *how* he came to do what he did matters.

When you think of being yourself in that kind of way, you're using another notion of what it means to be you. In this case, you're thinking that a person can't be authentic if his choices don't flow from his nature as the kind of being he is. Most people you talk to will likely argue that rationality is an essential component of being human. As a result, they have a hard time seeing Chris's choices as emerging from a fundamental aspect of his true nature, and as a result, they think that Chris's nonrational choice-making bars him from authenticity.

Although existentialists don't demand that authentic choices or lives follow from a commitment to rationality, this example highlights a fundamental notion of their understanding of authentic identity. What they want you to be concerned with is the issue of finding out the type of being you are and then approaching life in a way that is consistent with it.

One way to put this is to say that existentialists are concerned with your *existential situation,* which is your nature as an existentially existing human being; it's what comprises the template that tells you who you are. After you discover that, existentialists want you to make choices by using the right procedure; that procedure involves making choices, and living, in a way that accurately represents your existential situation.

The central truth about who you are: Humans are absurd beings

If one central fact explains who or what we are, it's the fact that we're fully absurd beings. We exist in the world in a fundamentally different way from other things. Rocks and chairs just sit there and take up space, and that's really all that defines their existence. Your existence involves more than that. You live in the world; you take on various plans and projects. Some people choose this path in life; others choose another. But the world that you exist in is indifferent to the paths that you choose. There's no reason in the world why this rather than that path is ultimately the right one to take. You have to take full responsibility for your choices.

Existence is absurd. It demands making choices (representing yourself through living), but you have no choice but to do so in a universe that provides no foundation for those choices.

That's who we are. It's written into us in a much more fundamental way than our genes or our personality could ever be. As Thomas Hobbes (who wasn't an existentialist but who did seem to get this part right!) once put it, "The privilege of absurdity: to which no living creature is subject, but man only."

And that's exactly what the existentialists want you to embrace — that absurdity is your lot and that you shouldn't have it any other way. The only way to deny this fact, to see life as not absurd, is to live inauthentically. But that means rejecting your own nature as a free, individual being. Why do that? The existentialists think facing up to yourself is preferable. Human existence may include having a personality or having a certain genetic code or biology, but it's really defined by your way of existing in the world as an absurd creature. That can't be changed without fundamentally altering the human race and making everyone into something radically different — an object.

The many truths of your absurd nature

Being authentic means making choices, or representing yourself in the world, in a way that follows from the right procedure. Part of that means to reflect your absurdity in the ways that you approach life (we talk more about that in the next section). But the existentialists say that being absurd actually means that other facts are true about your nature because they're either required for, or follow from, absurd existence. So being authentic means understanding all the basic truths that flow from your absurdity and embracing them in the way that you live your life.

Given that these basic truths are covered in more detail in Part III of this book, we just quickly survey each of them here. If your choices fail in some way to represent even one of these truths, your way of existing in the world is fake or artificial. You're as counterfeit as a $3 bill! Your job, according to the existentialists: represent accurately all these facts about yourself in your way of living.

Absurd existence takes place in the world

Absurd beings have a unique relationship to the world. For one, what we are requires that we exist in a world. The fact that our existence must take place in the world means that we're always faced with the continual task of representing ourselves by giving meaning to our own lives and to that world we exist within.

At the same time, your way of existing in the world isn't determined by the way the world is; it's for this reason that the world is indifferent to your choices. If the world did determine who you were, you'd have all the reason to be one way and not another (you'd lack free will, though!). Thus, without this unique relationship to the world, you wouldn't be absurd. So although being in a world is fundamental to you, you're not just another object in the world. You're different from rocks and chairs. Part of existing means taking a free position or stance on how to position yourself within the world (we talk about this in Chapter 6).

Absurd existence is passionate

Unlike rocks and chairs, which can't represent themselves in the world, we care deeply about how we represent ourselves and the world around us. As a result, human life must be passionate. Living in an authentic way means taking seriously your capacity for making decisions about how to live life. Living authentically requires making decisive commitments about how to forge your own individual path through life. Living in an uncommitted way is to forfeit the gift of your unique kind of existence and to live in the way that rocks and chairs and even animals must. It's living in an undignified way (we talk more about this in Chapter 7).

Absurd existence is free

We're free; no constraints or meanings inside the world dictate to us how we ought to live. The matter of what you do is always up to you. People may attempt to continually make excuses for their choices by attributing power to things or meanings they see as external to them. But an authentic existence within an absurd world reflects the fact that you always choose who you want to be, because meanings seen to be in the world are ultimately without foundation. Your way of existing in the world is always up to you (although this idea is discussed throughout the book, we give it special treatment in Chapter 8).

Absurd existence is individual

Given the way that you're immersed in the world — seeing the world from the inside out — you unavoidably have a very particular perspective or point of view, a way of interacting with the world that you may share with others, but that's fundamentally unique to you. Consequently, to embrace your choices in an individual way means striving to reflect your uniquely experienced world within your specific way of living.

Specifically, an authentic person represents himself in a way that reflects the fact that he's more than the mere sum of his parts. So even if you're part of a community or part of a world, the existentialists hold that as a uniquely individual thing, what you are is always more than just that. Individual existence succeeds in standing out (we discuss two ways of understanding this task, one religious and one atheistic, in Chapter 10 and 11, respectively).

Absurd existence is finite

We don't live forever. We're finite; our existence in the world has temporal limitations. You're born at a particular time, and at some point in the future, it's certain that you'll die. Your nature as an absurd being relies on this fact. Thus, some existentialists argue that the choices you make in life must reflect your continual awareness of your unique past — and how it functions as the background for your ways of understanding yourself and your choices. At the same time, many argue that authentic living must also reflect your conscious-ness of the inevitability of your own impending death (we tackle this topic at length in Chapter 9).

Absurd existence is social

Absurd creatures, living in the particular world that they inhabit, are forced to come to the realization that they aren't alone. Absurd creatures don't live in a world populated only with inanimate chairs and rocks, but in a world populated with other entities for which these existential truths also apply. The fact that other absurd creatures are in your world, existing in just the same way that you are, means making choices in certain ways.

Authenticity 102: Living Inauthentically Means Running Away

Although existentialists claim that life has no inherent meaning, they all divide ways of living into authentic versus inauthentic. Someone living inau-thentically refuses to accept the basic fact that life is absurd. Different exis-tentialists have different ways of talking about this situation, but it all comes down to a kind of dishonesty. The truth is that life is absurd — people want to find order and meaning, but there is none. If you live inauthentically, you refuse to accept this basic truth, and this, the existentialists say, is dishonest.

However, although all the existentialists view authenticity as a form of strength or health and inauthenticity as a kind of weakness, they don't agree as a group about whether living the authentic life is better than living the inauthentic life. Some of them think that an existentialist shouldn't claim that authentic living is better. As a result, some existentialists take other exis-tentialists to task for claiming, as far as they can tell, that authenticity is better, or of more value, than inauthenticity. Sartre, for example, thinks that Heidegger's notion of inauthenticity is evaluatively loaded. Heidegger insists that it isn't and for his own part argued that Sartre's notion of bad faith (his version of inauthenticity) is judgmental. Sartre insisted that it isn't. When you read the existentialists, however, it's tough to get away from the idea that authenticity is in fact to be preferred.

From one perspective, it's hard to imagine why anyone would fail to be authentic. People love authenticity. They want to see it in everyone around them. It's hard to imagine people who would honestly argue that it's not important to them. Can you imagine someone who champions being fake, someone who argues for the importance of *not* being who you are? Still, according to the existentialists, most people are *not* authentic. Why not?

Because it's hard to do. Existentialists tend to agree that authenticity causes a lot of personal discomfort, and for the most part, human beings tend to want to take the easy path in life.

Table 5-1 lists some of the terms the different existentialists use to distinguish between authentic and inauthentic ways of living.

Table 5-1	Authenticity and Value Judgments	
Philosopher	*Authentic*	*Inauthentic*
Camus	Revolt (Consciousness)	The Chain (Unconsciousness)
Kierkegaard	Faith	Despair
Sartre	Good Faith	Bad Faith
Nietzsche	Nobility	Slavishness
Heidegger	Authenticity	Inauthenticity

Inauthentic people take the path of least resistance

According to the existentialists, most of the time when people fall into being inauthentic or fail to be true to themselves, it's not because they *want* to be inauthentic (as we said before, people do crave authenticity), but because it's hard to be authentic and because, frankly, it's so easy to be inauthentic. It just works that way. It's a fact of life!

So why are people driven away from authenticity if they crave it so deeply? If a person craves X but chooses Y instead, you have reason to think that Y is a more powerful motivator than X on that person's behavior. In this case, existentialists may suggest that if you're driven away from authenticity, something must be discomforting about it. Well, that's true! Consider the following:

✔ Pursuing authenticity is difficult because it

- Requires relentless self-examination

- Exposes you to things about yourself that you may not want to know

> • Simply causes friction with others
>
> In short, authenticity hurts! But this isn't enough. In addition, a person needs to make a choice.
>
> ✔ If you're driven away from authenticity, you choose the avoidance of discomfort over your own desire for the admirable status of authenticity.

Existentialists are united on this point: Inauthentic people just can't hack discomfort, and they strive to avoid it at all costs. The more inauthentic a person is, the more prevalent his desire to avoid discomfort. Instead of being themselves, inauthentic people want to avoid the normal friction of everyday life that being themselves just naturally brings. They avoid self-examination, they lie to themselves, and they tend to rationalize their own behavior. The path of least resistance doesn't lead to authenticity. If inauthentic people have a motto, it's this one: Ignorance is bliss.

These motives for acting inauthentically actually reveal a little more about what makes people crave authenticity. It's not *just* that living authentically means living in accord with the person you are; living authentically also seems to require mastering yourself so that you don't give in to your baser desires to escape discomfort (at least when it's inappropriate to do so). Giving in to desires seems to indicate a lack of control, whereas an authentic person appears to be in control; he doesn't let desire for comfort or pleasure rule living.

In practice, people usually deny the truth by running away. When they can't face the fact that life is absurd, they find a way to hide or escape from that fact. The thought that life is meaningless, despite how much you yearn for meaning, can be scary. It's not surprising, then, that many, perhaps most, people respond in a way that existentialists would call inauthentic. As Camus points out, people can respond inauthentically in two ways. The most extreme method is to commit suicide. This response may not be common, but the existentialists take it very seriously. Less dramatically, people can deny absurdity by putting their faith in systems — philosophical, religious, or scientific — that cover up or explain away the absurdity of existence.

Suicide is not the answer

Suicide may actually seem like a rational and authentic response to honestly facing the absurdity of life and finding it unacceptable. Perhaps the most authentic response to absurdity is to *not* participate in worldly tasks at all! As it turns out, however, existentialists aren't in favor of suicide.

Some people may argue that the most genuine response is a specific kind of global disengagement — actual suicide. After all, recognizing the truth of the absurdity of human existence can be disquieting. It can certainly throw you for a serious loop. Surely you didn't think life was meant to be this way (that's part of what makes it so darn absurd; it's like spending your life trying to put a square peg in a round hole). You were sold a false bill of goods; you thought you fit in the world, that in some way you were playing a big, meaningful role in some large scheme, maybe even in the creation of something bigger or better than yourself.

If life just isn't worth living if it's absurd, suicide may seem like an authentic response. If absurdity is actually true of humanity, but it's an affront to the dignity of human life, some may argue that suicide may be the right way to go. You may think that by committing suicide, people *accept* that the truth of human life is absurdity, but they refuse to *will* (or embrace) the absurd life by choosing its continuance (through living it).

According to the existentialists, suicide doesn't really represent absurdity because representing something fully, or embracing it, involves accepting it as a whole being. The suicide acknowledges absurdity only partially and also partially rejects it, and thus isn't embracing the absurd.

The accepting part is purely intellectual. I see that absurdity is a truth about me. But I dare not face it as a matter of will. Instead, I avoid absurdity in its fullest sense by ceasing its continuance through death. The fact that this isn't enough to represent the absurd shows that the existentialists believe you can discover a truth about humans here, namely:

Melville's Bartleby: Accepting, but not willing, absurdity

A wonderful short story, Herman Melville's *Bartleby the Scrivener* (1853) is a favorite of the existential (or absurdist) minded. The story tells about a young 19th-century Wall Street copyist named Bartleby. As the story goes on, Bartleby becomes more and more strange, slowly opting out of daily tasks by responding, "I would prefer not to." Bartleby's refusals take on more and more serious consequences, as he loses his job, becomes homeless, and then finally dies because he "prefers not to" eat. Although an explanation of Bartleby's behavior is disputed, one reason hinted at in the end is that Bartleby has glimpsed the absurdity of human living. He never recovers, and as the story goes on, he loses his ability to partake in any human endeavor whatsoever, with tragic circumstances. For Camus, Bartleby would have accepted absurdity but not embraced it through his will.

- ✔ We are, in part, thinking, intellectual creatures.
- ✔ We are also, in part, willing creatures.

If both of these parts are necessary, you can't claim to embrace or accept the truth of absurdity by merely recognizing it on an intellectual level. That leaves out willing, which is also an essential part of what you are. To embrace something is to embody it in all you are. In this case, part of willing absurdity is to will its continuation through your continued absurd life!

Suicide fails to be absurd. Suicide acknowledges absurdity but refuses to fully embody it, so it doesn't fully accept absurdity. As a result, a person choosing suicide is misrepresenting who he is; he presents himself as not-absurd (by choosing to die in the face of the indignity of his nature) when that isn't what he is. As a result, suicide can't be authentic. True authenticity must see the truth of human existence *and* will that truth through continued life. Only such a way of being absurd is authentic.

Covering up the truth won't save you

The important thing is not to be cured . . . but to live with one's ailments.

—Albert Camus, "The Myth of Sisyphus"

Merely living doesn't automatically mean someone has willed, or embraced, the absurd. People often see absurdity and continue to live, but only on the grounds that the absurdity they see is somehow (or in some way) denied. To them, the world seems absurd, but there's a mysterious divine plan. Or maybe they believe *this* world is absurd, but an ordered, rational world is waiting for them after they depart this one. Or perhaps they say that the world seems absurd, but only because science hasn't finished providing all the answers.

Camus calls all such denials *philosophical* (as opposed to physical) suicide. It's philosophical because it uses fictions and illusions to hide the fact that life is actually absurd. It's suicide because, like physical suicide, it denies or renounces life as it actually exists. Religion, science, and many philosophies typically provide reasons and plans for the universe so that its irrational character is removed. That has the comforting effect of making the apparent absurdity of your situation into the illusion. But this kind of comfort prevents people from living authentically, because it misrepresents who they are.

In "The Myth of Sisyphus," Camus says, "[T]he doctrines that explain everything to me also debilitate me at the same time. They relieve me of the weight of my own life, and yet I must carry it alone." For existentialists, then, philosophical and physical suicide are both ways of running from the true absurdity of life.

Embracing Absurdity: "The Myth of Sisyphus"

In his most famous philosophical essay, Camus uses a guy named Sisyphus to vividly illustrate the life of absurdity and what he feels is the proper reaction to it. Sisyphus is a man in a horribly absurd situation who overcomes it through embracing that situation. Embracing the situation requires a special approach that makes him a fitting role model. Through a special kind of rebellion, he's able to reject certain aspects of his situation while staying true to who and what he is.

Sisyphus and his punishment

Sisyphus is a hero in Greek mythology. He's famous for being punished by the gods, condemned to roll a huge boulder up a hill for all eternity. He rolls this heavy boulder up the hill; then it comes back down, and he starts all over again. All his work is aimed at doing a job that's doubly pointless.

First, it's pointless because rolling a boulder up a hill is meaningless in itself. Who cares whether the boulder is at the top or the bottom of the hill? Perhaps you can imagine special circumstances in which it might matter — maybe if Sisyphus were a landscaper building a Japanese rock garden, for example. But, in itself, it's meaningless. On top of this, of course, is the fact that the rock comes back down, and he has to start all over again. The task is never completed.

Camus, who had great respect for the troubles of the working class, compares this situation to the plight of factory workers who do menial, repetitious tasks all their lives, only to find at the end that they have nothing to show for it. But really, he thinks we're *all* in Sisyphus's predicament.

What we share with Sisyphus is our existential situation. If the world is really fundamentally without order, or irrational, all the importance (order!) you attach to all the things you do is pointless. All your projects, employments, and relationships — whatever you toil to accomplish or achieve — are as empty as rolling a boulder up a hill. The world just is; it has no inherent value.

So your existential situation is that you're an absurd being, and you can't escape this fact about how you're related to the world around you.

The existential description of your situation can seem pretty bleak. You can see why the existentialists got a reputation for being real downers. They were famous for sitting in coffee shops, wearing black turtlenecks and chain-smoking — not lounging on beaches, sipping fruity cocktails. Suffice it to say there's a reason existentialists aren't often invited to party at the Palms with Jenny McCarthy (Greg has tried and failed). For now, we just want to warn you against wrongly interpreting the existentialists. They actually see the absurdity of life as being no reason for being depressed at all — quite the opposite, actually.

What usually doesn't get reported about the existentialists' attitude is the twist they add: the optimistic side of their attitude. All the doom and gloom about the meaninglessness of life are just the beginning. This may be your existential situation, but Camus and the other existentialists don't really think they're saying anything profound or new by describing that situation. What's important to existentialists, and where they feel they have something to say, is in how you respond to this situation. The optimism of the existentialist response to absurdity can be seen in Camus's description of Sisyphus's response to his situation. For him, Sisyphus wasn't just an example of a man struggling with absurdity, but a hero who overcomes and even conquers that absurdity.

Rebel without a cause . . . but a smile

Rebellion cannot exist without the feeling that, somewhere and somehow, one is right.

—Albert Camus, The Rebel

Sisyphus is a bit of a rebel. He defies the gods on multiple occasions and is particularly fond of tricking death. In one instance, he's said to have actually put death in chains. So Sisyphus doesn't just defy the gods; he also rebels against death itself. Rebellion is very important to Camus. Sisyphus is a rebel and has an attitude both in life and in death. Now, understandably, it's hard to have an attitude and be a rebel when you're pushing a heavy boulder up a hill. You're too busy sweating! Similarly, most people don't have time for existential concerns while they're scrambling to meet deadlines or get the kids into the minivan.

For Camus, Sisyphus's situation gets interesting when he's at the top of the hill, the boulder rolls back down, and he starts to go back down to do it all again. At this point, he has a choice. Should he give in to despair? Should he let the gods win and mope over his eternal fate? Or should he thumb his nose at them, embrace this meaningless task, and refuse to see it as a punishment? For Camus, Sisyphus's scorn saves him. He overcomes his situation because he stands in revolt of it. Sisyphus is a rebel, and because of this, Camus is convinced that you have to imagine him smiling as he walks down that hill.

What it means to be a rebel

A rebel is someone who refuses to surrender. In *The Rebel,* Camus explains the difference between a rebel and someone who simply renounces his situation. Renunciation is a form of surrender. A rebel, on the other hand, draws a line in the sand; says, "This far, and no farther"; and stands up to defend that line. You've probably known people who complain about their jobs or their lives constantly but do nothing, or can do nothing, to change their situation. They belittle their situation and themselves for living in it. They're in despair because they refuse to either accept their situation or act against it. They've simply surrendered. You probably know others, however, who hold their heads up proudly and refuse to be defeated. They declare that something is unjust in their situation and that they deserve better treatment — that it's their right.

So being a rebel really has two parts, a yes and a no:

- ✔ **No:** The rebel rejects something as an unacceptable intrusion upon his rights.
- ✔ **Yes:** The rebel asserts himself as someone who has value, as someone who has a claim to these rights, and as someone who can judge the situation as unjust.

For Camus, you can't be a rebel unless you stand for something, something you believe others should accept. Screaming at the cop and saying, "You can't do this! I don't like being in handcuffs!" isn't enough. A rebel asserts that something is unjust, something is wrong with the situation — "You can't do this; I have my rights!" By asserting rights, the rebel is asserting the existence of a value.

So when Sisyphus rebels against the gods, when he walks down the mountain feeling scorn for their sentence, he's also doing these two things: rejecting and asserting. What, then, is he rejecting? The gods expect that the best Sisyphus can do is to acknowledge his fate but feel resignation as a result, to hate what his life is. That's where the punishment lies.

The gods assume that only labor or work that has meaning outside itself, only labor that fits into a larger scheme of things, is dignified work. Outside serving as a punishment, Sisyphus's labor has no larger meaning. That's the whole point: It's meaningless! As such, the rock-rolling is meant to trap him for all eternity in a life that has no dignity at all. Thus, according to the gods, resignation is the best he can muster; as a matter of fact, the more resigned he is, the more intense the punishment is.

Rebels stand for something

Everyone loves a rebel. But if all you do is drink and smoke, listen to punk rock, or drive a Harley, what kind of statement are you making? Nietzsche once said, "Don't tell me what you're running from, tell me: what are you running to?" A real rebel stands for something, wants to build something. Gandhi stood up to the British and stood for the sanctity of life and the effectiveness of nonviolence. The Rev. Martin Luther King Jr. stood up against racial injustice and oppression, but he also stood for a dream of racial harmony and a United States that stood by the values expressed in the Declaration of Independence. True rebels, it seems, aren't merely *negative;* they also express *positive* ideals. Gandhi and King weren't necessarily existentialist rebels, but existentialist rebels share their penchant for asserting values.

But Sisyphus rejects this entire construction of the situation. He rebels against the gods' assertions that his task must be meaningless and that his only response is despair. He accepts his task as being inherently meaningless, but he refuses to let it remain so. He refuses to give in to resignation.

Sisyphus rejects

- ✔ The gods' view of his situation
- ✔ That his situation is incurably meaningless
- ✔ Resignation and surrender

Instead, he revolts, and in defiance of all that is, he asserts his own worth and the worth of his task. He lives for the challenge, for the struggle, when there is nothing else. Sisyphus, in his scorn, asserts himself as a being capable of judging, of deciding, of valuing, of creating. Although he rejects the gods and their punishment, he asserts his own dignity and value. At the same time, he chooses to embrace his situation and his task. He gives them value not because they have it inherently or because the gods conferred it, but because he, Sisyphus, willed them to have it.

He can't change his situation, but through an act of will, he re-creates what it means and what it's worth to him. In a real sense, Sisyphus takes full responsibility for his life. He embraces absurdity by embracing what is and making it his own. Thus, rolling the rock up and down the hill when nothing will come of it doesn't rob him of his life; it actually gives him his life. His rock is, as Camus told us, "his thing," and Sisyphus is the one who made it so.

Sisyphus asserts

- ✔ The value of his life
- ✔ The meaningfulness of his task, his rock, and the endless struggle itself
- ✔ His own worth and dignity as a human being
- ✔ His ability to judge these things and make them matter through an act of will

Rebellion can give life meaning

So why is Sisyphus smiling? Simple: He has a meaningful life. He recognizes his own value and the value of the actions that make up his life. It wasn't given to him that way, but he embraces his life for what it is, embraces even the absurdity of it, and dives into it as something he has made his own. And he does so without any inauthenticity. This is what makes the rock, and his task, truly his. He's living the life he chose, the life he created. Isn't that what everyone wants? You may say, "Hey, wait a second; he didn't choose that!" But in a sense, he did. He didn't choose to be punished for all eternity, but in his rebellion, he chose what it means.

No gods have condemned you to live this way. But death cruelly conveys meaninglessness onto everyone's projects. Camus thinks that you, like Sisyphus, can rebel against death. Don't expect an extra 20 years, but if you reject death and embrace your projects despite the meaninglessness death confers upon them, you embrace life and give it a value and even a kind of meaning. This is the meaning and the end to embracing the absurd and living authentically.

Part III
Living a Meaningful Life in a Meaningless World

The 5th Wave — By Rich Tennant

"I suppose it's just my way of finding meaning in an absurd and meaningless world."

In this part . . .

In Part II, our focus is on the themes that describe the problems the existentialists see themselves as addressing. This part covers the existentialists' responses to these problems. Taken as a whole, it presents a "how-to" manual of existential living. It clarifies the concerns that form the core of what existentialism is all about. The existentialists aren't big on final solutions, but they do generally agree that there's hope and that human beings can find a way forward.

Part III presents what the existentialists see as the way forward, the way to deal with the absurdity the world confronts us with. Each chapter develops a different existential theme, a different component of that way forward, primarily through the lens of one existentialist's philosophy. Don't consider these discussions the final word of the existentialists as a group on that topic, but you get an idea of why each of these themes is important and how at least one existentialist develops that theme.

Chapter 6

Understanding Our Unique Way of Existing in the World

In This Chapter

▶ Surveying different ways to think about existence

▶ Investigating how you're connected to the world

▶ Understanding who and what you are

*I*n this chapter, we talk about the meaning of human existence by analyzing Martin Heidegger's central existential work, Being and Time (1920). To crack the question "What is the meaning of human existence?" you have to look closely at what it means for you — the entity you are — to exist. What makes the uniqueness of human life possible?

Look closely at what it means to engage in life. Existentialists such as Heidegger point out that the proper method of understanding life isn't scientific because science looks at things from the outside, and you can understand life only from within. As a result, they propose using the phenomenological method, a way of investigating life from the inside.

We explain that existentialists such as Heidegger see life as grounded in an intimate immersion in the world. That means understanding the meaning of existence requires acknowledging the ways in which we're immersed in activity within the human worlds of significance that we occupy.

We end with a problem that arises from this description of life. Namely, we ask, "Where are *you* in all that immersion within the social and human world? Where's the individual?" In response, Heidegger points out that your basic, most fundamental way of living isn't as an "I" but as a "They." Basic, everyday living is a mirroring of the group or social climate that you live in. This doesn't mean that it's the only way for you to live; you can be authentic within life and express your individuality. But you need to first realize that your basic, normal mode of existing is what Heidegger calls "fallen" — existing in the world as a "They."

Different Ways to Investigate Existence

Heidegger was interested in the really big questions, like "What's the meaning of existence?" Yeah, that's big! To investigate it, Heidegger thinks you need to look closely at the particular mode of existence of specific beings — namely, beings just like you.

To investigate your own existence, start by recognizing that the capacity to ask questions about your own existence is unique to your way of being. Who and what you are matter to you. You participate in life in a way that no other being can. You wonder, you ponder, you ask questions about living. What does it mean that you can do that? What are you? What's the structure of the kind of life that defines you?

If you want to investigate life, you need a method. But how do you dig into the nature of life itself? Science seems like the wrong method, because it wants to examine life from the outside. It can't grasp what it means to wonder about and question existence — to actually experience living. Instead, Heidegger argues you need to analyze your existence — or participation in life — from the inside and try to understand its meaning from that insider's perspective.

Investigating the meaning of existence

Of all of the big questions, perhaps none is bigger than "What is the meaning of existence?" If you think about it, things *are*, a fact that's actually pretty darn amazing. Why isn't there nothing instead? Existence is pretty cool!

According to existential thinkers such as Heidegger, it's helpful to start by clarifying exactly what you want to investigate. To begin, note the different ways to talk about existing. As Heidegger puts it, you can ask about the nature of existence, or you can ask about the nature of beings. As he sees it, the difference involves the following:

- When you talk about *beings*, you mean things that exist. Cats, tables, chairs, you — these are all beings, not existence itself.

- When you talk about *existence*, you mean the mysterious fact that a being shows up or makes an appearance at all. Existence isn't itself a being.

Heidegger wants you to look at existence itself. Unfortunately, Heidegger thinks that most people have forgotten the question or left it behind. You may forget the question for lots of reasons. Perhaps you take the answer to be obvious (what's more obvious, you think, than the meaning of *is*?). Perhaps you blow the question off, suggesting that it's just plain unintelligible or silly.

Heidegger thinks that sometimes, people forget the question by mistaking questions about existence with questions about beings; they get things all mixed up, confusing what he calls *ontic* investigations (into the nature of beings) with *ontological* investigations (into existence).

Heidegger thinks you need to reinvestigate the mystery at the heart of things — existence. Now you just need to know how to get started!

Knowing existence means knowing you

Asking about existence is about as abstract as you can get. So how can you gain access to the issue? Heidegger thinks that you have to inquire about existence through an investigation of the existence of a particular kind of being. The best being to pick, he argues, is one just like you!

Why investigate a being to investigate existence itself? Can't you just deal with big, hard-to-grasp abstractions? Fortunately, no! Heidegger says, "Being is always the Being of an entity." What he means is that if you want to think about existence (being), you have to think about the existence *of* something that already exists. In a way, that's where existence is going on. Beings get you access to existence.

So what being should you use to investigate existence? A beer mug? Well . . . that's not the best route. Heidegger thinks it helpful to investigate a being whose existence is defined by the fact that it questions its own existence. You're that being. You engage with your existence. You wonder about it. You ask, "What kind of being should I be?" as though the *way* you exist is up to you.

This way of existing, which is unique to us, causes us a lot of anxiety because the Shakespearean question "To be or not to be?" is never settled. It's always there, demanding to be reengaged again and again. It makes life painful, but at the same time it opens the possibility for the exhilaration or thrill of life that your beer mug, which can't exist in this way, can never experience. The beer mug's existence doesn't include that kind of possibility (well, not *our* beer mugs, anyway!).

Why does investigating your type of existence help you? Why does it matter that you ask questions about life? Heidegger has his reasons. He says:

1. **You ask questions about existence.**

2. **Asking questions about existence involves understanding existence on some level.**

3. **So in the way that you engage with life by questioning it, you must already understand existence on some basic level.**

Heidegger's reasoning here is interesting. He thinks if you ask a question like "What *is* existence?" or "What does it mean for me to be?" you already have an understanding, on some level, of the meaning of *is* (*is* is in the question, isn't it?). But *is* means existence! So to ask what existence *is* already means being acquainted with the answer in some way to start.

With this insight in mind, Heidegger proposes that if you can investigate the very way in which you exist as the specific being you are — the fact that you wonder and question what to be — you may come to know a bit more about existence as a whole, or at least get some clues about it.

You want to investigate what it means for beings like you to experience life in the way that you do. After all, that's what life is — being engaged with what's around you, wondering about it, and asking lots of questions; directing your life one way or another; or being anxious; or being exhilarated. Life is trying to figure out how to situate yourself or how to *be*. It's hard work, but it's your inescapably existential duty and obligation.

So to investigate the meaning of your existence, look under the hood, and try to see how this sort of life runs and ticks. Not many questions are more existential than that!

Science: Analyzing life from the outside

If you want to ask about life, you first need a method to use to investigate it. The existentialists tend to be united on one point: The scientific method doesn't work well here, because it's committed to analyzing things from the outside, from a distanced perspective. Thinking about life from the outside, however, just seems to look at life the wrong way.

Don't get us wrong — we're not hating on science. We love science! In fact, science is clearly a very valuable method of investigation. Without science, you wouldn't have an iPod, and you'd have to walk to work because you wouldn't have a car. One of the reasons science is so effective, frankly, is because it analyzes things in a detached way. Science prides itself on learning about things from an impartial and unbiased point of view, and that view works when you care about technological advancement.

But that's not the best method of investigation for *all* inquiries. How does science approach the questions "What does life mean?" and "What makes life possible?" Open any science textbook that deals with humans, and take a look. What does it say? Lots of things: that humans are mammals, that humans are *homo sapiens,* that people have specific sequences of DNA, that the brain is composed of neurons. That sort of thing. That's what human life — as it's studied by biology from the detached perspective — turns out to be.

But when you pose the question about the meaning of life, is that the kind of response you're looking for? When you ask, "What makes life possible?" or "What does it all mean?" does the biology text help you out?

No doubt you get the unmistakable feeling that this is fundamentally the wrong kind of response. If you've read the book *The Hitchhiker's Guide to the Galaxy,* by Douglas Adams, you'll remember that a bunch of mice build a supercomputer to figure out "the answer to life, the universe, and everything." After billions of years, it gives its answer: 42. It's funny, but why? It's not 42 that you're laughing at (well, maybe you are a bit). Instead, you're likely laughing at the fact that the scientific language of the answer just doesn't fit the personal language of the question.

Life, as a way of existing, can't be analyzed from the outside. Life isn't biological life; neither is it chemical life or life as understood by physics. It's *experienced* life. Try as it might, science just can't grasp that. It can't address what it means to ponder, question, and wonder. But you want to know what it means to be that kind of thing — what makes it all possible or what it means to exist as the kind of being you are. Whatever the answer, we know one thing: Life won't be illuminated at all for us by talk of atoms or chemicals or neurons . . . or the number 42.

Viewing life from the inside out

Science doesn't do a good job of explaining life because scientific investigations are too impersonal. To get at the more personal dimension of life, you need a method that can analyze the actual experience that is life. You need a method that can get on the inside of the experience of life and analyze it from there.

Edmund Husserl (1859–1938) thought that he had just such a method. According to Husserl, to really understand the sort of life particular to human beings, you have to be a human being. You need to actually be an experiencing entity to get a grasp on what it means to experience and exist in a human way. In fact, this idea seems right. No matter how many scientific facts you accumulate about humans, you never get much of a clue about what it means to actually live or exist in the sense that you want to investigate.

Husserl proposed a method called *phenomenology* to rigorously study the actual insider's experience of living or existing. Phenomenology is a big word, but it's easy to understand. It breaks down into two Greek terms, *phenomenon,* which means *to appear,* and *logos,* which means *to make sense of* or *to give an account of something.* So *phenomenology* means to make sense of (or explain) what appears as you experience life from the inside.

What's it like to be a bat?

In 1974, Thomas Nagel, a philosopher who studies the mind, posited an interesting thought experiment. What if, he wondered, you knew everything there was to know about the physical scientific facts involved when a bat uses echolocation? In such a scenario, he asked, would you know what it was like to use echolocation? Nagel's answer was no — that the actual experience specific to bat life couldn't be fully reduced to the sorts of facts that science collects, even if it had them all to study.

Think about it. If you agree with Nagel's conclusion, it seems to suggest that what it's like for you to exist, experience the world, or participate in life can't be understood from the outside through scientific investigation. Instead, because knowing what it's like to be a bat would require *being* a bat, you have to take seriously the actual inside experiences of the human being. Knowing what it's like to participate in human life requires looking at human life from the inside and seeing how it ticks on its own terms.

The phenomenologist tries to pay close attention to how things look from the first-person point of view because that first-person point of view is so integral to what it means for you to exist. From there, the phenomenologist can analyze what appears to determine what makes the phenomena possible. The existentialist hopes that you can use phenomenology to gain access to important clues about the actual structure of life.

Living in Your Everyday World

Existentialists think that understanding what it means to exist as a human being is important. As we discuss in the preceding section, this exploration requires analyzing the experience of life as it looks from the inside of a being who experiences life as you do. In this section, we look at what Heidegger claims to find in his analysis of the phenomenon of human life and what makes your unique way of existing possible.

Heidegger's first claim is that our existence is what he calls a *being-in-the-world*, a very deep and intimate way of being connected to your environment. We take apart the phrase *being-in-the-world*:

- Look at Heidegger's claim that being connected (or being-in) from an existential point of view means being involved and committed to a world through concerns and goals. All these ways of being disposed toward the world are ways of responding to the question of what it means to be or to exist.

- Consider *world* to better understand what your concern is immersed within or about. In other words, what's the context within which you ask about your own existence? Heidegger's answer is that life takes place in social worlds; only within social environments is the human kind of existence possible. Worlds provide the kind of languages needed to interact with existence in the way you do.

✔ Connect being-in to the existential notion of *world*. According to Heidegger, being in-the-world always means engaging with life through a participation with your projects and goals. Heidegger argues that this is accomplished through seeing and responding to the particular social worlds we find ourselves within in terms of the tools that those social worlds provide and are composed of. From Heidegger's perspective, your most basic relationship to life is not only social, but also practical and activity-oriented.

The nuts and bolts of your life

Existentialists are centrally concerned with understanding what it means to live the kind of existence you do. Time to start investigating. When you think of life, what are the most basic components or parts? When you pay attention to it as a whole, what does life always seem to involve? For Heidegger, the most basic answer is that human life is a way of being-in-the-world. Human life, he thinks, means always being radically situated somewhere, being directed or focused intimately on what's around you.

The notion of being-in-the-world

Heidegger really *loves* hyphens. Seriously. He absolutely loves to connect long strings of words with them. No, he isn't grammatically deranged. He actually has a philosophical reason: He thinks that the hyphens draw attention to certain features of your basic existence. To see, compare these two ways of expressing this:

✔ Being in the world

✔ Being-in-the-world

In the first item, the grammar implies that *being* and *the world* are separate things connected by the word *in*. This implies that a being can exist and then be put *into* a world. If that's right, each of the two (*being* and *world*) can exist independently without the other. When thinking about *human* existence or human life, Heidegger strongly disagrees that this is possible.

Beings like us exist in a way that's better described by being-in-the-world. The hyphenated connections imply that what's connected by the dashes should actually be thought of as a unitary phenomenon. So you can't exist first and then be put in the world, because for you to *be* in the first place implies being connected to the world in an intimate way. Your very way of existing is worldly.

Dasein: The notion of existing-there

At the simplest level, what does it mean to say that life, or your unique existence, is essentially worldly? For the existentialists, learning about life or existence is phenomenological (see the earlier section "Viewing life from the inside out" for more details). So you should be able to simply look closely at how experience looks or appears and try to generate some basic clues from there. Go ahead. Take a look at your experience. Don't look at this or that particular experience. Instead, focus on what all your experiences seem to have in common. What basic features seem to always be present?

Well, at the core, living or being *in-a-world* always involves being *situated* in a context and a location. Human life is a being-somewhere!

Look around; test it out. It's so obvious that you tend to miss it. At no time do you ever exist and then wind up in some situation, one that you then experience. Instead, an essential part of your existence is being situated. You always find yourself in the midst of this particular experience or that, one that has this history or that one, this cultural background as opposed to that one structuring it as significant, and so on.

Heidegger stresses this point by using the German word *Dasein* to name the kind of being that you are. In German, the term breaks into two parts: *Da*, which means *there,* and *sein,* which means *to exist.* Together — yup, here comes another hyphen! — *Dasein* means *existing-there.*

The fact that we understand this on some level is reflected when you ask someone, "How's life?" You often mean "How are you situated lately?" People seem to acknowledge this basic, situated aspect of what they are (their existence). But you need to dig deeper into this notion of being essentially in-the-world. In particular, look closer at what it may mean to be in something from the standpoint of human life. Specifically, what does it mean to say that life is a way of being intimately connected to the world?

Space, the final frontier of life

Life is always situated. Using Heidegger's lingo, this means that one of the necessary aspects of Dasein (the kind of being you are) is being-in (the *in* part of *being-in-the-world*). The way Heidegger sees it, this means that *space* is central to existence and life. This is odd, because space is typically understood scientifically, and existentialists don't tend to understand human existence in scientific terms. So if an existentialist says space is essential to your existence, you can bet that there's an existential way of being spatial or "in space."

As Heidegger puts it, "Being-in is not a 'property' which Dasein sometimes has and sometimes does not have, and *without* which it could *be* just as well as it could with it." Ah, those hyphens! There he goes again! Just remember that the hyphen means the things connected are inseparable. So if *being-in* is hyphenated, life always incorporates a dimension of "in-ness." You don't first exist and *then* wind up in a spatially defined situation.

Think about the ways you typically use spatial terms. You say that your car is *in* the parking lot, that the cars are all *next* to one another, that each car is *2 feet from* the one that is *next* to it. What you should notice, though, is that this way of talking is restricted to objects seen from an observer's third-person point of view. For existentialists, people aren't objects, so you must understand your existence from the first-person point of view. You don't understand life from the observer's view, but the *participator's* view.

As a result, you need a way of understanding how space corresponds to that kind of existing. You need a participatory, existential notion of space. Clearly, it doesn't involve thinking in terms of maps or a ruler.

Does language give you any insight here? Yes! As it turns out, people often use spatial terms to imply a way of being *concerned, involved,* or *immersed* within relationships. You may say

- ✔ "Oh, she's just *in* love."
- ✔ "What's she gotten herself *into*?"
- ✔ "So are you *in* or out?"
- ✔ "Why does she find it so hard to stand *by* her family when in need?"

The frequency with which you use this kind of language reveals an existential way of understanding space. After all, when you think of *life,* it makes sense. Life just seems inconceivable without paying close attention to involvement. Isn't it fundamental to life? To be *in* stuff? To be *up to* things? When you think of pondering, defining yourself, or coming at life, the *in* of being-in-the-world is what's being implicated. It implies that you're always necessarily immersed with life. It matters to you. Because you're in the world, those concerns or immersion take the form of participating with this or that plan, goal, role, or relationship.

Life is fundamentally spatial because you're always touched by what's around you in ways that matter to you. Some concerns are closer to you than others, whereas others seem more distant (or foreign) to you. It's just what you are; you're spatial *through* and *through*!

Meaning: Life's requirement

Heidegger thinks that existential living means being involved. It means being concerned with your existence and therefore being disposed toward the world around you in a way that highlights how things *matter* to you. But what makes such mattering possible? According to Heidegger, it requires that you reside in a world in which things around you have a significance. Residing in such a world is the foundation of existential life. Immersion in such a world allows your concerns and disposition toward existence to take concrete form. Because worlds are social in character, Heidegger's point hints at a further claim: that your existential existence depends upon the existence of others.

Consider these two different ways of talking about worlds:

- The collection of existing physical entities
- A shared social way of structuring experience so that your environment is revealed as significant and meaningful in a way that allows you to live an intelligible human life

As we discuss earlier in this chapter and throughout the book, many existentialists, such as Heidegger, highlight how some words (such as *in*) can have a scientific meaning and an existential meaning. In the preceding list, the first use of *world* is clearly scientific. It means everything that physically exists. It's the sum of everything. Existentialists prefer the second use of *world* because they want to understand life the way it's experienced.

The second way of talking about the world hints at the fact that an existential world is a human world as opposed to the physical world. It's like a large web or social language in which you can become immersed. Think of times you've said something like this:

- "When is she going to join the real *world*?"
- "What *world* are you living in to do something like that?"
- "Alas, the business *world* is just not for me."

In each of these uses, you're implying that actions and ways of responding to things take on different significance depending on the kind of language or *world* of meanings that the person is immersed within. Understanding behavior as meaningful in a *human* sense, it seems, requires understanding the specific world that it arises from and that gives it meaning.

For example, to live "in the business world" is to experience, see, and respond to the environment (and the self) in the way that the social practitioners of business do. Perhaps, for example, someone in the art world and someone in the business world would react to a painting differently, because one person experiences it as an aesthetic work and the other experiences it as a good investment. It isn't "in truth" one or the other; the significance it takes on depends on the viewer's *world*.

Life involves a way of being affected by (and responding to) things in your environment in ways that matter to you. It's also a way of wrangling with the question "What does it mean to be?" Without worlds to exist in, these kinds of practical, meaningful, and highly existential engagements wouldn't be possible. Worlds provide a context and a language for you to *be* — for you to participate meaningfully in life. Only within worlds can you grapple with choices about what to be.

This truth about the need for worlds reveals, in addition, an interesting fact. Because the worlds you live in are mostly not of your creation, to exist *as* a human being requires the existence of others. Meaningful existential life requires, Heidegger thinks, a world of social significance to exist within.

Life's a workshop, and you need tools

Heidegger argues that your everyday life is *activity*. Being-in-the-world is essentially participating and acting in your environment in ways that embody the goals and plans that reflect your engagement with the question "What should I be?" This engagement is made possible, Heidegger argues, in the way that worlds reveal your environments to be filled with tools. In short, your worlds are just like workshops in which you respond to the question of your existence!

The activities of your workshop

Being involved, for Heidegger, isn't a mere attitude. It's a way of behaving. Involvement in life is practical. Your primary way of being immersed in-the-world is through accomplishing plans and goals that you have. If you're in the business world, you answer the question "What does it mean to be?" by defining yourself through projects that are meaningful in that world; if you're in the art world, you define yourself differently, in terms of the projects, concerns, goals, and roles that the art world makes available to you.

Being essentially practical, however, requires the use of tools that make participating in your goals, projects, and roles possible. For Heidegger, this means that in a world, you experience your environment not as composed of objects that you see and *then* assign functions or uses to. Instead, you experience the world *as* composed of tools and functions. Each tool's function is a part of the overall web of meanings that compose that world. Thus, being in a world means actively working toward goals made possible by that world, using the tools that world makes available to you.

Tools versus meaningless objects: What's in your workshop?

Heidegger claims that for a thing to "show up" in your experience (for you to notice it), you must experience it as *meaningful* in some way. To do this, you have to understand the thing through a particular world or system of social meanings. Cash registers, for example, exist in the world of commerce, and microscopes exist in the world of science. As Heidegger puts it, "an entity can 'meet up with' Dasein only in so far as it can, of its own accord, show itself within a *world*."

Heidegger's favored examples are about carpentry. Suppose that you want to build a house. Doing so means defining yourself as a carpenter and residing within the social world of the carpenter. In turn, because activity defines you as a carpenter, the process of defining yourself is done through some active project (the building of the house). In your activity, you encounter things (they show up) natural to that world, and in terms of their uses and relevance to your project. So you may encounter tools like hammers and nails (Heidegger says that people experience things primarily as *ready-to-hand*).

What the carpenter doesn't see, Heidegger insists, are wooden things and iron things (what the hammers and nails are made of). Be careful — this point is a radical one that's easy to misunderstand. People typically think that their experience is filled with meaningless *things* that they then react to by figuring out how to fit those things into their projects and goals. So you may think you see "iron thing" first and *then* interpret it as "nail."

Because Heidegger thinks thought of existence (or life) as an essentially involved immersion within a world of meanings, he rejects this picture of how you interact with your environment. Instead, he argues that from the start, you're involved with everything around you, seeing it as helpful or harmful to your way of engaging with your immediate goals and projects. You experience the world *through* your projects. As Heidegger puts it, you look around and see "the forest is a forest of timber, the mountain a quarry of rock, the river is water power, the wind is wind in the sails."

Clearly, this *sounds* strange. But think about it and inspect your experience. Pay attention to how your experiences look (or feel). How do you experience the world? When you move around and operate within your local environment, don't you simply respond to things in ways appropriate to the immediate task at hand? Don't you see uses, not meaningless objects?

Doing without thinking: Look, no hands!

Heidegger says that your fundamental existence in the world is practical and active. You respond to your existence through an immersion within the world through projects. In fact, Heidegger says that you can get so immersed within the everyday world that you stop noticing the tools you're using and instead see only the aim you're focused on. During these times, you aren't even conscious of yourself! So Heidegger's point is that your everyday mode of existing is practical and not even explicitly self-conscious.

Hold on a second! How can you navigate your world if you aren't self-consciously directing yourself? Wouldn't that imply arbitrary action? What would that look like? Nothing would make any sense! You'd be bumping into walls and making a fool out of yourself!

Many real cases actually seem to support what Heidegger is talking about while also dismissing these initial concerns. Think of a champion ice skater. How does she perform so many moves so quickly and effortlessly? The last thing she says is "I consciously directed my body during every part of that routine!" In fact, the more she thinks about what she's doing, the less successful she'll be. Such complicated activity almost seems to require that you *not* think about it. It needs to just happen, in a way, to work.

Most of the time, isn't this how you exist? Sure, you may not be doing triple axels, but you're often doing everyday tasks and navigating your social and practical worlds in ways that are actually just as complex without explicit, conscious thought. In fact, it sure looks like most people aren't consciously thinking about what they're doing most of the time. Instead, they operate under a mode of awareness that Heidegger calls *circumspection*.

Here are some small examples of circumspection:

✔ When you need to get into your car, do you think "Ah, key. That goes *here* in the keyhole. Right. Now turn it. Ah, yes, and now open the door"? Or do you just seem to do it, fixed instead on your task — *getting into the car?* Circumspection, Heidegger thinks, allows you to do what's appropriate to the task, given your environment. You see what tools around you are important (the key, door, keyhole), how they work, and how they relate to your task. In circumspection, you manipulate the world around you without thinking in light of your goals.

✔ Another example is language. After all, language is a tool, isn't it? Most of the time when you're speaking, do you have to think about how to make what you want to say come out in English? Or do you just speak, and out it comes, surprisingly correct? It's as though the language becomes part of you. Well, you've embodied the tool of language, so you don't need to notice it anymore. It's as though you work through it.

The ability to use language appropriately without thinking is *fluency*. Regular tools in your environment often work in the same way for you. When you're fluent in a world (say, the world of the carpenter), you can use the tools within that world in a way that allows them to disappear as you use them skillfully. They become *transparent* as you work through them.

I do, therefore I am?

Heidegger seems to think that our very basic way of existing is a kind of activity that's deeply immersed in the world. This view of the relationship between self and world, however, hasn't always been popular. In fact, it's a fairly radical way of understanding the self, although it's more typical in the East than in the West. Historically, Heidegger is opposing a very ingrained tradition that says *thinking* is primary — a view that sees the self or existence as private and subjective, and fully contained within one's own mind as a thinking and conscious being. This view comes from René Descartes (1596–1650). Descartes argues that the fact that you exist is shown conclusively by the fact that you think. As he famously points out in his book *Meditations,* "I think, therefore I am." For Descartes, you think first and *then* you engage in practical, worldly activity.

Heidegger reverses this, suggesting in a sense, "I do, therefore I am." Conscious thought comes *after* practical activity, specifically (for him) when practical activity *breaks down!* You start to consciously notice objects or even yourself as a thing when some practical activity that you're engaged in breaks down for some reason. So for Heidegger, although you have the capacity to think, or be self-conscious, it's not your essence at all, as Descartes thinks it is.

Oddly enough, Heidegger thinks that as this happens, *you* become transparent as well — just as much as the tool you're using does. When you're really immersed, nothing seems to exist but your goal. It's like you're in a trance. Sports players have a name for this: *being in the zone.* Through your goal, you're tuned in to the world like a champion ice skater. You respond without thinking, even about yourself. You're just *doing.* Weird!

Coming to Grips with Who You Are

Heidegger thinks that your existence is a being-in-the-world or a way of being intimately connected to the world. Check out the earlier section "Living in Your Everyday World" to see exactly what that means to Heidegger. For now, keep in mind that Heidegger notes that existing *in-the-world* means existing alongside others. Without them to structure and create the worlds you can live in, you couldn't exist in a meaningful way. The "They," or the faceless masses or others, make human life possible. Without "Them," you're nothing.

Of course, it's easy to lose this point because Heidegger also thinks that we get lost and entangled in our worldly immersion, and he thinks we also have to be capable of understanding our existence in a way not defined by "Them." Even though the world — as it's created by "Them" — is necessary for you to meaningfully exist, you don't need to get lost in the world of "Them." Of course, it's natural to do this; we tend to express the identity of the faceless, anonymous mass. In the everyday, we tend to fall away from what we are, existing not as individual "I-Selves" but as "They-Selves." Although "They" are necessary to your existence, don't forget that part of what *being-in-the-world* means is to maintain a sense of self *apart* from "Them" (we discuss this concept in more detail in Chapter 9).

This, of course, raises the question of authenticity. Can you be authentic? Is conformity your fate? Heidegger seems to stress that without a background of conformity, *you* as an individual couldn't really exist. Still, authenticity is possible if you can succeed in living in-the-world in a way that discloses what you are fully, and part of what you are is an individual. On the other hand, inauthentic people hide what they're capable of by happily living in a contented way as part of the "They."

Sensing others all around you

Heidegger thinks that one of the essential components of your existence lies in the fact that you're what he calls *being-with*. What Heidegger means by this is that existing in-the-world means also existing alongside other entities just like you. You're *with* them in the very way that you go about living your life, engaging with your daily existence, taking on roles, and working with tools.

Heidegger argues that the meaning of a tool is also connected to other tools. Understanding the meaning of a hammer means unthinkingly using it in a way that simply acknowledges that it's used *in-order-to-pound-nails*. But that means that you must understand what nails are too! And nails also point to other tools, and so on, until finally a world of significance forms around you, one that encapsulates you within a meaningful environment.

But tools point to more than just other tools, don't they? Sure, the hammer points to the nail, and the nail to the wood, and the wood to the house, but then . . . ? At some point, you reach a stage with no more *in-order-to* left! Instead, it then points to the *for-the-sake-of-which*. For example, at the level of a house, you understand that the house is built for other beings just like you.

Heidegger points out that this means your practical engagement with the world, your essential way of existing as the kind of entity you are, makes you aware, even if on a nonconscious level, of the existence of others. Simply by being-in-the-world, you're always sensing the existence of others in what you do. You make houses for *them* with the hammers *they* build. The electricity in your own house tells you that *they* are still at the job. At the end of your property lies the boundary with *the others*.

In short, engaging with your experience in a meaningful way demands that you sense *them*. In fact, even when you're physically alone, you're never by yourself. For human beings, existing at all always points to *their* presence. You're never really alone, even when there's no one actually around.

You're everyone and no one

In your most basic, everyday kind of living, you're deeply immersed in your tasks, in your routine, and in the roles you play in life. When you engage with life in this way, however, you're not really *you.* Instead, you're a living embodiment of what Heidegger calls the "They" or the "one." You become trapped within norms and roles and rules that you didn't create. You tend to passively embody the societal programming that structures and makes meaningful the things that you're doing.

Your social background is required for meaning

Heidegger thinks that a social environment or world must be in place for you to exist in a meaningful way or for you to live a human life as you know it. Before you ever come on the scene, deeply engrained rituals, norms, and rules are already in place to govern how, within the human community, people see things as meaningful or significant. As a result, the very existence of a meaningful life — the kind of thing people are interested in when they ask big questions like "What's the meaning of life?" — rely on the existence of this sort of social background. Without that background, you have no language in which to ask, or to propose answers to, those questions.

When you ask, "What's the meaning of life?" you typically want to know "How do I live?" When you think about these things, you ponder whether it's right for you to be a parent, or to be a musician, or to be a carpenter and build homes. You want to know how to dispose yourself toward the world.

But that world is a social one. Being a parent is a meaningful option because it has a social and cultural history. Carpentry is meaningful because of the hammers and nails — made by others — and because they're supposed to be used in certain ways for certain things. You typically don't pick up a hammer and use it to open your car door. That's not what (intelligent!) people do. Parenting is understood as having children and in acting and being disposed to them in certain ways. That's what people do when they're parents. So when you ask those big questions about the meaning of life, you ask them while immersed within that context.

You're a robot in everyday life

So who are you when you're plugged into that everyday way of living in the social world that makes things meaningful for you? When you reach for that hammer to drive in that nail, who is that hammer for? Is it for *you,* or is it for *anyone?* It's not for *you* as an individual. Clearly, hammers and nails (and parenthood and artistry) are roles and tools that are lying around for *anyone* to use. They make meaningful life possible, but they don't speak to *you.*

When you use those tools or take on those roles, in the everyday sense, you do so *as anyone.* As a result, Heidegger's answer to the question "*Who* are you, in the everyday of your life?" is interesting. He says, "Everyone is the other, and no one is himself."

You use the hammer as *anyone* would. You parent as "They" do. You decide to be an artist because it's a path authorized and structured by "Them." Heidegger puts it this way: "The they, which supplies the answer to the who of everyday Dasein, is the nobody to whom every Dasein has always already surrendered itself, in its being-among-one-another."

Yeah, that sounds as weird (and as chilling!) as it should. In your everyday existence, you're a bit of a robot. That's right. In your everyday mode of life, you're plugged in to the world of the general public in a way that you *become* that faceless mass. That means that the "They" isn't something foreign to you. It *is* you. When you're within the "They," doing what "They" do, as "They" do it, an odd kind of concern overtakes you, one that guides your way of inter-acting. It's called *distantiality.* Within the "They," you're concerned not to stand out in any way. You seek to mirror the norms and behaviors of others, and you don't focus on cultivating differences of any kind.

That's right. You're not a victim here of the "They" — you're the perpetrator in your everyday way of living. In your everyday life, you're a representative of the *one* (or the "They") for others. If someone tries to do things differently, you react in a way that tries to reinforce the right norms without deviation (what *one* does to accomplish that, of course!). You may say something or just make a facial gesture.

It's important to grasp Heidegger's main point. He isn't saying that what's most basic to your existence is a *you* that then gets overrun by the "They." Instead, the most basic aspect of your existence *is* the "They." In the everyday, you're not an "I-Self" — you're a "They-Self." Your most basic mode of being is a kind of robotic conformity. Still, if you want to be an individual (which we discuss in Chapter 9), this is where you must start; your individual self must emerge from your life in the everyday. Without an everyday self to function as the backdrop, your own individuality isn't really possible.

Falling away . . . from yourself

Heidegger says that an essential part of what you are is a *being-in-the-world.* This means that your concern with your own existence and life always has a worldly character. Your concern always manifests itself in your concern with your projects, roles, plans, and undertakings. However, you can easily get lost in that world, tranquilized by the chatter of the crowd or the spectacle of worldly entanglements. You get absorbed, forgetting that part of what being-in-the-world means is *choosing* how to define yourself instead of relying on the crowd to choose for you. It's your existence; you can't farm it out!

In an interesting passage, Heidegger notes "Being-in-the-world is in itself tempting." Tempting? Why's that? Being tempted implies that there's a place you're being tempted *from* and then a place you're being tempted *toward*. If you're on a diet, you're tempted away from moderation in eating toward hitting the buffet and living it up. So what does Heidegger mean by temptation?

In this chapter, we talk a lot about the immersion aspects that Heidegger stresses in his concept of being-in-the-world, but it's essential to remember that, for Heidegger, an essential aspect of being you is being the type of entity that asks questions about *your* existence and life. Don't forget that. We stress it all along, but in the following sections, we flesh out some of the implications of that claim.

Searching for mine-ness

Heidegger thinks that being concerned with how to live life, or asking what to *be,* is something you're always doing. Even when you're immersed entirely within the everyday, you're doing that. In the everyday, however, your concern about life is manifested in involving yourself in projects that "They" do, in ways that "They" want them done. But that's not the only possibility for you.

An essential part of your existence lies in its *mine-ness.* What does that mean? Simply that your life is *yours* and no one else's. It means that when you ask the question "What does life mean?" or "How should I live?" you're asking a question that can be finally answered only by *you* as the particular being that you are. It's your life, and you have to live it. Of course, you can choose to live your life not as *you* but as "Them."

Avoiding the fall

When you "fall," as Heidegger puts it, you tend to find yourself in a way of engaging with the world that asks questions about life (you're still engaged with the world, after all), but you're asking them in a way that obscures your nature as mine-ness. You're asking, "How does *one* live?" or "What do *They* think life means?" When you do that, you're forgetting the essential question that's fundamental to what you are, which is "Who and what am I?"

Heidegger calls this difference — between asking questions about life (through living) in the mode of the "They" and in the mode of "you yourself" — the difference between

- Being-in-the-world
- Being-in-the-midst-of-the-world

Chit-chatting your way through life

Heidegger thinks that it's normal to forget that you're an individual who should take a personal stance on how to live in the particular world you find yourself in. He thinks that when you fall (as he calls it), you tend to disengage with and step away from your own existence. He says that this can happen in two ways:

✔ **Idle talk:** When you engage in idle talk, you do what *one* does. In a way, it's like deciding to *live* as an embodied gossiper. You're not concerned with how well (or if at all) what *one* does connects to your world (or *the* world). Instead, you live in a way that just passes along the gossip of what *one* says to do by doing it and preaching it yourself.

✔ **Curiosity:** Curiosity is similar to what Kierkegaard (in Chapter 10) calls *rotation method*. It means being overly attracted to novelty and to superficial engagements with different things in the world. Instead of finding a task that's right for *you* and committing to it, you satisfy your curiosity by dabbling through shallow, nonrisky, and nonengaged living.

If you sit back and are really honest with yourself, how often do *you* engage in these different forms of living? Is your life engagement superficial? How immersed within what *one* does are you, anyway?

When you're a being-in-the-midst-of-the-world (Wow! That's one monster hyphenated term!), you obscure your mine-ness. You start to think of what you are as being simply defined by the projects that you undertake and how they're structured by the public, by others, or by society at large. You think of yourself entirely in terms of how "They" dictate that things are. As a result, you don't take responsibility for deciding the direction of your own life. Heidegger says you get entangled in your concern with the world.

When you're being in-the-midst-of-the-world, you've lost the *being* part of your existence. An essential aspect of you, your individual directedness or concern, has been lost. All that's left, in a way, is the in-the-world part. Your being has fallen *into* the world and lost its own distinctive character. Heidegger thinks that you're intimately tied to the world, even to the everyday, but you're not *identical* to those things; don't forget that a specific *being* is *in-the-world*. When you fall, that's what you forget; you cease to ask questions about *that* being's existence.

Being authentic: Determining the shape of your life

Heidegger's way of talking about the ways of living makes it easy to talk about the possibilities you have for being *inauthentic* and for being *authentic* (see

Chapter 5 for more on authenticity in general, and see Chapter 9 for Heidegger's own take on authentic living). Though the terms sound judgmental, Heidegger insists that neither is "better" than the other. If anything, one term *(authenticity)* simply better discloses what you are as a whole being. Still, it's important (don't forget it) to realize that being inauthentic is needed if you want to be authentic. Heidegger can't be telling you to leave inauthenticity behind forever. That can't be done. At the same time, inauthenticity is the ground that makes the emergence of authenticity possible.

Although the existentialists don't all agree on this topic, Heidegger insists that these categories shouldn't be understood as judgmental. You're not bad or lowly (or sinful) if you're inauthentic. And being authentic doesn't mean reaching some kind of superior state of being. Being inauthentic and authentic are both possibilities for you, so both are equally real.

Instead, think of it this way: When you're *authentic,* you're fully disclosed in your way of living. Everything you are is laid out in full view. You embrace life in a way that takes full responsibility for what *you* are. You see that what *one* does is just one way of doing things, not the only way, so you take an active role in determining the shape of your life.

Inauthentic existence tends to do the opposite. It cedes responsibility for living to others, to the "They." The inauthentic try to farm out or outsource what it means to exist to the crowd. This way of living does highlight the worldly part of life, but it obscures its individual aspect.

According to Heidegger, being inauthentic is perfectly natural. It's where you start. Never forget the social character of what you are. Without a social environment that makes the meaningful character of human life possible, you couldn't exist in a significant fashion. Authenticity is a way of responding to becoming too immersed (or lost, or fallen) in that social environment. But without inauthenticity, and the falling that's natural to it, you couldn't exist at all.

Chapter 7

Not Tonight, Honey: Why We Need More Passion in Our Lives

In This Chapter

▶ Comprehending passion as engaged living

▶ Analyzing the key elements of engaged life

▶ Grasping the link between passion and truth

▶ Viewing Kierkegaard's attacks on the modern age

All existentialists believe that living with passion is important. Whereas most people take living with passion to mean living frantically and doing lots of impulsive things, that's not what passion means from the existential point of view. Instead, passion means living life in an intense and deliberate way, one that flows from grappling seriously with the significance and meaning of your own individual life.

A core ingredient in living passionately is finding a cause or giving your life meaning. The meaning you find for your life should be one you're willing to die for, one you're willing to commit to organizing your whole life around. To be truly passionate, such a choice must also embrace a degree of mystery or uncertainty. By making these kinds of choices and commitments, you can make sure your life embodies the kind of risk that passion thrives on.

Kierkegaard thinks that living a life that's passionate is directly connected with the notion of truth, suggesting that the passionate life *is* truth. In talking this way, Kierkegaard introduces a new notion of truth, one that differs from the typically accepted scientific version. To live truly and passionately, you have to embody your life's purpose and let it transform who you are. In this way, truth turns out to mean more than a case of intellectually acknowledging that some reality external to you matches an idea that you have of that reality.

Unfortunately, not everyone lives passionately. In fact, Kierkegaard thinks that passion is hard to find in the contemporary world. Most people just want life to be easy and safe. They avoid striving and want answers about life to be handed to them. They desperately seek to avoid the anxiety that comes with grappling with their own existence. The temptations of the media didn't help matters, Kierkegaard thinks, given that they work effectively to undermine passion by distracting people from the business of real living. If Kierkegaard were alive today, no doubt he would be equally critical of the Internet age for the same reasons.

In this chapter, we examine all these points. We start by looking closely at what Kierkegaard means when he says that a life of passion is a life of *engagement.* From there, we turn to how living a life of engagement requires finding a cause to guide your life. This discussion puts us in a great position to then examine Kierkegaard's notion of truth, one that suggests that truth is properly understood as a specific way of living. Only passionate life, he said, can be said to be "in the truth." Last, we examine why Kierkegaard thinks that passionate, engaged, truthful living is so difficult for us today in modern times. The present age, he says, is without passion.

Seeing Passion as a Life of Engagement

Each of us is free. Unlike other, nonhuman things in the world, you have the unique ability to actually take on the question of your own existence. And you can let your engagement with that question help you carve a direction for yourself through life. Who are you? What's the significance of life? Why are you alive? You're free to ask and answer these important questions. Count yourself lucky; not everything can do that!

So it's up to you. You can step up to the plate and start swinging, asking the big questions and deciding how to create the direction of your own life, or you can just stand around and watch the balls go by; it's your decision. The existentialists say, "Swing away!" Living passionately means taking the questions, and your responsibility in answering them, seriously. You have to take your life seriously and *engage* with it. Wrestle with it! Look it squarely in the eye!

A life of engaged passion reveals at least two qualities.

- ✔ A passionate life emphasizes *how* you go about living and not *what* you end up actually doing.

- ✔ Living passionately means cultivating a bond with your own life that doesn't approach it as a problem to be *solved,* but as a relationship that you need to involve yourself in and remain open to.

In this section, we discuss these issues in depth. We discuss the importance of cultivating your freedom, which means making use of your ability to not only ask about the meaning of your own life, but also use the answers you come up with to fashion the future course of your life. This way of living displays passion, a way of approaching life that's truly committed to caring about the actual quality of your existence.

Freedom reveals the individual

It's not surprising that Kierkegaard, as an existentialist, thinks *freedom* is an essential part of being a person. You're different from the nonhuman creatures that surround you, so the way in which you approach your own life should be seen as different from the way animals approach theirs. You should strive to live not as an animal but as a human — as the free creature you are.

One aspect of freedom involves the capacity for autonomous self-movement and self-directed behavior. Cats and cows aren't capable of that independence because they're purely *natural* beings; in other words, their behavior is always determined by worldly facts. What this distinction highlights is the fact that the physical composition of a cat, the environment the cat is in, and the natural laws that govern the world of the cat all work together to uniquely determine what the cat does at each moment of its life. The cat isn't free!

Think of arranging a series of dominoes in a row. Knocking over the first causes a chain reaction so that the rest fall, one by one, until the last one does. That's how the behavior of nonhuman objects works. The conditions in the natural world at one instant cause the conditions in the next instant, which cause the conditions in the next, and so on.

Seen in this way, nonhuman objects, being entirely natural in composition, don't make choices; they're not free. Even when an animal such as a cat appears to be making choices, like seeming to decide of its own free will to get up and walk over to its food bowl, its life is really just a complicated string of falling dominoes. At each moment the cat is doing what its biology and its environment dictate.

We admit it — you're a natural being too. Sometimes your movements are dictated by factors in the physical natural world. If you fall in the ocean and can't swim, you'll drown. If you touch an electric fence, you'll jump backward and shriek in pain. But you're not like the cat or the cow, whose behaviors are *always* explainable in these worldly ways. Instead, the existentialists think that there are always instances in which you *can* be self-moving. When you lift your arm, it raises up because *you* decide to lift it. For the existential-ists, this *intentional* action isn't the result of some set of environmental con-ditions in the world. When you do act intentionally, which includes deciding how you face up to your impending future, your actions are up to you alone and nothing else.

Of course, your freedom to choose how to act in the present and face the future has limitations placed on it by the world you live in. If you're very fat, you won't be able to run very fast. But you can always make the choice to lose weight so as to run faster, even if you'll still encounter an upper limit on just how fast you're able to run. (Sorry — you'll never outrun that cheetah.)

The unique nature of your freedom shows that although you do live in the world and are subject to its influences, you also transcend the world because you're not determined by it, as the cat is. Of course, when the existentialists say *transcend,* they don't mean that you float above the world like a disem-bodied spirit. They just mean that you can rise above the physical cause-and-effect explanations that seem to govern nonhuman things. (We talk more about Kierkegaard's view of this topic in Chapter 10.)

Because freedom is an essential part of what you are, it's a facet of your *existence* that you must cultivate if you're to live in an honest, truthful, or authentic way. You must be true to this special aspect of what you are. This cultivation requires that you take the question of *how* to face your future and your existence very seriously.

Cultivating a sense of passion

It's centrally important that you embrace the kind of existence that's proper and specific to you, one that has freedom at its core. Face it — unlike cats and cows and tables and chairs, you're *not* a passive object. You're an active *subject.* Living with passion means embracing your subjectivity. When you succeed in embracing your nature as a subject, you cultivate passion.

What does passionate life look like? Most people mistake passion with reck-less impulsiveness. For them, living passionately means living life to the full-est by going to lots of parties, skydiving, and bungee-jumping from bridges.

Now don't get the wrong impression — the existentialists aren't against fun. Bungee-jumping can take place in a passionate life. But activities of that sort don't *define* passion. In fact, passion isn't something you can necessarily say a person has by simply looking at him and watching what he does. Passion isn't an externality; it centers on a kind of focus and intensity, a type of deliberate-ness about how you go about things. Kierkegaard calls it *inwardness.*

To Kierkegaard, passionate people are inward because they strive to *be* and to *exist* as subjects and not as objects.

> ✔ An *object* is passive in its existence because it has no choice about *how* it exists. It does what its world dictates that it do. Objects like rocks or cats don't take on the question of their own existence, or how to face their future, because they can't; they don't have the ability.

> ✔ A *subject* is active in its existence due to its capacity to choose how to exist or how to face its future. Subjects can direct themselves and can interact with the question of what it means to exist. Unlike objects, they can decide for themselves how to be in the world.

Passionate people take their very existence seriously. In cultivating their passion, they seek to develop their *subjectivity,* or existence as a subject. When you immerse yourself within subjectivity, you exhibit a deep sense of care about who you are, about the way in which you exist. You realize that you've been handed a gift — the power of self-determination — and you use it.

Passionate people are purposeful. Their sense of care about their own existence creates an intensity in them, a level of depth not seen in people who simply go with the flow.

You may think passionate people sound pretty grim because they're so serious about life. Not so. What *is* true is that passionate people recognize that each decision they make plays a role in determining who they become. Because they care about themselves, they refuse to treat their lives in trivial ways. For them, not being passionate about life is what sounds grim!

It's not what you do but how you do it

One way to understand passionate life is to draw the distinction between living as a participator and living as a detached observer. For a participator, living a full life is more about *how* actions occur. For the observer, living a full life is about *what* gets done. Passion participates rather than observes.

Imagine that a person saves a child from being hit by a car. A question arises: What's important here, ethically? Is it *that* the person saved the child or *how* he came about doing it? For some people, all that matters is that the child was saved. They focus on *what* occurs as ethically meaningful.

Similarly, for some people, living to the fullest or living meaningfully always means doing things. Did you do this? Did you do that? Did you go to the party? Did you ride on the roller coaster at the park? The answer to whether a person really lived a full life always comes down to something that anyone can see from the outside. If you want to know whether you yourself are living passionately, you can do so by floating above your body and just watching yourself to see whether you're doing the right things. For the nonpassionate observer, whether Bob lives a full life, or a meaningful or significant life, can be determined by following Bob around all his life and just observing what he does.

Existentialists like Kierkegaard disagree with this nonpassionate observer. Passionate life isn't just about doing certain things. What's missing is *engagement*. People centrally concerned simply with *what* a person does, Kierkegaard says, have "forgotten what it means to exist, and what inwardness signifies."

To really exist requires engagement. Think about the child-rescue example again. Some people focus on *what* action is performed, but others focus on *how* that action took place. Maybe the person saved the child but did it for a reward only. For some, this way of coming at the action rules it out as ethical, regardless of what the action does, as seen from the outside. According to these people, ethical importance is centrally determined by *how* the action is carried out.

Kierkegaard's point about living a full life is similar. How you come at life is important. Are you resolute in your living? Does your action flow from a deep commitment to being a certain kind of individual? Does it fill you with a sheer excitement about life? These questions are integral for existentialists. In other words, *how* something is done matters! In fact, for Kierkegaard, the *how* is always more important than the *what*.

Note that this principle opens a tremendous number of possibilities for you. Because living a full life isn't restricted to doing a certain set of actions, figuring out what path to follow is up to you. At that point, existentialists are concerned with *how* you pursue it! So it's important to remember that:

- It's up to you to figure out what path, out of all the ones possible for you, to take.

- After you choose that path, the existentialists urge you to pursue it with passion and engagement, with a fire of lived intensity.

Truly Passionate Life Finds a Cause

Your coauthors like to think that existentialists believe in the importance of cultivating a beautiful relationship with your own life. Like all meaningful relationships, that's not easy to do. Beautiful relationships take work.

First things first. You must find a cause to be engaged in through living. This means that you must grapple with existence and figure out how to approach it. In a way, you must find your existential calling; you must continually try to determine how to live in a way best suited to your individual self and the very concrete world you find yourself in. Because the integrity of your very existence is at stake, this cause must be something that you're willing to die — and live — for. Anything less disrespects your own relationship with life and cheapens it by refusing to treat it with the seriousness that comes with real passion.

Finding an ideal or cause that's worth living (or dying) for also requires taking a position on your own existence that embraces mystery and risk. The more your position on life or your commitment is understandable, the less mysterious it is and, as a result, the safer it is. Instead, you have to take big chances in staking out your existence, because that's what life expects from you. Playing it safe with your life is really just waiting around to die. To the existentialists, *that* is depressing and grim!

For the existentialists, a passionate life includes not only committing resolutely to a path you're willing to die for, but also doing so in a way that embraces the fact that you can never be sure that you picked the right road to tread. As a result, passionate living means opening yourself to the vulnerabilities of life. You realize that life is, in a way, bigger than you are. You'll never be able to truly figure it all out or have it under your control. Passionate life is intense, it's committed, it's risky, and it's vulnerable — open to the mysteries of existence and of life.

Your cause should express your life

Cultivating a beautiful relationship with your own existence requires you to choose a direction in life that expresses your individuality. No two people can share such a direction. Because passion requires that you express your *own* freedom and subjectivity, you must revolt against allowing your choices and projects to flow from any influences outside your individual nature.

At the most basic level, being passionate means being very aware of the very particular, concrete world that *you* live in. Living passionately means putting your foot down and saying, "This is the way I will respond to my world."

Each of us is faced with this demand at each moment of our lives. Most of us try to avoid facing up to it; instead, we let those in different situations, or even the crowd, choose how we live. When you do that, your life is no longer an *individual* expression; instead, your cause (if it deserves that name) reflects *them* (the others). You know the drill. You go to work for a certain company and marry such and such a person. You do your best to avoid this or that belief or behavior because doing otherwise would upset the larger group you have similarities with.

Why does this happen? Well, maybe it's your parents you want to mirror. Maybe it's your town. It doesn't matter why you conform or to whom; what's important to remember is that the fastest way to destroy passion and begin merely observing life is to treat yourself in this way. When this happens, you become existentially undignified. You're a subject, but you refuse to treat yourself as one. Instead, you treat yourself as a passionless object. When you allow what's external to you to determine your existence, you step out of the driver's seat and become a passenger; maybe you're even in the proverbial backseat of your own life!

When coauthor Chris was a kid, he was forced to play softball in gym class. He didn't feel comfortable playing because he was afraid he'd be bad at it. So when it was his turn to be up at bat, he would just stand there, never swing, and strike out. The coach would yell at him, "Chris, are you gonna swing the bat or just be a looker?"

Coach's existential message was clear: If you don't swing, you strike out anyway. Being on the field and just watching isn't playing the game. You may as well swing and throw yourself totally into it while you're at it. Give it your best shot. You may miss, but you'll always be engaged with the game. In sports, this mindset is called heart; in existentialism, it's called passion.

It's up to you to step up to the plate. You don't have any choice; you're on the field of life, and you can't get off (well, unless you commit suicide, and that seems like the wrong alternative to us; see Chapter 5 for Camus's view on suicide). If you start swinging by striving to express your own individual nature, you'll be plugged into the world in an exhilarating (though scary!) way.

Of course, the alternative is to stand at the plate and watch the balls go by, allowing others to make your decisions for you (perhaps because you're afraid of striking out). Yeah, it's easy. It's safe. But it displays no passion. No heart. No excellence.

You should commit to a cause worth dying for

Kierkegaard puts it succinctly: "The thing is to a find a truth which is true for me, to find the idea for which I can live and die." Although living with zest or living life to the fullest is often an excuse for living fast or partying a lot, it's really about the need to find a reason to live that you're ready to stake your life on. If you pick any lesser goal, you're just playing at being serious about your life. Your relationship to existence, or to your life, isn't beautiful; it's undignified.

Try this yourself: An honesty quiz

Don't put off the question of intense living. Right now, put this book down and ask, "What's the overarching goal that gives meaning to my life?" Ask yourself a few questions.

What's your aim in life? In other words, what's the most important thing in life to you? What's the one thing that seems to give meaning and purpose to all the things in your life? Now ask yourself whether you're willing to die for this cause or ideal.

✔ If your answer is no, ask yourself, "Am I really living? Or am I merely persisting and going through the motions? Am I just sitting around waiting to die?"

✔ If your answer is yes, ask yourself, "Is my life organized intentionally around that goal and cause? Or is it disorganized, sometimes in accordance with that goal and sometimes not? If it's disorganized, doesn't living life to the fullest mean doing something about that?"

Dealing with such questions doesn't make you morbid; it makes you intentional and purposive. A person who succeeds at living in the face of death this way truly deserves to have on his tombstone the words *I lived.*

People often ask, "Is that worth dying for?" when they want to know whether something is really worth the kind of time and commitment the goal requires. The question is fundamentally serious and important, perhaps the most important one you can ask about proposed paths in life.

Face it — you *will* die. Assume that just before you die, you have the chance to look back on what you did in your life and reflect so as to take stock of what you've become. You want to be able to say that your life, or the way in which you engaged with the world, was worth living so that you can embrace your quickly approaching death.

Many times, people fritter away their choices and time (as the old Pink Floyd song "Time" suggests), ignoring the fact that they'll die. When they behave this way, their lives start to lack cohesion and unity; they become superficial and lack intensity. (We talk more about the importance of embracing death — and even the aforementioned Pink Floyd song — in Chapter 9.)

But you will die, whether you ignore death or not. You have to face up to that. Your life is made up of a finite number of moments, which means you can't do everything. When you choose one option, the other options are gone forever. There are no mulligans in life; at the end, you simply die, and your time to pick paths and roads ends abruptly.

If life, as we mention earlier, is about swinging the bat and trying to connect with the ball, passion requires keeping death in view and realizing the importance of your present choices. That means realizing this may be your last time at the plate, so swing for the fences. Perhaps the character Andy in the movie *The Shawshank Redemption* puts it best: "Get busy living or get busy dying." Of course, this same saying is in the Bob Dylan song "It's Alright Ma (I'm Only Bleeding)," in which the lyrics read, "He not busy being born is busy dying." Dylan and Andy have the same message: Playing it safe with little goals you aren't willing to die for isn't the way to go about living. It's the way to be dead while you're alive.

Choices must include mystery and risk

Cultivating a passionate relationship with your own existence requires making commitments you're willing to die for. It also requires you to make choices whose significance and worth can't be definitely established. This means embracing mystery and uncertainty into the core of your life. Because nothing less important than the meaning you place in existence hangs in the balance, because you never know whether the path you choose is the right one, it means taking the greatest risks and not playing it safe.

Think of a relationship with a loved one. Romantic relationships contain lots of mysterious elements. After all, you're dealing with a *person,* not a thing. And when you're dealing with people, you can never say you know them completely. Who knows? You can never know whether things will work out as you planned. After all, relationships are composed of *free* subjects, so you can't determine what will happen. Maybe this person will change tomorrow unexpectedly, and all the years you spent in the relationship will seem wasted. That's why relationships are risky. To enter into a relationship in a meaningful way, you have to take a chance. After all, you can't fully control a meaningful relationship. You have to give yourself over to the uncertainty that passionate relationships harbor so as to truly experience that relationship. You should approach your existence in the same way.

Much as you try to accumulate evidence in favor of your choices about how to live your life, you can never know for sure that you made the right decision. The existentialists believe that there's nothing external to you that you can use to see whether your choices are actually meaningful or significant. That task is yours alone. As a result, an element of mystery always comes with trying to figure out how you should engage with your own life. The kinds of big questions about life just don't have clear-cut answers. Doing math may be black and white, but asking about the meaning of life, or how you should live, seems to have a lot of gray in it. In fact, the farther you seem to dig into the significance of life, the more perplexing it seems to become!

Try this yourself: How do you love truth?

The German writer Gotthold Lessing (1721–1781) once introduced an interesting dilemma: What if God offered you a choice? In his right hand, he would have all truth, and in his left hand, he would have only the capacity to strive for truth, coupled with the possibility for error. You simply need to choose one hand.

If God were to present you with this question, which hand would you choose? Lessing suggested that he would choose the left hand. From an existentialist's perspective, choosing the right hand means choosing an existential death. In possessing all truth, you would destroy the very possibility of existing as a human being, an existence that requires the kind of passionate striving that includes mystery and the kind of risk that comes along with it. To know all truth would be to control existence, but at the cost of losing all passion for life. You would become forever detached from the business of actual living.

This doesn't mean you shouldn't ask questions — quite the opposite. After all, you're grappling with your existence here! But you shouldn't ask or pursue those questions with the intention of *controlling* existence and shaking the right answers out of it so that you can feel more confident in the way you live.

David Hume, a famous 18th-century philosopher, once said about life that "The whole is a riddle, an enigma, an inexplicable mystery." Camus (whom we talk about in Chapter 5) feels strongly that "doctrines that explain everything to me also debilitate me at the same time." Camus's great point captures what we're saying: He feels offended by the desire to *explain* everything about life, because such explanations would "relieve" him, as he put it, of the "weight of my own life." Mystery and risk are what give life that weight; they're the fuel from which the fire of passion burns.

As 20th-century existentialist Gabriel Marcel once put it, don't think of life as a problem that needs to be solved. That's not what it means to be in a relationship with life. Instead, it's what it means to be in a *confrontation* with life. It's hostility! How to live life isn't a puzzle that you try to conquer. Instead, life is something you need to strive to *be* — to get involved with. Face it — your relationship with life is the most intense bond you'll ever have. Figure out how to cultivate that relationship in just the right way. Treat life with the respect that it deserves.

The more you do this, the more you'll become *open* to your own existence. Of course, this openness means being shaken by the fundamentally insecure position you find yourself in as a chooser. Basically, living passionately means choosing to be vulnerable in the face of your own life. It means recognizing the insecurity that surrounds your life choices, but also recognizing that those choices still need to be made with solid resolution and committed force. If you think about it, isn't that what all truly passionate relationships turn out to be?

Truth Is Passionate Living

For existentialists, embracing a passionate existence is important. It means finding an individual direction for yourself that reflects your own particularity. This direction must retain a maximum appreciation for the mystery of life; as a result, choosing it means taking a significant risk with your life.

Kierkegaard, however, goes further; he also makes the more radical claim that if a person succeeds in engaging with life in a passionate way, that person exists in the *truth*. This statement takes the discussion of passion to a new level. Is Kierkegaard being metaphorical? Can a *way* of living — separate from *what* is done — be related to truth? Seeing what he means requires analyzing the notion of truth in general. From there, you can see that just as a notion of truth exists for objects, Kierkegaard thinks that a notion of truth applicable to *subjects* is appropriate as well.

Kierkegaard's claim that passion and truth are connected leads him to rethink truth as a matter of *appropriation*. This means that for something to be true, you must make it your own, an active way of approaching truth very different from the common notion that sees truth as something discovered. Due to his specific way of understanding truth, Kierkegaard also argues that immersion in the crowd, which lacks passion and appropriation, is really what he called *untruth*.

What is truth?

Most people would agree that striving doggedly for truth is important. But what's truth? At the most basic, common sense suggests that truth looks like a special kind of representing. Specifically, you say that if X is "true," what X represents truly exists.

Representation is easy to understand. For one item (X) to represent another item (Y) is to say that X stands in for Y. For example, a map of New York *represents* what the map is supposed to be about (New York) when it accurately depicts the actual distances between fixtures in the actual landscape, when the roads on the map accurately represent the real highways, and so on. In such circumstances, most people are willing to say that the map stands in for the actual landscape of New York and so is true.

Most of the time, people use truth to talk about sentences, which are like maps in a way. When someone says, "The moon circles the earth," he makes a claim about objective reality or about what things are. What makes the sentence true is objective reality itself. Is the situation in the objective world just like the sentence says it is? In other words, does the moon really circle the earth? If it does, the sentence is true; if it doesn't, it's false.

Note, however, that this way of talking about truth seems to deal exclusively with *objects,* or with what things are. For most inquiries, this kind of truth, dealing with what things are — or what Kierkegaard calls objective truth — is perfectly appropriate. Most of the time, you want to know whether "the tornado heading this way is big" or whether "the water is boiling." In these cases, all you want to know is whether the sentences you're using map onto the world around you.

Whether an objective truth exists doesn't require any personal involvement on your part. Being detached from the situation doesn't create a problem. For example, claiming that "water is boiling" is true can be verified by observing (in this case, visually) whether the object (the water) referred to in the sentence really has those properties (boiling). If so, the statement is true. What would your involvement add? After all, if the water is boiling, that's true *independently* of you. So the issues of you and your life and the existence of objective truths about things are entirely separate from one another.

Most of the time, people want this separation to be the case. Think of science. Science is supposed to give you knowledge about the truths of the world that you live in. You don't want those truths to depend on the existence of the scientists or on anyone in particular. If chemical XYZ is bad for your health, you want that to be a fact that's independent of the personal existence of everyone. You want it to be a brute, impersonal truth you can count on.

But think this belief through for a moment. If one kind of truth pertains to the existence of objects, does another kind of truth pertain to the existence of subjects (subjective truth)? If so, truth can actually exist in a way that's completely independent of science. Because subjects are defined by *how* they exist, a notion of subjective truth would have to take the engagement of the person into question. As such, these truths wouldn't be independent of you because their very existence would require your own deep involvement in the world.

Truth is subjective

Most people are *positivists,* which means that they accept one kind of truth — the kind that science prizes. If science can't authenticate something, positivists say, it's not worth talking about because it's just nonsense. The existentialists, however, reject positivism. Instead, they claim that the way that we talk actually reveals that we believe in another type of truth, which Kierkegaard calls subjective truth. These truths relate to the kind of *how* (subjective) existence that human beings possess as living, engaging subjects. The existentialists think that when we say that we must dedicate our lives to truth, subjective truth is what we really mean.

To highlight the two different kinds of truth, it's helpful to think about the different ways that you use the verb *know*. The connection between knowing and truth is a tight one; if you say that you know something, you mean that you're in some way connected to the truth about that item. Different ways of knowing imply different types of truth. With this in mind, think about these two ways the verb is used:

- ✔ You claim that you know that God is X, Y, or Z.

- ✔ You claim that you know God.

What's the difference? In the first example, you know that God is this or that. Perhaps you know that God is good, or that God is all-powerful, or something of that sort. You're claiming that some sentence like "God is X" is true because what it claims exists externally to you. If God is omniscient, for example, that's truth independent of you and independent of whether you know it to be true.

How do you come to know these kinds of truths? The method is pretty straightforward. You look at the sentence and then you look at the object. You notice through distanced observation that they match (the form of distanced observation can differ; perhaps you use logic or reason, or perhaps you simply use your eyesight). In the end, *you* as a subject have nothing to do with whether the sentence is in fact true.

Now think about the second use of the verb *know,* which is very different from the first. When you say you *know* God, you're not implying that you're comparing sentences with objects and seeing whether they match. Instead, you're claiming that you're in a *relationship* with God, that you're *involved* with God in some way. "Knowing God" in this sense has a meaning like "living life intimately with God as your co-pilot" or something very much like it. "Knowing God" means letting God inform the way that *you* live. Clearly, this kind of truth isn't independent of you!

So what does *truth* mean in this second sense? Instead of comparing sentences to objects, *subjective* truth compares ways of coming at life with existence itself. As Kierkegaard puts it, "What is truth, but to live for an idea?" As such, for a subject to exist *in the truth* means to have a cause or ideal worth dying for and to passionately engage with life through it. When your ideal is worth dying for, and when you're related to it in the right way, truth is *embodied* in the way that you live your life.

Kierkegaard's passionate pagan versus the hypocritical Christian

The existential notion of truth really relates to the relationship you have with life. The more your way of living accurately represents what it means to be a subject, the more truth you find in it.

Kierkegaard uses a great example to explain how this principle works. He says that the pagan who prays passionately to a false God shows more truth than the Christian who prays falsely to his real God. As a Christian himself, Kierkegaard is making a powerful point. To live *for* an idea is to dedicate your life to it in a passionate sense.

The pagan is *living* for his idea, even if the idea itself doesn't match anything in reality. In the case of the false Christian, his idea is of something that really exists (according to Kierkegaard), but the *way* he's living isn't true to what it means to have that idea. The false Christian has no true relationship to God or to his own existence, because he has the wrong relationship to the idea in question. The pagan has the right relationship to his existence, living in a way that's *true* to the ideal, whereas the Christian doesn't. As a result, one lives in truth and the other in untruth.

Recall Kierkegaard's distinction about truth. Praying to a God whom you believe exists but who doesn't transform your identity isn't to live in truth; truthful existence is the kind of living that's literally transformed by what it engages with. Praying to a false God who *does* transform you is living in truth. The false Christian has no transforming relationship to his God as an ideal, so it never touches him.

Do you agree with Kierkegaard? If you had a choice between believing in the wrong ideas faithfully and truly, and believing in the right ideas falsely, which would you choose? Most people would likely choose the second option, thinking that objective truth is more important than subjective truth. What about you?

The paradox of living in truth

Kierkegaard claims that truth is a *paradox* (dilemma or puzzle). Although Kierkegaard's notion of paradox varies, one version of it is this: Although a person who lives in truth cares deeply about the actual objective reality of what he believes in, he isn't motivated to engage with it for the purpose of gaining external assurances that it really exists. A tough way to live!

Kierkegaard is clear that subjective truth deals only with what he calls *essential* truths about your own personal existence, such as morality and religion. Subjective truths concern the questions and issues surrounding walking the right path in life.

Living in the truth, however, requires an interesting mix of states internal to the person in question. For one, to be passionate about an ideal means *wanting* that ideal to correspond to something in reality. If you believe in God, you want God to actually exist. Passionate people don't dismiss such concerns; they take them very seriously. This intense gravity and seriousness that attach to life choices cause them to spark anxiety in you. After all, you want there to be a real aspect to what you devote your life to, don't you? No one *wants* to pursue a nonexistent fiction!

At the same time, living in the truth means not being motivated to pursue that idea on the basis of objective evidence or proofs. In fact, Kierkegaard is adamant about one thing: The more you can prove the objective reality of your ideal, the less passion you attach to it, and the less it seems worth pursuing. As a result, the more assured you are about the *objective* truth of the ideal, the less *subjective* truth will be embodied by pursuing it. Similarly, the more you *pursue* evidence for your ideal, the more it will appear that you lack passion about it.

Thus lies the heart of one sense of paradox at the core of subjective truth. Living in the truth or with passion requires firmly embracing and committing to ideals that you keep in a state of uncertainty. Passion requires not knowing whether that ideal is objectively true. As Kierkegaard puts it, "Passion and the paradox fit each other perfectly." Here, you see Kierkegaard's attempt to link a dimension of truth to his requirement that a truly passionate life requires uncertainty and risk. Truth and passion require mystery.

Making truth yours alone

When you find ways to address the question of how to live and commit to those ways passionately, you live in truth. But what specifically makes such a life a true one? It can't be that what makes your path true is the presence of evidence for it; Kierkegaard thinks passion requires embracing the uncertainty of what you pursue. Instead, he thinks you must make the truth yours alone by appropriating it and allowing it to transform your identity and your life.

In a famous quotation, Kierkegaard says, "Here is such a definition of truth: an objective uncertainty held fast in an appropriation process of the most passionate inwardness is the truth, the highest truth attainable by the individual."

Truth is the holding fast of an objective uncertainty. That part is easy enough; it just means that you embrace the lack of certainty that what your ideal or idea corresponds to objectively exists. But how do you hold that uncertainty fast in an appropriation process? To see what he means, we need to distinguish two ways that Kierkegaard thinks people can approach a truth. He calls them

- ✔ **Approximation:** The method of knowing that's characteristic of objective, scientific truths about things.
- ✔ **Appropriation:** The method of knowing that's characteristic of subjective, essential truths about your own personal existence.

Approximation: The scientific route

Suppose that you approach your ideal through approximation. You've looked at all the rational reasons why living by such an ideal makes sense, and you've accumulated evidence in its favor. You know it's not certain, but you think the evidence is compelling. You have enough evidence to feel confident about pursuing your ideal. In fact, with each new piece of evidence you collect, you take yourself to be closer and closer to the truth.

This is approximation. The problem with this method, Kierkegaard thinks, is that it treats truth as something external to you. Whether you take your ideal to be true depends on evidence, and evidence is public and common. And that means the truth of that idea isn't reliant upon you at all. Anybody who sees the evidence should be convinced of its truth. Essentially, the motivation to pursue this ideal doesn't need to come from you.

But if the truth of that idea or the motivation to pursue it doesn't depend on you, how can you be passionate about it? Essentially, Kierkegaard's claim is that the better the evidence gets, the less the truth is *yours* and the less it can function as the object of your passion. Think about it: How excited do you get about the fact that water freezes at 32 degrees Fahrenheit? Probably not very! Well, it *is* objectively true, so why not? It's clear — certain objective truths just don't inspire a whole lot of passion in us.

Because of this problem, Kierkegaard insists that the approximate route to truth is a dead end when it comes to dealing with the personal questions central to your existence.

This conclusion shouldn't surprise you. When you turn to approximation to deal with personal questions about life and about existence, it's clear that you don't want to be deeply involved in the issue of your ideal's truth. That would be too risky and would put too much responsibility on you. Turning to approximation shows a lack of courage. You don't want risk or mystery. You want assurance from the outside that your choices are the right ones. You want life to make sense. You want your existence to yield to reason.

Appropriation: The existential route

Do yourself a favor. If you're going to use the method of approximation, save it for when you buy a new saw or for when you need medical advice. When it comes to choosing the ideals to live your life by, use appropriation instead. Instead of seeking evidence and proof to determine the truth of your ideal, recognize that really living your life requires that the truth be yours alone and that your motivation for pursuing it come from you, not from public evidence.

The only way to make a truth your own is to embrace it through sheer commitment and inward passion; you need to make the decision to embrace this ideal with all you are. To embrace an objective uncertainty in appropriation means to live the truth, to make a leap of faith, and to commit to something not justified or grounded in evidence. That's the leap, after all. You must leap over the uncertainty that opens between you and your idea; you must leap over it and bridge the gap between the two through a willed, passionate commitment.

Through the leap, you forge that ideal into a central component of your whole existence. The ideal becomes part of what you are and so becomes true through your way of embodying it and letting it shape your life. Essentially, although scientific truths have to be discovered through approximation, subjective truths are created through appropriation.

Be honest. Haven't you had moments like this, even if they were brief? Didn't you feel *real* at such moments? As though only at that moment you really began to exist and to live? As though you finally had truth on your side? For the existentialists, only during such times are you a true embodiment of what it means to be an authentic person. In appropriation, you've given up the attempt to make life easy and understandable. You're forging ahead into the world of the unknown, truly blazing a path of your own.

The crowd is untruth

Kierkegaard writes, "There is a view of life which holds that where the crowd is, the truth is also, that it's a need in truth itself, that it must have the crowd on its side." The existentialists (and most reasonable people, if you ask us) are fiercely opposed to crowd-driven conformity. Sadly, most people don't act until they know what the crowd thinks. For them, the crowd *is* truth. For Kierkegaard, it's the opposite: The crowd is untruth.

In arguing against conformity, Kierkegaard points out St. Paul's suggestion in the Bible that "only one receives the prize." Although St. Paul's meaning is clearly religious, you can take Kierkegaard's point in a more general way (having nothing to do with the *Highlander* TV series, by the way; existentialism isn't about cutting off people's heads). Kierkegaard suggests that living authentically, or living in truth, can occur only to an *individual.* Passionately living life to the fullest can't occur for a person as a member of a group because in the crowd, you aren't an individual. As a result, "the prize" must be claimed outside the hands of the crowd. To win it, you must face existence alone.

As we explain in the next few sections, Kierkegaard has some reasons for thinking that crowd-dwellers are forever losers in the game of life.

The crowd believes only what's authorized by many

The *logical fallacy* (form of bad reasoning) known as the *appeal to the people* occurs when you suggest that something is true because a majority of people believe it's true.

Although clearly problematic (the earth isn't flat even if lots of people say it is), Kierkegaard is more concerned with the way of approaching life that this fallacy embodies. Specifically, crowd-dwelling requires a detachment from your own life. The crowd-dweller avoids (mostly due to fear) grappling with how to respond to the very concrete and particular situations he lives through. The crowd-dweller doesn't want to take on the risk of embracing an individual path. Instead, he detaches from his own existence and seeks to express what's common to *everyone's* experiences, losing touch with his own particular life. What he does and his motivation for pursuing it aren't his own.

The crowd embraces anonymity

As you detach from the realities of your own individual life and seek to submerge yourself within the crowd, you begin to live as a shadow without real substance. Your desire to live as an expression of everyone means you reject the need to be a particular person with a particular name. You take no positions on existence that reveal you as an individual chooser. As a face in the crowd, you're successfully hidden and anonymous. When you do take positions, you simulate living by taking on false commitments as a group member. For example, *you* don't commit to fidelity to your spouse; "good Christians" do! Simulated life is like the life that you watch an actor portray on stage. The actor is playing a *role.* The actor isn't committed as an individual to what he's doing. When you do things "as good Christians do" or "as good fathers do," you're playacting through life. As an individual, you don't exist.

The crowd is cowardice and false courage

Individual existence requires great courage. You have to stand on your own two feet and face up to the mysteries and risk involved in making your own decisions about living. After you're safely hidden within the group, your choices can't be risky, because *everyone* understands and approves them. Best of all, if your choices don't work out, everyone is at fault, and all can share the blame.

Socrates the crowd-hater

If you want to live in the crowd, you need a few skills. You need to be good at appeasing those around you. You have to make them feel good about themselves. You need to be a good social chameleon, to be sure your way of acting assures others that you're one of them. If that means moving from one belief or behavior to another in different situations, do it. You need to become what the ancient Greeks called a *sophist*. Sophists were notoriously uninterested in truth and cared more about persuasion and rhetoric. Socrates lived as an antisophist, and he paid the ultimate price for doing it. Socrates avoided crowds and preferred to speak only to individuals. He felt, as Kierkegaard did, that truth wasn't in the domain of the crowd but belonged only to individuals. In fact, Socrates felt that individuals needed to free themselves from the crowd's alleged wisdom and learn to approach existence truthfully. In spurning the crowd in this way, he made lots of enemies, some of whom put him to death on false charges. In fact, in his defense trial (described in Plato's *Apology*), Socrates told the Athenian assembly — the crowd that would judge him — that he would not treat them in the ways crowds like to be treated. He told them that he would not flatter them and play to their cowardice.

As Kierkegaard puts it, in the crowd each individual "contributes his share of cowardice to 'the cowardice' which is the crowd." Of course, although the crowd is cowardice, within it people quickly acquire a false feeling of courage. No wonder: Within the crowd, people become willing to carry out actions that they otherwise may not. Think of a crowd riot. Although it's possible that no one person has the courage to riot, you can hide behind your anonymity as a crowd dweller and avoid the consequences of your actions. In your hidden form, you've become unaccountable. You draw a false strength from your invisibility and from the sheer numbers around you.

Performing an action when everyone's in it together is easy; performing an action in isolation and in full view, when everyone knows it's you, is really living. Real courage comes from within, not from without. If risk, mystery, passion, and devoted commitment to a path that gives expression to one's individual existence are what mark living in truth, living in the crowd is clearly the sign of untruth. You must take the business of individual existence seriously; the more people who are around, the harder getting down to that business in a meaningful way will be.

Why Modern Life Drains You of Passion

To Kierkegaard, the *present age* — the world of his time (and our own) — had lost its fire and passion. Unlike the more revolutionary times of past, the present age prefers the easy life. Those within it look for ways to distract themselves from the difficulties of engaging meaningfully with existence.

Kierkegaard's Fire Chief

To hammer home the message of crowd cowardice, Kierkegaard talks about the Fire Chief. When a fire happens, he says, it's serious business. The Fire Chief knows that when he arrives at the scene, the surrounding crowd will be brandishing useless pitchforks and buckets. They're not serious about the fire, but they want to play at being serious because that's what crowds do. At best, they're a nuisance to the firefighters, but at worst, they're dangerous and get in the way. As a result, the Fire Chief rightly uses the police to disperse the crowd.

In developing this analogy, Kierkegaard is asking a simple question: Are you willing to take your own existence seriously, as the Fire Chief treats the business of putting out fires? If so, you'll have to make passionate commitments about how to live. Of course, when the crowd hears that you're addressing how to live your life, it will immediately show up to prove that it takes the issues under consideration very seriously, and it'll demand that you pay attention to it as proof of your own seriousness. However, just as in the scene of the fire, the crowd is merely waving figurative pitchforks; it's dangerous to you in your quest because it wants you to live in untruth.

What will you say as the Fire Chief in charge of your own life? You can't call the police (unless the crowd is waving real pitchforks). You have to send them away on your own if you plan on living in a meaningful way. Will you? Do you have the courage?

One of the focuses of Kierkegaard's attack on the modern age is the printed media. Through it, he feels, people are tempted to become part of the larger abstraction known as the crowd or the public. The main concern is that the media entices people to become superficially involved in trivial issues distant from their own lives. Because passionate people are deeply engaged with the *concrete* lives of their own circumstances, these temptations drain you of your engagement with your own particular life. As a consequence, they help make you dispassionate, phony, and shallow.

To end this chapter, we look at whether Kierkegaard's attack on the media, and his attack on the modern age, would be extended to the Internet age that we live in; we're pretty sure it would have!

The present age is so dull

Kierkegaard is convinced (and Nietzsche too — check out Chapter 11) that people are living in an age of putrid mediocrity. In the present age, people don't want to live; instead, they want to *feel* as though they're living. The present age is attracted to *simulation*. In short, the present age loves playacting about life and therefore enjoys self-deceptive fantasies about life. What could be duller or staler?

In his criticism of modern times, Kierkegaard draws a distinction between two different approaches to life. He calls one the present age (which is the modern period) and the other the revolutionary age. Kierkegaard says that the *revolutionary age* is marked by

- ✔ A devotion to subjectivity

- ✔ A commitment to action

- ✔ A willingness to embrace great passion

- ✔ A cultivation of risk and danger

The revolutionary age is one that's deeply rooted in subjectivity and truth, which we discuss earlier in the chapter. In the revolutionary age, people take their existences seriously. They take chances with their lives. They make ambitious plans and live them out, and the people around those who live this way applaud them. Passionate people in a revolutionary age are *exemplars*.

One way to think of the revolutionary age is to think of the Klingons in the TV series *Star Trek*. The Klingons are a warrior race dedicated to fighting battles. Every day they seek out danger, trying to constantly push the envelope. When they die, others sing songs of remembrance — testaments to their right (and true!) way of living. Klingons don't fear death; to them, it's a necessary part of living. Their motto: "Today is a good day to die!"

Not in the present age. According to Kierkegaard, people in the present age adore

- ✔ Objectivity and science

- ✔ Endless deliberation but no decision-making

- ✔ Safety as opposed to danger

- ✔ Appearance and not reality

In the present age, people like to feel alive but don't want to make the kinds of decisions needed to really live that way. Kierkegaard says that in the present age, people meet and plan rebellions, deliberating furiously over details about what should go into the revolutionary document. Tired, they call it a day and go home to dinner *feeling* as though they've done something, as though they actually participated in a rebellion. Maybe they'll do it all over again tomorrow.

People in the present age love science and reason and don't trust themselves to make decisions about how to live. They spend lots of time in the self-help section of the bookstore, looking for those how-to books that tell them how to live their lives correctly. Essentially, they dedicate themselves to the pursuit of distraction because it gives the illusion that they're actually doing something when they're always really standing still.

To use another *Star Trek* analogy, the present age would love the holodeck. In the Star Trek universe, the holodeck is a computer simulation that allows you to live any kind of experience you want, no matter how dangerous, at no actual risk to yourself. You can simulate dangerous life at no cost. In the revolutionary age, people actually did the things the present age plays out in the holodeck. In the present age, people who simulate life effectively are seen as smart. They exhibit "good sense" by playing it safe. To those in the present age, those seen in the revolutionary age as exemplars are really total idiots.

Kierkegaard's attack on the media

Living with passion is a central existentialist concern. Of course, one way to erode passion — life in the crowd — will always exist as a possibility in the world you live in. However, as technology increases, the ability — and pressure — to incorporate yourself into the crowd becomes harder and harder to avoid. Technology makes the crowd more and more a part of the everyday world so that it's no longer something you have to seek out.

Kierkegaard is very worried about the growing presence of the printed media, because he sees them as the voice of the crowd or the public. Before the media's emergence, the influence and temptation of the crowd were limited to word of mouth. The size of the crowd was limited to the number of people who could congregate. But the printed press allows the crowd to reach out to and pull in even more people into its clutches through the media.

The main issue Kierkegaard has with the media is their ability to serve as a temptation to detach from actual lived existence. Think about it. Newspapers, television shows, and talk radio tempt you to superficially involve yourself in topics that you know little about and that have no relevance to the concrete issues that you, as an individual, ought to be grappling with. Instead of becoming committed to living your own individual life, you're hypnotized by what "They" say about Paris Hilton and Britney Spears or by what's going on politically in an area 2,000 miles from where you live.

The media demand that you have more and more opinions about more and more topics. They seek to divide your attention until it's so thin that you can spend only minutes on each topic, essentially making your connection to the issues superficial. Of course, another reason the media are so dangerous is that they give the crowd an ever greater appearance of strength, scope, and objectivity. Eventually, the temptations of the media are too great for many to resist. Eventually, as the Borg says in *Star Trek: The Next Generation*, resistance is futile. The omnipresent temptations of the media eventually assure that all people are eventually assimilated into "the public."

The Corsair incident

Kierkegaard's antagonism toward the media originated out of personal experience; he knew well how the inner workings of the press functioned. Copenhagen had a number of what were most likely tabloids circulating in Kierkegaard's time, the most popular being *The Corsair*. Like some modern tabloids and television shows, *The Corsair* took it upon itself to publicly lampoon high-status residents of Copenhagen with insult and ridicule. Kierkegaard, who had long had a favorable relationship with the journal, invited the journal to attack him. It did, maliciously running attack piece after attack piece insulting his physical appearance and his demeanor and exposing him to a high degree of public ridicule. Did Kierkegaard actually *want* this separation from Copenhagen? Perhaps the philosopher who so strongly championed individuality felt he wasn't sufficiently separate from the crowd. In any event, his separation from society did, in fact, result in a remarkably productive period of writing, some of which discussed how certain kinds of communication typical of the media frequently exhibit inauthenticity.

Think of the number of people deeply trapped in the pages of *The National Enquirer* and *Star Magazine* or angrily perusing the editorial pages of the newspaper, upset about people's opinions concerning topics distant to their localized world. Funny thing is, they can't seem to pull themselves away from it! It's like a drug addiction. People are drawn to the *safety* of dealing with others' issues rather than their own.

The media also tempt you to participate in gossip-mongering or opinion-trading. They invite you to insert your opinion without having to make any real commitments and without any real risks. In the media of Kierkegaard's time, newspapers allowed for the highlighting of opinions and beliefs that had no identifiable source; authors used pseudonyms.

Just as hiding in the crowd creates a false feeling of courage, Kierkegaard writes that through the press, a man can profess "things which he perhaps did not in the least have the courage to say personally in a particular situation; every time he opens up his gullet — one cannot call it a mouth — he can *all at once* address himself to thousands upon thousands."

Kierkegaard fiercely believes that real passionate living means a nonsuperficial, real involvement with issues that affect your life. It means investing your time and your commitment in choices, because you don't have unlimited time, and real involvement requires you to dedicate yourself to one pursuit as opposed to another. The press allows you to avoid making those either/or choices. You can do it all! Dabble a little here and a little there. No commitments needed, no choices. No time investment. No consequences. The press functions to undermine real commitments and in so doing, it undermines you.

The Internet: A modern passion-killer?

Although Kierkegaard is probably right that the modern media tend to succeed in distracting people from the task of grappling with their own concrete existence, a new foe has emerged on the horizon: the Internet. Should Kierkegaard's attack on the media extend to the Internet? Our answer (as is the opinion of Hubert Dreyfus, a contemporary philosopher who has written extensively on this subject) is yes!

Knowledge: No passion required

First, think of the question of knowledge. Whereas knowledge was once the realm of committed experts who passionately dedicated their time to studying concrete issues and took the risks that such dedication requires, the Internet has introduced a different view of knowledge. Instead of understanding that *knowing* something requires time and effort, people now have billions of Web sites to choose among. They just need a search engine.

The fact that perusing this information requires no risk, no commitment, and no time investment invites people to become what Kierkegaard calls "intellectual tourists." You dabble here, you dabble there; no degree of superficiality is low enough to stop a person from becoming an expert in everything. Don't like what an expert said about X? Type it into a search engine, and in 10 seconds you can play at being a serious devotee to that question. On some sites, *anyone* can be a contributor, no expertise needed. You can act just like an expert in no time without actually getting involved. Sure, you don't really understand the issues, but armed with your informational sound bites, you look like you do.

Relationships: Idle and superficial

And what about relationships with others? No need to actually get involved with people anymore — you can just use the social-interaction Web sites that so many people use. After you're there, you create your own identity, whether it accurately represents you or not. You acquire as many virtual friends as you can. (You want to be Net-popular, right?)

Clearly, these friendships aren't necessarily real. You can't just press a button and be friends with someone. One site even allows the user to join up with causes. That used to mean actually doing something in support of the cause. What does it require now? Press the button for the cause you desire; your identity profile now lists you as a supporter for everyone to see. You're playacting again, and all from the easy comfort of your computer chair!

Is the Internet helping make your relationship with the world and with others more superficial? Do you find yourself on instant messenger often, having long conversations consisting of five-word sentences? What are these conversations about, other than just a desperate attempt to keep from being bored? Are you reducing your relationships to mere chitchat, to what 20th-century existentialist Martin Heidegger calls "idle talk"? (Check out Chapter 6 to read more about what Heidegger says.)

Kierkegaard surely wouldn't have wanted to banish the Internet. These technologies often have *positive* effects on relationships and human interaction. For significant numbers of people, using these sorts of media may actually help reinforce existing networks of friends and family. So they don't have only the negative effect of helping people escape real-world relationships to engage in a risk-free fantasy world.

Kierkegaard, if he were alive today, would likely acknowledge this. But he would have wanted people to be very careful about how they use such technology and to be always mindful of its tendency to distract them from the realities of living as human beings. In short, he would have thought that the Internet is like all other technological gadgets we can become so addicted to; we should make the Internet work for us, not allow it to absorb us and distract us from living in a really passionate way.

Chapter 8

Sartre's Existentialism: Learning to Cope with Freedom

In This Chapter

▶ Understanding the importance of Sartre's "Existentialism"

▶ Living with your freedom

▶ Creating value and meaning

▶ Coping with existential psychology

*V*ariously known as "Existentialism," "The Humanism of Existentialism," and "Existentialism Is a Humanism," Jean-Paul Sartre's most widely read essay was an attempt to clarify the meaning of the existential movement at a time when its popularity was near its zenith. Although not written for professional philosophers, like much of his work it's meandering, frustrating, endlessly brilliant, and at times opaque. One of Sartre's main goals was to defend existentialism from attacks and misconceptions, many of which persist to this day. The two groups he most clearly addresses are the Communists and the Christians. In today's terms, you may say he was fending off attacks from both the Left and the Right. Sartre himself identified more with the Left. We discuss politics more in Chapter 12, but for now it's sufficient to point out that Sartre was personally committed to socialism and that both he and his philosophy were overtly atheistic.

Partially due to the fact that "Existentialism" (as we refer to the essay) was meant to be a defense of his philosophy, Sartre focuses on the optimism inherent in the existentialist movement as he sees it. It's a strange, tough kind of optimism, but in the end, it *is* optimistic. The source of this optimism, for Sartre, is the freedom of man. We use more gender-neutral language in the rest of the chapter, but we think it worth throwing that in there to make a couple of points about Sartre. First, it's the language Sartre used, but, more important, we feel in his case that it wasn't *just* a product of his time. People love to debate whether and how much of a sexist Sartre was, and also how significantly his gender and his issues with masculinity and with women slanted his philosophy. We don't go deep into this kind of analysis, but we think many of Sartre's literary and philosophical ideas are distinctly masculine. Which ideas, and how much so, we leave to you to decide.

In this chapter, we discuss some of the major themes and ideas of "Existentialism," particularly as they pertain to the idea of freedom, which is central for many existentialists. Because Sartre sometimes lights on a subject and then moves on, bringing in details from his wider philosophy helps make sense of what he says. Sartre is kind of like that philosophy professor who starts talking to you about the squirrel problem in his backyard and then six topics later comes back to the squirrels, dismissively saying, "But that problem is really just a side effect of the military–industrial complex's hold on the current administration." Uh-huh. We help you connect the dots back to the squirrels (in a manner of speaking).

We start with an examination of what it means to be free and why Sartre has such a strong and unrelenting notion of the breadth and depth of our freedom. Then we explain one of Sartre's most important concepts — the idea that our existence precedes our essence — and what this principle has to do with our freedom. (Hint: everything!) As we mention earlier, "Existentialism" presents a tough-minded optimism. We explain why freedom is such a tough road, why Sartre thinks — to use another of his most famous phrases — we're "condemned" to be free, but also why freedom is so important and why it's a source of hope. Like many of the existentialists, Sartre was concerned with human psychology and how one copes with a life without any inherent meaning. He was particularly influential on a movement in psychology that aimed at dealing with this issue. In Chapter 14, we discuss these folks and how Sartre influenced them.

What Does It Mean to Be Free?

We hear and talk a lot about freedom. Everyone wants to be free, right? People fight wars for freedom on the assumption that everyone wants it. Sartre and the other existentialists may take issue with that assumption, but the first question you have to answer is what freedom *is*.

In one sense, freedom is living without constraint. This is a popular way of thinking about freedom today. You're free if nothing gets in your way: Mom and Dad, oppressive regimes at home and abroad, your boss (you know, *the Man*). You can also point to internal constraints such as mental illness, drug addiction, and maybe even genetics. If you're genetically disposed to like potato chips more than tomatoes, are you free to lead the heart-healthy lifestyle your doctor recommends? If all humans are genetically disposed to prefer the chips, if preferring them is part of human nature, everyone is in trouble. Judging from the rising heart-disease rates, something like this scenario just may be the case. The question constantly asked today, then, is "Are people free?" Was this or that person free when she performed a certain act?

Sartre rejects all this business about constraints. His answer to the final two questions is yes. It's always yes, because people are always free.

Freedom means always having a choice

Freedom means different things to different people. If you can quit your job without starving or losing your home, you have economic freedom. If you can go to the church, mosque, synagogue, or temple you want, you have religious freedom. Many devout Christians crossed the Atlantic to exercise that kind of freedom in the New World. Some of them lost no time once they got here exercising their freedom to discriminate against others. In Christian and other theologies, each person has a choice between good and evil. What all these notions of freedom have in common is choice. If you have economic freedom, you can choose to quit your job, or choose to go to the Bahamas and stay at a first-class resort. If you have religious freedom, you can choose which religious services to attend or maybe to not go at all. A big enough group of people may even have the freedom to choose to curtail the freedom of others.

You're *free,* then, when you have a choice. The exact nature of that choice can vary, but when you have a choice, you have freedom. Sartre contends that people always have a choice and therefore are always free. Having the constant luxury and responsibility to make a choice is part of the human condition. Why? Because no matter what your situation is, you choose that situation. Sartre believes this for four main reasons:

- ✔ You choose how to interpret your situation.

- ✔ You choose how to react to your situation.

- ✔ In particular, you choose whether to remain in your situation.

- ✔ Any part of your situation that you don't choose is irrelevant.

That last point may seem like a bit of a cheat — as though anything that doesn't fit into Sartre's way of thinking just "doesn't count" — but it's integral to not only his worldview, but also to the existentialists' view in general. The existentialists are absolutely committed to a vision of honesty that insists upon facing the world, facing life *as is*. Even the Christian existentialists tend to see traditional religion as a dodge for facing the hard truth that life is fundamentally meaningless. Nietzsche says, "God is dead" largely to stress that no God or heaven could give meaning to life after the fact. If life is to be redeemed, it must be *this* life as it's handed to us. That's not to say you should refuse to engage in life, that you should accept life as it is and not try to change it. Quite the contrary. Sartre thinks that such engagement is crucial. What you must do, however, is engage the world on honest terms, starting from a view that acknowledges what your starting point really is. Saying, "But if I weren't poor . . ." or "If I hadn't been born in a time of war . . ." is no better than saying, "But if God could have given us a miracle . . ." or "If I were a superhero and could fly . . ." You start from where you are, but you move forward. In that moving forward, you always have a choice.

Free choice means free action

In other works, Sartre refers to everything you *can't* control as your *facticity*. The list of things you can't control is fairly broad. For example, although Sartre says that there's no human nature, he does concede that people have temperaments, such as a quick temper or a nervous or shy disposition. Your nature, what you are, is something you create, but your temperament may simply be an uncontrollable fact you have to live with. Your native nationality, whether you were born rich or poor, the political circumstances you live in — these factors are all out of your immediate control.

Your facticity is at once very broad and very narrow. Take a look at your life in 360 degrees. *Look* at everything, but don't *think* about it. Look at it as a frozen movie still. Your job may require that you be at work at 8 a.m.; you may be an American, French, or Chinese citizen. Your parents and upbringing may be rich or poor. You may have inherited a quick mind from your mother and an impatient temperament from your father. At this writing, you live in a time of uncertainty and war, and this environment may affect your life directly or indirectly. All this composes your facticity at this moment.

Now unfreeze the snapshot. As soon as things start moving, you get involved. The 8 a.m. start time isn't just a fact; it's a fact that you live, and in living it, you choose it in a number of ways. First, you choose it because you don't quit your job. "But I need to pay my rent," you say. Then you choose it to pay the rent, but you choose it nonetheless. You could choose another job to pay the rent, or you could risk homelessness while searching for another job. Or you could even choose homelessness. The fact that a choice is unattractive to you doesn't mean that it isn't a choice.

You also have a choice in how you see the facts of your situation. Do you to see the 8 a.m. start time as an inconvenience? As a way of jump-starting your day? If your constitution is like coauthor Greg's, you aren't a morning person, and you may see an 8 a.m. start to your day as a hideous inconvenience and proof of a vengeful God intent on punishing you for your existential ways. (Greg sympathizes; he feels this way some days.) But even if you have Greg's constitution and not coauthor Chris's popping-at-the-crack-of-dawn disposition, you can still view your 8 a.m. start as an opportunity.

As Sartre points out in "Existentialism," "There's no such thing as a cowardly constitution; there are nervous constitutions. . . . A constitution is not an act; the coward is defined on the basis of the acts he performs."

And it's in such acts that Sartre sees the fullest expression of freedom. Fundamentally, free choice is about action. No matter what confronts you, no matter what your constitution, you have a choice in how to respond, in how to *act*.

Sartre brings all this together in the story of a young priest who had lived through a series of setbacks. He had grown up in poverty and experienced many humiliations stemming from this status. He hadn't done particularly well in school. Later, he botched a love affair and failed in his military training. Now, as all these events were happening, the young priest certainly made a number of choices, but that wasn't Sartre's interest in the story. After your past has happened, it's unchangeable and becomes a part of your situation to which you must respond. The young man in this story chose to look at all these trials and failures as a sign that he wasn't meant for worldly success, and he entered the priesthood. You may think Sartre would reject this religious interpretation, but he actually embraces it as a perfect example of the freedom to choose how to view the facts that confront us and how we choose to act in response to them.

Of the young priest, Sartre wrote, "It was a sign of something, but of what? He might have taken refuge in bitterness or despair. But he wisely looked upon all this as a sign that he was not made for secular triumphs. . . . Who can help seeing that he alone decided what the sign meant?"

In many respects, life is something that happens to you, but you always choose how to interpret and respond to it. You are, therefore, always free. In any situation, a number of choices are available to you. Admittedly, some of these choices may be extreme or unpleasant, but they're present nonetheless.

Our most basic choice is living

One of the characteristics that makes us free is the fact that we can always pull out of a situation. You can quit your job, you can accept not paying the rent, you can say no. The ultimate expression of this fact is, for many of the existentialists and Sartre in particular, that a person can always choose suicide. (Check out our cartoon in Figure 8-1.) Therefore, every situation is one you choose because you could always get out of it.

Try this yourself: Freeze frame

Think about your life, and freeze it for a moment. Look around at all the facts that make up your life history and current situation. Find ten things that you didn't decide upon and can't control. Now, like a movie, set the scene rolling again, and look at your relation to those ten things. Ask yourself the following questions:

✔ How do I see these ten facts about my situation?

✔ Can I look at them another way?

✔ Can I walk away from them?

✔ Can I choose how to respond to and interact with these aspects of my situation?

Sartre says the answer to the last three questions is always yes. Therefore, you're always free and always choose your situation.

Figure 8-1:
The notion that suicide is an alternative to your every choice seems rather absurd.

Suicide is always an option, albeit an unpleasant one

At first, this theory may seem extreme. Who looks at the alarm clock and says, "Well, I could get up and go to work, or I could kill myself"? We hope you don't. Putting this argument into context and understanding a bit about Sartre's life and times may make this argument seem more natural. Sartre didn't just live through World War II; he was active in the French Resistance against the Nazis during their occupation of Paris. The war is a constant theme in his writing and a constant source of examples for him. As many of the French (including Sartre) saw it, those who lived through that time were sharply and simply divided between those who collaborated with the Nazis and those who resisted and said no to the situation that faced them.

When Sartre speaks of suicide, then, he isn't raising it simply as an abstraction, but as a genuine choice that faced many of his countrymen and women. Many of those who resisted literally chose death rather than betray their fellows. As unthinkable as choosing death is for many people, Sartre is adamant that people must acknowledge that it *is* a choice that's available. For the collaborator to say "I had no choice" is dishonest because that choice was available, and others had the courage to make it. Strictly speaking, though, they didn't have the courage to resist; they chose to act in that way, and in so doing made themselves courageous. (We discuss this concept further in the later sections "What Sartre Means by 'Existence Precedes Essence'" and "Freedom Is So Important Because It Brings Hope.")

Facing mortality means engaging in life

Still, you may say that talk of death and suicide makes sense in the context of war but not in most people's lives today. What relevance does the choice of suicide have for healthy, well-adjusted folks who are choosing whether to get a second mortgage on the house? The short answer is: everything. For the existentialist, you make every honest choice with the knowledge of your own mortality in the background. That's the most fundamental element of your situation. The significance for Sartre is that death is always an option, always an available choice. It may not be one you would readily choose, but that doesn't change the fact that it exists. After you honestly face the existence of that choice, the rest of your choices open up. If simply living is an active choice you make, how much more so is the choice to keep your job? To pay the rent? To go to work at (God help us) 8 a.m.? If you acknowledge that you could choose death, how can you deny all the other choices available to you, whether it's leaving a spouse, angering your parents, or performing an honest act in the face of duress? If death is a real option, hard choices like these are real options, too — and saying that you couldn't do this or that is disingenuous. Facing the reality of your own mortality is, for Sartre and the existentialists, an awakening experience. If you respond to it properly, if you don't run from it, it heightens your awareness of your own inevitable engagement in life: the degree to which your life is a choice and the degree to which that choice is yours.

Human nature versus the human condition

Sartre repeatedly says that he doesn't believe in an inherent, universal human nature, but he acknowledges a human condition. The difference is that the *human condition* is a set of facts that confront all people. We all live in a world with other people, we need food and shelter to survive, and we're all mortal; this last item is the essence of the human condition for all existentialists. *Human nature,* on the other hand, is what it means to be human. It arises in large part from the meaning human beings choose to give to all the facts of the human condition and how they choose to respond to those conditions.

Human beings may have a lot in common, but none of this has *meaning* until we confront and live through those facts. It's only when we start acting that we define our nature both as individuals and as human beings. It's through those acts, performed in relation to a condition shared by other people but unique to ourselves, that we create human nature and our own nature. Are human beings cowardly? Are we inquisitive? Good? Evil? In what sense? Do we strive toward something as human beings? These are the types of questions that Sartre thinks pertain to human nature and that he believes have no answer until human beings start making choices and acting in the world.

What Sartre Means by "Existence Precedes Essence"

Sartre argues in "Existentialism" that all existential thought is summed up in the phrase "Existence precedes essence." Not everyone agrees that this is *the* definition (Heidegger, whom we discuss in detail in Chapter 9, was mortified by the assertion), but it's certainly an important concept. To be more precise, what he's saying is that, for human beings, our existence precedes our essence. Much clearer, right?

It will be clearer if we just get a handle on the notion of essence. When you say something is essential, you're saying it's necessary. If you make New England clam chowder and leave out the clams, well, you haven't made New England clam chowder. (We've both spent a good deal of time in New England, and we won't even be discussing that other chowder.) Clams are just part of the definition of clam chowder; they're essential to making clam chowder what it is and not some other soup. The *essence* of something, then, is whatever makes it what it is. So by saying that existence precedes essence, Sartre means that human beings exist — are born and are conscious of their lives — before they really "are" anything. No crucial, necessary ingredient defines what a human being is. Nothing, in short, serves as an essence or nature that forces all human beings to *be* a certain preordained way. You have no human nature; there's nothing you're called or meant to do. You quite literally start as nothing.

We explain in the coming sections exactly what this means and what significance it has, particularly for human freedom, responsibility, and value. You can think of freedom as a blank on a form you have to fill out. It's there, but it exists only to be filled in with something else. In the case of human beings, that something else is who and what you are.

A human being is not a watch

Sartre explains the meaning of his most important phrase by comparing a human being with a manufactured item. We use a watch; Sartre uses a paper cutter, but the point is the same. A watch has a set function: It exists to tell time. Although some watches may be digital or contain pocketknives, if something didn't tell you the time, you wouldn't call it a watch. You could say (if you were feeling all philosophical) that telling time is a necessary feature of being a watch; that's what makes it what it is. Furthermore, this function already exists in the mind of the watchmaker before he actually creates any given watch. No one sits down to make a watch without thinking, "I'm going to make something that tells time." The watch's essence — what it is to be a watch — precedes its actual existence because that essence, that purpose, was in the mind of the designer before the watch came into being.

Two interesting characteristics about watches, then, are

- ✔ They have a fixed essence or definition. That is, at least part of what it means to be a watch is that a watch is an "object that tells time." Doing so is a necessary part of being a watch.

- ✔ The essence is present before the actual watch is. The essence exists as an idea or a plan before the watch is created and actually guides its creation.

Sartre dramatically claims that if God doesn't exist, this order is reversed for at least one object in the universe. Because God didn't design us, we weren't created with a plan in mind, as the watch was. Unlike the watch, we weren't meant to serve a set function or realize a set pattern. When we're born, we're simply there, with no reason or meaning. No designer had any essence in mind, so we exist before that existence has any meaning, purpose, or definition.

So according to Sartre, we're unlike the watch in two crucial ways:

- ✔ We have no fixed essence or definition. Being a human being has no inherent meaning; human nature doesn't exist.

- ✔ We exist before we have any definition, purpose, or meaning.

Although the watch starts as an instrument for telling the time, we start as *nothing,* as a great emptiness or lack. Our only definition is that we're beings that lack definition. But notice the words *fixed* and *before.* Definition, meaning, purpose — for human beings, these things come later. You aren't born with them but must develop them on your own.

That's why existence *precedes* essence. A human being is essentially a creature that creates its own essence. You must define yourself through your choices and actions. It's only after exercising your free will and choosing how you'll act in the world that you start to define yourself and develop or create a meaning to your own existence.

Being human means being free

The most obvious consequence of the lack of human nature is that we're free to create what we'll become. But this makes it sound like you can choose who you'll be if you want to. Rather, it's more accurate to say that this freedom to make yourself, and your acting on this freedom, are what you *are.* In his more hyperbolic moments, Sartre goes so far as to say that a human being *is* freedom. He rejects the notion that this construction is a way of secretly acknowledging a human nature he claims doesn't exist. To the extent that freedom is a nature, it's only an empty nature waiting to be filled in. Think of your freedom as a blank on a form you have to fill out. It's there, but it exists only to be filled in with something else.

Of watches and watchmakers

William Paley, an 18th-century Anglican priest and philosopher, made very different use of the idea of a watchmaker in his attempt to prove the existence of God. Paley's argument asks you to imagine that you found a watch on the ground. Its complexity and the fact that this complexity was clearly developed with a particular function in mind would indicate the existence of a watchmaker who designed that watch.

Similarly, he argued, the complexity of human beings and the clear functions to which their various parts are adapted prove that they must be the creations of a cosmic designer. For example, the human eye shows evidence of design because it's a complex object with an obvious function (seeing). Human beings, in this view, are the products of a cosmic designer who had a plan or function in mind for them.

Notice, however, that although the function of a *part* of a human being — such as a heart or an eye — seems clear and obvious, the function of the human being as a whole is less clear. Sartre was living after Nietzsche announced the death of God (see Chapter 3 for more on this concept), when the rightness and order of the universe were no longer accepted as a given. He wasn't willing to so easily accept the notion that human beings have a divine origin and that this origin gives them a ready purpose as surely as a watch has one. On the contrary, Sartre turns the example on its head and states that human beings have no designated purpose or function precisely because they have no such "watchmaker" to build that purpose or function into them. They simply start as an emptiness, a lack of these things, a nothingness.

Freedom, according to a certain singer-songwriter, is just another word for nothing left to lose. If existence precedes essence, we're not only free to create ourselves; we're also free of any inherent, built-in baggage. Because we're nothing, nothing is compelling us or prejudicing our choices or our actions. Any choice is possible. That kind of freedom can be overwhelming, and Sartre doesn't think it's anything to take lightly.

In the next section, we explain why freedom is a great weight and why being free isn't as simple as catching a wave and living a carefree existence. Sartre was no hippie, but a serious, even austere thinker with the soul of a moralist.

Condemned to Be Free (And Responsible) Whether You Like It or Not

Like Nietzsche, Sartre is wonderfully quotable. He's the author of a deep, complex, and highly detailed philosophy. But perhaps because that philosophy is deeply relevant to the project of living that everyone must undertake, Sartre expressed some of its most important and relevant tenets in short, powerful, and highly suggestive (if not particularly clear) language. We discuss the meaning of the highly important phrase "Existence precedes essence" in the preceding section. Another central tenet of Sartre's philosophy is that human beings are "condemned to be free." To some extent, the phrase is rhetorical; no judge sentences you to freedom. Certainly, the atheist Sartre didn't believe God was behind it! What he means, in part at least, is that being free is a fundamental part of the human condition and that we can't escape our freedom.

Being "condemned" sounds pretty ominous, though. (We include a little cartoon about it in Figure 8-2.) And Sartre calls this an optimistic philosophy? Well, yes, he does. But it's always an optimism about where we can go from where we start. This discussion deals with the human condition — the starting place, which he admits can look pretty bleak at times. The sense in which that starting place (freedom) is something we're "condemned" to basically has the following two aspects:

✔ The first aspect is the aforementioned inescapability of that freedom. You're free in life to make many choices, but whether you'll be free isn't one of them. It's an inescapable part of your human condition, like it or not.

✔ The second aspect is the weight of freedom. You experience your freedom as a great burden because it's a tremendous responsibility. If your freedom is inescapable, so is your responsibility.

Responsibility is the other side of the freedom coin, and it's also at the heart of Sartre's philosophy, which asserts that you're totally free *and* totally responsible. Responsibility itself has two elements:

- ✔ If you're responsible for something, you (ideally) have some kind of power or control over the outcome. If your boss said to you, "Johnson, you're responsible for sales for the fourth quarter, but you won't have any authority over the sales department. In fact, you'll be working for maintenance fixing toilets," you'd be understandably confused and probably a bit peeved.

- ✔ Further, being responsible for something suggests that it matters somehow, that something is at stake. It's only with a bemused grin to other adults that parents give children "responsibility" for tasks like counting the number of blue cars they pass on a long road trip. Real responsibility involves things you care about in one way or another.

In the case of freedom, the responsibility you bear is, in a very real sense, for *everything* you care about. If you want to know exactly what's at stake and why freedom is so important, read the section "Freedom Is So Important Because It Brings Hope," later in this chapter. For the rest of this section, we explain why this freedom and this responsibility you bear for your choices are inescapable.

Figure 8-2:
Freedom means responsibility, and that can be tough to face.

The inescapability of choice

Choice is inescapable because of the type of beings we are. Unlike a stone or a watch, we're conscious. We have what Sartre refers to as *subjectivity*. His notion of it is taken directly from the French philosopher René Descartes, who famously said, "I think, therefore I am."

"I think, therefore I am"

Most people have heard this famous quotation, but few really know what it means. Think of that weird, late-night discussion you've probably had (unless maybe it's just us existential types) in which someone eventually asks, "But wait — what if all this is just a dream?" Strange-flavored brownies may or may not be involved in such discussions. Descartes, although probably brownieless, was trying to figure out how we can be certain of anything. How do you know whether what you believe is true? To answer this question, he performed a thought experiment in which he tried to doubt every belief he had. He was looking for one belief he absolutely couldn't doubt. He found he was able to doubt quite a lot, including the existence of the entire physical universe and his own body. The only thing he couldn't doubt was the existence of a thinker (himself) who was doubting. So he proclaimed the one fact he could be certain of was that he existed: "I think, therefore I am."

In building his philosophy, which is all about knowledge, Descartes starts with this subjective viewpoint, with his own consciousness, and builds everything else from there. This creates a separation in his philosophy (and in many later philosophies) between consciousness and the rest of the world. In this view, the human body is conceptually distinct from the human mind, or consciousness. You look out at the world, you see it, taste it, smell it, and interact with it, but you seem somehow different. Unlike most of the objects you perceive, you're *aware* of yourself and of other objects. Most important, you look out on the objects in the world and make *judgments* about them. For Descartes, the main judgments involved are "believe" and "don't believe."

Consciousness is constantly choosing

Sartre adopts this point of view — the view of starting with consciousness — not on particularly existentialist grounds, but simply on the basis of the fact that he thinks Descartes is right. Sartre thinks that our own consciousness is the one certainty we all start with and that it's from this subjective viewpoint that we each look out onto the world. But although Descartes thinks we fundamentally judge statements to be true or false by looking out from our consciousness, Sartre feels that our fundamental act is to choose how to interpret and interact with the outside world.

For Sartre, the first act of consciousness is to choose. Consciousness, in itself, is nothing. It becomes something only as it makes these choices. This is what makes us different from all the other objects in the universe. Most objects simply are what they are. They're complete, in a sense, in themselves. A rock is a rock. It doesn't need to do anything or have anything added to it to be what it is. In other words, the universe is filled with objects that, if they could talk, would sound a lot like Popeye, saying, "I yam what I yam, and that's all that I yam."

Human beings are, in one sense, objects in the world. As such, they simply are what they are — 5-foot-2-inch, pinkish, hairy blobs of tissue, bone, and blood, for example. But unlike other objects, we also create what we are and what we'll become. We're subjects — conscious beings — that create what we are through the choices we make. The point isn't simply that consciousness *can* do this, but that this is what consciousness *does* by its very nature. Whereas other objects, like rocks and watches, simply *are,* a consciousness is constantly *creating* itself by constantly choosing.

	Existence- Essence	*Subjectivity*
Emptiness	Because human existence precedes human essence, human beings start as nothing. You're nothing before you start making choices.	Consciousness, or subjectivity, in itself is nothing. It becomes something only as it makes choices.
We're different from objects	An object's essence is predetermined, but human beings create their essence only later.	Objects simply are what they are. In one sense, humans are objects, but as subjectivity, human beings create what they are.
Our nature, to the extent that we have one . . .	. . . is to create ourselves, because we have no essence.	. . . is to choose, which is the activity that allows us to create ourselves.

You bear sole responsibility for your choices

Because to live is to choose, you're perpetually under the weight of this responsibility to choose. Not only can you not avoid choosing, but you also can't avoid the responsibility for that choice. The subjective position that Sartre's philosophy starts with is a very lonely position. Many things come before you for your consideration; you need to review many things for interpretation and response. But like Harry Truman said, the buck stops here, with you, and with each of us. As things parade by you for your consideration, nothing compels you to make any *particular* choice, and nothing can comfort you by taking responsibility for that choice away from you.

Imagine your consciousness as a chief executive officer at a big desk. The facts and situations of your life continually parade across your consciousness, like proposals for your consideration. No one is sitting next to you in your consciousness; no one helps you interpret what comes across or decides for you what to approve, what to reject, what to choose, and how to respond. It's up to you to review each "proposal" and make the decision.

As an atheist, Sartre can't accept God as the justification for our actions. But really, even if God exists, it makes no difference. Like everything else that crosses your desk, the word of God is just one more thing you'd have to interpret for yourself and choose how to respond to. The truth of this principle becomes evident if you consider the vast number of religions and interpretations of the Bible, Koran, or any other holy work. You may say you choose something because God or your preacher says so, but really, you choose how to interpret and respond to what God or the preacher says. You even choose which preacher at which church to listen to in the first place. This is why, even if God exists, the situation from the human perspective remains the same. Choice is still ultimately in your hands alone.

Sartre calls this sense of being alone in decision-making *forlornness.* He illustrates it beautifully with a story about a student who came to him for advice. The young man's mother absolutely lived for him; she had no one else. The son didn't want to betray and abandon her, but he also felt a responsibility to his countrymen to fight the Nazis, and felt he could best do this by traveling to Britain to join the French air force based there while France was occupied. The young man couldn't decide what to do.

Connecting the dots: Subjectivity and "existence precedes essence"

If you read "Existentialism," you may be mystified by Sartre's claim that the notion that "existence precedes essence" is the same as saying that "subjectivity is the starting point." After all, he never really explains exactly how this is so. Because we promise in the introduction to this chapter that we'll help you connect the dots, we're taking a moment to connect these two big ideas in Sartre's philosophy. Although we're leery of saying that these two statements are the same (American philosophers are notoriously slow to admit that two different things are really the same, no matter what famous French philosophers say), what Sartre is trying to express with both of these statements is that *human beings start as nothing.* To make the connection between each of these statements more clear, take a look at some of the parallels that exist between the story of subjectivity we just described and the notion that existence precedes essence.

Naturally, no ethical system has the answer on page 691, under "Your Mother or Your Country: Which to Choose?" Even if such a book existed, it would be up to you to decide whether to accept its conclusions. But really, any ethical system can give only vague rules that you have to interpret and apply. Sartre wants us to see that whether we acknowledge it or not, we're always involving ourselves in our decisions. Whatever doctrine, advice, or other external influence we may point to, in the end, we're always the ones making a number of choices, whether it's what action to take, which advice or doctrine to listen to, or how to interpret them. In this case, the student chose to go to Sartre for advice as opposed to someone else, and he got the advice he chose to get. Sartre's response? "You are free. Choose."

Coauthor Greg was a perfect illustration of this point himself. In college, he had a favorite professor he went to for advice. But in a sense, Greg knew perfectly well before he went what the advice would be. The bottom line from this professor was always the same: "Follow your heart." On some level, Greg already knew what he wanted to do and what he wanted to hear by the time he went to the professor. Sartre thinks all decision-making is a more or less transparent version of this. That's not to say nothing ever influences you. That influence is never *determinative* — that is, it's never so strong as to force you to accept its direction and thereby eliminate your freedom to choose. You take all the available input and make a series of choices: weighing the information, interpreting it, and finally deciding.

Freedom Is So Important Because It Brings Hope

Winston Churchill once said, "The pessimist sees difficulty in every opportunity. The optimist sees the opportunity in every difficulty." Existentialism isn't an easy philosophy; it doesn't see the world as an easy place to live, and it doesn't propose easy solutions to living in it. It is, however, a philosophy that sees an opportunity in the difficulties it examines. For Sartre, the greatest difficulty and the greatest opportunity in life both lie in human freedom.

Freedom means always having a choice, and where there's a choice, there's hope. This is the optimism Sartre's philosophy offers — not that the world will be perfect, not that your choices will be easy, but that you'll have a choice, and with that choice an opportunity to change yourself, your situation, and your world for the better. Sartre rejects all forms of *fatalism,* which suggest that our human nature dooms individuals or human beings as a group to be stuck in our situations.

Cowardice was one of Sartre's obsessions and an example he regularly returned to; after all, he did live in a time of war and fought for his freedom with the French Resistance. Many of the characters in his examples and his fiction are cowards who run from their responsibility or from standing up against totalitarianism and injustice. But the point Sartre continually comes back to is that the coward is a coward by choice. It isn't any one decision that makes the coward a coward. A coward is someone who continually makes the decision to act in a certain way. But Sartre thinks this fact is the good news. If the coward is a coward by choice and is constantly faced with choices (which is the nature of life), the opportunity exists for the coward to change and choose to be courageous. No matter what your past, no matter what choices you've made, there's always hope because you're free. But this philosophy is a hard road, and that constant sense of possibility cuts both ways. The courageous hero is no more secure in her courageousness than the coward is in cowardice. Choice is a constantly recurring opportunity for both success and failure.

Free choice creates value and meaning

If God doesn't exist, no eternal, objective measure of value exists, and nothing has any inherent meaning. This doesn't mean, however, that life has no meaning or value at all. It's just that every meaning and value is a human meaning or a human value. And because human beings have no human nature and no inherent values or meaning, we're constantly creating those human meanings and values.

Opening Pandora's box

In the story of Pandora's box, Pandora receives a box that the gods tell her not to open under any circumstances. Curiosity and the lure of the forbidden are too much for Pandora, and she eventually opens the box, which releases all the ills and troubles of the world. At the bottom of the box, however, is hope. As often interpreted, hope is the one consolation allowed to humans for the host of troubles facing them — the one consolation we have to help us through life.

In a sense, when existentialists announced the death of God, they opened a Pandora's box, out of which flew the troubles of meaninglessness, anguish, and forlornness. But at bottom, what the existentialists offer is hope — hope that by opening the box and facing these hardships that, after all, were sitting there waiting all along, we can find a way of coping with them. For Sartre in particular, the hope at the bottom of the box is freedom.

That creation happens when you make choices. Sartre is all about action. It's all well and good to think that poetry, philosophy, opera, and art museums are the best things that life has to offer, but what does that mean if you choose to spend all your time watching *Three's Company?* Your choices are the only expressions you have of what you value. On the other hand, if your choice wasn't free, it wouldn't be an expression of value. To value something means to view it as better in some way than an alternative. Without freedom, then, nothing would have value; where you placed your value would be determined for you. Because we appear to be the only creatures that express free choice, we're the only creatures that can value one thing over another.

Choice, then, is a creative act. The meaninglessness and valueless-ness of the universe are, in a sense, only the starting points. We say *in a sense* because nothing creates absolute, eternal values. Those don't exist. Through freedom, though, human beings have the power to escape the utter lack of values that's our starting point in the universe. But this escape isn't easy. It's an act of will that people naturally shrink from. We want someone to provide a set answer — a fixed, eternal meaning — for us, and we don't really want the responsibility that comes with creating values for ourselves.

Sartre's response is sympathetic. He says he's "vexed" by the lack of a God to provide eternal truths for us, but he points out that this is simply how it is. This is the situation we find ourselves in. Existentialism, as he sees it, doesn't create that situation; it just creates an optimistic path through it.

How your choices affect you

As you choose, you create value. In doing so, you create yourself. For Sartre, freedom is the source of human dignity. Although it's true that we start as nothing, we have the power to make something of ourselves and the freedom to determine what that will be. A rock or a watch can't change what it is. This distinction is why Sartre rejects the notion that his philosophy debases human beings. He's not a naturalist who equates human beings with animals or sees a human being as miniscule speck of dust before the grandeur of the universe. The universe is filled with objects that are conscious of nothing, feel nothing, choose nothing, and value nothing. The Milky Way, for all its vastness, is as dumb and senseless as a rock. Only human beings make choices and make themselves into something.

But you're no more than what you choose. Sartre rejects the idea of human potential. He considers it meaningless to say that an author, for example, had another great book in her that she never wrote. The only measure of what a person is capable of is what she actually does. A human being is, after all, essentially nothing. All that exists at your center is an ability to choose.

Therefore, you're no more than the sum of your actions. Because you're constantly choosing and acting, you're constantly creating who and what you are. This power is why, instead of your choices and actions being meaningless (as you may expect from only a superficial understanding of existentialism), Sartre feels that your choices matter deeply.

This importance is why Sartre considers freedom to be the source of human dignity. What makes us different from and more dignified than a rock or a watch is that what we are is in our hands. We have the freedom and the responsibility to create who and what we are. If you think about it, this corresponds with our everyday notion of responsibility. When someone holds you responsible, it is in one sense a burden, but it's also a sign of respect. Holding someone responsible indicates that the person is capable or competent. Children are in many instances considered incompetent. Adults don't consider them capable of making decisions or choices. Although they may feel compassion for children, they don't give them the respect they'd give a competent adult. For Sartre, existentialism isn't an affront to human dignity — philosophical and religious systems that would deny human beings their responsibility are.

Choice and consequences

Although Sartre is optimistic about our ability to make choices and, consequently, our ability to make good choices and change, nothing in his philosophy extends this optimism to the realm of consequences. You can act heroically, but this heroism doesn't guarantee any particular end result. Chance, facts about the world, and the freedom of others can all conspire to bring to ruin the effects of our noblest deeds.

But Sartre insists that, in some respects, these consequences don't really matter. You're free to make choices that create who you are. You can't control the conditions in which you make those choices, and you can't control the outcome. What you can control is sandwiched in between, on the one hand, the situation you find yourself in and, on the other hand, the effects your actions have on the world after you make your choices. If you make good choices, if you choose to live honestly and courageously, you've made of yourself an honest and courageous person. That's all you can do and all you can hope to do.

Sartre presents a great example of this principle in his short story *The Wall.* In it, protagonist Pablo Ibbieta has been arrested and sentenced to death. He repeatedly refuses to give up the location of resistance fighter Ramon Gris, even as his cellmates are taken out and shot one at a time. In a final act of defiance, he lies to the guards, saying that Gris is in a cemetery. Ibbieta is later confused that the guards allow him to continue living, until a recently captured man named Garcia tells him, "They got Gris." How? Garcia tells him that Gris left his hiding spot and fled to the cemetery Ibbieta led his captors to. Ibbieta is overwhelmed by the absurdity, the tragedy, and even the comedy of the situation. Ibbieta's situation isn't unique. He couldn't control whether the Fascists came to power, and he couldn't control the outcome of his actions, which in this case were absurdly tragic. But in between, he chose to resist, he chose to act courageously, and so exercised his human dignity to make something of himself that he could call good.

How your choices affect the world

Every choice is an act of creation. Because Sartre doesn't believe in God, eternal values, human nature, or an inherent meaning to human life, he's committed to the idea that meaning, value, and your own character can arise only from your own choices. When you make a choice, you create in three ways:

- ✔ **You create who you are.** Each time you choose to tell the truth, for example, you contribute to the creation of someone who tells the truth.

- ✔ **You create values.** If you choose to tell the truth rather than lie, you have chosen to value truth. That value may have existed before you because others made a similar choice in the past, but it doesn't exist apart from human choice. In that sense, your choice contributes to the creation of this value.

- ✔ **You create what it means to be human.** If human nature doesn't exist, what human beings are and what it means to be human are simply an amalgamation of what individual human beings choose to make of themselves. In a very real way, then, when you make choices, you're choosing what it means to be human. For Sartre, this fact was at the heart of the weight of responsibility that hangs over us.

Kant and the Categorical Imperative

Sartre's philosophy, particularly as presented in "Existentialism," owes much to the German philosopher and ethicist Immanuel Kant. Nowhere is this influence more evident than in Sartre's assertion that when you choose for yourself, you're choosing for the entire world. Kant wasn't an existentialist. His philosophy was concerned with the search for universal ethical principles that he felt should guide all action, and such objective moral laws are precisely what the existentialists deny exist! Kant called the ethical principle he developed the *Categorical Imperative.* According to the first formulation of this principle (the two others aren't important here), whenever you make a decision, you should act as though you're creating a law for all human beings to follow. The question you should ask yourself is, "Can I will the principle behind this action to be treated as a universal law that everyone should follow?" Basically, should it be a rule that everyone act this way? Sartre takes a very different path but arrives at this same principle. For Kant, this imperative is an objective moral law, discovered by rational inquiry. For Sartre, it arises simply from the nature of our situation. Because you are, in fact, choosing for all human beings, if you're honest, you must acknowledge this fact and accept the responsibility that comes with your choices.

We discuss the first point earlier. Sartre often speaks of the next two points together. The world of value and meaning is a human (and human-created) world. Because when you act, you're helping create this world, Sartre feels that, in a sense, you aren't making choices just for yourself, but for the whole world. When coauthor Chris makes a choice, he's creating a value, and he's defining what it means to be human. Sartre believes we have a great responsibility to consider this fact as we make our choices. It's natural, therefore, for you to ask of your choices, "Do I want this choice to be a human value, for all people?" "Is this what I believe human beings should be?" Sartre isn't so much saying that you *should* ask these questions but that these questions will naturally arise in your decision-making process if you honestly look at the facts — namely, that in choosing, you're creating values that extend beyond yourself. The questions themselves are simply a natural expression of the responsibility you have in creating values with your choices.

Freedom is the highest good

In one sense, Sartre, like the other existentialists, doesn't believe in objective values. He argues in "Existentialism," however, that you can identify one thing that logically must be considered not only valuable, but also *the* most valuable thing; in that sense, this thing is the highest good. Naturally, this thing is freedom. His argument is fairly straightforward. Because you give something value only when you freely choose it, all value comes from free choice. A rock or an ant may go left or right, but it doesn't care which way it goes. It doesn't choose the direction; the direction is chosen for it by a complex series of physical interactions. Without the ant's active engagement in its own motion, it's simply a mechanical process. Value arises when you express a preference for *this* over *that* through your freedom to choose *this* over *that*. Nothing is more valuable than freedom, then, because everything else that has value derives that value from freedom.

For Sartre, to value anything is to value the thing that gives it value. If you value courage, for example, you have to value free choice, because courage wouldn't be valuable without it. To some extent, this argument is familiar. One of the traditional arguments for the greatness of God is that God is the source of all good things. If you love life and all the blessings of life, you should thank God and worship him as the source of all these good things. As the source, he's higher and better than any one of those things. Without God, nothing has inherent value, not even life.

Similarly, by choosing life or anything else, human beings confer value upon life and the other things we choose. But what makes our choices value-creating, as opposed to the choices of, say, an aardvark, is that human beings have free choice. We make one choice *rather than* another, and so value one thing *over* another; we confer value upon this rather than that. So freedom is the highest good because it and it alone allows us to confer value upon various things in life. Without it, life wouldn't just start without any inherent meaning or value; it would stay that way.

Chapter 9

Finding Authenticity: Facing Death, Conscience, and Time

In This Chapter

▶ Understanding why facing death is essential to an authentic life

▶ Appreciating the importance of listening to your conscience

▶ Seeing why authenticity requires the right stance toward time

*W*hen you think of existentialism, you probably get an image in your head of people sitting around muttering to themselves, dressed in black and depressed about their impending deaths. Well, some existentialists, such as Martin Heidegger, do think facing death is extremely important if you hope to live an authentic life that's true to who and what you are. But it doesn't mean going Goth and moping around all day being depressed.

Instead, as most existentialists suggest, living authentically means engaging with life in a way that honestly reflects what you are. This includes reflecting the ways that you're limited as an existing being — and death is one of those limitations. In fact, as far as the existentialists see it, when you embrace death, you become liberated for the possibility of actually living. From this angle, it's actually those who avoid the confrontation with death who end up living superficial lives that aren't worth living. If you ask us, *that's* what's depressing — ignoring death!

Still, living authentically is no easy task. It's especially hard if the existentialists are right that most of the time, you're deeply immersed within the life of the crowd and the masses, far removed from confronting the important questions about life that you need to ask if you hope to live authentically. Luckily, for Heidegger, no matter how lost in the world you get, you'll always have an existential conscience that calls upon you to shun the crowd and return to living in accord with who and what you are.

In this chapter, we show how this conscience reveals even more ways, in addition to death, that our existence is limited. These limitations reveal more aspects about what you are that you have to embrace if you're going to live authentically. This discussion of death and conscience leads to Heidegger's claim that embracing your limitations — or living authentically as a whole, undivided self —involves having just the right stance toward your future, your past, and your present.

Specifically, authenticity requires living in a way that unifies your whole existence, bounded on one side by birth and on the other side by death, in the way that you engage with life in the moment through your actions. Authenticity is a way of giving your life wholeness across time.

Embracing Death as the Key to Life

Existentialists such as Heidegger think that a meaningful, authentic life requires an embrace of your own mortality. Given the importance of embracing death, we must ask, "How can you face it if you'll never actually experience it?" After all, the moment death occurs, you no longer exist.

Well, Heidegger agrees that although you can't know the actual *event* of your death, you can face up to the awareness that your end is an inevitable part of your future. This means recognizing that death is a possibility for you at each moment. Thus, authentic living is living *toward* death, actively embracing the fact that the Grim Reaper is always right up ahead.

- ✔ Facing up to death is something you can only do alone.
- ✔ Facing death individualizes you, separating you from the crowd and forcing you to take seriously the task of making meaningful, individual choices about how to live.

Given these points, avoiding death is what's depressing, because it leads to a superficial, conformist life that's not worth living at all.

Confronting death is essential

Generally, people think death is a depressing subject that should just be avoided. "Why focus on it? Just live!" they say. Heidegger disagrees. Confronting death is essential to living an authentic life. Still, some have argued that death can't really play this central role because it's entirely unknowable. After all, how can you face something you can't even know?

The argument that you shouldn't focus on death comes from an ancient school of philosophy called Epicureanism, which flourished around 300 BC.

In a nutshell, the Epicureans thought that death was something that couldn't ever really touch you at all. So they counseled that you should be, at best, *indifferent* to death.

Their reasoning is actually pretty simple, and something like the Epicurean argument is adapted by Jean-Paul Sartre. The argument suggests that death isn't really a possibility for *you* because when death arrives, *you* are gone. As a result, death isn't something that you can experience, because you and death can't be in the same place at the same time. Because you can't experience death, you have no reason to be concerned with it.

There's something to this argument, isn't there? If what you fear is the event of death, if you worry about what it'll be like, the argument makes a good point: If you and death can't be in the same place at the same time, it seems to make no sense to take up a position or an attitude toward it. Sure, you may worry about *dying* (you may say, "I hope I die in my sleep," for example), but that's a concern with the suffering that may go on just *before* you die, not a concern with death itself.

For Heidegger, however, it's neither dying nor the actual *event* of death that he thinks you need to face up to. Instead, what's central to living authentically is facing up to what the event implies: One day, you won't be around.

If you think about it, it's a curious fact that only human beings are capable of realizing this aspect of their *finitude* (the fact that they'll one day end). Your plants and your pets will die, but they have no awareness of it. Dogs and cats may get sick and grow uncomfortable, but they have no idea how that sickness may eventually play out. People do. As a result, Heidegger thinks that it's an undeniable part of what you are: *Being-toward-death* is a possible way for you to be.

Facing up to your being-toward-death doesn't mean sitting around worrying about death, brooding over it, or becoming morbid. It doesn't mean going Goth and buying the standard existentialist gear (all black clothes). Instead, being-toward-death simply means never losing sight of your future finitude; it means letting that awareness affect the way you live your life.

Keeping an eye on the inevitable: The Grim Reaper is up ahead

Existentialists agree that humans are essentially forward-directed beings. Your existence involves always being one step ahead, planning, seeking out, and working through the possibilities that present themselves to you in any given situation. You're always thinking, "What next?" But the Grim Reaper is up ahead, too, as one of those possibilities. As you push forward into life, you push forward into death. Each second is one in which death may occur.

We doubt anyone reading this right now is muttering to himself, "I'll never die." If you are, you may want to read *Self-Deception For Dummies*. We've got news for you: You most certainly *will* die. Unfortunately, Heidegger thinks, most people think of death inauthentically. They treat it as an event *way* off in the future, something distant from life itself. You may think, "Heck, I'm only 20 (or 30, or 40, or 50 . . .). I still have X number of good years left in me, provided I don't get hit by a bus!" This isn't embracing death — it's avoiding it.

Heidegger puts it this way: "Death is a possibility of being that Dasein always has to take upon itself. With death, Dasein stands before itself in its own most potentiality of being."

Essentially, Heidegger wants you (collectively, we're "Dasein"; see Chapter 6 for details) to see that you shouldn't treat death as an event that's coming closer to you with every passing moment, like a train slowly approaching from the distance. Thinking this way has the effect of putting distance between you and your death, making it something foreign and external to you and to what it means to live your life now, for you to *exist*. It's inauthentic because:

- ✔ It makes death an external event instead of an internal way of being.

- ✔ It makes death a passive happening as opposed to an active way in which you can actually live.

Authentically embracing death doesn't mean waiting for the event to occur; it means running toward it. Only by taking the bull by the horns and taking an active stance on death can you live a life that's truly yours. Odd as it may sound, you have to learn to make death into a way to live.

Hold on a second. Heidegger isn't advocating suicide. Running toward death doesn't mean you're seeking it out or trying to make it more likely in the near future. Instead, it means pushing into the future, or choosing among your possibilities while keeping in view the fact that one of those possibilities is always that you'll die.

Living with death means thinking, "Hmm. I could do A or B. Or I could die." You acknowledge that the possibility of your own impossibility, or the fact that one day your possibilities will end, is always present now; you live with it, so it's not a distant, future event. If you can seriously do that, Heidegger thinks, death may well have a serious impact on the way you live.

Can you do that, honestly, and not in a halfhearted manner? Can you embrace your finitude? Really embrace the fact that Porky Pig could rip through the screen of your life now and say, "That's all, folks!" Can you keep it up in a way that incorporates it into the way you live?

Making choices becomes monumental in light of death

Few things are truer than this: When something is rare, it tends to be treated as valuable. When something is common, it tends to be viewed as cheap. Life is no exception. If you think that you have a lot of it to go around, you won't value it as much. The less you think there is of it, the more you'll take it seriously. In short, death makes life valuable!

Anyone who has had a near-death experience can tell you that afterward, things just look different. Of course, in a way, everything around you is the same. But it all feels different; the way the world matters to you has changed. You become afraid of the danger of treading superficially in life. You desperately want your choices to matter.

When you have all the time in the world, life is frivolous

Recall those times when an awareness of the possibility of death wasn't present to you. What happened? You treated the moments before you superficially. It happens all the time. Have you ever been in the midst of some project that you think you have to do while promising yourself that when you're done, you'll get back to that other project — the one you think is more important and that you've been neglecting? Maybe it's your work; it gets in the way of your spending time with your family. Maybe it's something else, but the story is always the same: You always have time later. This is the essence of treating life superficially.

Understanding how this happens is easy. Think of the future moments of your life as something you want. You have a demand for life. Now consider the law of supply and demand to see how much those moments of life are worth to you. When you treat death as an event that's far off and distant from you, you're clearly reasoning that that you have a decent amount of supply (of life) lying around. You're convinced that even if you're going to die, it won't be today or tomorrow or even next week! You see supply as high, so the value of life winds up being low. That's why the important stuff gets put off. You think you have plenty of time get back to it. You live frivolously.

The inevitability of death invigorates life

Now imagine something different. Say that you thought you had half that time left to live. Or a quarter of it. Or perhaps that you had two weeks to live. Would your way of interacting with life change? It should! The reason is obvious: The demand for life remains constant, but the supply of life just got drastically smaller! As a result, the value of life goes up in response. Choice starts to matter.

The moral of the story is clear: When you *live* with death, as part of the very way in which you approach life, you take your life more seriously. The embrace of death invigorates life. You invest each moment with seriousness. You ask real questions about why you should live in this way as opposed to that way. Each moment matters. After all, you realize that you aren't going to get a mulligan or a do-over at any point. When you make choices in life, it's like the sign in the store window: "All sales are final."

Death increases life's value

Perhaps you're thinking, "Maybe death is part of life, but wouldn't it be better if it weren't?" If the supply-and-demand theory of life is accurate, the answer is no. The supply of life would go up, infinitely! But if that's right, the value of life drops infinitely as well! As a consequence, immortality doesn't sound particularly attractive. Sure, you'd have an infinite amount of time to experience things. But you wouldn't value the moments. You'd forever put things off. Why not? You could always do the important stuff later. The immortal would live with no zest. No passion. Not for us, thanks! We'll choose death!

Time and death on the jukebox

Artists probably think about death more than most folks. One music band that seems to revel in the desire to grapple with death authentically is Pink Floyd. The recognition that we can often become aimless and without direction as a result of failing to take our finitude seriously is captured nicely in the appropriately titled song "Time." A partial listing of the lyrics reads

Ticking away the moments that make up a dull day,

You fritter and waste the hours in an offhand way.

Kicking around on a piece of ground in your home town,

Waiting for someone or something to show you the way.

Tired of lying in the sunshine, staying home to watch the rain,

You are young and life is long and there is time to kill today.

And then one day you find ten years have got behind you.

No one told you when to run, you missed the starting gun

And you run and you run to catch up with the sun, but it's sinking

And racing around to come up behind you again.

The sun is the same in the relative way, but you're older.

Shorter of breath and one day closer to death.

The song perfectly gets at the point Heidegger advances: When you fail to acknowledge death, you become frivolous, spending the moments you have without purpose. When you think that you have time to "kill," it means you aren't coming face to face with your death. And that means that your life ends up wasted. You "fritter and waste the hours in an offhand way."

After you look at things in this way, you start to see that the possibility of living with death — or acknowledging your finitude — is a gift. It gives you the possibility of taking your life seriously. Without it, meaningful life would be impossible. Of course, that doesn't mean that everyone uses the gift he's been given. Most people, sadly, live their lives as though they're really immortal.

Meeting death alone: It's inevitable

Facing death leads to an inevitable confrontation with anxiety (check out Chapter 4 to read more about anxiety). Not surprisingly, death anxiety has a useful function within existentialism. It causes you to recognize that you're individual. After you become aware of this fact, you sense that the ways that society and "They," or the others, live life doesn't speak to you as a unique individual. As a result, death anxiety makes responding to death by hiding within a life dominated by what "They" do difficult. That means that facing death involves re-questioning how to live, doing it alone.

Living resolutely

Facing up to the reality of your finitude and death has a very jarring effect on a person. It tends to make you think of the individual choices in your life as serious and monumental; you no longer want to approach life in a superficial way. Essentially, death instills in you a desire to be resolute. You want to approach the question of how to live with determination and force.

But how do you actually carry that out? What should you resolutely do? The anxiety that facing death brings doesn't tell you. It simply forces you to realize that it's *your* life to live and *your* death that you need to face up to. Of course, "They" have ways that they'd like you to deal with death (which means to avoid it!). And "They" have ways that they'd like you to live. But in anxiety, "They" don't appeal to you; "They" have no persuasive force, and you can't get over the fact that "They" are artificial.

Making choices on your own terms

To face death authentically — to live your life — means to face the challenge of your finitude on your own terms. Yep. Apart from "Them" and apart from their schemes, their distractions, and their ways of trying to get you to avoid the subject of finitude. This can be a bit scary. For the first time, you feel radically alone. The choice of how to live is only yours.

But it's also scary for another reason: When you distance yourself from "Them," you also remove the possibility of making any choice that you're assured is certainly the right one. That's what "They" offer. "They" provide the security of obvious choices because what you must and should do in the eyes of the public is clear. Individual life, on the other hand, is risky. It's not safe.

Heidegger's message here is simple: Dealing with death by finding an individual path to resolutely follow can't be farmed out or outsourced to the "They" or to others. Embracing the eventual ending of your own existence, expressed through your way of making resolute choices, is something that you have to deal with as an individual, without any assurances that you're living your life in the right way.

Confronting death means feeling vulnerable and threatened in the face of life. When you confront death, you have nowhere to run. But that's what living authentically means. To live freely. To feel truly alive. You ready for that?

Conscience Nags You to Be Yourself

Existentialism puts a high premium on highlighting the possibility of living authentically. Recognition of death is integral to understanding and grappling with the finitude of your future. But surely you don't need to have a near-death experience to have the kinds of insights required to be authentic, do you?

Heidegger's reply is that everyone comes equipped with an existential conscience that calls to them to live authentically. This conscience turns out to be you talking to yourself about yourself. Conscience is you trying to shake the part of you lost in the crowd out of its stupor and conformity. When you heed the call of your conscience, you take a necessary step toward embracing yourself and living authentically.

According to Heidegger, conscience shakes you from the inauthentic life of the crowd by reminding you of your guilt, which in turn points out to you your responsibility for taking ownership of what you are as a self or as a being.

Specifically, your existential conscience nags you to own up to the fact that part of what you are is a "lack" or "nullity." What this means is that your conscience wants you to own up to the fact that as an existing, choosing, self-determining being, you're incomplete in some key ways, such as the following:

- ✔ The possibilities available to you for self-definition aren't limitless; in fact, the options you have are structured by the historical and cultural world you're born into.
- ✔ You can't make all the possibilities available to you a reality.

Essentially, your history gives you a context in which your task of self-definition must be carried out; in addition, when you make choices, you're forced to further limit your possibilities by always ruling out other paths for yourself forever.

The voice of conscience is always there

Highlighting the possibility of living an authentic life is clearly important to existentialists. However, they also recognize that people are often deeply wrapped up in inauthentic living. So this raises a problem: If you're often lost in your routines, how can authenticity be an ever-present, live option for you? What wakes you up? Heidegger says it's the presence of your (existential) conscience. It calls you to be authentic, but listening to it is up to you.

Heidegger thinks this existential conscience has a clear function. As he puts it, "Conscience summons Dasein's Self from its lost-ness in the They." It's inside you, like a built-in voice always in operation, one that calls you to find your way out of your zombielike, inauthentic routine.

You've likely heard the voice of your existential conscience. It nudges you to realize that you transcend the crowd and the routines you get lost in. It makes you feel uncomfortable in those routines when you get a bit *too* comfortable in them, pushing you to feel fake and untrue to yourself. It nags you with an awareness that you aren't living up to your true potential. This voice isn't comforting because it disrupts the secure, but artificial, tranquility you find in the inauthenticity of crowd life. As a result, Heidegger thinks that conscience always feels like an imposition, as if it comes against your will. No doubt — it pierces through that artificial bliss you're enjoying in the "They"!

In a way, your existential conscience is like your *moral* conscience, which also is like a voice. Your moral conscience, however, tells you that some actions are wrong, whereas your existential conscience isn't concerned with what you do at all. Instead, it focuses on how you go about living. Moreover, your moral conscience and your existential conscience don't need to agree (we outline Kierkegaard's claim that such a disagreement occurs in the case of Abraham in Chapter 10). After all, according to the existentialist, your moral conscience may be nothing more than the internalized voice of the crowd, a feeling of shame that warns you that you're not doing "what one does."

Your existential conscience reminds you that no matter what path you choose to take in life, the possibility exists for you to take that path authentically or inauthentically. You can choose it because that's what "one" does, or you can choose it as an expression of your unique individuality. It's up to you.

Conscience: You talking to you about you

Where does this mysterious existential conscience come from? Who's speaking? Who specifically is being spoken to? How does the conscience get its message across? Oddly enough, Heidegger thinks that all these questions are answered in the same way — in a word, "you." You're the caller. You're being called, and the message is to point out you to you! Existential conscience is you holding up a mirror to you so you can see your true nature.

Think of the call of conscience like a phone call. On one end you have the person dialing (the caller). That's you. But it's the you who's always in there, in your life, always capable of authenticity (no matter what you do, unless you magically turn into a stone or an animal, this part of yourself is always present). That self always capable of authenticity is the caller. We call it the "You-Self."

The You-Self is dialing up the you who is presently lost in the crowd. It must: Heidegger says the call can't be addressed to the They-Self. The They-Self is the self of the everyday — the self within you that represents the voice of the crowd. The They-Self is the everyone-self that has no identity of its own, the identity you take on when you become steeped in your conformist routines. The They-Self actually *avoids* the call. In fact, as Heidegger puts it, in the call of conscience the They-Self "gets passed over in this appeal." When Heidegger says that the call of conscience passes over the They-Self, the implication is that in passing over the They-Self, the call dislodges the You-Self that's trapped within the They-Self. In dislodging it, the call allows the You-Self to see itself as something separate from "Them."

But how does it work? If you had an FBI transcript of the call, what would be on it? Well, nothing actually; it wouldn't say anything in words. This makes sense, because the call doesn't address you as a father or as a worker or as any of the designations the "They" offers you to understand yourself. Instead, conscience wants to communicate to you as an individual — to the you behind those roles. Thus, the call operates in silence in refusing to address the They-Self and forcing you to recognize that you're different, that you're capable of more.

In a way, the call is like the You-Self (as possible authenticity) yelling to itself (the You-Self actually trapped in the crowd or the "They"): "Hey! Buddy! Remember me?" In the call of conscience, the You-Self is desperately trying to free itself from its own entanglements in the world, in inauthentic life in the "They."

Face it: You're guilty!

Your existential conscience doesn't instruct you to take on any specific paths in the world. It doesn't tell you, "Hey, be a doctor" or "Look, don't steal from others." Instead, in calling you to be yourself, the existential conscience wants you to face up to what you are apart from the crowd. At the core of this effort, it wants you to see that you're guilty. But guilty of what?

Moral guilt versus existential guilt

Typical intuitions of what it means to have a conscience are associated pretty closely with notions of guilt. People say things like "Oh, my conscience wouldn't let me do that," meaning that it invoked feelings of guilt, preventing them from following through with the action. In such cases, you're dealing with your moral conscience and with moral guilt.

Existential conscience calls you to recognize your guilt — not moral guilt, but existential guilt. Here's the difference:

- ✔ **Moral guilt:** Moral guilt typically acts as a spotlight of sorts. It's a result of performing some shameful action, and it points to an absence of something in you. When you steal, moral guilt pains you because it makes apparent your lack of honesty. Moral guilt makes clear to you that you're incomplete or limited in some important way.

- ✔ **Existential guilt:** In contrast, existential guilt doesn't point to an action, but to you as a being. Moral guilt points to a lack in you that causes that action, whereas existential guilt points to an absence that's a fundamental essential part of what you are as an existing being. The lacks that moral guilt point to should be filled in; the lacks that existential guilt points to should be embraced.

Heidegger calls these lacks or limitations that are central to what you are *nullities.* Existential guilt brings you face to face with the fact that you're fundamentally incomplete. Moral guilt can spotlight lacks that can be filled in (by becoming honest, for example), but your existential nullity is an essential aspect of you. It can't be removed. As a result, you're always guilty.

Existential guilt calls you to take responsibility

If you're always guilty, what's existential guilt calling on you to do? Guilt typically calls upon people to take responsibility. In the case of moral guilt, it calls upon you to take responsibility for your lacks by owning up to them and then taking the appropriate steps to fill them in.

Existential guilt also demands that you take responsibility for your nullities, but in a very different way. Because you can't fill in those nullities, taking responsibility for them means owning up to them as you. In other words, taking responsibility means living in a way that honestly strives to express the nullities in the way that you live your life. It means embracing your guilt.

Chin up! Face your limitations!

The existential conscience calls you to face up to what you are. This means recognizing and embracing the ways in which your existence as a choosing, self-defining being — a being who puts possibilities for itself in play — is limited. One of those limitations points to the fact that you don't control how you come to *have* the possibilities to define yourself. The other points to the reality that you can't *be* all your own possibilities. Instead, choosing something always negates and narrows down what's possible for you to choose later on.

You're a chooser, and choosing means destroying

Before turning to how you're limited, we give a basic definition of what you are. Existentialism embraces the idea that you're a choosing, self-determining being. You're special in that your existence is always at issue for you, so existing always means being in the process of defining yourself through the choices you make. With that in mind, how can this kind of being have limitations?

As a self-chooser, you're always faced in a situation with a set of options to choose among. We call them A, B, and C. Your first limitation or nullity emerges right here: Although these are all your possibilities from which to define your life, you can't embrace them all. You must forge forward and choose. You have no escape. When you choose A, you must choose *not* to fulfill choices B and C. So being a chooser means electing one possibility and destroying (or nullifying) the remaining ones. Just as death limits your possibilities for self-definition going forward (because your possibilities will end!), actual choice involves the destruction of the possibilities that exist now. After an option is gone, it's lost forever.

Recognizing this element of your finitude, or this sense in which your existence as a chooser of possibility contains a nullity, can be frightening. You see all the possible selves laid out for you to be, but you can't be them all. Sometimes you may try to escape this. You may try to have it both ways by desperately trying to figure out a way to actualize everything at once. Or you may try postponing the need to decide. Either way, you're trying to escape from one of the fundamental aspects of what you are as a self-defining being. Forging into possibility involves destroying possibility. No two ways about it. To create, you must destroy!

Don't expect any assurances

The fact that choosing kills some of your possibilities forever leaves you wanting assurance that you've done the right thing. Well, you can't ever get that kind of assurance; this is revealed by the second nullity at your core as a self-defining being.

To be completely assured that your choice is right, you need to be able to step outside any context that may influence your way of looking at things. What you want is a timeless, God's-eye view of your situation. From this standpoint, you could objectively and dispassionately sort through the possible options and figure out which option is right. Heidegger's point, however, is that when you truly see what you are, you see that this will never happen. You can never step outside your biased framework to see with assurance what's right.

Heidegger's point here is that as a self-defining being, you have to make choices within an historical and cultural framework — one that structures not only what's possible for you, but also how you think about those possibilities. What's possible for you, in a given situation, is different from what was possible for an ancient Roman. You don't share the same world or the same history. Moreover, ancient Romans saw and experienced the world differently than you. You inevitably respond differently even to the same situations.

Heidegger calls this being *thrown*. Being a self-defining being requires being thrown into a certain historical situation, a certain time period, a certain culture, and a context that makes a specific set of lives possible. Heidegger thinks that although this does function as a constraint, because your power of self-definition is indeed limited, it isn't something to complain about. Instead, it's the very ground of your freedom! To want to create yourself from the ground up should be seen as inauthentic — essentially obscuring and refusing to face up to the fact that your human existence is a situational one. All lives have a *context* in which they should be understood.

The Importance of Living in Time

Heidegger thinks authenticity demands embracing your existential nature, which means acknowledging the finitude or set of limitations specific to you as a self-choosing, self-determining being. As he sees it, living authentically requires that you have the right orientation toward the past and toward the future. After all, death lies in the future, your historical context lies in your past, and you must make choices in the present.

To investigate this idea, however, we first need to think about what it would mean to be oriented toward time. We look briefly at two different ways in which you can understand time:

- ✔ What we call everyday time treats time as something that's outside you, external to your life and to your experiences. Everyday time sees the past, present, and future as separate and disconnected, like a series of independent moments.

- ✔ The existential view sees life itself as immersed within time and also holds that the experience of the past, present, and future aren't separate, but intimately interrelated.

Because authenticity requires that you be oriented toward time in living, you need to discard the everyday notion, which sees time as external to living. In fact, for experiences within life to be truly meaningful, they need to be experienced across time — something only the existential notion of time can explain.

The everyday view: You're in time

According to the everyday view, time is something external to you, a kind of medium that you travel through. This everyday standpoint on time also sees the past, present, and future as disconnected and also sees only the present as having any real significance.

In the everyday sense, time is captured when you think of the clock. As the hands move, you think, "Wow . . . that thing is *measuring* time." But what *is* this clock time? What's being measured? Hard to put your finger on it, isn't it? The following three points seem to be true of the human way of thinking about everyday time:

A. Time is external to you.

B. Time is a series of identical, disconnected, "now" moments.

C. In time, only the present exists, so it's the most important.

In the following sections, we think these points through.

Time is external to you

Start with (A). Do you typically think of time as something that you're *in,* like water can be in a cup or like a medium that you can move through? It's like space, in a way. Just as you may say, "That pen is 2 feet from that lamp," you think, "The American Revolution is more than 200 years *away* from me." Events far off are distant from you because they're farther away in the medium of time than others are. This way of talking leads you to think that you're in something temporal right now, and other events are in other temporal spots so that you can measure the distance between them (in terms of minutes or hours or years).

Time is a series of identical, disconnected, "now" moments

You'd probably say that you're "in a moment" — the now. Wait. Now you're in a different now, and you've left the former now behind! And again! Sit still, won't you? Here's where point (B) comes into play, which suggests that you jump from one identical "now" moment to the next, leaving behind past "now" moments and looking forward to new "now" moments yet to come. From this view, all time is really the same, because all the moments are just identical "now" containers that stuff can be put into. But if you think about it, it also suggests that the past, present, and future are disconnected. The present is here, whereas the past (or future), is over there, in the (temporal) distance.

In time, only the present exists, so it's the most important

From here, point (C) becomes clear. When you're in a "now" moment, you exist in the present. But you can't, according to this view, be in a "now" moment in the past or in the future. Then you'd be in two different spots at once! Maybe you were, and maybe you will (ideally!). But according to the everyday view of time, the past "now" moments are gone and buried. And the future ones don't yet exist. Only the present, then, can really exist and have any real significance.

If you think about it, everyday talk about time is helpful in many ways. You do need to coordinate appointments, so using the clock is valuable. But clock time doesn't seem to have much to do with how you experience life, other than dating certain things that happen to you in life. The existentialists, however, don't want to say that living or existing comes first and then is placed in time. Instead, they want to say that living itself is temporal. As a result, it's not surprising that they have a different conception of time!

The existential view: Lived time

Existentialism approaches existence from a personal perspective, from the first-person point of view, so we're interested in the role that time plays in understanding life from the inside. What's it like for time to be part of you? Existentialists such as Heidegger stress that human life requires a way of existing that's spread across time.

You can't separate life from time

Heidegger's view of *lived* time is different from the everyday time measured by the clocks on the wall. To start, in opposition to the everyday conception of time, Heidegger doesn't think that time is external to you. It's not some feature of the world, and it's not something that your life can be in. Heidegger says that life and time can't be pulled apart in a way that would allow one (life) to be in the other (time). Time plays too intimate a role in what it means to live for that to ever be possible. Life is temporal at the core.

The past and future are meaningful

Think of the way in which you experience life. Are you jumping from one "now" to the next, as the everyday conception of time suggests? Not very likely! Instead, life seems to have a kind of meaningful flow, as if within life as you experience it, the boundaries between the past, the present, and the future aren't as sharp as the everyday conception suggests.

Say that at the moment (right now), you're getting your passport photo taken. How is it possible that this action turns out to be meaningful to you in the way that actions in life can be? From the existential perspective, the meaning of that action relies on the experience of the present *including* an experience of the past and the future at the same time. If that's right, the existential past isn't dead, and the existential future isn't yet to happen. Rather, they're both present in your experience with life right now.

Think about the example a bit. Getting your passport photo taken is significant to you because *later* you'll be in Greece, a possibility you're pushing into and experiencing. So the action is connected to the way that you're projected forward into future possibilities. In Heidegger's view, this means that in your experience, you're always outside the present, already reaching forward into the future.

At the same time, your action is meaningful because "ancient Greek philosophy *has always* appealed to you." Your past likes and dislikes, your upbringing, and your history aren't dead events in the past. Instead, they shape you and the way you experience your world and the possibilities of your worldly situation. These are elements of what you are that set the stage for actions that you perform to be meaningful. Actions tend to be meaningful when they play a role in a story, one that has a past, a present, and a future.

Take this point further. If it's true that the self can be meaningful and significant, a meaningful (authentic) life will live in a way that stresses its past *and* future. Human life, or your existence itself, is temporal. It would make no sense to say that you exist and then you're located in time! A meaningful human life is connected across time.

Pulling Yourself Together through Time

Heidegger opposes the everyday view of time because it views time as external to your life and because it views time as a series of unrelated now moments. Neither seems true, however, of the way that you experience life temporally. Lived, existential time seems very different; time is central to your way of existing, one in which moments in the past, present, and future are related to one another in the way you experience life as meaningful. Existing for you means living across time.

With this notion of existential time as your guide, when is your life meaningful, whole, or authentic? What's the right approach toward time? Heidegger's answer is that your life is authentic when, in the way that you engage in certain actions, you embrace your entire future *and* past. One way to see it is to note that the self has a dimension not only on the present, but also on the past and future. Because authenticity means being yourself, your way of existing must strive to *live* all your past and future specific to you as a self, in your present acts. Only in living this way can you hope to succeed in pulling together your whole self and achieve authenticity.

In this section, we investigate what it means to embrace and unify your future, past, and present. We show that unifying yourself across time connects to our earlier point that authenticity for Heidegger requires embracing the finitude specific to you as an existing being. Along the way, we also view the inauthentic ways of living across time as ways to reject our various finite limitations. As you may expect, failing to unify the self by rejecting either the future or the past (or both) aspects of what you are, or rejecting your own finitude, results in the type of life specific to being lost in the crowd.

You always exist in the future . . .

Although the everyday conception of time sees the present as the most significant part of time, Heidegger thinks the future has clear priority when understanding who you are as a being. Fundamentally, people are self-defining beings always focused ahead on what's possible for them; in Heidegger's jargon, you're a "being-ahead-of-itself." Given this fact, you can live authentically or inauthentically toward your future.

Pay attention to the way you're existing right now. Are you just in the moment? Or are you always looking ahead into the future, trying to see where to go next? You're always reaching ahead of yourself into the next moment. It's a good thing, too. If part of your way of actually existing weren't one step in the future, you couldn't be a self-defining being always striving to address the question "Who am I?" After all, asking such questions involves looking forward to possible ways of addressing the question.

Heidegger thinks that the possibility of living in an inauthentic or authentic way is always before you. If self-definition of forward-directedness is essential to you, you should expect that there will be inauthentic and authentic ways of doing it.

The inauthentic future

For Heidegger, the inauthentic future is precipitated by the refusal to embrace death. That means you refuse to live in a way that recognizes that being projected forward into new possibilities should be accomplished in light of the fact that your efforts might, in the next second, end. Of course, living inauthentically in the future still means being focused toward possibilities and choosing (you can't help doing that). But in refusing to face up to your death, you reject your own finitude, and as a result, you refuse to face up to a part of your own self as a self-defining being. You can't live in a whole way when you do that because you disown a large and essential part of yourself.

As far as Heidegger sees it, when you flee from this anxiety-laded recognition, you run straight into the tranquilizing arms of the "They" or the crowd. In the midst of the "They," you don't need to deal with these issues. You don't need to tackle with the urgency of self-definition in the face of your inevitable end. Instead, you can focus on measuring up in the eyes of the public at large. You forfeit the kind of individuality that emerges from a courageous facing up to death, but in exchange you get the snuggly, warm, and fuzzy kind of bliss that's associated with crowd-based, robotic conformity.

How does this happen? Perhaps you focus on the possibilities that relate to keeping up with the Joneses. Perhaps you focus on redecorating your house, hosting parties, and making sure that you're always running with the right people. In a way, insecurity (anxiety) about your finite future (death) is replaced by a different sort of worldly insecurity: fear about succeeding in the mass-generated, public world of success that you've embraced.

Heidegger calls the inauthentic mode of being toward the future *awaiting*. He uses a passive term for good reason, because those who await see their own possibilities only in terms of the successes or possible failures of their worldly projects. When you await, your way of thinking about the task of self-creation is dominated by the question "What should *one* do now?"

The authentic future

Authentic being-toward-the-future is very different. Heidegger calls it *anticipation*. Where awaiting is passive, anticipation is active — a way of running toward your future. This involves a recognition that you will die.

This recognition tears you away from the "They" and from complacent modes of living. You see the possibilities for existing in the future as far exceeding the possibilities that are offered up and dictated by "Them." As a result, you see the future in terms of the always unsettled question "What should *I* do now?" — a question that necessarily requires your involvement in the answer. You no longer wait but drive forward in an active sense, resolute to forge courageously toward your death by living as an individual in light of the projects you commit to. Although your future possibilities are fixed in the inauthentic future, in the authentic future they're open, and you take an active role in determining what they are.

. . . And you always exist in the past

Although your primary mode of existence is toward the future, Heidegger reminds you that your existence always has a distinctly embedded location. As he puts it, you're "already-being-in-a-world." This means that you push forward into the future *from somewhere*. In a sense, your attempt at resolute self-definition always has a starting point, one that Heidegger sees as your historical and cultural heritage. Whether you embrace your heritage (and your finitude) as a part of your way of existing, though, is up to you. You could also choose to try to forget it or to dismiss its importance in your life.

Think of the angry child who cries out, "I didn't *ask* to be born!" In actuality, the child is verbalizing a profound truth that applies to everyone. Not only didn't you ask to be born, but you also didn't ask to be born *here*, in *this* time, or in *this* culture. And that means that the way in which you understand your continual task of self-definition is heavily dependent upon the way that possibilities are made available to you (and the way that they're framed and understood) *in* that context. This fact, if you recall, is one of the types of finitude that your conscience reveals to you, if you listen to it.

This fact fits easily into Heidegger's way of thinking about your existence as temporal. If being authentic means thinking about your future as aiming toward your eventual death, it also means thinking about your past as pointing toward your historical and cultural birth. Quite literally, it's a recognition of what you, as a self, emerge out of. The 19th century gave birth (say) to one way of engaging with the project of self-definition; Rome in the fourth century gave birth to a very different way of being a self; and your own time and culture gave birth to yet another. As a result, your way of engaging the question "Who am I?" is always tied to that context. As a result, that past is alive in you right now — in the way that you exist, in the way that you approach the future.

But how does this fit into the notion of having to embrace your finitude if you want to live authentically? Just as much as death functions as a limitation on you as a self-defining chooser (your possibilities will end, after all!), your birth does too. The limitation is clear; not everything is possible for you. Much as you may want to be the supreme master of who you are, it's just not possible (Kierkegaard called this desire *demonic*) because you can never get your past under your control in that kind of way. Even thinking about your past is influenced by your past. Try as you might, you can never self-define the very conditions that make your attempts at self-definition possible.

Forgetting: The inauthentic mode of the past

Heidegger's name for facing your past inauthentically is called *forgetting*, which is appropriate, because it seeks to obscure your existential relationship as a chooser to your past. In the inauthentic past, you refuse to recognize the connection between how you push forward into the future and your historical and cultural birth. When you forget, you disown a part of yourself, and as a result, living as a whole self is impossible.

When thinking about forgetting, remember that inauthentic views of time view time as a sequence of disconnected moments, and that the present is always central. From this view, the past is what's dead and "no longer." Seeing the past in this way separates the past from any kind of actual interaction with what's meaningful in the present. In a sense, the past is nothing more than a museum of archived events on display.

Inauthenticity is always a flight away from the task of individual self-definition, a headlong rush into the lifestyles prescribed by the crowd — by the "They." How does this translate into the inauthentic way of living with the past? Well, it means living toward the past the way "They" demand.

How are the projects and roles and rules prescribed by "Them" presented to you? Does the crowd see its own fads and wisdom as following from a limited set of possibilities that history had laid out? Do people in the crowd think, "If we'd been in a different context, we'd have different wisdom!" "No!" says the "They." They see what "one does" as *universally* valid. As timeless. If their truths are connected to history at all, it's as the culmination of history's trials and errors. If so, what's the point of the past, other than to view it as a sort of amusing curiosity?

Repetition: The authentic mode of the past

Engaging with your past authentically is very different. You don't see your past as *dead* — as a set of moments you're forever separated from. Instead, the past is open and alive in you now. The past is in you, giving significance to the present (and the future) and shaping the possibilities for you to define who you are and who you will be.

As a result, to authentically engage the part of your self that's "past" requires refusing to see the significance of what's possible for you now as self-contained within the wisdom of the "They" and their so-called timeless fads and wisdom. This preset menu of choices that "one follows" isn't *the* way of living, but *one* way of living.

Authentic engagement with the past also recognizes that "They" do their best to obscure the fact that history and culture make available to you a whole host of different ways to live, examine, and understand your life. When "They" focus on history, it's selective. "They" remember what supports their fads and trends, and forget (or bury) the rest. It's in their best interest to hide the different possibilities for self-definition that culture and history make available because failing to do so would highlight that their way is merely *one* of many. So the authentic view of the past reveals that your existence is in an inevitable tension with the "They." To be authentic, you must do battle, using the past as a way of re-understanding the present in a way that allows for a criticism of their way of presenting the world, and your role, to you.

For Heidegger, this means that you need to reveal what's been hidden or obscured in your heritage (which *is* you, after all!). You must claim your heritage as your own and employ it to create unique possibilities for individually facing up to your present life in a way that avoids "Them" and their way of understanding what is possible. Authentically engaging with the past thus opens possibilities and allows for individuality. After all, your past *is* you, so you need to learn to dig in and figure out a way to own it, highlight it, and live it in the present.

First, as a self-defining chooser, you need to embrace that your options are limited to the ones made possible by your contextual birth (your heritage). Don't see this as an unjust limitation on you. After all, it *is* you! It's your unique birth that makes being an individual possible. To embrace this, you need to reach back into yourself (in your own history) to discover what was obscured by "Them" as options for you to understand and grapple with your life and your future. Heidegger calls this method of authentically engaging the past — by using it as a way to try to understand the present — *repetition*.

When Heidegger tells you to engage in repetition, he isn't telling you to dress and talk and act like people from the past. You don't want to literally repeat the past and walk around with a bizarre wig on your head, acting like you're George Washington. Instead, you want to look back in the past and observe how people lived their lives — how they thought and how they approached things. What possibilities were open to those people to face life? All these various ways of existing present possibilities that are part of your heritage, and they're available for you to take up as an individual. You can then adapt these options to the present circumstances of your own life or the question of how to forge ahead into your future.

Given the fact that authentic engagement with the past opens new roads to you to approach your future, repetition can be invigorating. Think about what happens when you learn more and more about your own culture and its history. Your way of understanding your present world opens up. The current fads or conventional wisdom become just one interpretation of the world (maybe even a superficial one). Investigation of the past reveals new ways to understand life, a new undiscovered country to explore. In fact, after you do this, the thinking of the "They" seems stale and dead. Embracing your past, in bringing part of you to light (your birth), brings a sense of liberation to life. The possibility of a creative interaction with your own existence — as an individual — becomes possible.

The importance of choosing your own hero

Heidegger thinks you should look back into the past of your heritage to uncover new possibilities, other than those offered by the crowd, for understanding how to engage meaningfully with life. One of Heidegger's suggestions is that you need to choose your hero from the past, an exemplar that you can use to help guide you in interpreting and responding to the situations you find yourself in with a sense of purpose.

It's a cool idea. You find a historical hero, and in a sense, you have a dialogue with that hero about life. Of course, Achilles, who sees battle as the way to live an excellent life, would be baffled by the world you live in. But thinking about Achilles and the struggles he went through in his world can help you see your world in different ways, in terms of possibilities not offered by the crowd. By having this kind of dialogue with your hero, you make him relevant to today's world, making him live through you in the modern world as a guide. Of course, the process works both ways: The way you view your present world also affects the way you think about and interpret your hero as a historical figure.

Joining future and past . . . in the present

Although Heidegger sees the future as central, he also sees the present as the focus point in which the authentic life comes together into a whole across time. Specifically, he thinks that in your actions, the span between your birth and your death is tied together in a way that allows you to see and engage with your world free from the dictates of "Them." Heidegger calls this way of understanding the present the *glance of the eye*. You're committed and resolute, and in light of your engagement with the past, you have an ability to see how the present situation is meaningful, to see the possibilities it discloses for you. In light of your engagement with your future and with your death, you're resolute and committed in your choices.

Remember that for Heidegger, as for many existentialists, authentic life requires engaging with the world in a way that fully embraces what you are as an existing being. One aspect that existentialism thinks is central is engagement. Your existence is fundamentally action-oriented. As well, your existence has a span in time; it ends in the future (in death) and begins in the past (in terms of your history, culture, or heritage). As a consequence, you should expect that existing in the present can have inauthentic and authentic forms. Action in the present can seek to represent that full unity, or it can fail to bring the self together and allow only parts of it to be represented in the way that you live.

The inauthentic present: "Making present"

As you probably expect, the inauthentic past means an immersion in the "They." But how does this play out in the inauthentic present? For one, resoluteness doesn't exist. In its place, you lack commitments. You have no connection with life and instead you float superficially over it.

In Chapter 6 we talk more about this, in the phenomenon Heidegger calls *falling*. He argues that your way of engaging with life can be marked by a kind of disconnection, a being "lost in the world." Think of the way gossip works; how it passes from one person to the next; how with each person who repeats the gossip, the person's connection to life itself becomes more and more distant. This is how the inauthentic present works. When the gossip changes (when what "one does" changes), so do your actions. As a result, your identity has no self-defined character. As an individual, you aren't plugged into the world in an active way. You coast along, determined by the external currents of opinion around you.

The inauthentic present is marked by shallowness. No sense of *you* is implicated in what you do. Your actions don't implicate your sense of mission in life or your sense of self-determination. You don't bring to the present a *way* of structuring what's possible that's individual to you. Your actions don't highlight your past and future. Instead, they express the chatter of the everyday world. To the person lost in the inauthentic present, death is an abstract subject, and the past has no impact on what's being done now.

Imagine a person with an addiction — drawn to a continual flow of new, pleasurable experiences (similar to what Kierkegaard calls *rotation method* in Chapter 10). He runs from party to party, from one fun event to the next. Like a bird mesmerized by shiny objects, this kind of person is caught up in the glitter of the passing experiences in the "now." The past, the future, and how they implicate and inform your own sense of self — all these things are of no importance at all. Not for us, say the existentialists!

The authentic present: The glance of the eye

Heidegger calls the authentic way of existing in the present *Augenblick.* In German, this means *glance of the eye.* It's an odd phrase to use, but it actually does make sense. In the authentic present, the world is transformed and seen in a new way. Your world, and your existence, take on a very particular kind of significance right before your very eyes.

Heidegger thinks that in the *Augenblick,* in the way that you interact with the world, the following four things come together:

- ✔ Your embrace of death means that your actions are *resolute.*
- ✔ You're committed to the task of forging ahead into the future as an individual.
- ✔ You forcefully seek to engage that challenge in the way that you live.
- ✔ Your way of seeing what's possible for you in your situation is disclosed by the way in which you're continually engaging authentically with your past.

But how? In what way should your resolve express itself? Imagine a resolute person with his fist thrust in the air defiantly raised against the "They," yelling "Yes!" But yes what? All you know is that you can't live through "Them." To take that route is to become irresolute and to give up on the seriousness of life and on the task of defining your own path. Thus, in your resolute commitment, you turn to yourself — to your past and your heritage — and find possibilities to help you engage with the situations in life in a meaningful way that allows you not to become lost in the world, or lost in what "They" dictate.

After you find new options and possibilities in the past (and perhaps a hero to team up with; see the nearby sidebar "The importance of choosing your own hero") you return to the present, where it all comes together in the moment or in the glance of the eye. In the *Augenblick,* your resolute embrace of death and seriousness of choice are joined with your penetration of the past, your heritage, and your selection of new possibilities. This joining of the two sides of your existence (past and future, birth and death) is now expressed in the way you act in and see the present. Your life as a whole is unified; your present situation and your action make sense in a story that connects your past and your present and your future. You're finally an authentic individual. Well, at least for the moment. You have to keep it up, you know!

Chapter 10

Kierkegaard: The Task of Being a Religious Existentialist

In This Chapter

▶ Investigating Kierkegaard's notion of the self

▶ Analyzing despair, or the failure to be a self

▶ Discussing Kierkegaard's three main spheres of life

▶ Exploring why Kierkegaard believes only the religious life is truly authentic

*O*ne of the easiest misconceptions to fall under when you encounter existentialism is to think that it's incompatible with religion. If you've been thinking this very thing, it's understandable, especially given some of the strong antireligious attitudes that many of the existentialists display. If you're religious, Kierkegaard is your guy; he believes strongly that existential concerns and religion are strongly connected.

Like all existentialists, Kierkegaard argues that striving to exist in a passionate fashion, by making real individual choices and commitments about the direction of your life, is essential. Kierkegaard also shares the key existential belief that real authentic choices about the big questions in life require risks, because you can never be certain that the path you choose or the answer you embrace is the right one. His reason is typically existentialist: The world itself contains no truths, values, or signposts that can tell you what to do. Questioning life and choosing a path to follow must be performed alone, as a solitary individual.

Existentialists believe that an awareness of this radical freedom to choose among different paths in life produces strong feelings of anxiety in people. More times than not, they try to escape those feelings by denying the freedom and responsibility at the core of what it means to be a self. People do this by turning to inauthentic modes of living that seek to blot out individual choice, commitment, or risk. Of course, by blotting these out, you also deny the core of what it means to exist as the individual you are.

In this chapter, we look at Kierkegaard's notion of the self and then turn to how the challenge to be a self can go wrong and one can as a result fall into despair or sin. We then look at Kierkegaard's notion of the three stages of life, examining how each of these stages or spheres of life represents a different way in which a person can approach the task of existing. Two of these stages, the aesthetic and the ethical, are inauthentic. Only the third, the religious, allows someone to truly become a self and to authentically exist. We turn to the Biblical story of Abraham and Isaac to make this point clear.

Although this stance isn't shared by all the existentialists, for Kierkegaard only an embrace of religious faith can avert false attempts to hide from anxiety or from the task of being a self. True passion, commitment, and risk can be found only in a leap of faith that embraces the aspects of your existence that you can't in any way rationally understand. In short, a true religious life is the attempt to embrace the *absurd* (a central existentialist notion) that lies at the core of your existence, an embrace that will in the end acknowledge that your existence is dependent upon something greater than yourself. In Kierkegaard's view, that's God!

Sickness unto Death: To Be or Not to Be Your Self

The existentialists are centrally concerned with *the self* and with issues of freedom. Kierkegaard says that being a self is a task that requires embracing your freedom, something that you have to continually work at. To do this, he argues, you must make choices about how to engage with life, and those choices must express honestly both what you presently are (what's fixed about you) and what's possible for you (what's open to you). In addition, being a self requires acknowledging your dependency upon the divine.

Unfortunately, people often reject this task because coming face to face with their freedom causes anxiety. Seeking instead to flee what they are, they allow the different elements of the self (what you are and what you can be) to fall into disarray, with one side becoming overrepresented in comparison with the other. When this happens, your life choices express a false view of what it means for you to exist as the whole being that you are.

Kierkegaard calls this fall away from wholeness *despair*. From his perspective, because the various ways of failing to be a self all share a fundamental refusal to acknowledge what you truly are, which itself includes a recognition of your relationship to God, despair turns out to be a way of living in sin.

The self: A tension of opposites

Kierkegaard believes that being a self is something you have to work at. It requires what he calls *spirit,* an effort of will directed at holding together what Kierkegaard sees as the different parts of the self. One way to think of those parts is to refer to the difference between what a person *is* at any given time and what that person *can be.* Being a self means being conscious of that tension within you and striving to grapple with, in the concrete situations that you live through, what's fixed and what's possible by working to represent them both in how you approach those situations.

Clearly, a lot of facts are true about you. You were born into a certain culture with a certain history. Some physical facts are true of you. You feel pleasure and pain. Some facts are true of your social world and your position in it. You were born into a certain family. You have a certain genetic makeup with certain talents. When you think of it this way, it is clear that at any given specific time, it's true that you *are* a certain particular person. Being in a concrete situation involves finding yourself in a very specific, real world.

Kierkegaard uses a number of terms to express this aspect of what you are, sometimes saying that it represents what's finite, bodily, necessary, or temporal. All these highfalutin terms come together to point out that you live in the real world, so they point to the need for you to acknowledge realities on the ground.

But don't worry; fear not! You're not *just* a pile of fixed or finite facts. You're also a *soul.* Although certain fixed realities always make up you and your world, different paths are always open to you in any concrete situation. In other words, you have a capacity for self-determination. Part of being a self is the ability to think outside the box about your own life. After all, you always get to choose how to *view* the facts in your world. You're free and have the capacity to choose who you can or should be, how to carve a path for yourself within the reality you live in. To describe this, Kierkegaard uses a different set of terms — infinite, soul, eternal, and possibility — to get at this aspect of what you are.

For Kierkegaard, for you to be a self partly turns out to be a way of living that emerges from grappling honestly with your own freedom — with your own ability to think outside the box about life, at the same time always acknowledging the context that forms the basis for the real, actual world you live in.

The hard work of being a self: Bringing together polar opposites

Kierkegaard thinks you need to work hard at being a self. Being finite means that at any given instant, some things are always fixed about you. But because you also embody the infinite, or the possible, you transcend or can think outside the box about your own existence. So although your finitude constrains you, it doesn't determine your path. To be a self means to work to keep those two aspects as close together as possible in the way you make choices or in the way that you choose to approach your life.

When coauthor Chris was a kid, he was intrigued by magnets. If you take two magnets and try to connect similarly charged ends, they repel each other, so you have to work hard to bring them closer and closer together. Kierkegaard thinks that the aspects of the self work in much the same way. They repel each other because they're opposites, so you have to work to bring them closer together in your choices.

Philosophers think that opposites can't exist in the same place at the same time. If a person is 6 feet tall, he can't *also* be 6 foot 2. If an object is round, it can't also be square. You can think about Kierkegaard's task of being a self in a similar way. Can the self be finite *and* infinite? Can it be what's necessary *and* what's possible? Can it be body *and* soul at one time? Can you be something fixed but at the same time transcend what you are?

The parts of the self are opposites, so they strongly repel one another. In the self, the temptation is always to allow the parts to come apart and become distant from one another. This happens by over-representing one side of the self over the other when you make choices. In doing so, you lose sight of what's involved in your real, concrete existence, which always includes both elements.

Think of the two possibilities available for overrepresenting one side over the other. First, you can too heavily weight what's fixed in your situation to the detriment of representing what's possible. Typically, this results in living passively, as though you're a prisoner of fate who has no active role to play in your life. At the same time, overrepresenting possibility to the detriment of what's fixed means living in a daydream world about what could be. In this case, you lose touch with the real, concrete world. What you need to do to truly exist as a self is to strive to choose in a way that grapples with what *both* aspects reveal in a given concrete situation.

Of course, the closer you bring them together, the harder it is to keep them that way or to bring the opposites closer together still — just like those magnets. The harder you try, the more you feel the strong repulsion between them, and thus, the stronger you'll feel the temptation to let the opposites become distant and disconnected by overrepresenting one to the detriment of the other.

If you think about it, Kierkegaard is telling you that being a self requires living with a spirit of resolve and resistance. The task of being a self means fighting to refuse to let yourself give in to that temptation to let the self fall apart.

Being a self before God

Part of being a self means honestly representing what you are and what you can or should be. Kierkegaard thinks, however, that being a self requires something more — at some point, you have to recognize that you can't fully succeed at being a self without divine help.

For Kierkegaard, the ultimate goal is to become a self, or to live in a way that ultimately expresses what you truly are. It's to be authentic, being true to what you are and what you can be. But Kierkegaard thinks that this task, at a higher level, is too much for anyone to handle on her own. As Kierkegaard puts it, at some point the self, to be what it truly is, must acknowledge the "power which constituted it." He's saying that you must recognize that your selfhood is ultimately dependent upon a power that's independent of you. What this means is that the authenticity you strive for in your existence is, at some point, beyond your control.

Later in this chapter, we talk about the specific way in which you come to this recognition or acknowledgment. For now, it's important to see that Kierkegaard thinks a central component of being a self requires the action of reaching out and seeking divine assistance. What this means is that making real choices incorporates an aspect of submission before God. Authentic selfhood, at its core, has a religious dimension for Kierkegaard.

Despair: Attempting to escape your true self

People often fail at the task of being a self, resulting in despair or a condition Kierkegaard calls the "sickness unto death." Despair occurs when the opposites that compose your existence, between what you are and what you can be, fall out of proper balance.

One reason you may want to escape the task of selfhood is anxiety. Anxiety can be a very disorienting and discomforting feeling, one that various existentialists have described as the kind of uneasy "dizziness" you feel when you sense the true nature of your freedom (if anxiety is something you want to investigate further, see Chapter 4 for more!). The point is simple: The more you strive to engage with life in an honest and authentic way, the more you become fully conscious of the burden of the responsibility of selfhood.

That means that in striving to be a self, you become aware of your role in giving what's possible and what's fixed in your world its own proper place. Of course, you also become aware that there's no rule book to show you how to do it right. You simply must choose on your own. That's scary and is sure to cause a little anxiety!

Think about your life. Every time you choose, the set of what's fixed and possible for you in a concrete situation changes. Each moment of your life, your destiny is in your own hands. Every time a door opens and you choose it, the others close forever; now new doors, specific to the choice you've made, open. Thought of in this way, choosing is really a heavy responsibility, and the consequences of choice for your own identity are monumental.

Choosing your own path is exhilarating. But it can also feel disheartening when you face the fact that Kierkegaard thinks that you can't lean on any signs or truths external to you for support. The way in which you choose to represent what's fixed or possible in a concrete situation can never be verified as being right. You'll never know for sure that the doors that opened to you, which are based on how you interpreted what was fixed and possible, were appropriate to the situation.

Every time you choose, you do it alone, with only yourself as support. True authentic choice, especially when it deals with the question of determining the character and direction of your own life, is inherently risky. For some, the anxiety that results from these facts is too much to take. So they let one element in the self become overrepresented in a way that makes them feel better about their situation.

Say that your friends are advising you about some bad situation you've gotten yourself into. They say that you'll need to make some tough choices and try to create a different possible future for yourself. Instead of facing the anxiety that stems from taking control of your life, you withdraw into passivity, claiming that your lot is just inevitable, given the facts about yourself and your situation. You wind up overemphasizing what's necessary and fixed, and as a result, you give yourself an excuse to refuse to take an active role in your life as a free and responsible individual.

You may accomplish the same aim of escaping the anxiety of freedom by overemphasizing the possible in your situation. When you're in that bad situation, you don't think about what you can do to fix it. Instead, you withdraw into a different kind of passivity, into a daydreaming kind of existence. You spend your day picturing all the people that you could be, but without ever making any of the actual choices needed to try to make one of those possibilities into reality.

Either way, Kierkegaard would say that you've chosen the path of despair. You have the worst kind of sickness, a sickness of the *self* — one in which you desperately try to escape being who you are and thus lead yourself into a way of living that's existentially unhealthy. If holding the self together is a portrait of wholeness, despair is what happens when you fall apart.

Despair: The path to sin

Kierkegaard thinks that the task of being a self requires two things:

- ✔ Properly holding together in a state of tension the different aspects of what you are as a self
- ✔ At some point, achieving this goal through a recognition of your dependency on the divine

Although the two are closely related (you can't do one without the other), this way of framing the issue provides two reasons for you to see why a person might fall into despair. It also reveals that for Kierkegaard, always the Christian existentialist, despair takes on a religious dimension — namely, sin.

Weakness

Kierkegaard says that the despair of weakness is motivated by a desire to *not* be the free self that you are. You realize on some level that you're free, but you give in to the weakness of allowing the oppositions within yourself to become overrepresented. Perhaps you give in to the desire to see yourself as a victim of fate or to disappear within a dreamlike world of possibility. Either way, you give in to a weakness so as not to have to face up to the conditions of your actual concrete existence.

Defiance

You can also fall into despair by overemphasizing your own freedom and power. Here, Kierkegaard says that you're motivated by a desire *to* be what you are; you *want* to be self-determining. You even become prideful about it. This is the despair of defiance; you believe that you can do the job of becoming a self all on your own. You refuse to recognize your dependency on God to be what you are or to succeed at the task of selfhood. You refuse, as Kierkegaard says, to "recognize that you are brought into being by that power." In fact, for Kierkegaard, the Devil is the most extreme case of defiance; although the Devil recognizes the existence of God, he refuses to acknowledge his dependence on him.

Both holding together the oppositions within you and seeking out divine assistance to complete the task are required to be a self. So whether despair is weak or defiant (Kierkegaard actually states that all despair is a mixture of both), it all comes to the same thing: By failing to be a self, you turn your back on God, because your true state or condition is that of being a self *before* God. If you understand sin as turning your back on God, it becomes clear that choosing to exist in despair *is* sin.

Misunderstanding this point is easy. Clearly, to despair doesn't require *doing* anything sinful in the ordinary sense. By saying that despair is sin, Kierkegaard doesn't mean that it entails treating someone badly or causing anyone pain. Instead, saying that despair is sin is like saying that you've willfully oriented your self toward *existence* in the wrong way. It means being guilty of not treating your life with the seriousness that it demands. It means choosing not to be whole. A churchgoing person who has never broken a law or entertained a single thought of doing anyone any harm can still live in a completely sinful state in this way. You can be in despair and still be a morally good person (a subject we talk more about at the end of this chapter).

Inauthentic Life Stages: Aesthetic and Ethical

Kierkegaard says you should strive to make choices in a way that highlights the nature of your individual, concrete self. Concrete selves don't give either aspect — fixed or possible — too much emphasis. Instead, they properly represent both aspects in the way in which they make choices.

Sadly, people often fail at being their concrete selves and instead live in despair, falling into one of the two inauthentic life stages that Kierkegaard calls the *aesthetic* and the *ethical*. Each stage represents a different way of failing to be a self. Only the third stage, the religious, is authentic and free of despair.

The aesthetic stage: Life without choices

Aesthetes refuse to pull together the opposing aspects of the self in choice, so they fail to meaningfully represent what's factual and possible within their actual lived experiences. Aesthetes avoid *all* commitments and simply refuse to choose a path in life; they lack spirit and direction, and thus have no self at all. They're like small children who refuse to grow up and choose *who* to be in life. Aesthetes don't take an active position in determining the significance of their existence. Instead, they find significance and meaning in their lives through the enjoyment of passive experiences.

For Kierkegaard, it's important to remember that being spirited, which the aesthetic person lacks, requires at least the following two things:

- ✔ Actively struggling with the question of what and who you are; taking an active role in determining the significance of your life
- ✔ Striving to integrate the status of that ongoing struggle into your life through choices and commitments about how to live

Struggling with the question of the very meaning of your own existence isn't easy. In fact, it's painful. It requires a lot of self-analysis, a lot of self-criticism, and a great deal of honesty about the role that your own freedom plays in determining your own destiny. Because this struggle with existence isn't pleasant, and because it often involves anxiety, most people jump ship and fall into a life of despair.

Aesthetes jump ship by refusing to take their lives seriously. They refuse to acknowledge that they're existing beings with the freedom to carve a meaningful path for themselves through life. Embracing a life of freedom would mean making spirited commitments about the direction your life should take and holding yourself accountable to them. If you've committed to being a certain kind of person, you think of the future as composed of a set of situations in which you'll strive to remain faithful to the self-identity you've chosen. The aesthete wants to avoid all this. The aesthete doesn't want accountability or to feel obligated to any commitments she made in the past. Instead, the aesthete wants to live carefree, in the moment, with no sense of unity over time or direction or clear purpose.

Spirited people take an active role in finding meaning in life. They come at life through their self-determining choices. The aesthete is the opposite; she seeks distraction. Instead of making a commitment, she chooses to be entertained by pleasure or to pursue what's agreeable or interesting. Basically, aesthetes want to detach from existence or life and watch it from afar. They're like spectators. They want to experience life like it's a movie. In other words, they don't participate *in* life; they want to eat from a bucket of popcorn and kick back and enjoy the experiences life throws at them — all from the safety of their theater seat, of course. The aesthetic life is inherently passive.

The aesthetic life just won't work

The aesthetic life can't sustain itself. It's ultimately self-defeating. It typically posits the meaning of self-fulfillment in some form of rotation method — in learning to cultivate experiences of either pleasure or interesting possibility as a way to escape from the emptiness of not engaging with the fundamental human task of being a real self. But these escape attempts are futile.

No one has the ability to keep it up. Think of how it works. You start by feeling an emptiness right at the center of your life. It calls on you to embrace your freedom and take up the question of the meaning of your life. But it isn't pleasurable. So you use aesthetic distraction, either through hedonism or mental mind manipulation, to try to avoid it.

But no matter how good you are, the pleasure of an experience ends; now you're back at the beginning all over again. Oh no. That means . . . back to anxiety! The answer? Quick — find another distracting experience! It ends, and more anxiety follows. Aestheticism never *cures* or even faces up to anxiety; it just desperately works to keep it at bay. As a result, the aesthetic life just seems to burn itself out. It's like doing drugs; the more you do, the more you *need* to do. You always need bigger and better experiences to do the job. It's not sustainable. Eventually, you run out of gas and collapse!

In addition, the aesthetic life takes self-fulfillment and hands it over to the world. No matter what you do or how good you are, the world will always hand you experiences that will frustrate your attempts to live in pleasure. You can't control the world. This will leave you bitter and may lead you to start wrongly thinking of the course of your life as being dictated by fate or destiny.

Finally, the failure of the aesthetic life can simply be seen in its lack of dignity. All aesthetes, on one level or another, try to withdraw from active participation in life. An aesthete doesn't want to be a real engaged self, charting a determined course into the future on the basis of her choices. In the end, the aesthetic life just seems to reduce human existence to a type of animal life. Aren't you better than that? Isn't life more than pleasure, the agreeable, or the interesting?

The unconscious aesthete: Sleepwalking through life

One way to be an aesthete is to be an *unconscious aesthete*. This is a particularly curious form of aestheticism. This type of aesthete is unconscious because she's not particularly self-reflective about what she is. She interacts with the world, but with no real notion of self. In a sense, the unconscious aesthete is like an animal, moved in this direction or that always as a result of sensing what's agreeable or disagreeable in the situation at hand. At times, Kierkegaard uses the fictional character Don Juan as an example of this aesthete, a person pulled by the forces of his bodily needs (in this case, by his sensual impulses). However, the unconscious aesthete can also be a social being, one who lives in mindless conformity to what's agreeable and away from what's not.

To understand Kierkegaard's point, think of a laboratory rat. Set up a maze, and put cheese in some corridors and electric shocks in other ones. Now place the rat inside. Quickly, the rat learns how to move through the maze to avoid the shocks and get the cheese. How? As purely natural or bodily creatures, rats are biologically programmed to avoid pain and pursue pleasure.

The unconscious aesthete is like a rat, but she lives in a social maze rather than a laboratory maze. Quickly, she learns where the shocks and the cheese are located within society. If you're a woman, tan often, because then men will look at you approvingly. Buy more stuff, because you want to keep up with the Joneses — the people most approved of! You go to church not because you *feel* a real connection to God, but because in a Christian community, that's what Christians do. After all, what would "they" think if you didn't? You know — you'd get shocked by the pains of disapproval!

As far as Kierkegaard sees it, the unconscious aesthete has no view of herself as spirit or as an actively self-determining being who can take charge of her own existence. Instead, the spirit in these people lies dormant and is sleeping. They live like the rat *must* live, moving this way or that simply as a result of the type of experiences those different paths offer up. Of course, this aesthete always has a choice, but she seems to have no consciousness of herself as a being capable of real self-direction. In a way, the unconscious aesthete is like a child, driven by what's agreeable or disagreeable.

Isn't this particularly undignified? As Kierkegaard sees it, it's like choosing to live in the dingy basement of a beautiful home (the self) and choosing never to occupy its more sophisticated upper floors. Clearly, no one would literally do that with a real house. So why do some live that way with respect to their own selfhood? Living like a rat when one is capable of much more?

Think of this kind of aesthete as being conscious of her surroundings (she doesn't, of course, run into walls!) but not *self*-conscious, similar to the rat (only the rat doesn't have a self to be conscious of!). She isn't conscious of the possibility of spirited, free living. As a result, she's like a zombie — the *living dead.* She understands what she is only in terms of what she does. As Kierkegaard puts it: "The man of immediacy does not know himself; he quite literally identifies himself only by the clothes he wears, he identifies having a self by externalities."

Unlike the rat, you aren't *just* a creature in the natural world, determined to act in accord with the cravings and desires of your body. The way of being lost in the body, or in a view of existence that values only agreeable experiences, can take different forms within society, like a slavish robotic devotion to the following:

- Acquisition of material goods, such as money or possessions
- Attainment of approved social positions
- Cultivation of the majority's beliefs and opinions

The hedonistic aesthete: Pleasure is king!

Some aesthetes are more conscious of their despair, so they realize on some level, even if only minimally, that they aren't living in a dignified way. They show a glimmer of self-consciousness about themselves and so about their own condition. They know, on some level, that a spirited free component is part of what they are, and as a result, they know that the aesthetic life, which is passive and nonspirited, is undignified. Still, these aesthetes don't want to acknowledge this truth fully and deal with it, because it's painful. As a result, they strive to cover up their own lack of dignity by distracting themselves with hedonistic pleasures.

When do you think the intuition that you're spirit tends to become clear? Probably when you're alone, not doing anything, and faced just with your self. You see that there's a self that you should be, a self that takes control of its own existence, chooses itself, and gives its own life a passionate direction. Of course, this realization comes with a healthy dose of anxiety, so that's not pleasant.

As a result, a conscious aesthete needs a plan, a way to avoid those self-realizations and escape anxiety. The typical plan of the aesthete is to stay *very* busy. That allows her to avoid those painful moments of self-reflective clarity.

In his work *Either/Or,* one of Kierkegaard's fictional characters, an aesthete amusingly called "A," expresses this insight. He suggests that "boredom is the greatest evil" and advises what he calls *rotation method* as a response. One type of rotation is called *field rotation* — in short, learning to cycle through faster, more frequent, and more intense entertainment as a means of keeping boredom, and the clarity about the nature of the self and with it one's own despair, at bay. Life for the field rotator is about lots of distractions and pleasures. The more you can get, the better and more significant life is. Party on, dude!

Obviously, the field rotator avoids commitments. Why bother? You should always live for the moment, the field rotator suggests, and at any moment you need to be on the lookout for better and more intense experiences. That means always living in the moment. Coauthor Chris knew a guy who would never commit to coming to a party at his house. If he did intend to come, Chris would know it only when he arrived. As a field rotator, this guy clearly thought, "Why make a commitment to go to Chris's when something more pleasurable might come up in the meantime?" To the field rotator, commitments are totally illogical. As an aesthete, you'd never commit to do X tomorrow when you don't know whether some other option Y might pop up that would be more exciting and intense than X.

Freeze frame: Try this yourself

Are you a field rotator? Ask yourself:

✔ Do you find yourself often talking about how bored you are?

✔ Are you always in search of something to do?

✔ Do you find inactivity painful and stressful?

✔ Do you sense a feeling of anxious emptiness when you're doing nothing?

✔ Do you avoid commitments and decisions until the very last moment?

✔ Do you have a difficult time being alone?

✔ Do you find yourself text-messaging often just to be able to do something?

If you find yourself answering yes to too many of these questions, chances are good that you're an aesthete and most likely a field rotator. According to Kierkegaard, the more this is true of you, the more you should expect your personality to be disorganized and fragmentary and your life without clear purpose. Because you're oriented only toward the enjoyment of the moment, you don't try to cultivate any coherent personality around any kind of life goal.

The reflective aesthete: Lost in the imagination

Imagine a person who suddenly awakens from a long deception, one that hides from that person the fact that her future isn't determined. This kind of person would awaken more self-conscious than ever before and would be amazed at the new world of possibilities that emerges before her. The spirited person would learn to make responsible choices by carving out a self from the possibilities presented. But the reflective aesthete doesn't do that. Instead, when she becomes more and more aware of her self as a self-determining power, she becomes more addicted to her newly found world of the possible that opens before her. It becomes a new way to escape.

Because the reflective aesthete *is* an aesthete, she's still devoted to enjoyment. Like other aesthetes, the reflective aesthete is also devoted to *not* living in an active sense; instead, she's passive. In the case of the reflective aesthete, that passivity is demonstrated by a withdrawal into the mind and into the world of the possible that the imagination can provide. As one of Kierkegaard's fictional reflective aesthetes puts it, "The essence of pleasure does not lie in the thing enjoyed, but in the accompanying consciousness." The reflective aesthete doesn't just want to experience pleasure as a result of being affected by pleasurable things in the world like a field rotator. Instead, this aesthete wants the pleasure to come from ways of imaginatively manipulating the world. The goal of this aesthete is the mental cultivation of interesting experiences.

The reflective aesthete, Kierkegaard suggests, does this by using the world as fodder for the creation of different ways of thinking about things. The reflective aesthete is so interested in possibility, in thinking *about* things in the world, that she becomes largely detached from the way things really are; fantasy is all that matters now. As one of Kierkegaard's aesthetic characters says, with a tinge of addiction in his voice, "Pleasure disappoints; possibility never. And what wine was so sparkling, what so fragrant, what so intoxicating, as possibility!"

It's pretty clear how the reflective aesthete fails to make commitments. To be committed to a task or to a particular identity, you have to choose a concrete identity and path. You have to select a possibility that gives meaning to your life and make it actual. In other words, possibility is meaningful when it plays a role in helping you figure out how to live in the actual world you inhabit. Real choices give you particular direction in your concrete world. But the reflective aesthete isn't interested in this because she has no desire to live in the real world at all. She wants to live in her head, fantasizing about and cycling through all the different ways that particular things *could* be. Kierkegaard calls this *crop rotation*. Instead of cycling through different worldly experiences (as the field rotator does), you take one experience and cycle through different ways of thinking about it or envisioning it. You get creative, even artistic, about the way you think of the world.

Freeze frame: Try this one too

Are you a reflective aesthete?

- Do you find yourself lost in the intense pleasure of daydreaming?

- Do you get resentful that the real world can get in the way of how you like to think of it?

- Do you fantasize often about your past, reimagining it in different ways?

- Do you avoid making choices because you like thinking about the possibilities the alternatives make available to you?

If you answer yes to too many of these questions, you likely have some reflective aesthete in you. In fact, a lot of people you know probably say that you live inside your own head!

You know the type. You're always saying to the person, "Hey, come back down to *reality*" or "Earth to Chris . . . you in there, Chris?" They're *in* there all right — in their heads, imagining possibilities — and that's where they want to stay!

The ethical stage: Finding your meaning within roles

After *aestheticism,* which is noted for its lack of spirit and its refusal to make choices and commitments about how to make something of one's life, the next stage of despair is the ethical. In this stage, a person has moved out of the aesthetic stage and is finally ready to make commitments and choices about who to be and how to live. The ethicist does this by freely electing to take her place in a larger social and moral structure — what we call the Universal. The Universal is the set of objective moral truths that functions as the foundation of meaningful and appropriate worldly interaction. After you choose to subordinate yourself to the Universal and to accept your role within its overarching system of meaning, you have a road map to understanding how to engage with life in a meaningful way.

Although the ethical stage is an advance on the aesthetic life, because it embraces the necessity of choosing and committing to a way of life, the ethical stage is still a form of despair, or a way to avoid being a self, for the following two reasons:

- The ethical stage assumes that a person can find the answer to the question "How do I engage with the world?" without the need for any contribution by the specific individual herself. Instead, the Universal has all the answers and provides the rule book for living meaningfully. For Kierkegaard, however, this means that you haven't truly held the tension within the self together, because meaningful choices always come alongside the feeling of risk — to the extent that you can't tell whether you've made the right choice. The ethical life, however, seems to suggest that you *can* know what the right choice is, so risk as an element of individual (and spirited) existence disappears. Life is too ambiguous for that!

✔ Kierkegaard thinks that the ethical life inevitably leads to a return of despair because its goals are ultimately unattainable. Thus, although the ethical life suggests that we can attain happiness by subordinating our individual desires and needs and wants to the dictates of the Universal, we just can't ever seem to be able to do this. The ethical life, as a result, leaves us feeling perpetually guilty; frustrated; and, in all likelihood, miserable.

The importance of choosing yourself

The ethicist thinks of the aesthete as someone who wants to be free to do whatever she wants, whenever she wants. As the ethicist puts it, the aesthete is a *multiplicity,* or an assortment of faceless masks. She's all style, no substance. Because she refuses to choose a stable identity, one that actually makes demands on her, she's actually *no one.* Moreover, the aesthete secretly knows she's in despair because she can't avoid the nagging truth that she's living in an undignified way.

According to the ethicist, the aesthete has an either/or choice to make. *Either* she can remain in this hopelessly passive life, knowing that it's futile, *or* she can choose herself by embracing a stable identity and committing to it. To make the choice to leave the aesthetic realm, however, the aesthete must first experience its final futility. The aesthete must separate herself from that life and judge it unworthy, as something subordinate to the ethical life. The aesthete can give up this life only by renouncing it.

Are philosophers reflective aesthetes?

One of the interesting claims that Kierkegaard makes is that philosophers, especially those who tend to deal in large-scale concepts and theories, are reflective aesthetes trying to avoid the world. Funny enough, this is what most people say — that philosophers live in an ivory tower and avoid the real world. Is this true? Well, the craft of philosophy does typically deal with abstractions. Philosophers construct a number of abstract concepts that they claim represent the world and then they try to see what relationships obtain between those concepts. Essentially, they develop ideas about the world and then they just deal with the ideas from that point out. Of course, you may object that these abstractions aren't really the concrete world at all. So philosophers take a bit from reality and then use their imaginations to construct a more interesting world to play in. Ideas turn out to be the philosopher's sandbox, not the real world. As Kierkegaard might say, philosophers like to think about existence, but that's it! They're not as interested in experiencing existence. The world within the mind is so much more interesting, and as a result, they show no interest in the real world.

The ethical life demands that you need to first choose yourself as a chooser. You must give up on the aesthetic method of letting experiences and sensations rule your life. You need to step up to the plate and commit to taking up the question of your existence. In doing this, the first step is to commit to *not* being an aesthete. It all starts with committing to growing up! The aesthete simply refuses to take herself seriously, so that's the first step in being a self: taking yourself and the task of living seriously. Only on this foundation can you begin to choose a more specific identity for yourself.

Choosing yourself by embracing a system

When you decide to live in the ethical stage, Kierkegaard thinks, you can't just choose to choose. You also have to make specific choices about who you're going to be. Specifically, choosing the ethical life means making a free choice about joining a social and ethical system — one governed by objective rules and structures.

The way the ethicists see it, the structure of the world — and society — is very rational. Science shows them why interaction in the physical world makes sense or is meaningful. Lucky for them, the ethicists see rules that govern the way individuals should interact with their world. Philosophy, using reason, can figure out the objective structures that govern human action. We can stamp a name on the whole collective set and call it the Universal.

It's Universal because those structures and rules apply across the board to all individuals. The Universal says that if a person is in an X type of situation, she should do Y. Because the Universal transcends the particularity of any specific person, however, you as an individual get factored out. What a person should do is always a function of the social roles she occupies.

Think of a math formula like "X times 0 = 0." It says that no matter what number you plug into X, you always get the same answer. Similarly, the Universal suggests that the nature of the specific individual just doesn't factor in to the equation. So your individuality isn't important when you're trying to figure out how to live meaningfully in the situations you find yourself in. All you need is knowledge of the Universal — of the objective rules that govern human interaction in the world and knowledge of your social role in the situation you're in. For the ethicist, because human interaction is meaningful or significant only when it matches the Universal, a person who wants to have a meaningful life has to embrace the way of living that it dictates. Essentially, you must learn to subordinate yourself as an individual *to* the Universal.

We sense an objection. Perhaps you think that if this is true, living meaningfully means being robbed of individual choice, because the only way to exist meaningfully is to rigidly conform to the dictates of the Universal.

The ethicist thinks that if that's the way you see it, you've left out something important. You don't just fall into these social and ethical roles. You freely choose them as a self-determining being. To freely choose a role means to see the self as significant when it conforms to those roles. Perhaps that means that you choose to take your place within society as a son and a husband, as a friend, a teacher, and many other things. You decide to fulfill your social destiny, in a way. But don't forget, the ethicist says, you freely choose your place.

According to the ethicist, this way of choosing to live life is a perfect way to bring together the oppositions within the self in just the right way. When you choose to submit to the Universal, you freely consent to the necessity found within that life and its rules and structures.

Including beauty and pleasure in the ethical life

If you're aesthetically inclined, you no doubt think that the ethical life is boring! There's no beauty or pleasure in choosing to conform to the objective rigid rules and structures that govern the human community! The ethicist thinks you've got it all wrong. The ethical life isn't just beautiful, but also artistic and pleasurable. So it should be appealing to all you closet aesthetes out there. So the aesthetic life has a *place* in the ethical, but its place is subordinate to the ethical.

Think of marriage. Although the aesthete sees marriage as boring because it demands commitment to a certain way of life, the ethicist sees it differently, thinking that true beauty and pleasure can come into being only with commitments.

Is the ethicist right? When you choose to marry, you promise to love and to care for and to be faithful to a person. This vow is more than a reference to now. Instead, a marriage commitment stretches across the past and the future. As a married person, you'll see your past as a married person would. In addition, you'll see the future that way too. Specifically, you'll see it as containing opportunities to be, or fail to be, the kind of person you've committed to be. In each new situation you're in, it's up to you to succeed at being the way a married person should be (how that role is structured in that society) in that circumstance.

The work of striving to become what you've committed to be is similar to treating yourself like a bonsai tree. If you find yourself tempted to be unfaithful, you learn to prune those desires out of yourself and to cultivate new ones — like the desire for fidelity. Your aim is to prune and cultivate your character and your desires so that eventually you have only the desires appropriate to being a husband or wife. Being a married person is something that you work to *become*.

Now think of your choice to join the ethical in the same way. Basically, if you choose to take your place within the structures of society, you aim to shape your own wants and desires so that they perfectly match what your social roles expect of you in any given situation. Each time you're in a new situation, you'll want to feel, see, experience, and act (in short, exist) in the world just as those roles demand. You'll want to be the perfectly pruned social and ethical bonsai! Pruning a bonsai tree is an artistic craft, and so is the craft of pruning the self. Clearly, the ethical doesn't reject art and beauty — it transforms it!

The ethicist also thinks that you'll get a lot of pleasure out of your social life. What your roles demand and what you want are in harmony if you're successfully doing your job pruning yourself, so you'll get a great amount of pleasure out of performing your roles.

If the ethicist is right, the ethical life contains pleasure and beauty. So the ethical doesn't jettison the aesthetic; it contains it, but in a way that doesn't let the aesthetic view of what life is predominate. The ethical person claims to be in control. She makes choices and commitments. She chooses an identity for herself and follows through, creating herself in an artistic way to become the person she chose to be.

Using ethics to hide from yourself

The ethical life has a kind of seductive quality. C'mon, don't lie — we know you like it! It seems so peaceful, so pleasurable; it's even artistic. And so harmonious! You find your place and meaning in the universal ethical rules that govern the social roles that constitute your larger community. It's just like a big jigsaw puzzle in which all the pieces fit together and you've finally fit your piece — namely, *you* — in! Yet if you're reading an existentialist, and suddenly things get all warm and fuzzy, you should suspect something is amiss.

One problem is clear: The ethicist requires that you choose to freely subject yourself to a bunch of societal rules and structures governed by the Universal, which is itself determined by the impartial dictates of reason. The Universal contains the final answers and rules to living a meaningful and significant human life. You can have that life if you submit to it.

But what is the job of the individual self here? Where in the ethical life is the part where the individual self has to continually grapple with the question of how to engage with life, of how to exist in the world in concrete situations? Of course, the ethicist suggests that the individual plays a role through continually recommitting to living in this way. But that's it.

If you look at it this way, it looks as if the ethicist has decided to hide from the responsibility that she has, as an individual, to grapple with the hard work of being an active, spirited self. But this requires grappling with situations as a particular individual in that situation. Turning to a meaning and significance found in something external to you won't do.

As we discuss later in this chapter, this concern also expresses itself in Kierkegaard's attack on the ethical stage from the standpoint of religion. If, he argues, the individual's relationship to God must be central to a meaningful life, the individual herself can't be exhausted by the ethical. The individual must still have a significance *outside* the ethical.

Of course, Kierkegaard's attack on the ethical life isn't unexpected. Existentialists don't believe that universal values and truths like the Universal ever exhaust what you are. As an individual, you must continually struggle with the responsibility of finding your own way.

Failing to capture the ambiguity in life

To choose to subsume the self under the Universal — to strive to live life by objective moral rules or structures — really means choosing to cease to live as an individual. But here's another problem. The ethical life claims to deny a central facet of existence — that it's essentially ambiguous.

Think about the times you've made big decisions in your life. Doesn't it seem that rule-following fails to do justice to what you actually did when you made your choice? In really important situations, it's rare that a cookbooklike response will suffice. Somewhere along the line, you have to fudge a little to make the rules fit *that* situation. It's as though the concrete situations that you live in are round holes and the rules are square pegs. You need to do a lot of cheating to get that peg to fit into that hole. Kierkegaard's point here is intuitive. The answers to big questions about life (such as "How should I live?") can't be prepackaged and given to you.

The ethical life fails to deliver on its promises

One of the central claims of the ethical life is that it promises a kind of wholeness, or a life of happiness within the secure confines of society and the roles that you elect to take on. If you decide to be a father and a teacher and a friend, you'll find ultimate happiness and significance in life when you've successfully learned to discipline the self so that its desires conform perfectly to what those roles demand.

But can that ever truly happen? It seems that this promise of fulfillment is one that can't be cashed in. As an individual, you resist being stuffed into those constraining roles. As a result, you always seem to have desires and hopes and aspirations that rub up against those categories and so cause friction in your life. As a result, the ethical life doesn't deliver on its promise of fulfillment and happiness. Instead, it leaves you feeling guilty, frustrated, and possibly even miserable. It's an unattainable ideal. When we realize that, despair is inevitable, but we have nowhere to turn.

Does Kierkegaard think you should be unethical?

Much as Kierkegaard criticizes the ethical life, he's not telling you to seek to be unethical or bad.

To start, keep in mind that Kierkegaard doesn't say that you should, in moving past the aesthetic stage's unhealthy attachment to experiences, reject those kinds of connections to the world. Rather, he's saying that you shouldn't define yourself and your life in terms of those experiences. Essentially, it's okay to have aesthetic tastes or to flavor your life with a variety of pleasurable or intense experiences. You simply can't make aesthetic experience a false idol, something you bow down to as though it were God, allowing it to determine the meaning of life.

Similarly, you shouldn't strive to move to the woods and avoid social life and ethics. Of course being a mom or a friend or a colleague is important. Kierkegaard just thinks that the ethical life doesn't define you or give you significance. Just as much as the aesthetic life shouldn't become a false idol, the ethical life shouldn't become one either, because it's not your final aim or purpose or meaning. So again, go cultivate those ethical bonds. But remember that you are more.

In short, it may be the case that you can and should add ethical (and aesthetic) elements to your life. But don't make the mistake of thinking that the aesthetic or the ethical exhaust what you are. You're much more than either one, separately or taken together.

The ethical life is too full of pride

The last problem with the ethical stage connects with the next stage, the religious. According to the ethical life, self-fulfillment and wholeness, even if difficult to achieve, are always ultimately in the hands of the person. In other words, you can *be* a self simply through your own power — through self-discipline. If you read what we say earlier in the chapter, however, Kierkegaard believes that being a self is a task that we need to take seriously (which the aesthetic life fails to do), but at the same time we must realize that we do not, on our own, have the ability to complete the task. Instead, for that we must turn to God. Seen in this light, the ethical life contains too much *hubris*. It's stubbornly prideful about the role of the self in its own creation, a pride that ultimately leads to despair.

Fear and Trembling: Embracing the Religious Life

Kierkegaard clearly thinks the task of being a self isn't easy. He identifies various ways in which you can fail at the task and end up in what he calls despair. He also identifies different life stages that people can wind up in and that exemplify despair.

At this point, we make the turn to the final and ultimate stage, the *religious*. Only when a person enters this stage is Kierkegaard willing to say that she's finally succeeded in becoming a self (even if she'll have to keep at it).

Consistent with the basic tenets of existentialism, Kierkegaard thinks that in this stage a person truly embraces all the aspects of what she truly is and thus lives an authentic life. That means embracing, through a leap of faith, the fundamental absurdity of existence. For Kierkegaard, embracing this fundamental absurdity can be truly accomplished only through a leap of faith into the religious life.

Whereas the aesthetic stage privileges feelings and the ethical privileges reason, the religious favors faith. Theology often struggles in the attempt to understand faith. What is it? Kierkegaard turns to the Bible to help figure out an answer, specifically to what is often taken to be the ultimate story of faith: the saga of Abraham and Isaac. Kierkegaard thinks that this story hides the answer to two related questions: "What is faith?" and "What does it mean to be a self?" An analysis of that story brings us a bit closer to our answer.

The strange story of Abraham and Isaac

Imagine that one day, you're tending to your job programming computers, executing stock trade orders on Wall Street, or just reading a *For Dummies* book. Everything in your life is going just fine. You have a spouse and a son, and you love them both very much. You enjoy your job, and you're a happy member of the community in which you live. You try your best to live a very moral life, and you contribute often to the poor. You attend church regularly and consider yourself to be very religious. And then one day, something very odd happens.

You hear what you take to be the voice of God. No one else can hear it, just you. In a way, this isn't odd — you've spoken with God before. But this time the voice disturbs you because it tells you to go home and sacrifice your son to it. What would you do?

Of course, as the story tells us, Abraham does as he was ordered, though God sends an angel to stop Abraham at the last second — as he draws down the knife on his son Isaac. Consequently, for passing the test with flying colors, Abraham is understood to be the father of faith.

Kierkegaard wants to know what it *means* to say that Abraham is the father of faith. This is important, because the way in which Abraham engages with his existence is what you have to pull off to become a self for Kierkegaard (no, you won't have to sacrifice anyone . . . well, at least not necessarily).

For Kierkegaard, the movement of faith is the final link, the final piece in the puzzle that you've been missing all this time. Authenticity isn't gained through feeling, or through reason; it's attained through faith.

Giving up the earthly: Killing your son

Kierkegaard thinks that an important part of Christianity — or of being a self — is being willing to give up the world. What this means is that you shouldn't think that what gives your life meaning can be found within the world. Instead, Kierkegaard thinks that life's meaning is found in a relationship with God. This doesn't mean removing yourself from the world, however. It means loving the world passionately while renouncing it for the sake of God. That's the first step!

Kierkegaard doesn't deny that you exist within the world and that as a result, you have earthly or worldly attachments. As the same time, given that Kierkegaard thinks being a self means keeping what's fixed (or finite) and what's possible (or infinite) about you in tension, seeing your significance as located solely in the world ignores one important aspect of your self: that what you are always transcends what's given in your worldly experience.

One way of being overly attached to the world is seen in the aesthetic life, where you see the significance of life in they way you're affected by things. As some aesthetes have it, pleasure is king. Kierkegaard doesn't want you to become lost in those experiences, because they become idolatrous, which means mistaking the wrong thing for God (or for what's ultimately significant). In the case of the aesthetic, when your experiences become your "God," you have a problem. Instead, you need to be connected to the world in a healthy way that recognizes its importance but subjugates it to what's superior.

Abraham: Father of faith

The story of Abraham is an early one in the Bible, told in the book of Genesis. Although the story is a central one to Christianity, it also functions prominently with the Jewish and Muslim traditions. As the story goes, Abraham, who was an old man, entered into a covenant or agreement with God. In return for Abraham's devotion to God, God made him a promise — that he would be the father of countless generations of people on earth. The promise was understood in a specific way: Abraham (who was actually pretty old at the time) and his wife, Sarah, would have a son, Isaac, and Isaac would be the line through which that promise would be fulfilled. Although Sarah was very old at the time of the promise, it came true; she got pregnant and gave birth to Isaac. Years later came this story: God demanded that Isaac be sacrificed as proof of Abraham's faith.

This viewpoint can help you understand why God asked Abraham to sacrifice his son. After all, Isaac represents the object in the world that Abraham is most attached to. God doesn't oppose Abraham's love for Isaac (or the experience of happiness that it yields for him). He just doesn't want Isaac to become an idol that replaces him. What Abraham really is as a self (his relation to God) transcends the world, so he must be prepared to separate himself from his attachments to the earthly in a way that demonstrates a recognition of that true nature.

Embracing the God who's beyond ethics

Abraham is in a serious pickle; he has to sacrifice his kid! Put yourself in his shoes. What's he thinking after he hears that voice? What would you think if you heard that voice? Of the many ways to respond to this dilemma, two specifically would rule Abraham out as the father of faith.

One way is to simply deny that it's the voice of God. If the voice persists, you go to see a psychiatrist and ask to be put on medication. A second way is to acknowledge that the voice is God's, but to deny that God is telling the truth. Both responses have a similar foundation; they refuse to accept that God would ever ask you to do something that seemed so vicious and evil and for no apparent greater good.

By thinking in these ways, you reveal that your relationship to God is mediated through an *idea* of God that you have. This doesn't mean you know everything about God, but it means that you *do* know at least some things, such as the fact that God doesn't command anyone to do evil.

This is a common way of understanding God. But think about it. Doesn't this mean that you are dictating that your God relationship be conducted on *your* terms? Isn't part of this *your* claim that God must conform to your conception — funneled through reason — of what the good is? Really, you're demanding that God be subordinate to ethics, subordinate to your idea (or your society's idea) about how actions should be performed in the world. You're really using reason to understand God. This creates a second idol (next to Isaac, in this case) to worship: the ethical.

But if God transcends the world, why should he be constrained by ethics? Isn't suggesting that God must fit into a preconceived notion of what the divine is awfully presumptuous? If you think about it, you can see a lot of hubris in this view. *Hubris* comes from ancient Greek, and it means something like exaggerated self-confidence. In ancient Greek tragedies, characters who are hubristic all but inevitably get into deep trouble. In this case, thinking in these ways would be pretty hubristic!

If Abraham understands the voice from this hubris-based perspective, you can't find much faith in him at all. If he refuses to sacrifice Isaac because what the voice says makes him think that it's not God, he's lost his faith and found an idol: worldly ethics. If he's on the way up the mountain but just going through the motions — because he knows God is putting him on — then he has no faith either, for the same reason! On the other hand, if God is above ethics, he'll have to look at the situation in a whole new way.

Experiencing ethics as a temptation

Usually, sin is understood as the turning away from virtue. So we typically say that sinning is the performance of actions that are ethically unsound or vicious. But Kierkegaard doesn't think of sin as a failure of virtue. He sees sin as a turn from *God*. Because God transcends ethics, it must be possible that in a certain situation, sin may turn out to be not turning away from virtue, but being tempted toward it!

Kierkegaard's new way of thinking about the God relationship shakes up people's intuitions, because most Christians think that being a good Christian is synonymous with being a good person. Because being a good person means aligning yourself with the ethical structures that govern the human community, being a good Christian means playing your proper social role in just the right way. Good Christians tell the truth, they're kind to others, they're generous, they're kind and caring parents, and they feed the poor.

Clearly, by this view, sin means giving in to the individual desires that you have that are opposed to those of the ethical community. Thus, to sin is to defiantly assert that you're meaningful and significant apart from ethics (apart from society or the Universal). Thus, Christianity interprets sinning as acting selfishly, of ignoring the larger whole.

With Kierkegaard's view of sin in your pocket, rethink Abraham's situation. If he's called by God to kill his son, his possible sin isn't to be pulled *away* from ethics to do something those ethics reject. Instead, because for Kierkegaard sin is always primarily a rejection of God, Abraham's sin in this case is giving in to the temptation *toward* ethics. Clearly, ethics demands that a father not kill his son; it's not virtuous. So here, ethics and virtue tempt you *away* from God. The result is clear: In Kierkegaard's view, ethics and sin can be in opposition.

According to Kierkegaard, God's command, if Abraham hears it right, forces him to recognize that his relationship to God is independent of ethics (the world). When someone stands in relationship to God, it's not as an individual *within* the ethical; it's as an individual standing above the Universal, *alone*. Ethics isn't the medium through which you have a relationship with God. In a relationship between you and God, ethics is a fifth wheel.

If Abraham hears the voice of God correctly, he understands that in his relationship to God, he (Abraham) and God are outside, and higher than, the

Universal. Abraham realizes that he shouldn't reject ethics entirely, but he should learn to perform what Kierkegaard calls a *suspension of the ethical* when God calls for it, because only in God does Abraham find his true significance and meaning.

If God transcend ethics, God quite possibly *does* want you to kill your son (or mother) and *will* follow through on the request. If you can accept that, and embrace that kind of relationship with God and with the world, Kierkegaard thinks you're starting to get somewhere. Abraham has to see himself as an exceptional individual, one who must strive to see the foundation of his own existence as, to use Nietzsche's phrase, *beyond good and evil.*

Renouncing your worldly self

A faithful Abraham believes that God will take Isaac from him. He has to be bummed about it. But Abraham could kill Isaac and see it as something any good person would have to do in his position. But true faith, Kierkegaard argues, means Abraham must sacrifice the possibility of finding any comfort in what he does. He must not have a worldly way of rationalizing his murder of his son to make it more understandable. He must sacrifice even this kind of connection to the world.

Missing what Kierkegaard means is easy to do. To help clarify, look at the ancient Greek story of Agamemnon. Agamemnon is the king of Mycenae, and his country is at war with Troy. To fulfill his duties as a king, Agamemnon has to sail his fleet to Troy. But he has a problem. Some of the gods have demanded that he murder his daughter, Iphigenia, to provide the wind needed to get his ships there.

Agamemnon's in a pickle. Ethics makes two demands on him, each motivated by different parts of his worldly identity as a king and as a father. One role demands a sacrifice; the other role prohibits it. These tragic dilemmas were common in Greek plays of the time, typically dealing with clashes of duties like the one Agamemnon faces. In a tragic dilemma, there's no way out; either way you turn, you do something wrong to do something right.

Agamemnon does kill his daughter (don't worry — his wife kills him later when he gets back from Troy). Like Abraham, Agamemnon has to give up or sacrifice the worldly thing that he loves most: his daughter. He must make this sacrifice to affirm his more important ethical relationship to his people as a king.

That's where the similarities with Abraham end. Agamemnon sacrifices his daughter, but he doesn't have to give up his worldly identity as well because his action makes sense in terms of worldly ethics. According to the ethical structures governing Agamemnon's world, his daughter's murder was required of him as a king, so it actually served the greater ethical good.

Faith and Kierkegaard's love life

Philosophers in general have had a pretty sorry relationship with love. In fact, Nietzsche (who had serious issues in this area too) joked that the married philosopher "belonged in comedy." Kierkegaard was no exception, but his story is a famous one.

Early in his life, he became enamored with a young girl named Regina Olsen. The couple became engaged, but after a short time, Kierkegaard broke off the engagement. One reason was that Kierkegaard wasn't sure he could do God's work — his writing, and trying to wake people up to authentic life — and be

married at the same time. To him, it seemed like an either/or choice; he had to choose one. It was a decision that haunted Kierkegaard for the rest of his life.

Many think that within Kierkegaard's discussion of the Abraham story is the story of his own tortured relationship. He felt that he had been called upon to sacrifice (luckily, not literally) Regina for God. He waited all his life hoping to get Regina back, as Abraham got Isaac back, but it never happened. She, unlike him, moved on and married another man.

Although he's unhappy, Agamemnon can resign himself to the loss of his daughter because it was demanded of him by the Universal. He acts in a ghastly fashion, but not immorally. So Agamemnon — and those around him — can rest on his worldly conception of what he's done to understand it. People can pity Agamemnon and be glad that they've never been called to do something similar.

Abraham can't rest on world ethics, and that's why his situation calls for more than just a sacrifice of a child. Unlike Agamemnon's, Abraham's temptation doesn't come from within the ethical realm (in Agamemnon's case, the temptation is to act as father). Thus Abraham has no worldly self to whom he can turn to justify what he's doing. When Abraham acts, he leaves his social and ethical world entirely behind him.

As a result, Abraham embraces his choice as one that can't be understood or justified within the world. In terms of the world, Abraham is a murderer. Thus, in terms of his worldly self, Abraham can't comfort himself at all. He must simply do it because he's chosen to heed God's call. Essentially, he's prepared to sacrifice his own worldly self as well as the life of his son. It's also worth noting that for Abraham, his son *is* his immortality. There's no Christian afterlife. So this really is a big sacrifice!

This is pretty devastating. Abraham has no safe harbor, no excuse to use. He stands before his relationship with God in fear and trembling. He must choose as an individual alone.

Believing the impossible: The knight of faith

Abraham is resigned to the fact that God will take Isaac from him. But if that's where the story ends, Abraham is just a resigned guy, not particularly happy. However, he also believes, Kierkegaard argues, that he'll get Isaac back again. He seemingly believes the impossible! That requires faith. It's his faith that allows him to be happy as he travels to the mountain.

Abraham is resigned to the fact that he's going to lose Isaac. He knows that it's not a game and that God isn't messing around. As a result, Kierkegaard says that Abraham makes the "movement of infinite resignation." He's sacrificed the world for God. But can you be resigned to losing the world and also believe that you'll get it back? If Abraham is actually thinking this, he's really grasping onto something that doesn't make any sense at all; Abraham is embracing the absurd.

With God's help, Abraham finally holds together what's fixed and what's possible in his action. He's resigned to the loss of Isaac and the world (the fixed) but also hopeful that he'll get Isaac back (the possible). It's an absurdity, but that's what's needed to live as a true self, to open yourself to the mystery that in God all things are possible. Thus Abraham ceases to try to force existence to make sense. Instead, he opens himself to the mystery of the divine.

Why faith must be offensive

Although many existentialists weren't religious, for Kierkegaard, the greatest way of living in truth was to embody the life that contained the greatest passion — and to do that required faith. For Kierkegaard, this makes sense: Living passionately means making a commitment to a life that's full of risk and mystery, like Abraham's, one that requires real courage to will. As it turns out, for Kierkegaard Christianity is the greatest passion.

If you make a commitment to being a good person, you can never entirely explain why you made that commitment in terms of reasons and evidence. Even if you claim to have reasons, those reasons themselves require reasons. At some point, you need to make a commitment to this way of life through a leap. Because the leap itself lacks reasons, it requires risk and embraces mystery. Leaping into life embodies passion.

Even if reason can't tell you that being a good person is best, choosing this path surely isn't offensive to reason. The problem is just that at some point, reason has to say, "I don't know." As a result, for Kierkegaard the ethical life doesn't embody the ultimate degree of risk and mystery that a person can take on. Instead, he takes the Christian requirement of belief in Jesus to raise the anxiety that comes with passionate choice to a fever pitch. He calls this ideal the *absolute paradox*. Reason isn't indifferent to the absolute paradox; it's offended by it.

Kierkegaard has a point, doesn't he? Imagine the Christian who stakes her existence on a belief in Jesus as the son of God. If her ideal is correct, God, who's eternal, actually became man and made himself temporal and finite. What is wholly transcendent and sacred (God) became profane and ordinary (man). Jesus is the living embodiment of a contradiction!

Unlike belief in goodness, belief in the incarnation of Jesus is an outright rejection of reason. Reason doesn't want to reject ethics, but according to Kierkegaard it *does* want to reject the Incarnation. The absolute paradox doesn't just lack reasons to embrace it; there can't *be* any reasons, because it makes no sense.

Here, in the realm of the absurd, you find infinite passion. As Kierkegaard puts it, "The supreme paradox of all thought is the attempt to discover something that thought cannot think." In the Incarnation, it has found just that paradox. Kierkegaard says that faith requires that you ". . . remain out upon the deep, over seventy thousand fathoms of water, still preserving my faith." The deep, of course, is the absurd. It's as though what Kierkegaard wants us to do is walk out over an empty abyss, with no foundation beneath us to give us security, and travel from one question mark about existence to the next, in a passionate and committed way.

Kierkegaard is suggesting that committing to Christ means shattering the use of reason as the way to forge a relationship with your own existence. To truly exist, and so to live in total truth, you must embrace the absurd. Although Abraham lived before Christ, he too forged a relationship with the absurd. He committed to a sacrifice while believing that what was sacrificed would be restored to him. Neither belief rules out the other; it's paradox that's kept alive by willing both with equal force. That's faith.

Proving that God exists

What would Kierkegaard have thought about the contemporary fuss over intelligent design — the claim that the complexity of life on earth is explained by pointing to the guiding hand of an intelligent designer — and evolution, which suggests that this complexity can be explained by using merely natural forces?

Although Kierkegaard lived before Darwin and wasn't exposed to evolutionary theory, he was dismissive of intelligent-design theories because he rejected the need to point to evidence for God. For Kierkegaard, a person's need for objective proofs of God is a clear sign that the person's faith is lost. To strive to place a rational foundation under your faith removes the demand for inwardly grappling with the paradox of living religiously. Kierkegaard was also dismissive of a trend toward using historical evidence to prove Jesus's validity. He believed these attempts demean faith and have a common goal: relieving the task of taking responsibility for your faith and placing it on something external, like reason and intellectual analysis.

Here's where people need God's help. Abraham must kneel before God and submit to God for help in achieving this movement. In doing so, he'll become himself. He must humbly ask for God's grace.

Why Abraham is an existential hero

Why is Abraham an existential hero? What Abraham does, in essence, is learn to live the life that all existentialists think you should embrace. For all existentialists, living authentically means one thing: embracing the absurdity of your existence (check out Chapter 5 for more on that). You shouldn't shy away from that role; you should joyfully embrace it.

Surely Abraham embraces absurdity by being willing to sacrifice his son and believing that his son will be restored to him. But Abraham's existential journey continues long after he leaves Mount Moriah. You may expect that afterward, Abraham would never be able to reconnect with his world again. He would find no passion in his relationship with his son, and he would from that point think of his social roles, and the ethical rules that structure them, as totally meaningless. A lot of people would expect, quite naturally, that Abraham's situation would ruin him by turning him into an angry, disgruntled person.

But if Abraham continues to be a knight of faith, this can't happen. Instead, Abraham must love his son with the same passion that he did before he renounced him. And he must embrace his social and ethical world with as much vigor as he did before. But he must do this while recognizing that the significance of his life doesn't lie here, because he transcends the world in his relationship with God.

Abraham doesn't return to the world and accept it in the way that a person might accept a broken gift. Instead, Abraham joyfully rejoins the human community. This is the central existential dilemma: trying to figure out how to exist in a world without ultimate meaning while engaging with it passionately (you might find an interesting analogue here with the story of Sisyphus in Chapter 5). How do you live in a world that you know you transcend but still live in it meaningfully? For Abraham, or for you, the way you do it can't make sense, and that's why it's absurd. But everyone has that task before her — one that, according to Kierkegaard, you can accomplish only with God's help.

The problem with contemporary Christians: They lack faith

As an existentialist and as a Christian, Kierkegaard is concerned about your relationship with existence and, hence, with God. From his point of view, however, the problem isn't that people strive to be like Abraham but fail.

Instead, Christians in today's age don't even bother to try. Kierkegaard felt that modern Christianity was watered down by the church, so the question of grappling with existence just doesn't arise anymore. It's taken a backseat to other (most likely aesthetic) pursuits.

Kierkegaard's beef with the church is based on his distaste for attempts to make Christianity palpable or rational and so more digestible to the crowd. In the end, Christianity winds up being used as a way of giving the social rituals of everyday life a larger context. Christianity becomes less about an anxiety-laden individual's commitment to God and more about being a good husband, or a good business partner, or a regular churchgoer. Religion becomes about what you do, as opposed to a *way* in which you're engaged with your existence. As a result, in Kierkegaard's view, religion is made common. Kierkegaard starts by distinguishing two things:

- **Christendom:** The modern descendant of Christianity
- **New Testament:** The actual way of life required of Christians as Kierkegaard sees it outlined in the Bible

Christendom, as a term, gives the impression of a state or an empire — but not a religion. This is Kierkegaard's point. In 19th-century Denmark, citizens were members of the state church, which was Christian, so Denmark was effectively a Christian state and society. Kierkegaard's worry, however, is that making Christianity into a social or political institution is contrary to its real New Testament aim: for the *individual* to forge a relationship with God. The two simply don't work together.

The need to give up the world

To live as a New Testament Christian, Kierkegaard thinks you must acknowledge your fundamental separation from the world. Being a true Christian means rubbing up against the world and living in a perpetual state of worldly friction. Because Christians are supposed to be at odds with the world, you must, as Nietzsche might say, live dangerously. As Kierkegaard sees it, the early Christians always saw themselves as outside the world, society, and politics. They saw that their true place was with God and not with the earthly.

As Kierkegaard sees it, Christendom is different. In modern Denmark, living well within the world requires that you be a Christian. In 19th-century Denmark, *everyone* was a Christian. To get along in society, you couldn't buck the crowd — and the crowd was Christian. The success of Christianity has become its greatest threat; when everyone is Christian, no one is truly Christian because the word doesn't mean anything anymore.

To Kierkegaard, Christianity has ceased to be religion and started to look more like a country-club membership that you need if you want to succeed or live well in a particular society. He has a strong point. In heavily Christian communities, being Christian is important if you don't want to be ostracized or seen as weird. Businesses pride themselves on being run by good Christians to drum up better business. In some communities, you'll have a hard time getting married if you aren't Christian. No one's parents would allow themselves to be known by the crowd as the people who allowed such an unacceptable thing to happen.

As Kierkegaard laments, in modern times the typical person ". . . is also a Christian, goes to church every Sunday, listens to and understands the pastor, yes indeed they understand one another; he dies, for ten dollars the pastor ushers him into eternity — but a self he neither was, nor became." Kierkegaard's description of the life of the typical Christian sounds stale and meaningless, doesn't it? That's Kierkegaard's point. Sure, most people attend church regularly. What for? Mostly to keep up appearances, to remind their social peers that they're still one of them — a socially acceptable person.

The meaning of Christianity has long since been lost. As Abraham's story shows, your relationship with God isn't found in your involvement with the world. A true Christian grapples with the individualistic question of what it means, for the individual, to exist and what it means to be Christian. Because the church itself is too heavily invested in the business of the world, it's focused on expanding its own membership. So it knows better than to make Christianity about anything that forces people to grapple with difficult subjects or topics or to prepare people to see themselves as separate from the world.

Dostoyevsky's existentialism: "The Grand Inquisitor"

A brilliantly written story called "The Grand Inquisitor" (part of a longer novel called *The Brothers Karamazov*, 1880) was written by Russian author Fyodor Dostoyevsky and has a similar theme to Kierkegaard's anti-Christendom message. In "The Grand Inquisitor," Dostoyevsky tells the story of how Jesus gets arrested by the Spanish Inquisition upon his return to the world. The bulk of the story is the Grand Inquisitor explaining to Jesus why he has been arrested. The Inquisitor tells him that he's protecting the people from Jesus, that they aren't strong enough to handle the freedom to grapple with and choose the right path that Jesus wants to offer them. Instead, the Inquisitor says this path leads to nothing but unhappiness and misery for people. If people want happiness, they need security and comfort. People need to be told what's good and evil by the authorities. They need to be given clear rules and rituals to follow that allow them to be not only free of the anxiety of choice, but also comfortable in their lives and happy through the stable and understandable life that the church provides them. The Inquisitor's way of framing the situation mirrors Kierkegaard's worry that the interests of the church and the interests of the individual aren't the same. For Kierkegaard and the Inquisitor, the question is an either/or choice: Is it Jesus's way, or is it the church's way?

Life isn't meant to be easy

Authentic, true living shouldn't be easy, Kierkegaard thinks. Cultivating a distance from the worldly things that typically make you happy is bound to cause you to reach for the aspirin bottle pretty often. As far as Kierkegaard sees it, the spiritual man of the New Testament understands this and embraces what's uncomfortable, unreasonable, or offensive about Christianity (and life).

Kierkegaard thinks most religious people don't fit this description. Instead, Christianity gets reinterpreted by organized religion so that it authorizes how people already want to live. The church doesn't calls for sacrifices anymore — other than the occasional $10 tossed into the offering basket. The life of Christianity within the church is passionless. No commitment. No risk. No fear. Faith is simple and easy. Just live your normal, socially acceptable, happy life, and the Christian part of your life follows along for free. Nothing needs to be difficult, because God wants you to be happy! From Kierkegaard's perspective, when faith and following Christ get easy, something's rotten in Denmark — pun intended!

Chapter 11

Nietzsche: Mastering the Art of Individuality

In This Chapter

▶ Seeing the self as an achievement

▶ Understanding why individuality involves power

▶ Grasping the life of the authentic noble

▶ Describing the life of the inauthentic slave

*E*xistentialists stress the importance of living in accord with who you are. So who are you? For one, you're the kind of being who's irreducibly individual. Every person has a particularity that's unique to him and that can't be understood by turning to meanings and values that are external to him. Because you're individual in this way, only you can give a proper expression of your own meaning. Existing as an individual requires that the purpose you give to your life reflect your individuality.

Because your experiences of the world and of yourself change, however, your unique individuality is always undergoing alteration. As a result, existing as an individual means always challenging the meaning you give to your life to ensure that it continues over time to honestly serve as an expression of your uniqueness. A lot of people have a difficult time living up to these tasks. Many times they give in to weakness and define their lives in terms of values exterior to them. Sometimes they reject the need to continually reassess the meaning they've given their lives by holding onto a fixed idea of themselves.

Living as an individual means embodying the path of a warrior. You must resist the values of the crowd by taking individual responsibility for creating your identity, and you must perpetually put that identity at risk by subjecting it to constant challenges.

In this chapter, we explain how Nietzsche views the self and why he thinks that living as an individual means giving your life a goal or meaning that's always in a state of flux or change. We discuss Nietzsche's archetype of individual authentic living, the *noble,* and we highlight what it means to live life in a noble fashion. We then discuss how the noble person seeks to create an individual meaning, direction or goal for his own life, one that he seeks to artistically express and cultivate by avoiding dogma and instead by seeking to increase the number of diverse perspectives on that goal. Such a pursuit means putting your own idea of who you are (your goals) under constant threat, which reveals Nietzsche's belief that a noble self meets the challenges that individual life entails, including the suggestion that noble living embraces the task of *living dangerously* by developing its own self in a way that puts the survival of that very self in continual danger and at risk of coming apart.

We round out the discussion by also highlighting Nietzsche's archetype of *failed* individual living — the *slave.* As we highlight, slaves and nobles do not merely differ in how they actually approach life but are also differentiated by the kinds of emotions that characterize their existence. Whereas the noble is dominated by a consciousness of self-love, the slave is overwhelmed by hatred, an emotion that produces a kind of resentment that Nietzsche sees in modern Christianity and that he thinks leads to the slave's rejection of individual living in favor of various strategies of self-deception. We finish the chapter by presenting a more passive way to fail to be individual — to succumb to the weaknesses of herd mentality, or to give in to the temptation to live in sheer conformity to what the crowd or the masses dictate.

Investigating Who You Are

According to the existentialist, your self is always changing. On one level, this seems an odd thing to say; don't you feel that there's a "you" that's survived all the changes your personality has gone though? Nietzsche, for one, doesn't disagree that it feels that way, but he thinks that it's a deceptive way of understanding what it means to be self.

In fact, Nietzsche thinks that behind that feeling of unified selfhood is the true you — a battlefield filled with hostile and competing psychological forces called desires (these are drives, character traits, instincts, or impulses). At any point in time, some stronger desires are dominating weaker ones. As a result, a hierarchy of desires forms that results in what you take to be your perspective on the world, or the way things look and feel from your point of view.

Nietzsche's view of the self leads to three central points:

- ✔ Being composed of desires, your self is always biased. You can't help but project meaning or value onto the world.

✔ Because changing experiences means developing different desires, the question of who you are is always an open one.

✔ Although you are, at any moment, a given perspective, you're never reducible to that perspective. Your identity is never fixed; new perspectives are always possible for you.

You can take charge of who you are

Underscoring the mystery of the self, Nietzsche says, "We are unknown to ourselves, we men of knowledge — and with good reason. We have never sought ourselves — how could it happen that we should ever find ourselves?" Commonly, we take our perspective, or our way of engaging with the world, as integral to our sense of our identity. If engaging the world as an individual is important, this would imply that you need to know what it would mean to have a perspective or identity that expresses your individuality.

Imagine that elements of your perspective were grafted into you by society. In fact, society may want you to uncritically accept certain ways of seeing things. If you do that, you're engaging with the world in ways created by others. Are you willing to call this perspective an expression of what you are as a unique individual?

Well, let's face it — you'd look like a robot programmed to perform a societal function. Society isn't the only thing that can get in the way of individuality in this way. Sometimes people deceive themselves into seeing things in ways that will cause them less pain, showing a key Nietzschean point: Being an individual and happiness aren't necessarily correlated. It's also a sad truth, but some people value feeling good over living as a unique individual. Nietzsche would probably see such cases as examples of the slang phrase *selling out*.

One thing is clear: If your way of engaging with the world isn't an expression of your own unique individuality, you're not in control of your own life. Knowing when you've been deceived is important, so living as an individual begins with understanding yourself, which Nietzsche suggests in the earlier quote we're not terribly good at.

Living as an individual requires the following:

✔ Engaging with the world in a way that expresses your unique self

✔ Living self-critically to control elements of your self that aren't reflective of you

✔ Being honest about the self at all times and avoiding deceptions

You're a sea of desire

Nietzsche wants to advance a new interpretation of what you are. He rejects the notion that there's a fixed "you" and suggests instead that you talk about the self as composed of a multiplicity or diversity of different desires. If that's right, you change all the time because your desires alter as you go through new, different experiences.

Something feels right about this concept. I don't feel in any way like the same person who occupied my body at 15, or 20, or 30, or 40 (all right, coauthor Chris is over 40!). What accounts for the difference? Well, your perspective on the world changes over time, and that's because the desires that compose your perspective have changed.

Nietzsche thinks that

- The self is composed of desires, and these always change.

- Those desires compose your perspective or point of view, or your way of engaging with the world.

- Your desires are always changing, so your perspective is always in flux.

Like the 18th century philosopher David Hume, Nietzsche feels that if you tried to introspect into yourself and follow a point of view or desire backward, you'd never find a mysterious self or "I" hiding out behind the scenes. Both of them feel this way because they're convinced that a unified "I" behind your desires doesn't exist. As a result, Nietzsche thinks that being an individual demands taking account of the fact that who you are is always undergoing alteration and change. As a result, being an individual can never attempt to express a fixed or timeless self.

Heraclitus's river

Heraclitus was a pre-Socratic philosopher who lived in Greece around 500 BC. He is known as the philosopher of *becoming* because he thought that the basic nature of reality was change. Everything, Heraclitus argued, was in a constant state of flux or alteration. Nothing was fixed, and the appearance of stability was really an illusion. As an example, because the exact water in a river is never the same, Heraclitus believed that you could never step into the same river twice. One of Heraclitus's philosophical opponents, Parmenides, argued the opposite: He denied that anything changed and said that the appearance of change was an illusion. He was a philosopher of *being*, and he felt that all reality was one fixed thing. Nietzsche sides with Heraclitus, and he incorporates beliefs about becoming into his own way of talking about the self.

You're biased: You can't help it; it's just you!

Today's culture thinks that if you try hard enough, you can escape your own biases and achieve objective or unbiased interpretations about the world. Nietzsche's claim that your identity is really a collection of desires conflicts with this because desires are inherently biased by definition.

In typical existentialist fashion, Nietzsche rejects the notion of a right way to see things. He sees no *objective* truth in the world for you to discover. Instead, he thinks you must understand the world through your perspective, one that always reflects your own specific interests.

Nietzsche puts it this way, "No, facts are precisely what there are not; only interpretations." Nietzsche surely doesn't think that this is bad; it's natural. Knowing who you are as a self requires embracing this fact. Nietzsche's view is called *perspectivism,* the view that all descriptions of the world are given from a biased or self-interested point of view.

In fact, even science and philosophy, Nietzsche thinks, inherently represent the interests of its practitioners; the belief that objective science or pure reason reveals the truth of things is a fiction! In fact, although most people tend to see science as fact, the existentialists view the truths of science as one perspective in the world among others.

You can change: Analyzing the false belief that you're a fixed object

One false belief that Nietzsche thinks gets in the way of your goal of living as an individual is the claim that you're a fixed, unchanging object. Still, most people *feel* as though an unchanging, fixed thing lies behind their thoughts and feelings and desires. Most people feel that the self is an independent thing that *has* those things. Nietzsche thinks that for us to live in ways that are more authentic to what we are, we need to tackle this false belief and the further falsities that it leads us to embrace. Here are a few of them:

✔ **False belief #1: You don't change.** If your self is just a solitary, unified thing, changing beliefs and desires won't change *you.* You'd be the same all the time, because you're different from your beliefs and desires; you're the thing underneath them.

✔ **False belief #2: Being a self requires no activity on your part.** If you don't change, you can't *cease* to be a self (well, unless you die). If that's right, it would be silly to say you have to succeed at being a self or that you could do something wrong and suddenly fail to be a self.

✔ **False belief #3: You can achieve an objective point of view on the world.** Being biased always means seeing things from one desire or other. But if what *you* are turns out to be something that's independent of desire, you're something that's essentially unbiased and objective.

Nietzsche wants to challenge all these false beliefs. For one, he wants to suggest that you're not an unchanging thing. Instead, you have lots of internal parts that are always changing and undergoing alteration. Second, those parts have to be arranged in just the right way for you to be a self. So being a self requires actual activity. Last, the existentialists claim that you're always biased in how you see the world. This is a basic truth of existentialism — that you're always projecting meaning of your own onto the world and that this is just an inescapable part of who you are (Camus and Heidegger both make this claim; see Chapters 5 and 6, respectively).

You can be fooled by your own language

Nietzsche thinks you have false beliefs about what you are for lots of reasons. Maybe society benefits by fooling you into thinking that objectivity is valuable and that its way of seeing things is objectively correct. Nietzsche thinks this clearly happens, and if you're going to be an individual, you need to be on guard against these kinds of deceptions. But another way in which you can fall prey to these false beliefs is more subtle.

Perhaps, Nietzsche says, language fools you: You become seduced by the ways you talk. You say things like "I went to the store" or "I desire a steak for dinner." These sentences have an object, the "I," and an independent action, the "went to the store" or "desire a steak" part. This way of talking suggests that some unified "I" object *does* or performs the action and that the self or "I" is separate from the activity of desiring or doing.

Use language like this frequently enough, and you'll start thinking that "I" refers to some object that's separate and independent from desires, wants, or actions. You soon start thinking that you're a fixed thing that doesn't change, that you don't have to do anything to be a self, and that you're capable of seeing things from an unbiased point of view.

Although language simplifies life, Nietzsche thinks you shouldn't let useful fictions (like the word "I") affect your way of understanding yourself. It may be helpful in society to *talk* as though you're a fixed object, but that doesn't mean you *are* that way. Because language usage leads into deceptions about what you are, you need to be careful not to allow language to affect you in your attempts to engage with the world as an individual.

Understanding the Self As a Chaos Made Orderly

Existentialism stresses the importance of existing as an individual and so emphasizes that individuality requires making fundamental life choices about the kind of life you find meaningful. So even if the self truly is a collection of desires, you need to learn to structure those desires so that they express your choice of life direction.

To understand the importance that choice can play in being an individual, you need to understand that each desire, or component of the self, is a different way of seeing the world. As a result, all your desires are always in competition. This recognition leads to the importance of choice: Being a self requires unifying those warring desires under a central purpose or meaning. So being a self requires mastering yourself by giving your desires a common direction.

This reveals two of Nietzsche's central points:

- ✔ The self begins as a kind of chaos of unorganized desire.
- ✔ Being a self requires the activity of mastering your desires and ordering them around a choice that expresses the meaning you've given your life.

Getting a handle on your unorganized desires

Your self is really a big collection of desires, each of which is aimed at the world in a specific way. A desire for pizza is aimed at getting pizza, whereas the desire for money is aimed at getting money. To be aimed at the world just means to see the world and to be motivated to act within it in terms dictated by what the desires point to. Seen in this way, the self turns out to consist in many different perspectives all aimed at the same world.

As an example, take courage — the kind of desire that can form a part of what you are. Any desire can partly shape your way of being in the world, which means that it contributes its unique way of being aimed at the world to your point of view or perspective. So when you look out at the world and respond to it in terms of emotion or action, courage, if it's part of you, plays a role in how that all happens.

Putting your desires into perspective

Think of each desire as having two components:

- ✔ The first reveals that the desire has a particular way of seeing the world that's specific to it. Courage literally sees the world in terms of its aim — courageous action. If courage is part of you, and you see a child in a burning building, you see this as a situation that calls for immediate action. In a sense, the desire points to the building and calls attention to it, shouting to you, "Hey! Pay attention! Courageous action goes here!"

- ✔ The second component of desire is that it's a way of being driven toward the world. As a result of having desires, you're literally pulled toward certain things and away from other things. The courageous person literally feels *pulled* toward the building and toward helping. He also feels emotional pain if he resists that pull, so being driven includes feeling, which shows that being you isn't just a way of thinking. You're an embodied entity, so you don't see things, and *then* feel a certain way and are pulled toward or away from things. They all occur at once.

One way to think of this concept is to consider a scenario in which someone shows you a picture of an animal that has a combination of both duck and rabbit features. To see the picture *as* a rabbit or *as* a duck means that you have a concept of those things to apply to the world. If you don't have a concept of a duck, you won't see the picture as a duck. You can't. The desires at your core work the same way. To experience the world in an X-way, you have to have the desire for X. Someone without that X-desire will see it in some other way, one according to the specific desires he has.

Now you may be saying to yourself that you have a lot of desires, but it always feels as though you have *one* point of view. How does that work? Well, if you're a collection of desires, that feeling of unity really represents a collection of desires that have come together in some way.

Embracing internal struggle as essential to you

Inside of your self, a vicious struggle is always under way between the desires that compose you. Each desire wants to dominate the rest, to take the lead in determining how you engage with the world.

How do warring desires interact? Say that you have a desire (or drive) for money and a desire for social acceptability. Now imagine that you're at a street corner, and a little old (wealthy) lady is standing there, terrified to cross the street. Your desire for money sees her as a source of possible satisfaction; she has lots of money in that purse, and the desire urges you to wallop her with a club and rob her. At the same time, you have a desire for social acceptability also fighting to have its aim represented in your way of engaging with the world. It sees certain things — like clubbing little old ladies — as unpleasant, so it pulls at you accordingly. If you have both of these desires, you feel them;

you sense a tension in the way that you see the situation, and you feel your body pulled to behave in contradictory ways.

How do you resolve these inner conflicts? Although desires are always in competition, Nietzsche says, they aren't all equally powerful. Stronger drives tend to dominate weaker ones. If the desire for acceptability is stronger than the desire for money, both end up having a place in that person's perspective, but the acceptability desire controls *how* the money desire gets to express itself. In Nietzsche's language, they fall into an *order of rank,* with one dominating the other.

In this case, that may mean that you agree to help the old woman across the street safely, knowing she'll offer you some money afterward. This way, both desires get expressed, but one rules the other (money desires are expressed in socially acceptable ways).

Now think about it — that's just two desires. But you're a bogglingly large number of desires — and they're all at war! Your way of engaging with the world is determined by the way that those internal battles play out.

Striving for selfhood through self-mastery

Everyone knows someone he thinks of as a psychological train wreck. The person seems to lack any kind of control over his desires. For Nietzsche, being a self requires *not* being a train wreck. It means that you possess a commanding drive that represents a choice about how to unify your warring desires under a single goal or purpose. It means giving your self a coherent sense of direction through self-mastery.

Maybe when the particular train wreck you know is in a certain situation, one desire takes control of him. When he's in a different situation, some other contradictory desire takes control. So in one situation, desire A has control of desire B, whereas in a different situation, B controls A. This kind of person seems to have no coherence or order within his personality. He seems out of control, unpredictable, and unstable — hardly the kind of person you'd want to be around!

This kind of person isn't the picture of what an existential individual looks like. Individuals have a sense of direction; they have a goal or purpose that unifies their lives. An individual decides that *this* is how he wants to engage with the world, and in making that choice, he rejects other ways of engaging. Then he sticks to those decisions. He's not a flip-flopper. Individuals seem to live with a sense of real purpose and direction.

Seen in this way, selfhood looks a lot like an achievement; it's something that you're always doing. Your stronger desires don't just tell your weaker desires to do something and then watch it happen. Those stronger desires have to keep making those weaker desires do what they want. In this way of speaking, the self needs a commander. It's a 24/7 job to keep all your desires in line.

Nietzsche thinks of self-mastery as a kind of art. He says, "Only one thing is needful; to give style to one's character — a great and rare art!" In a sense, when you strive to be an individual, you are at the same time the artist and the mound of clay. You fashion yourself into a sculpture. You look at the desires that compose you (the clay) and decide what goal or aim you want to posit for your life (what shape you want this clay to take on). This self-formation requires choice. You have to decide that the clay should take on some particular shape as opposed to some other. The self-as-artist then imposes upon his desires a sense of style by making them conform to that self-chosen shape. Of course, by *style* Nietzsche doesn't mean the imposition of some contemporary style or fad, but a notion of style as expressive of one's individual creative and aesthetic nature.

For Nietzsche, individuals

- ✔ See life as a kind of artistic project.
- ✔ Play the role of artist in creating a goal or shape that their life should take.
- ✔ Play the role of the clay because they're also being shaped.

Say that you want to fashion yourself as a studious person. Becoming a doctor is important to you, so you give yourself this goal. Well, this means that in different situations, you're capable of controlling your desires and keeping them in line. If you have a videogame console in your room, but you have an exam tomorrow, you need to be able to control the desire to play so that it doesn't interfere with your goal of being studious as a person. In fact, true mastery means that you've trained your desire to get entertainment out of studying! That's how individuals live. They choose, and then they hold themselves accountable to their own decisions. If you submit to the videogames each time, you're more of a train wreck, with no real, cohesive sense of self. You're all over the place, with no sense of direction or purpose.

This ability to give style to your own person requires a lot of inner strength. Treating yourself as a work of art isn't easy. Think of it like driving a chariot. The strongest charioteer (remember, this means the ruling desire, not a nondesire-based self!) can keep all the wild horses driving it pointed forward and moving in one direction — the direction that the charioteer wants.

Being an Individual Means Being Noble

Making a firm choice about how to give shape to your life is necessary to live as an individual, but being a self still requires more, because the meaning you give your life must be unique to you as an individual. To succeed at being a self means being noble; you don't recognize exterior values or meanings, such as those coming from institutional religion or societal norms, as having an authority over you. So you give yourself a self-created purpose.

Nobles truly embrace the existentialists' claim that value comes into existence with you and with your own choices. To become a noble self-creator means loving yourself and having reverence for who you are. You see your way of existing as the definition of the admirable. It also means seeing those people who fail to live as you do (nobly) as pitiful, contemptible, and weak.

Nobles are in control of themselves

Being an existentialist means organizing your life in accordance with a purpose or meaning that reflects your own unique individuality. Only in this way can you be said to truly control your own self. Nietzsche thinks of this person as noble.

The noble individual is autonomous, whereas the non-noble is heteronomous. The word *autonomous* comes apart into two Greek terms: the term *auto,* which means *self,* and the term *nomos,* which means *law* or *rule.* Taken together, the terms mean *self-ruling.* Essentially, an autonomous person gives himself his own rules to live by. If your way of engaging with the world doesn't reflect your own self-created rules and purposes, you aren't ruled by the *autos* (the self). In this case, you're *heteronomous* — a term that contains *hetero,* which means *other,* and again *nomos,* or *rule.* That's the description that sticks to the non-noble; he's *ruled by the other.* Non-nobles engage with the world based on the rules and purposes of others, so they aren't self-controlling.

Nietzsche isn't saying that the autonomous noble person (the individual) rejects the rules of those around him and tries to behave like a lunatic. In fact, the noble person may follow the laws of society, but only on the presumption that he has concluded that those rules are worth following. The noble person is always ready to step away from society's rules when they fail to cohere with his sense of how he should live his life.

Ask yourself what constitutes your ultimate worth and significance. Is it that you're a member of some group (society, your peers, your family, or your culture)? If so, what you are reduces to that. Without that group, you're nothing. If you don't reduce to that group, your ultimate worth and significance transcend it. The noble understands himself as transcending external groups. He may be in those groups, but he doesn't see his significance as wholly exhausted by them. That's why the meaning he gives his life — or how he organizes his desires — must come from what's inside himself.

To keep this distinction between different ways of understanding the ultimate significance of the individual, think of one as reductionist and the other as existentialist in character:

- ✔ If you're a reductionist, you believe that what you are — your ultimate value and significance — can be understood strictly in terms of something external. You *reduce* to those external things.

- ✔ If you're an existentialist, you reject reductionism about your own value. You may be related to other things, but your significance and value are unique and internal to you. Your value can't be explained away.

Living nobly isn't easy to do. It requires a willingness to stand alone and apart from the crowd. Could you endure solitude? Can you create your own meaning and purpose, even if they depart from everything you've been told is right and good? Most people will claim they do this all the time. But how many of them are really in self-deception? How much of an individual are you, in actuality? How much about you is mere reflection of the masses around you? How much in control of you are they?

Nobles in the arts

The existentialist self-creator is portrayed as separating himself from external notions of what's right. Not surprisingly, in literature and film this character is typically portrayed as dastardly and malicious (though for the existentialist, this isn't necessary; it just makes for good art). Two examples are Raskolnikov from Feodor Dostoyevsky's *Crime and Punishment* and Colonel Kurtz from the film *Apocalypse Now.* Both characters come to view themselves as freed from the chains imposed upon them by external values and decide to re-create their lives apart from those codes. Kurtz fights the Vietnam War in a way that's liberated from what he calls "lying timid morality" (with some ugly consequences!), and Raskolnikov plans and executes the murder of a pawnbroker, seeing himself as being above the straitjacket of morality imposed by those around him. As both characters learn, being a self-creator is difficult, because nothing outside you can offer a justification for your chosen way of living. You must function as your own source of justification, and that's not as easy to do as it sounds.

Nobles love themselves

A noble individual creates and gives himself his own meaning and never accepts value from the outside. To create yourself in this way is to become like God; you decide what value is and what expresses that value. The noble sees himself as the source of value itself, and not surprisingly, the noble loves himself.

In Nietzsche's words, the noble "experiences himself as a person who determines value and does not need to have other's approval." The noble does not associate the idea of value or meaning with what's external to him. Instead, value is something that he creates. He lives on his own terms. He writes his own rules.

This makes sense in the general existential picture. If God has died (which we discuss at length in Chapter 3) — and that means that the notion of value being external is no longer seen as believable — you can't honestly look outside yourself any longer to discover how you should live or how you should interpret the world. As a result of the emptying of meaning from the world, the noble creates his own meaning. As Nietzsche puts it, after God's death, "must not we become Gods ourselves?" The noble takes on the challenge and does.

If the noble creates his own meaning, he has to love and admire himself, because he sees himself as the new authoritative source from which meaning flows. Thus, Nietzsche says that when the noble contemplates the question "What is good?" he naturally thinks about himself and about the kind of life that he lives. His experience of himself is one of complete self-affirmation and self-love. His life just *is* the good.

Noble living requires that you do the following:

✔ Experience yourself as the meaning of the good.

✔ Be self-affirmative.

✔ Love yourself.

This may sound pretty egoistic and self-important. It is! But shouldn't it be? The noble has taken on the task of creating his own meaning in a meaningless world. He creates value and imposes value on the world through his way of engaging with that world. He's proud of what he does and doesn't hide from it. Should he be humble about his worth? Heck, no! Of course, you don't want to wrongly exaggerate your value, but you don't want to be shy about your value either.

Nobles have contempt for nonindividuals

What the noble, self-creating, authentic individual thinks of the other people in the world depends on who those people are. Some will turn out to be good, and some bad. Recognizing these distinctions, being noble means that you have to be harsh and judgmental. You don't see everything as the same.

Clearly, if you see other nobles in the world, you'll see them as also being engaged in the project of meaningful self-creation. Fellow artists! You see them as good, because they reflect your standard of what's valuable. As a result, regardless of what, specifically, those other nobles posit as their own goals and purposes, you'll embrace them as equals.

The vast majority of people aren't noble. They don't meet the challenges of life honestly. Some don't have goals; they're like train wrecks psychologically. Their lives are scattered and without direction and purpose. Others have goals, but they aren't self-created; as a result, they live in self-deception and hide from their role and responsibility as creators of meaning. Nietzsche calls these people *slaves* and suggests that the noble experiences them as the exemplification of the bad. What the noble means by *bad* is that slaves are common or lowly. They're deserving of contempt.

Isn't that mean? Not really. The noble believes that *everyone* wants, or at least should want, to be in control of his own destiny, to live as an individual. Who wouldn't? The slave fails at doing so and thus is seen as controlled by his weaknesses. Thus, the slave is a failure at life. Lacking the strength to posit a unique goal, he turns to the goals of others. But that's a pitiful way to exist, one that should be held in contempt. Slaves fail to tackle life head on in a courageous and honest way. They're cowards, and the noble is honest enough to say so.

You may feel that this viewpoint is a bit rough or judgmental. Well, frankly, it is. If you feel that it's not quite right — that no one should see anyone as beneath him — Nietzsche would say that the slave in you is talking and taking control of your perspective. You need to take control of that impulse before it takes control of you! Face it: Greatness is exemplary; it's individual. If you want to dare to be great, you have to recognize that some things aren't great; instead, they're weak or lowly. If you can't handle that kind of judgmental heat, get out of the kitchen, Nietzsche says! Perhaps slave life would be more comfortable for you.

Relishing Change As Essential to a Noble Life

An authentic existential life requires making hard choices about how to define yourself as a unique individual and then organizing the desires that compose you so that the resulting structure obeys the meaning that you've given yourself. However, it's also essential to the existential notion of the self that the meaning you give to your life make sense only in a context.

When your experiences change, so do your desires, and as a result, new ways of seeing things emerge. Being an individual requires that you're always challenging and rethinking your way of understanding yourself to see whether it remains an appropriate expression of who you are in the unique world you're living in.

Noble individuals embrace change not only in the world, but also in their own sense of self. They aren't afraid to give themselves new goals and purposes when their own unique individuality demands it. Nietzsche calls it the need for *self-overcoming.* To fail to acknowledge this need is to fall victim to *dogma,* a belief in the timeless value of one way of organizing the self or of understanding the world. Dogma always stifles individuality by leading you to reject change as an essential part of what you are, and in so doing causes you to fail to live in accord with the challenges of existentialism.

Nobles embrace change

The self is always in flux. As time progresses, you naturally experience new situations and come to have new beliefs, new desires, and new impulses. As a result, what it means to engage the world as a unique individual is always an open question.

The goals you gave yourself at age 15 or the way your desires were organized then likely aren't appropriate to you now. It would seem weird if you were always obligated to engage with the world in the way that your 15-year-old self did. You may have been noble then (probably not!), but that nobility was dependent on the way that self was internally made up and on the specific context that self lived in at the time. After you put a self into a wholly new world, its nobility must be re-created anew.

This reveals a key existential intuition: You're always ultimately responsible for the way you engage with the world. Saying that you engage with the world in a certain way because that's the way you've always done things is just as inauthentic as saying you interact with the world in a certain way because that's the way others do things. Just as much as the noble person is always ready to separate himself from the ways that society lives, you must be able to maintain a similar distance from your own past self.

One of Nietzsche's fictional characters, Zarathustra (from his famous work *Thus Spoke Zarathustra*), says, "And this secret spoke Life herself unto me. 'Behold,' said she, 'I am that which must always overcome itself.'" New situations, Nietzsche feels, call for new, fresh interpretations, and those new interpretations may require different ways of organizing the drives and habits that constitute who you are. Nietzsche calls this essential part of noble individuality *self-overcoming*.

Nobles embrace self-overcoming, the need to continually alter and move past the specific ways in which they engaged the world in the past.

In fact, the noble's sense of love for himself demands that he never rest content in an identity that he's already created. What the noble loves about himself isn't some set of meanings or goals that he created, but his role as a creator of meaning. The noble loves his ability to will himself, and he strives to maintain that will. Loving one's self means not abdicating that role.

Nobles reject dogma

Most people don't like the idea that being an individual means continually re-creating the self. They'd rather create a timeless identity and stick to it forever. Mistaking the noble love of the self as refashioning a changing flux or desires with liking some particular version of one's identity is easy to do. For Nietzsche, becoming wedded to some particular version of yourself or the world is hostile to life. Nobles must reject it vigorously.

Nietzsche thinks we need to face up to the fact that there are no timeless truths. There is no right structure to things in world or even to you. Instead, all truth and all value are really functions of a specific context. (As discussed earlier in this chapter, all truth is *perspectival*.) If this is so, there can't be some "one way" to always look at the world. But that's what dogma argues!

Always remember that for the existentialists, when you're tempted toward thinking that your self has an essential timeless structure, it's always a sign that some internal weakness in you is gaining expression. Why do people turn to fixed truths about the world and about themselves? Well, change is difficult; it requires adjustment, the constant reshuffling of desires, and the frustration of not satisfying some desires in you that are no longer seen as appropriate. Change is just painful, and for those who, out of weakness, prefer the security of happiness to being unique individuals (remember, for Nietzsche, these aren't necessarily correlated!), timeless truths are just what the doctor ordered! Unfortunately, that doctor isn't concerned with your *existential* health! Nietzsche, on the other hand, is.

Feeling as though you've found the right way to be or the right way to see the world is very comforting. It makes you feel you're in sync with some truth about things that you didn't create and that assure you that what you're doing is valuable. Imagine making a difficult decision. Isn't it easier to make that decision when you can authenticate it on a system of value that you didn't create?

How many times have you searched through the Bible, social code, or favorite book of philosophy to justify the way you see or interact with the world? Have you ever tried to justify your behavior in terms of what your own past self would do?

Maybe you should just get off that merry-go-round of self-deception. Aren't all these responses really just ways of avoiding your existential responsibility to choose for yourself? To create your own identity right now?

Life is self-overcoming. You must always see who you are in a particular situation as transcending the ways in which you've seen things before. The true individual noble rejects, Nietzsche says, "worship of the state, the tyranny of demagogues and the tyranny of the crowd." Most of all, they reject worship of their own past selves!

The noble life is a path, not a destination

Being a noble individual means organizing the desires that compose your self around a unique aim or project that gives your life individual meaning. It also means rooting out weaknesses within yourself that pull you toward conformity and dogma (whether about yourself or about the world) so that you always remake and reshape your own self as your experiences change. This path is so difficult that the archetypical noble — Nietzsche calls him the *Übermensch* (which means *superperson* or *overman,* the person who is beyond the form of current humanity) — has yet to exist on earth.

Nietzsche's pessimism about the actual scarcity of these individuals doesn't mean that you can't strive to be noble. But you have to keep at it. You stay on the road of nobility as long as you elect to do so. It doesn't really matter if you stay on the road for a year if you finally decide, at the end, to turn off it. It doesn't matter that you *were* on the road if you're not now. Being a self isn't something you *are;* it's something you *do.*

If you choose this road, many temptations will surface to distract you from the task of becoming an exemplary noble individual. The path will be highly frustrating at times, and painful, and you'll always be making things difficult on yourself (as will others!). But who ever said that being in control of your life and expanding on your own creative possibilities as a unique individual should be easy things? Aren't all great things worth striving for? Perhaps even suffering for? Nietzsche's fictional character Zarathustra puts it best when, in talking about the relationship between individuality and happiness, he says, "My suffering and my sympathy for suffering — what does it matter! Do I then strive after happiness? I strive after my work!"

Indeed, he's right, isn't he? Life isn't about aiming for pleasure or about things being easy or about being happy. These goals are for people who don't have the strength to live nobly. No, for the noble, it's all about the *work* of continually creating yourself into an individual.

Nobility Means Striving for Power

Existentialism argues that you must always subject your self-created goals to continuing challenge, opening the door to the ever-present possibilities of renewed self-creation. But how do you know if you're responding to new experiences in appropriate ways that uniquely reflect your individual nature? Nietzsche responds by suggesting that noble interaction cultivates and pursues power.

Power means that after you posit a goal or meaning for your life, you must seek out experiences and perspectives that differ from that goal or meaning; you must meet the new experiences and perspectives in battle, so to speak. Your aim is to learn to express yourself in new and more sophisticated ways — in other words, in the new ways made possible by encountering those new experiences.

The result of pursuing power is twofold:

✔ Your identity, or way of organizing your desires in line with a goal, is made more beautiful through the ever-more-complex ways it's capable of expressing itself through new, diverse experiences. Power is increased in this way, because it takes greater strength to hold together a self whose inner tensions are always being expanded through the incorporation of different viewpoints and perspectives.

✔ Living nobly means exposing the self to conditions that can make your life goal unstable. Noble living pushes the envelope and requires the cultivation of danger as a lifestyle — putting the current version of who you are in continual jeopardy. Putting your self on the line takes real courage and inner strength. Only in this way do you really cultivate a sense of power and embrace who you are!

Life is all about power

Nietzsche frequently connects life and power. In one particularly infamous passage, he suggests that "life itself is *essentially* appropriation, injury, overpowering of what is alien and weaker; suppression, hardness, imposition of one's own forms, incorporation and at least, at its mildest, exploitation . . ." Although admittedly harsh in tone, Nietzsche thinks that being a noble individual means accepting that life includes the desire for acquiring power in these ways.

How? What Nietzsche wants you to see is that acquiring power doesn't necessarily mean dominating other people. Instead, you cultivate a specific kind of self and a specific kind of life that displays or reflects a kind of inner power.

In *The Genealogy of Morals,* Nietzsche writes, "In the beginning, the noble caste was always the barbarian caste; their superiority lay, not in physical force, primarily, but in force of soul — they were more *complete* men." This is an illuminating quote, because in it Nietzsche is making two key points. First, he states that the nobles of ancient times were the most powerful physical force on earth (he's thinking perhaps of the early Romans), but he suggests that this kind of outer power doesn't explain why they were superior. So what did? He says that it lies in their *completeness.*

Here's an example to help clarify this point. When coauthor Chris was young, he endured a few situations in which he was bullied at school. His mom said that bullies aren't really powerful; in actuality, they're weak inside, and their weakness expresses itself as the desire to beat up smaller kids. The fact that they're big enough to accomplish this shouldn't fool you into thinking that they aren't actually weak, because it's really their weakness that drives their actions. Weakness — not strength — controls the bully and drives his behavior.

Chris's mom was onto something, Nietzsche might say. The weakness that expresses itself in bullies is an inner weakness or incompleteness. They lack real courage. They never put themselves at risk and actually challenge themselves. The ability to put yourself at risk — even if you may not survive — shows a kind of confidence that Nietzsche would say is needed for inner power.

Inner power has two elements. First, inner power expresses itself in the demand that you organize and place order on your desires through the creation of a passionate goal for your life. How well can you impose your own goal on your own desires and forge a sense of inner order? Second, inner power hates dogma and the weakness associated with it. Through inner power, the noble wants to see just how far his passionate goal can be expanded in the world against all challenges to it. How far can you overpower other perspectives and incorporate them into your goal and meaning? As a result, you see the following:

- ✔ Noble life requires making risk a part of your life.
- ✔ Noble life requires continual challenge.

True power seeks to develop internal beauty

Nietzsche thinks that you must live in a way that reflects your unique individuality. However, he also thinks that truly embracing your individuality means wanting to see how many new, diverse desires and experiences you can incorporate into your life. The ability to incorporate many diverse perspective within yourself but remain focused on a definite goal or purpose reveals true inner power through an inner beauty reflective of an artistry of living.

The way that you give your life a meaning is your way of interpreting and interacting with the world. But what's important isn't the goal you pick, but how you live that goal. Visualize the process of producing a painting. Say that you decide to paint a picture with a specific kind of content: the sea. The question now becomes how you can paint that picture in the most beautiful way. One idea may be to try to paint the picture with as many colors as you can, realizing that this method means producing that content in the most difficult way — the way that requires the greatest ability and power as an artist.

Now think of the goal or meaning that you give your life. That's the content of the painting. The question is how many desires and perspectives (colors) you can paint that goal with. The more conflicting the desire or perspective is to incorporate under that goal, the more beautiful that goal becomes when it successfully incorporates those new perspectives through self-mastery. Thus, the more power the self has, the more it seeks to express its meaning and goal through the most difficult situations. It wants to expose that aim or goal to experiences that seem to even contradict it, all in the name of seeking to make that goal's expression even more beautiful.

Imagine that you live a religious life. How would you live like this through the cultivation of power? Well, you seek out situations and perspectives that are, or at least seem to be, inconsistent with it. Perhaps you recognize that people say religion and science don't go together, so you strive to learn a lot about science. You aim, however, is to learn about science, which you view as dangerous to your worldview, with the hope of incorporating science into your way of looking at things — religiously! Of course, you may find your goal weakened and overpowered by what you seek out. That's the risk. You may find your self defeated, and you may turn into one of those psychological train wrecks we talked about earlier. For this reason, not everyone has the courage to expose his identity in this way.

If you think about it, what Nietzsche is really asking you to do here is to live your sense of who you are. If you really believe in your goal, really love it and feel passionate about it, you want to experience all the ways that it can be expressed (Kierkegaard talks similarly about the self as requiring *passion;* if you're interested, jump to Chapter 7 to learn more). In a way, it's like getting a new car and wanting to know how fast it can go.

Truly honoring your purpose in life is living it passionately — pushing it to go faster and faster, each time pushing it, and yourself, to the limit. For Nietzsche, the famous song lyric "It's better to burn out than to fade away" characterizes noble living.

Powerful nobles ignore neighbors

Some people like to choose friends who are pretty much exactly like them. They look for clones. Nietzsche says these people look to surround them-selves with neighbors. Nietzsche despises neighbor-seeking because it means looking to be surrounded by people who don't challenge you. Nobles don't do that, because they always seek to live their identities by exposing them to conflict and challenge.

Nietzsche's fictional character Zarathustra points out that "your neighbor-love is your bad love of yourselves. . . . You call in a witness when you want to speak well of yourselves; and when you have misled him to think well of you, you also think well of yourselves." What Nietzsche means here is that when you don't actually like yourself, or when you don't want who you are to be challenged, you seek people who will tell you that who you are right now is perfectly good and acceptable. Sartre would say that we run around trying to find just the right people — namely, those who will tell us exactly what we want to hear! When this happens, you become seduced away from living in a noble fashion by the good feeling you get from the compliments.

Embracing change means exposing yourself to new and different perspec-tives. The neighbor-seeker rests on his laurels and continues to think of his self in the same old tired ways. He hates change; thus, he hates that aspect of himself and tries to avoid it. Think of today's most popular, young, spoiled Hollywood stars. They're neighbor-lovers. They surround themselves with people who are essentially *paid* to tell them how great they are. Because of that, such people will have a hard time being noble.

People who seek neighbors fear that they're too weak to be themselves — which involves change — so they try to secure the longevity of some fixed idea of who they are. They fear, and often hate, the part of themselves that requires change.

Nobles cultivate friendships with their enemies

The noble seeks friends because they can help him on his path to becoming more powerful. A friend would ideally share the desire for attaining nobility and seeking power, but beyond that, a true friend likely will differ on the specific path of what being noble turns out to look like (which is required, because you're all individuals).

Nietzsche's character Zarathustra recognizes, at one point of the fictional story, that his disciples are looking to copy his specific way of living or his specific goal. As a friend, he must stop them from doing this because he knows that living by the goals of others stems from weakness and fear, and so isn't healthy. To help them, he prods them to leave him and find themselves as individuals. He says, "This — is now my way — where is yours? Thus did I answer those who asked me 'the way.' For *the* way — it does not exist!"

Nietzsche thinks that a great friend really acts like an enemy. As Zarathustra puts it, "In your friend, you should possess your best enemy. Your heart should feel closest to him when you oppose him." He's always looking for a weakness of yours to exploit, to expose you for your own flaws and imperfections. If you've unknowingly succumbed to some self-deception and weakness, the true friend will let you know! According to Nietzsche, the noble friend is a gift-giver; through his actions, he provides you with the ability to be great by challenging you. Given that all true friendships are reciprocal, you return the favor, of course!

Coauthor Chris likes to read about Confucianism, which holds that living life in a petty and selfish way is unacceptable. Every so often, Chris comes up with a way of interpreting something or acts a certain way in a situation, and his wife says, "Umm . . . isn't that how a petty person would see things?" This kind of realization hurts; it reveals to Chris that he's succumbed to a kind of weakness within his self that he hadn't yet seen. But this kind of comment is what makes Chris's wife an excellent noble friend. Her aim isn't to create the conditions for Chris's happiness but to create the conditions for his own nobility — to help him take charge of his self and be an individual.

What kind of people do *you* surround yourself with? Do you seek out friends who agree with most of what you believe? Do you get angry with your friends when they tell you the truth about ways that you deceive yourself? Do you *expect* them to do such things? Or do you really want to be surrounded by yes-saying neighbors?

Nobles live dangerously

In an interesting quote, Nietzsche says, "Live dangerously! Build your cities on the slopes of Vesuvius! Send your ships into uncharted seas! Live at war with your peers and yourselves!" You have to live passionately, always pushing the envelope.

No one could possibly think that Nietzsche actually means that you should literally sell your home and rebuild on the slopes of an active volcano (although the real estate on the slopes of Vesuvius may actually be pretty cheap). Neither is Nietzsche pushing you to go out and become an extreme sports enthusiast, jumping from bridges with bungee cords attached to your feet or leaping from planes and skydiving (he may not be opposed to it, either).

At the same time, though, he's saying something very similar: He wants you to engage in the existential version of those things. The bungee-jumper, the skydiver, and the Vesuvius home builder all have one thing in common: They don't view the best life as the longest life. Instead, they seem to always want to push the envelope. They view a good and excellent life as one that's always put at risk. That's the only way to truly value and honor life.

So how can you do that? How can you live on the slopes of Vesuvius? Simple: Go to the library. Read a book on a subject that completely disagrees with the way that you've chosen to live your life. Learn about your history. See whether you're the victim of self-deception. Seek to unsettle yourself; shake up what you think and believe. When you're in public, seek out the kinds of people who disagree with you passionately, and talk to them. Cultivate friendships with these kinds of people. Surround yourself with the seeds of your own destruction. Nietzsche once claimed, "I am not a man, I am dynamite!" Well, if you're dynamite, surround yourself with matches!

Nietzsche's noble is a warrior. He writes, "What matters long life! What warrior wishes to be spared!" Are you ready to be a warrior for your self-created identity and goal? Can you subject your identity to that kind of battle? Do you love yourself enough? Are you willing to die for who you are?

Being a Slave: Rejecting Individuality through Hatred

Nietzsche thinks that it's important for you to respond to the death of God (see Chapter 3) by giving your own life a unique and individual shape and meaning. This means, at least, not passively adopting external notions of what's valuable. But what about people who reject this challenge and define themselves in terms of what's external to them?

Nietzsche calls these people slaves. You can become a slave in two ways. One is through what Nietzsche calls resentment and the other through becoming absorbed into what he calls the herd. In both cases, you end up adopting life-negating values, but the way in which you adopt them is different. In this section we look at resentment, and in the next section, we look at the herd.

Turning to resentment, the subject of this section, we can say that the slave wants to be noble but finds it difficult to master his world; he can't engage with it in ways of his own choosing. This failure means that he's constantly frustrated, so he lives in pain and suffering. As a way of dealing with this situation, the slave focuses his growing hatred and anger on the noble and his way of living. Through resentment, he creates meaning for himself by negating everything that the noble stands for. Thus, although this gives the slave a negative goal to organize his life around — not being noble — the goal isn't unique and is also decadent, because it calls the slave to deny what he really desires: the pursuit of individuality and noble power.

Coping with oppression by changing your interpretation of the situation

Nietzsche thinks everyone desires, on a fundamental level, to master his own world. Everyone wants to be noble. This is a basic existential premise: Everyone strives to engage with the world on his own terms. Some people find this task almost impossible because they're oppressed in some way, perhaps by another group of people. Some people are simply too weak. As a result, part of these people's identity is forced into suppression, and as a result, they experience suffering. One way to fix the problem is to turn to self-deception.

Imagine that you live in a time when the group you're associated with is totally dominated by some other group (being a peasant in the presence of knights or being a Jew in the presence of Romans, for example). The dominant group sees and treats your group as the embodiment of what's lowly and deserving of contempt. It's no doubt true that the ancient noble isn't a particularly nice person. He pushes you around; he physically abuses you. He forces you to work 20 hours a day for a pot of gruel and a snickering promise to let you live another day. To him, you're just a tool, and you have no further function or meaning. Your life is one of perpetual violation.

The slave, however, is no different from the noble; he also wants to engage the world on his own terms. But he can't. So his life isn't just violation, but also frustration. Whereas the noble experiences himself as power and connection with the world, the slave experiences himself as weakness and disconnection.

Fortunately, you'll likely never experience the slave's circumstances, but you've probably felt like the slave in smaller situations in which you sense that you're completely out of control and ineffective in your life. When this happens, the feeling is just unbearable. On some level, you must acquire some kind of feeling of control over your life. But how can the slave do this? When you've been in these situations, how have you responded to them?

Well, you do have one thing at your disposal: You can change the way you see the situation. You can use your imagination to reinterpret the situation so that it no longer looks as though you're weak or not in control. If you can pull that off, this life isn't so bad after all! Heck, go for broke. Why not reinterpret it so that you come out to be strong! Nietzsche thinks that to live on, the slave learns to become clever, to cease living honestly in exchange for the ability to endure the unbearable suffering of his own existence.

Learning to see through the eyes of hate

To be noble means to experience yourself as the embodiment of power. To be a slave is to experience yourself as weakness. These different viewpoints obviously lead to different perspectives of the self and those around you.

A noble's love

The consciousness of the noble is filled with self-affirmation and self-love. On the other hand, the slave's consciousness is filled with hatred and self-loathing. This difference results in very different ways of evaluating the world.

The noble interprets and interacts with the world as he chooses. He's a self-creator, and he loves himself and his life. He enjoys navel-gazing, looking at himself and getting caught up in his infatuation with his own nature and life. You can imagine that nobles get together and have lots of parties celebrating their lives. Thus, it's not surprising that when the noble decides what's good and what isn't, he starts with what he's always looking at — himself — and he deems it to be good.

After doing this, he does remember that other things aren't noble. He then labels them accordingly; they're the bad, which just means "not like me." The noble's way of evaluating the world starts with the value he assigns to himself; then he understands everything else in those terms. Nietzsche calls this way of looking at the world *master morality*. It epitomizes in structure what it means to take up the existential challenge of creating meaning for yourself.

A slave's hate

The slave's life, on the other hand, is filled with frustration and pain and suffering. When he looks at himself and navel-gazes, he feels nothing but his own impotence and weakness. As a result, it's not surprising that the slave doesn't want to do a whole lot of navel-gazing. If anything, the slave needs a way to keep his attention away from himself so that he isn't continually reminded of who he is. So what does the slave focus his attention on?

Well, try to place yourself in the mind of the slave. What's the mood in there? Yeah, you guessed it — lots of pervasive anger and hatred (it's hard to blame him). So toward whom should the slave direct that anger and hatred? He could focus it on himself, but that means having to be reminded of his own weakness. But he has a better option: Focus it on the noble! The slave toils away in the field, always thinking of the master and how he hates him. Ever done this? Found yourself sitting at some hated job/school/home always seething and thinking of that hated boss/professor/parent and how evil he is?

Because the slave's mindset is so different from the noble's (as summarized in Table 11-1), it's pretty evident that his way of evaluating the world is different. If you're a slave, instead of evaluating yourself affirmatively and then evaluating everything else in terms of your self-created meaning, you start by evaluating the object that's always the focus of your attention — *the other* — and because you think of that object with hate, you evaluate it negatively. So you evaluate the object of your hatred as evil and then evaluate the rest of the world in those terms. Basically, you've learned to paint the entire world in the colors of your hatred. Nietzsche calls this way of evaluating *slave morality*.

Table 11-1	Noble versus Slave Mindsets		
System of Value	*Dominant Feeling*	*First Object of Evaluation*	*Honest and Authentic?*
Slave Morality	Hatred	The Other	No
Master Morality	Love	The Self	Yes

Using hatred to creatively reinterpret the world

When you find yourself oppressed and ineffective in your life, hatred and what Nietzsche calls *resentment* can come in handy. What's particularly impressive is that you can use your hatred at these times to reinterpret your world in a way that makes your own oppression seem like something that's actually valuable. Now, that's a feat!

How can you use hatred to reinterpret life and make it more bearable? An example may help. When coauthor Chris was young, he was very poor. Just as the slave actually wants to be like the noble and to master the world as he does, Chris wanted to be like the rich. They seemed to live life; they seemed fully effective in their own world. But being young, Chris had no way to be rich any time soon. So Chris knew his suffering and feelings of impotence were likely to continue for a long time. He wanted to feel effective and in control, but he couldn't. Like the slave, he was trapped.

But Chris, like the slave, was clever. He learned to reinterpret the situation. He began to mix his envy of the rich with an ever-present hatred of them (based on a jealousy about what he didn't have and couldn't attain), and the two combined to form resentment. Like the slave, he began to reevaluate the world through his hatred — in this case, his hatred of the rich. First, he decided that the rich were evil. The rich were inauthentic and stupid, out of touch with reality, and deluded in their splendor. Of course, he noted, no one in his right mind would want to be rich! Power, wealth, and opulence — they were all signs of what was wrong with the world.

Of course, this isn't the end of the evaluation of the world, because it hasn't yet produced its goal: making Chris feel effective and in control. In fact, this is the point at which his hatred (or resentment) gets really creative — and sneaky. Remember, what wasn't rich was good. So what was Chris? What a surprise — Chris, being poor, was good! Ah — suddenly his suffering became more bearable! By a brilliant turn of self-deception, Chris convinced himself that being poor was really, as the slang phrase would put it, keeping it real, an obvious sign of truth and authenticity. Poor people understood the real truth of things and weren't deluded. They were actual, real, truthful people. Alas, he figured, seeing the truth about things means enduring suffering. "Ah, well," Chris said to himself, "that's the cross I'll have to bear!"

What a brilliant move! Now, at long last, Chris's suffering, which was once seen as nothing but weakness and impotence, could be given a new meaning — one that had a positive connotation. Essentially, the more he suffered, the more authentic he was; suffering and lack of power were now signs of his own greatness! What a twisted artist Chris had become — how creative! Have you ever done *that* before? How much of your own values, when you're honest, are driven by resentment?

Letting resentment take control of your life

Nietzsche thinks when you're weak, you sometimes turn to creative deceptions to rationalize your life. Realizing that you really want something but are too weak to acquire it, you convince yourself that you really never wanted it in the first place or even that you worked hard to reject it. Afterward, you build your life around those deceptions and use them to give meaning to your life and the situations you live in. Still, as much as the slave is organizing his life around a goal, it's not an individual noble goal because it cedes control to something outside itself. So it fails the existential challenge to self-create as a unique meaning.

As we mentioned before, when coauthor Chris was young, he rationalized his own poverty and his suffering as something good by seeing the rich — or the drive to be rich — as evil. People use this deception all the time. The hopeful soon-to-be cheerleader gets rejected by the squad and then surprisingly discovers that cheerleaders are really superficial and that her rejection by them actually proves that she has depth. How many times have you done this in your life? We don't know about you, but we know that *we've* lost count.

Is this way of giving your life meaning individual and unique to you? It isn't. In this case, you allow some system of value external to you to decide what is and isn't meaningful. How so? In Chris's case, perhaps not surprisingly, he didn't major in business when he was in college. Why not? Well, maybe he'd already convinced himself that only the inauthentic are driven to pursue riches. So he majored in philosophy, in which you can't expect to ever make much money.

If you think about this "without prejudice," as Nietzsche would say, it looks as though Chris wasn't noble at all. Perhaps he didn't forge a courageous path of self-definition. Instead, he let his resentment against the rich structure the very ways in which he understood his own life. As a result, the value system of the rich controlled him, just flipped upside down! In a way, Chris's actual envy of the rich continued, but negatively. His self-deception allowed him to continue to mirror them, but in opposition. His entire way of looking at the world and interacting with it is still defined by the values of the rich. Chris deceived himself into thinking that he freed himself of the object of his hate, when really all he did was chain himself to it more securely.

What this story reveals is that it can't be the case that only those who *match* the behavior of some external source are conformists. Those who live their lives trying to be the *opposite* of that external source are conformists too. Think of pop culture. For some people, you can predict with uncanny assurance what their favorite music will be. Just look at the top-ten charts. Some people love what the music industry — and their peers — tell them to love.

But don't you also know some people who are the opposite? You can predict that whatever music is in the top ten, they'll hate it. Whatever clothes are chic, they'll wear the exact opposite. Whatever movies are in, they'll avoid. Aren't they just *negative* conformists? Appearances to the contrary, their lives aren't individual reflections of their own uniqueness. They're just as entirely defined by the values of what's outside them as the normal conformists are, just in reverse.

Clearly, if you become a slave, you don't live up to the challenges of existentialism, because you farm out the job of creating meaning or defining yourself to something external to you.

Interpreting Christianity as just more slave talk

One of Nietzsche's most infamous claims is that Christianity is slave-oriented. Christianity takes the idea that noble qualities like power, strength, pride, and self-love are evil and the idea that slave qualities like humility and weakness are good, and it gives those judgments a timeless, objective foundation in religion.

Religion's timeless truths

A central existentialist point is that values always reflect a context. So whether something is good or bad depends on the situation and the point of view or perspective you have when facing that situation. As a result, nothing is good or bad in itself. To argue that something is good in itself is to claim that value can exist in the world independently of people or of some point of view or of some specific context.

Slave morality has to deny that all values are contextual, so it must reject the basic tenets of existentialism. If the slave system is just one perspective among others, it isn't particularly persuasive to the slave as a self-deception — and the slave needs to believe it to justify his own situation. It isn't very convincing to the noble either — and the best interests of the slave include convincing the noble of slave values, of course. One way to accomplish both is to think of the values of slave morality as timeless truths grounded in the authority of God. If that's right, the timeless truths of the slaves are better than those truths that are dependent upon perspective — those of the noble. Slave values are objective and unbiased, whereas noble values are neither.

Christianity's slave morality

So religion is a good vehicle for slave morality, but how does Christianity fit in? According to Nietzsche, Christianity is the perfect embodiment of slave values because it justifies the slave's situation and behavior by suggesting that the slave acts and lives the way he does *not* because he's weak, but because this is the way God commands him to be. Sure, the slave would love to strike at the noble, to take revenge on him for his abusive treatment. In reality, Nietzsche says, the slave is too weak to do so. Christianity reinterprets the situation, however, and says that it takes strength of will to be able to "turn the other cheek" and to "love one's enemies." It's not that failing to strike back is a sign of weakness. Doing what God commands you to do is hard. So turning the other cheek isn't a sign of weakness — it's a sign of real power to do as God commands. Turning the other cheek is actually a sign of power and goodness!

Of course, Nietzsche notes, the slave's life *is* full of suffering. No matter how you reinterpret that, it still hurts; pain is pain, after all. So when does the slave get to be happy and free of pain? Well, says Christianity, your reward will come in heaven! As it (not surprisingly!) turns out, only those who live slavelike lives get eternal bliss. Only the meek shall inherit the earth, and it's harder for a rich man to enter heaven than it is for a camel to pass through the eye of a needle. In heaven, the slave will receive a lot of happiness — if he can just manage to stay a slave (as though he has a choice!).

Don't forget — the slave hates the noble. This fact is easily given a place; the slave's religion reassures him that hell and the final judgment will deal with the nobles *later on.* Sure, those nobles may be having a grand old time oppressing you now, but it'll work out in the end when they live on the lake of fire and have pitchforks jammed in their eyes for all eternity. As Nietzsche sees it, Christianity is a grand lie — a deception meant to serve the weak and allow them to justify their wretched, weak, and untruthful lives.

Nietzsche thinks that we're the descendants of the slaves — that our consciousness is permeated with slave values or what he considers to be the same thing, Christian values. This is why the death of God is such a historical event. History has provided us — with the growing sense of disbelief in the Christian God — the ability to free ourselves from these slavish lies and to once again take on the great task of becoming an individual, noble self. Ah, Nietzsche suggests, we can actually sense the possibility of being human once again, right there, just over the horizon!

We should note quickly that although Nietzsche's view of Christianity as a religion is pretty negative, he appeared to have respect for Jesus. In one work, he referred to Jesus as "the *last* Christian," implying that his followers go on to distort his message. From Nietzsche's perspective, Jesus had some noble qualities. He created his own values, and he stood alone against the crowd. However, the values he created were *decadent,* as they seem to call for the rejection of the sort of noble living that Nietzsche thinks is essential to authentic life.

Mediocrity of the Herd: Rejecting Individuality through Conformity

According to the existentialist, being an individual means creating a meaning for your own life that reflects your own uniqueness without the need to borrow or rely on external values. In the previous section, we discuss how a person can cede control of his life — and become a slave — by creating values through hatred.

In this section, we talk about another way to lose control and fail to be an individual: giving in to conformity through joining what Nietzsche calls the herd. Nietzsche believes that the *herd,* his term for the crowd or the masses, fears the emergence of the unique individual.

In response, the herd pressures people to cultivate a love for mediocrity and passivity. The herd does this by discouraging people from cultivating a sense of their own difference and uniqueness, instead urging them to develop only those traits that they share with everyone else.

The crowd takes away self-control

Everyone has succumbed to the pressures of parents or friends. They want you to do something their way, and you wind up doing it because they see it as right. When this happens, you allow external values to determine your direction and to take control of your life.

Sometimes you give up control not to a friend or to a parent, but to the crowd. Think of what your parents have probably said (or used to say) to you numerous times. They say, "Don't do that; what will *they* think?" or "Is that what *people* do?" Who exactly are they talking about? Who are "they," and who are "people"? They clearly don't mean particular people, but the voice of common opinion or of society in general.

If you cede control of your life to the masses by letting their values determine your life, you give up on being an individual (we also discuss Heidegger's view of this problem in Chapter 6 and Kierkegaard's view in Chapter 7). What's individual is necessarily in conflict with the motivation to simply conform to what's group-oriented. This doesn't mean that the individual and the group always do different things, but it does mean that the way in which they come to decide what to do is different.

The uneasy notion of hell

Many people, including some Christians, find themselves unsettled by the notion of hell, of a place for the eternal torment of those punished by God. Some seem to think that the idea of hell is inconsistent with the notion of a benevolent, loving God. For Nietzsche, of course, this is no accident; the point of heaven and hell is to provide a place for the slaves to get their rewards and the nobles to get their final punishments.

Are you bothered by this notion too? Does it seem strange to torment beings for eternity? As Nietzsche sarcastically comments, Christianity isn't a religion of love; it's a religion of hate. In fact, Nietzsche comments sarcastically on the writings of the 13th-century Italian poet Dante who, in describing the gates of hell, suggested that it has etched into them the sentence "I too was created by eternal love." Nietzsche suggests that it should have been rewritten to say "I too was created by eternal *hate*." Is Nietzsche right? Does the notion of hell make you wonder whether the person who created it, or the notion of it, was consumed by hatred?

To use an example, imagine that you want to group many objects in a way that's meaningful. You start with two red triangular objects made of wood. At this point, three properties give meaning to the group: red, triangular, and wooden. Then you add a third object; it's red and triangular, but made of steel. To add it, you can't use wooden as part of the group's identity anymore; now only red and triangular will do. Then comes another object, but it's blue. Now only triangular will do! Each time the group gets bigger, the identity of the group becomes more abstract and less and less individual.

The logic of crowd identity works similarly. The larger the whole grows, the more abstract the identity of the group becomes. When Mom asks, "Is that what *they* do?" it's this faceless, abstract identity that she's asking you to conform to. Maybe it's that "New Yorkers" think this, or "Christians" say that, or that "Americans" think this or do that.

Individuals make decisions based on what reflects the interests of the individual. What defines a person as individual is what that person, out of inner strength, decides is meaningful. As a result, if the interests of the whole become the values that constitute your own meaning, you start to interpret and interact with the world in a way that doesn't flow from who you are as an individual. Conformity requires that what makes you individual be left out of the equation so that you don't let it influence your point of view or your perspective. If that happens, you don't control yourself. You're a robot performing the interests of the faceless crowd.

The crowd represents the voice of the weak

Crowds or herds often come together and unify on the basis of some perceived threat. At times those threats are external, and at other times they're internal. In both situations, the group pressures people to develop and cultivate traits that answer to a need that the group has. The second kind of group uniting — on the basis of internal threats — is particularly harmful to the existence of the noble individual. The reason is that in such a case, the group pressures people to acquire what Nietzsche calls decadent values. In other words, these groups ask members to cultivate ideals of weakness over ideals of strength.

At times a group forms to meet a threat posed to it by an attack from another group external to it. In these situations, the group encourages its members to develop qualities that favor greatness and strength. Particularly, the group favors the cultivation of strong, warrior traits in its members — a love for exploitation, violence, suppression, and cruelty. If society can produce enough of these individuals, it can use them effectively to fight against the threat it has encountered.

If the group is successful, peace becomes prominent. At this point, the group is placed in an odd position. From the point of view of the group — what's common among its members — the presence of the strong, those who were originally beneficial to the group, is now seen as an internal threat. These members are a threat because what's different and unique tends to resist being identified with the group. As a result, the existence of individuals is a threat to the group's survival. Basically, the fate the group once feared from the external enemy, it now fears from the individuals in its own midst.

How should this new threat be faced? The group can't face this threat in the same way it faced the original threat. Instead, to succeed in keeping the group cohesive, it needs to change how it influences the development of traits in those within it. As a consequence, it will now teach its members that the capacity for violence or suppression is shameful — those same qualities that are required for nobility — whereas virtues such as kindness and humility will be seen as strengths.

Making the emerging new people within the group toothless has a function: it removes the possibility that they'll be a threat to the interests of the weak within the group. Herd values always flow from fear of what's noble and great. As a result, herd values must be resisted by the individual.

The crowd preaches equality and mediocrity

Nietzsche thinks that the crowd promotes the interests of the weak in part by preaching mediocrity. Because your nature calls on you to strive to be different, superior, and unique, the way of engaging with life cultivated by the crowd and the individual are natural enemies.

How does the herd or crowd convince its members to identify with the interests of the weak? One of the fundamental claims of herd morality is the claim that everyone is naturally equal or that everyone has equal rights. If so, no one has more worth than anyone else. To experience the world as the noble does is wrong because this view rejects natural equality. After all, the noble sees himself as a height and looks *down* at others who don't measure up. Those people who feel this way, the herd claims, are arrogant, shameful, and elitist. The herd strongly encourages this view in its members.

 We realize that you may like equality; it seems like a good idea to rear people with. But think about it for a second. Where does this way of thinking lead? If all people are always equal, regardless of how they live, you have no reasons to ever look up or down upon another being. But if that's right, your worth is always the same regardless of how you live. As a result, you have no reason to try to strive to be great. Action means nothing! In fact, striving to be great inevitably brings suffering and pain because it's challenging. But if being great isn't really admirable, what's the point of the suffering it brings? This view has chilling effects, Nietzsche thinks, on the ways you think of yourself and on the ways you think about the task of living life because it suppresses and condemns the effort to be an authentic person — a noble.

In opposition to the noble's ideal of the exemplary, unique, self-creating individual, the herd puts up a counterideal: the mediocre person. Whereas the noble claims that striving and suffering are natural parts of life because they follow when you pursue excellence, the herd says that no one should strive, because no one can really be better than anyone else. All striving is useless and brings meaningless pain, so instead, you should aim to be average. You should work at not distinguishing yourself and be just like others. Instead of working to distinguish themselves by creating their own meaning, the herd gives its members a different job: keeping sedated and busy through the pursuit of superficial pleasures. Thus, the herd preaches hedonism.

Nietzsche worries that one day, the age of what he calls "the last man" will arrive. This is the age in which everyone embraces herd thought, and the very possibility of the great, self-creating individual disappears. In the society of the last man, Nietzsche says, there are "no herdsman and one herd. Everyone wants the same thing, everyone is the same: whoever thinks otherwise goes voluntarily into the madhouse." In the culture of the mediocre, everyone claims that the goal of his life is to avoid pain and to be happy.

The age of consumerism

Some people suggest that society has been overrun by the desire for constant distraction. (We examine Kierkegaard's description of this state of affairs in Chapter 10.) People don't seek greatness anymore. If anything, their desire to be better than others is limited to making more money and gaining more possessions, not by the achievement of individual greatness.

To be great is to own a Lexus when your neighbor has a Mazda. It's to have a 5,000-square-foot house when your neighbor's is only 3,500 square feet. It's to vacation often in Acapulco so that you can show the pictures to your neighbor, who can't afford to travel. It's to make sure that you can get plastic surgery so that you look better than your friends. To strive for this kind of consumer greatness, people work harder to buy more things, and the more they buy, the more they need to work. They want to keep up with the Joneses and assure themselves that their neighbor's things don't outshine their own things.

Have you given up your individual passion for human life and instead become a consumer drone?

Beyond good and evil: Breaking away from the crowd

According to Nietzsche, the aim of herd mentality is to prevent the emergence of its great enemy: the exemplary noble individual, the self-created person. After you see that herd morality (just as much as slave morality) isn't an unbiased truth, but just another perspective (and one of the weak, at that!), Nietzsche thinks you can return to seeing your *own* perspective as valuable. After you do this, you'll see that you must break from the chains of slave and herd morality and free yourself from the straitjacket of its limiting customs. Once again, you'll want to create yourself! To regain control! To be what you are — a creator of meaning!

Nietzsche says ethical codes and religion have been used as weapons against you. To be fair, although Nietzsche focuses on Christianity, many religions from Buddhism to Hinduism to Judaism could easily be just as blamed in this way. What they have in common, Nietzsche would argue, is that they keep man mediocre and passive. They keep you harmless and toothless and unable to unsettle the weak. But why should your life become organized around goals that protect the interests of the weak? What should your revolution look like? Should you help members of the herd free themselves and become great too? Nietzsche has no desire to free the weak from their own systems of thought. For all he cares — and for all he thinks you should care — you should let them stay bound up tight in their straitjackets of morality. As he puts it, "Let the ideas of the herd rule in the herd."

You're different. As a potential exemplary individual, you're not obligated to live by those rules. You must learn the need to brave the cold, outside the comforts — and distractions — of the mediocre, hedonistic lives that society lauds. You must learn to leave the herd and take on the task of being a self, of becoming the exemplary noble individual you can be.

From Nietzsche's point of view. herd mentality has seeped into your consciousness and made you sick. Nietzsche's character Zarathustra, and Sartre himself, often talk about their *nausea*. How do you respond to it? You must begin the work of healing yourself. This means that you learn to live beyond good and evil — to see that what you are transcends the values of the herd. God is dead, and you should let the idea of external value — whether in him or in the herd — die. But as Nietzsche says, leaving God and external value behind doesn't mean that you'll learn to live beyond good and bad, which was the noble way of understanding value. You must once again regain the right to be noble, to experience yourself as the creator of what's good, and to see others who don't measure up as bad and pitiful. So moving beyond good and evil isn't a call for you to start going around saying, "Well, who's to say?" every time a question of value comes up. Instead, you'll recognize that *you* are to say!

It's high time, Nietzsche thinks, that you return to the hard work of being what you are, of meeting the challenge of creating meaning in a meaningless world.

Part IV
The Enduring Impact of Existentialism

The 5th Wave   By Rich Tennant

"You know, Socrates said, 'The unexamined life is not worth living,' however, in your case, Edwin, it might be a blessing."

In this part . . .

Existentialism had its heyday in the early- to mid-20th century. Although it's still alive and well today, to some extent it has returned to its rebellious, outsider roots. Mainstream English-speaking philosophers tend to ignore the existentialists all together. On the European continent, postmodern philosophers look to some of the existentialists as forerunners of their work, but largely reject what's most specifically existential. Still, existentialism has found new life in those philosophies that analyze and give voice to the situations of oppressed people, such as women, minorities, and the impoverished masses that make up much of the world outside of the former colonial powers. Outside of philosophy, existentialism has had a particularly strong impact upon psychology. Thinkers from the German psychoanalyst Ludwig Binswanger to TV's Dr. Phil have appropriated existential concerns and insights to further human well-being and mental health.

Chapter 12

Fear and Loathing in Existential Politics

In This Chapter

▶ Examining how your philosophy relates to your politics

▶ Addressing existentialism's relation to political evil

▶ Navigating the political environment underscoring French existentialism

▶ Seeing lessons in the political bickering between Camus and Sartre

There's no such thing as existential politics. As with most other things, existentialists don't have a unified view of politics. Further, no existentialist ever wrote a great political work like John Locke's Second Treatise of Government, which was widely read and admired by some British colonists in the New World who went on to use many of its ideas in drafting their constitution. Thomas Jefferson never had the opportunity to read Nietzsche and probably wouldn't have stuck a clause in the Constitution about the death of God if he had. Something in existential philosophy resists the very notion of politics. Yet the existentialists were real people who lived in the world, and they often couldn't help but be involved politically or at least have political opinions. For the later existentialists (particularly the French), these opinions often come out in maddeningly opaque references to politics in much of their work.

In this chapter, we give you some background and historical context to make reading or studying these philosophers a little easier. Politics has been a central source of criticism for all the existentialists. Often, but not always, this criticism has been undeserved. Basically, the criticisms leveled at the existentialists fall into three categories:

✓ **Existentialism supports Nazism:** This criticism is aimed mostly at the German philosophers Nietzsche and Heidegger.

✓ **Existentialism supports violent revolution:** This criticism is mostly a product of Sartre and de Beauvoir's left-wing politics. Even their friend and fellow existentialist Camus leveled this complaint at their version of existentialism.

✔ **Existentialism leads to quietism:** Existentialism leads to inaction, a refusal to engage in the problems of the world. This may be because it's such an individualistic philosophy, it leads to a lack of concern for other people (Sartre's philosophy was accused of this) or because it leads to resignation and acceptance of injustice in the world (Sartre accused Camus of this).

This chapter helps you understand what relationship really exists between the existential philosophies of these folks and their politics. In the process, we assess the justification for each of these criticisms.

In the opening sections, we examine how political the existentialists are as a group and whether existentialism as a philosophy lends itself to any particular politics. In the later sections, we concentrate on the politics of the individual philosophers and to what degree those politics were influenced by their existential philosophy.

Politics is a subject that's hard to separate from history. Although existentialism began in the 19th century with Nietzsche and Kierkegaard, it developed, flowered, and had its heyday in the 1930s, 1940s, and 1950s in France and Germany. For that reason, the philosophy couldn't help but become in many ways intertwined with the events of the time: the rise of Fascism, the Nazi Holocaust, and the cold war.

The horrors of the Nazis were devastating to the Europeans, and the events of the 1930s and 1940s colored their outlook for years to come. Their resulting bleak feelings became so intertwined with existential thinking (if not in reality, certainly in the popular imagination) that it has been said that existentialism isn't so much a philosophical movement as a mood. We don't agree with this assessment, but you can't dive into the politics of the existentialists without recognizing the towering importance of these events in that time and place. When we discuss these events, however, we do so to help you understand more clearly what their philosophy means as you read it today.

Are Existentialists Political?

The connection between existentialism and politics isn't a simple one. Pause for a moment and consider the type of philosophy existentialism is. Although it drives professional philosophers crazy, the truth is that philosophy tends to be linked in the popular imagination with the study of religion. For the more technical branches of philosophy, nothing could be farther from reality; subjects such as logic, ontology, epistemology, and a whole host of other long words that sound like they belong in a Harry Potter spellbook have little connection to anything like spirituality.

But existentialism — which can be said to have started, conceptually if not chronologically, with the death of God — has closer ties to the study of religion. It studies broad issues like meaning, purpose, and getting along in a world where these things aren't readily provided. For Christian existentialists like Kierkegaard, Marcel, and Buber, separating their faith from their philosophy is hard to do. Likewise, despite their occasional assertions to the contrary, the atheistic existentialists' philosophies are infused with the consequences of their rejection of any religious faith.

You're probably not surprised, then, to hear that the relation between existentialism and politics isn't direct or uniform. Like religion, politics seems to have a natural connection to philosophy. The sense is that the philosophy that informs your basic worldview would naturally affect how you see your relation to others and the society you live in. But as with religion, how a broad worldview gets translated into concrete action is by no means automatic or obvious. Also like religion, existentialism is a broad tent, with many different kinds of adherents under its banner. These differences can lead to wildly different expressions in the political realm and in differences in the degree to which existentialists even enter this realm. So are the existentialists political?

Some are political; some aren't

When dealing with philosophy and politics, drawing another comparison with the realm of religion is useful. Religion has priests and mystics. Priests are involved in various ways with other people, whether they're leading sacred rites, doing work for the poor, or arguing with other people about what the religion's rules should be (and then, in all likelihood, working to enforce them!). They're enmeshed in the fabric of their communities and in the business of their religious organizations.

Mystics, on the other hand, disengage from the world, go out to the desert, and try to have a direct experience of divinity. The thing to remember about mystics is that they're less interested in changing the way the world works and more interested in transforming themselves. They generally get involved with others only to communicate any wisdom they gain from this disengagement. But even then, their interest is generally to inspire other individuals to undergo their own personal transformations and see what they have seen. John the Baptist and Buddha are archetypical mystics.

Early existentialists: More mystical than political

Many of the existentialists — particularly the early founders, like Nietzsche and Kierkegaard — definitely had a strong strain of mysticism. Nietzsche didn't write most of his books while he was on appointment at a university or even when he was within the borders of his native Germany. The hero of his masterpiece, *Thus Spoke Zarathustra,* is a mystic who descends from the mountains to share the wisdom he gains in his solitude. We don't want to overstate their disengagement; both Nietzsche and Kierkegaard write to some extent within an academic and philosophical tradition and for a community that's part of that same tradition. And certainly, they want to influence that community and the wider culture with their writing.

But both take serious departures from traditional academic writing. Their works are deeply personal. Kierkegaard continually references a tragically failed love affair and criticizes mainstream philosophy for not paying sufficient attention to everyday life; Nietzsche often speaks of being misunderstood and of writing for only a few isolated individuals who may understand. Although they may have an interest in influencing other people and their culture, this influence is on a deeply personal, spiritual level. When reading these writers, you may feel that they're writing personal letters directly to you. If politics enters such writing, it's many levels removed from their immediate concern, which is how an individual faces the existential situation everyone shares.

Later existentialists: Politics comes into play

None of the existentialists is exactly mainstream (after all, the whole movement is a departure from the mainstream), but in the larger sense, many of the later writers in the movement were respected members of their university faculties or the broader academic community and were deeply involved in politics as well. These later writers weren't the thinkers who discovered existentialism on a secluded mountaintop, metaphorically speaking. Instead, thinkers like Heidegger and Sartre worked out the details of the earlier, more personal, more immediate writers and turned them into a more systematic philosophy. In doing so, they couldn't help but come face to face with broader political issues. The French existentialists in particular were extremely political. Sartre was no mystic, and his philosophy is especially obsessed with action, with *doing,* and much of this doing in his writing and his life is concerned with politics.

Does existentialism lead to specific politics?

We outline some of the philosophers' divergent politics later in this chapter, where you discover that the short answer is "no" — existentialism doesn't lead to specific politics. We address the specific allegation that it leads to Fascism in the next section. Here, we tell you why it doesn't lead to *any* specific politics. Three related characteristics about existential philosophy tend to push it away from backing any one political philosophy:

✔ Existentialism is more about form than content.

✔ Existentialism is extremely individualistic.

✔ Existentialism denies any ultimate truth that could lead necessarily to specific politics.

When your teacher asks you to write a paper, she usually has instructions for the form — "Make that ten pages, double-spaced, and be sure you have an introduction and a conclusion." — and a content — "Explain how Heidegger's concept of Dasein relates to the prevailing Zeitgeist of angst in prewar Germany as he was writing *Being and Time.*" Fortunately, the existentialists aren't that specific. They're concerned with how you understand your situation and how you do what you do. Unlike traditional religion and morality, existentialism tends to put little emphasis on the specifics of what you do or should do. Existentialists stress, for example, the importance of living with passion (see Chapter 7) and living authentically (see Chapter 5). But these concerns relate to the form, not the content, of your actions. The specifics of what a person should do are often left open to interpretation and individual choice.

The existential philosophers (like Sartre) who do venture into the political generally do so only in the most abstract and formal terms (in their philosophical writing, at least). Sartre thinks you should "maximize freedom," but that's pretty broad. Americans may tell you that democratic capitalism affords the most freedom and that the poorest man in their country is a king, because he's master of his own destiny. But a socialist may argue that the lower classes are condemned to long work hours, little rewards, and little real freedom to choose how they'll live or what they'll make of themselves. They may argue that the American "king" is a mere "wage slave" who's alienated from the products of his labor. Only a workers' revolution that achieves economic equality for all can free the workers to fulfill their full potential. The form of existentialism's conclusions leaves open a wide field of political content.

From the beginning, existentialism has been an extremely personal and individualistic philosophy. This individualistic nature affects existentialism's relationship with politics in two ways:

✔ First, as political as some of the existentialists may have been personally, the philosophy itself is naturally resistant to this move. The focus of politics is on groups and living within and among those groups. It's about what systems, rules, and ideals everyone should adopt. Strong individualists, and extremely individualistic philosophies, often resist the pull of politics toward this group concern.

A right way to act politically?

The existentialists say that there's no ultimate meaning, truth, or morality. So you probably think they have no ultimately right politics either. Strong-willed and opinionated human beings, however, can rarely avoid slipping into dogmatism, self-righteousness, and the assertion of absolute truths, even if their avowed philosophy asserts that there are none.

Read Nietzsche, and see whether you don't marvel at the dance he does, bombastically condemning this and asserting that, all while denying the existence of truth. Most of the existentialists assert the rightness of their own political philosophies (those who have them, at least) and the natural connection between those philosophies and their fundamental existential commitments.

Most often, however, existentialists argue that their individual politics are *consistent* with their existential commitments, not that they follow *necessarily* from those commitments. That is, these individuals tend to defend themselves against the charge that they're contradicting themselves — which would be dishonest, and very unexistential.

They generally don't try to assert that anyone who accepts their existential philosophy has to think this or that way politically. Generally. They are, after all, only human.

✔ More important, the individualism of existentialism finds expression in the belief that individuals do, and should, interpret and navigate the world for themselves. So presenting an argument for this or that politics is kind of antithetical to the nature of existentialism. Doing so suggests that there's one way of moving through the world, one way of interacting with others. But the existentialists don't have one ultimate truth about anything, so they can't have one final answer to political questions.

So on the whole, existentialism has an apolitical bent and doesn't lead to a specific politics. But a human being, as Aristotle noted, is a political animal. Even when the philosophy espoused by the existentialists wasn't overtly political, there were always those on the outside interested in assessing its political ramifications. The French existentialists were determined to make existentialism political from the inside because for circumstantial and personal reasons, they each had a great concern for the subject. So despite its apolitical bent, existentialism has become intertwined with two political philosophies in particular: Fascism and Communism. In the remaining sections, we assess the relationship between the existentialists' individual philosophies and their real or imagined politics.

Does Existentialism Lead to Evil?

In upcoming sections, we discuss the concrete, historical accusations leveled against some existentialists and their politics. The underlying issue may be better stated as a question: Does existentialism lead to evil? We address part of the answer to that question in the section on Nazism, but a significant piece of it also rests in the final section on Camus and Sartre, who were decidedly *not* Nazis.

By *evil,* we have in mind things pretty much everyone agrees are *very* bad things: murder, extreme cruelty, violent oppression. We specifically have in mind the way these things are justified and perpetrated on a *political* level, as they were in the regimes of both Hitler and Stalin. The accusation is that the existential philosophers and the philosophies they espoused gave support to political leaders who were evil in this way. The question of whether existential philosophy has a natural tendency to support this kind of political evil is perfectly reasonable. After all, if it does, you can understand why some people would want to hide it from the kids. More to the point, it would undermine the claim we have been at pains to advocate: that the goal of existentialism is to afford human beings a more successful and healthy means of coming to terms with and plotting a course through their lives. If existentialism leads to evil, you would be rightly suspicious that either this isn't the goal or that existentialism fails miserably.

But existentialism doesn't lead to evil any more than religion does. The latter has perhaps been more widely abused and twisted to justify atrocities than any other form of human endeavor, inquiry, or expression. The sad fact is that human beings, whatever their religious or philosophical bent, have a tendency to involve themselves in evil and to search for whatever method is most ready at hand to justify that evil. Ironically, humanity's best intentions and highest aspirations are often what lead us astray. It's true that existential philosophy (usually in misunderstood form) has been used to justify evil. It's also true that with the best of intentions, existential philosophers (particularly Sartre) have danced with the Devil in hopes that something good would come of it. But as we argue in the preceding section, existentialism as a philosophy has no particular political bent in itself. It is what people sometimes use it for, as with any human idea, that sometimes leads to misery.

Real and Imaginary Flirtations with Nazism

In 1933, a gang of violent thugs gained control of the nation of Germany and quickly started institutionalizing a mythology they had created around their charismatic leader, their race, and the nation they claimed to be saving. To serve their needs, they co-opted every facet of German history and culture that they could co-opt, and destroyed or covered up everything they couldn't co-opt. This maelstrom of mythologizing and propaganda sucked in the thought of two of existentialism's greatest thinkers: Friedrich Nietzsche and Martin Heidegger. Critics often attack or simply dismiss the thoughts of these two thinkers on the basis of their alleged connection to the most hated movement in Western civilization.

But the issue is deeper and broader than this alleged historical connection with Nazism. Existentialism is often seen as a godless philosophy that *naturally* leads to evil. For two of its greatest thinkers to be supporters of Nazism, which to many people is the embodiment of evil, would seem to support this allegation, especially if their *philosophy* supports Nazism.

Nietzsche wasn't a Nazi!

You'll forgive us for being a bit peevish on this topic, but really, give the guy a break. Adolf Hitler formed the Nazi party in 1919; Nietzsche died in 1900, after years of mental and physical illness in an asylum. Okay, maybe it isn't quite that simple. Nietzsche generally isn't charged with literally being a Nazi, but some claim that he influenced Hitler and helped inspire his movement, that his philosophy naturally leads to Nazism, and/or that he held many of the ideals of the Nazis, so he was a Nazi in spirit if not in name, and he glorified in his writings the ideals that the Nazis would later put into practice. Some even throw out terms like *proto-Fascist* or *proto-Nazi,* which just mean that he was an earlier or original version of these unsavory things. We think if he's a proto anything, it's proto-existentialist.

Nietzsche didn't influence Hitler

It has been said that Nietzsche was *the* philosopher of the Third Reich and that his philosophy underscored much of the thinking of Hitler and the Nazis. This simply isn't true. There's no evidence of any such influence or of the Nazis taking his thinking particularly seriously.

The connection between Nietzsche and Nazism was largely a creation of his sister, Elizabeth Foster-Nietzsche. Through her efforts, Nietzsche became a celebrated thinker in Nazi circles, though not necessarily an influential one. Elizabeth held extremely conservative, anti-Semitic, and nationalistic views. In keeping with these views, she married an avowed anti-Semite. Nietzsche hated him.

Unlike Nietzsche, Elizabeth lived well into the 20th century — long enough, in fact, to become a Nazi and even meet Hitler. Although she was never particularly close to her brother in life, she took full control of his estate — including all his manuscripts and perhaps more important, his public image — after his death. Among her more damaging activities were publishing many of Nietzsche's unfinished manuscripts, editing (and even rewriting) them to make them more congruent with her own political views and those of the Nazis.

But Hitler's Germany wasn't much about reading; it was about icons and images. It was about reaching back and claiming (read: co-opting) the greatness of Germany's history. By the time of the Nazis, Nietzsche had finally started to receive the recognition he had long been due, and his name was added to the list of "great Germans" to which the Nazi party claimed to be the heir. Partially due to his sister's influence and campaigning, Nietzsche achieved the dubious distinction of being accorded a special seat at this table. To cement the mythological connection between Hitler and this great thinker of Germany's past, Hitler made a trip to the Nietzsche archives (run by Elizabeth, naturally) in 1934 and posed for a famous photograph with a bust of Nietzsche. In the picture, the Fuehrer stares at the bust in deep and serious thought. Nietzsche doesn't stare back.

But just because the Nazis claimed him, or the picture that his sister presented of him, doesn't mean Nietzsche did, or would have, claimed them. (More about this in the next section.) More to the point, just because the Nazis claimed an affinity with Nietzsche for political ends doesn't mean they read, understood, or really cared about anything he actually said. There's no evidence that Nietzsche had any real influence over Hitler or even that Hitler read Nietzsche.

In short, the real connection between Hitler and Nietzsche had more to do with propaganda and political maneuvering — both Hitler's and Elizabeth's — than with ideas. Elizabeth sold the Nazis a bill of goods on her brother so that she could profit from it financially and, more important, in terms of her personal prestige.

All this iconography, posturing, and propaganda were based on the assertion of an affinity between the thinking of Hitler and the Nazis and the thinking of Nietzsche. Even if you reject the notion that Nietzsche had any real influence on the Nazis, asking whether this affinity of ideas really exists is completely fair. See the next section for details.

Nietzsche didn't share Nazi ideals

Here are three general points about Nietzsche that are relevant to the accusation that his philosophy shares or glorifies Nazi ideals:

- ✔ **Nietzsche is very easy to misinterpret:** Nietzsche's philosophy is loud, highly critical, uncensored, and often harsh-sounding. He's also intentionally opaque, impish, and playful in his writing. Often, his meaning can be very different from, even the exact opposite of, what it appears to be at first glance. To read Nietzsche out of context or in sound bites is to almost guarantee misreading. In today's society, think of a politician who constantly talks from the hip in passionate and uncensored words. This kind of person is guaranteed to be shredded by the media and her political opponents as they quote bits of her speeches out of context, magnify the significance of minor asides, and give the most sinister interpretations possible to her words. Nietzsche is like this, except that his words are never poorly chosen; rather, he seems to *court* misreading. Perhaps because he wants to be read carefully or not at all.

✔ **Nietzsche is fundamentally apolitical:** Nietzsche's writing is concerned with the personal and obsessed with the individual and individuality. He critiques societies, as he critiques everything else, but his concern with them is largely with whether they foster or hinder individuality and personal greatness. His tone when discussing social or political topics, even as he dishes tremendous criticism, is often distant and scientific. History is one of Nietzsche's areas of fascination and expertise, and he often looks at such topics from an historical or anthropological viewpoint. But it all comes back to individuals: What does what you learn about the human species from these cultural investigations tell you about what the individual is capable of?

✔ **Although Nietzsche isn't a Nazi, he's not Mother Teresa or Abe Lincoln either:** One of coauthor Greg's philosophy professors once said, "If reading Nietzsche doesn't disturb you, then you aren't reading Nietzsche." Nietzsche proclaimed himself an immoralist and an antichrist. Although these claims include a certain amount of hyperbole — and impishness — you can't expect the moral terrain to be all warm and fuzzy, or even familiar, when you're reading about Nietzsche. Prepare yourself, because here there be monsters!

There isn't one central accusation against Nietzsche concerning Nazism. The accusations don't come from one central place, and they aren't centered on one particular idea in his philosophy. Bits, pieces, and themes in his philosophy have at various times been accused of having Nazi overtones or worse. In the following pages, we review some of the accusations against Nietzsche as they relate to specific dimensions of Nazism.

Racism/anti-Semitism/nationalism

Hitler asserted that the Aryan race (basically, Germanic and Scandinavian Europeans) was superior to other races and that mixing of the races, either culturally or genetically, could only do damage to the superior group. The Germans, of course, were considered to be the finest example of the Aryan race. Hitler's racism was particularly anti-Semitic — that is, targeted at people of Jewish decent. It was the Jews who were accused of being the greatest racial threat to the Aryans. Hitler used the Jews as scapegoats and villains to unite and distract the German people with hatred and fear and to promote his version of German nationalism.

Nationalism generally indicates a concern with a national identity, usually thought of in terms of ethnic or cultural connections. In Hitler's case, this was a belief in the greatness and unity of the German people.

Accusation: Nietzsche believed that many character traits are inherited, and he regularly criticized groups of people on racial grounds. He's particularly critical of the Jews and refers to their morality as a "slave morality."

This info is all basically true, but

- ✔ **Nietzsche is an *almost* equal-opportunity offender; he skewers pretty much everyone.** We say *almost* because his favorite target is probably the Germans, whom he ridicules mercilessly, particularly for their pretensions to superiority. He would've found the Nazis' arrogant nationalism laughable and inane. Also, he believed the mixing of races was a good thing, because each race had its strengths; he wasn't an advocate of racial purity.

- ✔ **Nietzsche had mixed feelings about the Jews, which was typical of his attitude toward most things.** He had great admiration for the Jews and their society. As someone whose philosophy asserts that human beings must be creators of value, he saw Jewish society as powerful and original. As he saw it in historical terms, they were creators of a morality that was vastly influential. Most of his criticism of them was directed at the content of this morality, which he saw as being at the heart of Christianity, of which he was also very critical. Pretty much every attack he made on the Jews, then, was also a criticism of the Christians and by extension, his society at large. He had no special animosity toward the Jews, and he certainly didn't see them as inferior.

- ✔ **Nietzsche detested anti-Semites and railed against them regularly.** One of the major reasons he split from Richard Wagner, one of his early idols, was over the latter's anti-Semitism. It was only Nietzsche's sister's anti-Semitic warping of her brother's philosophy that ever gave this accusation any traction. Certainly, the source of his viscous feelings toward anti-Semites was partially aroused by his deep respect for Jewish culture. He also detested anything common, which anti-Semites, unfortunately, were during his time. In the end, however, we like to chalk this one up to simple good taste.

Fascism

Fascism generally refers to the confluence of a number of authoritarian beliefs, such as totalitarian rule, a disdain for human rights, and an obsession with military superiority and police power. These powers are usually said to be part of a hypernationalistic and often racist agenda of national unity and superiority.

Accusation: Nietzsche was an elitist who was obsessed with greatness and with the creation of the Übermensch (or superman). He believed great individuals go "beyond good and evil" to accomplish their ends. Finally, he had utter disdain for Western democracies and their notions of equality and egalitarianism.

Again, this accusation is mostly true, but

- Fascism tends to be nationalistic and racist, and Nietzsche was anything but. (See the previous section for details.)

- The Übermensch is largely misunderstood and is more of an individual and spiritual goal. (See Chapter 11 for more on this.)

- Nietzsche *was* an elitist, and he believed people should strive to be great. His picture of a noble, however, is of someone too busy *being* great, asserting positive values, and slapping herself on the back for being so wonderful to really give a lot of thought to criticizing, let alone oppressing, the inferior people around her. Nietzsche's major criticism of Judeo-Christianity is that it spends too much time decrying evil and making people feel guilt and shame. Indeed, he feels the greatest evil someone can do is to cause another shame. No noble, therefore, would ever treat the Jews, or anyone else, like the Nazis did. This is certainly another source of Nietzsche's vehement anti–anti-Semitism.

- Nietzsche wasn't a big fan of democracy or equality. He felt very strongly that the worst thing a person could be — to her own detriment, as well as everyone else's — is part of the crowd, and he believed democracy encourages this. Despite this belief, he never supported any particular alternative, and certainly not Fascism.

The cult of power and militarism

At the end of the day, the Nazis believed in one thing: power. Their understanding of power was principally the simple brutal application of thuggish force. But force wasn't just something to be used pragmatically. It was something to be reveled in and glorified, in speech, in action, and in the arts.

Accusation: Nietzsche is obsessed with power and strength and believes that all human beings are guided by a will to power.

Here, perhaps more than anywhere else, you can find ample quotes that seem to support the accusation. That's probably because there's some truth to it. Nietzsche spent much of his life in a sickly and weak state, and like it does with many in that condition, strength and power became a bit of an obsession with him. But the will to power is no more a political thesis than Darwin's survival of the fittest. (See Chapter 11 for more on the will to power.)

For Nietzsche, this obsession with power, like most of his obsessions, was ultimately turned inward. He ultimately came to glorify the spiritual strength of the individual, not the simple-minded brutality of Fascists like the Nazis. Ultimate power is discovered and exercised in self-overcoming, not the abuse of others.

Romanticism

The story Hitler told about racial superiority and nationalism included romanticism about nature and about the German people. He said that what's natural is good, and that the Germans, particularly the German farmers, were the most natural of peoples. Although Hitler utilized technology, particularly military technology, to brilliant and terrible effect, he constantly admonished people to be on guard against moving too far from their rural roots. He glorified *natural* man and derided the Jews as not only an inferior but also an *unnatural* people.

Accusation: Nietzsche, like the Nazis, glorified nature and insisted that human beings should accept their basest nature rather than accept the limits imposed by a civilized society. This leads to a barbarous politics.

Although romanticism is hardly the greatest of the Nazi crimes, it's not one Nietzsche is really guilty of at all. As an existentialist, Nietzsche believed you must accept what is and create value out of what you have instead of assigning it to some heavenly other world (see Chapter 3 for more on this idea). No existentialist believes nature is inherently good, because no existentialist believes nature is *inherently* anything. Nature is simply what *is;* it's the situation you live in. Because the existentialists believe your project is to create value, they believe your project is to create value in the natural world — because that's all there is. Nietzsche doesn't glorify nature. He simply refuses to start where so many other religions and philosophies start — with the rejection of the natural.

This acceptance of nature would lead inevitably to a barbarous politics if barbarism is all that humans, as natural creatures, were capable of. If people are nothing but voracious, wanton, little id monsters, hungry to loose their darkest desires on the world, something like Nazism is probably going to be the result. But if that's true, if that's what people are, *no* philosophy can lead to anything but barbarism! But Nietzsche doesn't just embrace the darkest passions; he embraces everything natural within you, including your will, your self-control, and your highest aspirations. The French, who were far more political than Nietzsche, later approached the problem of political terror with a humanistic attitude firmly grounded in Nietzsche: All problems are human problems, and any solution possible must be a human solution.

Return to the past

Like many demagogues, Hitler won over supporters by touting a return to a mythical, glorious past. He made much of the greatness of Germany throughout history and strove to connect himself and his movement at every opportunity to great figures of Germany's past.

Accusation: Much like the Nazis, Nietzsche glorified Greek culture and advocated a return to the Greek way of thinking. Such backward-looking thinking leads to ultraconservative politics, fearful of the present and the future.

All existentialists thought something had gone awry in philosophy and that it had lost touch with real life and real living. Nietzsche especially found great wisdom and nobility when looking back at the Greeks. But as with everything else, his feelings were mixed. Nietzsche's project was really to mine everything for the good that could be found in it. It was never to walk in lockstep with any set of ideas — past, present, or future. This individuality of spirit is actually what makes Nietzsche and the later existentialists particularly resistant to the "charms" of Fascism and Totalitarianism.

Murder, cruelty, and horror

Murder, cruelty, and horror are the real legacy of Hitler's regime, its true meaning, and the real taint that hangs over those associated in any way with his reign. If existentialism is guilty of supporting these things, it's null and void as a philosophy to all civilized people.

Accusation: An immoralist, someone guilty of the excesses described earlier, such as his elitism and his obsession with power, is capable of supporting anything, including the horrors of the Holocaust.

Claiming that an immoralist *could* support such things may include a certain truth, but it simply isn't true that Nietzsche *did.* Furthermore, based upon all the points we make throughout this section and the personal, positive nature of his philosophy, we assert that he *would not.* Nietzsche simply isn't guilty of the excesses he's accused of. At least, he's not guilty in the simple-minded way his accusers generally consider him to be. This is significant, because it's often stated that such untenable attitudes are the natural result of an existentialist viewpoint. The fact that even Nietzsche, the immoralist, and the other existentialists resoundingly reject such ideals suggests that you must look elsewhere for the source and justification of the Nazi horrors. It also suggests that no necessary connection links existentialism to the acceptance of repugnant behaviors and belief systems like Nazism.

Accepting existentialism doesn't necessarily mean someone *will* accept horrid moral systems or behaviors like Nazism. Unfortunately, accepting existentialism doesn't necessarily mean someone *won't* accept a horrid moral system like Nazism.

The Heidegger problem: A Nazi in the family

In a way, Heidegger and Nietzsche present opposite cases. Nietzsche, especially in small doses, sounds like he *could* be a Nazi. He shares Hitler's love of colorful rhetoric, and he often rails violently at his enemies. But he was the farthest thing from a Nazi (see the earlier section "Nietzsche wasn't a Nazi!" for a fuller discussion of Nietzsche's "Nazism"). Reading Martin Heidegger (1889–1976) is more like reading a Chinese dictionary in German. His intellect is dizzying, his philosophy dense and highly abstract, and the connection between that philosophy and everyday life unclear. Yet Heidegger was, in the most literal sense, an active member of the Nazi party during Hitler's Germany.

This membership has posed a problem for people who study Heidegger. Should they dismiss this great thinker and his philosophy? Should they view that philosophy as tainted and noxious?

Partially because Heidegger's philosophy is so dense, the exact significance or meaning that his Nazism has on his philosophy has never been clear. Also, philosophers and academics are always huge fans of anything so immensely complex that no one seems to fully comprehend what it means. They're kind of like Bob Dylan fans.

Heidegger has always had a huge contingent of followers and defenders who are quick to say, "Yeah, but he wasn't *really* a Nazi" or "Yeah, but it doesn't show up in his work."

The Heidegger problem actually breaks down into two sets of questions:

- What was the extent of Heidegger's involvement in the Nazi party? How much of its philosophy did he agree with? Did his views on Nazism ever change? How *much* of a Nazi was he?

- How did Nazism relate to Heidegger's existential philosophy? Did Nazism influence his thought? Does his philosophy naturally lead to Nazism?

The first set of questions seeks to determine to what extent Heidegger is guilty of anything and the second to determine to what extent the man can be distinguished from his philosophy.

Not a Nazi in name only

Heidegger was a Nazi in a fairly robust sense. He never committed any atrocities, and he wasn't a concentration-camp guard, but his involvement in the party wasn't trivial either. For years, that involvement was philosophy's dirty little secret, generally swept under the rug. As he and his supporters told the tale, Nazism was a youthful mistake, something Heidegger was never that involved in. He was also often excused by virtue of the fact that he lived in a one-party state where everyone who wanted to advance joined the party. Really, the story went, he wasn't guilty of much more than living in Germany in the 1930s and 1940s.

But Heidegger wasn't just some clerk. On May 27, 1933, he was inaugurated as the rector, or leader, of Freiburg University. This was four months after Hitler came to power and 26 days after Heidegger joined the Nazi party. He wasn't a high-level party insider, but he was viewed as loyal, right-thinking, and acceptable. His appointment was part of the reshuffling the Nazis did to put people they could count on in positions of power.

And Heidegger turned out to be perfectly adequate in that capacity. Starting with his speech at the inauguration, he established a pattern of rhetorically supporting the regime and its legitimacy. At the inauguration, he gave a stirring and impassioned speech about the spiritual decay he saw in his country and in the world, and the need for leaders — like himself and the Fuehrer — to lead first the nation and then the world out of this decline. By all accounts, Heidegger believed what he was saying and believed that the university, as well as the nation, needed strong leadership.

Heidegger would provide that leadership in the way political appointees generally do, by enforcing the policies and mandates of their patrons. Although he seemed to take pains to protect the positions and privileges of some of his professors — including some Jewish professors — he generally acted as a Nazi tool to gradually weed out Jewish influence and the influence of "bad politics." In this regard, he acted as both a bureaucratic enforcer of Nazi policy and as a stool pigeon, reporting on the political associations of others.

Not an advocate of bloodshed

The best that can be said of Heidegger's involvement in the Nazi party is that it ends here. In fact, Heidegger resigned his post in the summer of 1934, after what's often called the "Night of the Long Knives," when the Nazis killed hundreds of Hitler's political enemies in one night. (Think of the end of *The Godfather* on a massive scale.)

Evidently Heidegger could stand for dictatorship, exclusion, and the ruining of reputations and careers, but not bloodshed. We say *evidently* because Heidegger almost never spoke of these matters, which makes their significance even harder to assess.

In a 1966 interview, he spoke briefly about that time, but he never mentioned the Holocaust or gave any indication that he regretted or withdrew his support of the Nazi party. Heidegger was ever the obscure academic, and the only criticism he leveled at the Nazis was abstract and philosophical. (The interview is discussed further in the following section.)

Loose connections between his philosophy and Nazism

No argument has ever clearly made the case that Heidegger's existential philosophy was influenced by, or led him to, his Nazi sympathies. Of course, with a philosophy as dense and abstract as Heidegger's, making that case is hard for two principal reasons:

> ✔ The more dense a philosophy is, the more interpretations it is subject to. One of those interpretations may lead to Nazism, but which one? And is it the right one? Just because you know Heidegger joined the party doesn't mean you know exactly *why* he did it or what philosophical justification he may or may not have seen in his own philosophy.

> ✔ The more abstract the philosophy is, the farther removed it is from everyday life, and the harder it is to say what consequences that philosophy has in the real world.

The only certain connection was revealed by Heidegger himself in an interview with the magazine *Der Spiegel* in 1966. There, he states:

> . . . I see the task in thought to consist in general, within the limits allotted to thought, to achieve an adequate relationship to the essence of technology. National Socialism, to be sure, moved in this direction. But those people were far too limited in their thinking to acquire an explicit relationship to what is really happening today and has been underway for three centuries.

Heidegger believes technology alienates human beings from their *being,* from what they most essentially are. Perhaps, then, Nazism's romanticism and the promise of a return to the past (both covered in the preceding section on Nietzsche) were what appealed to him. Certainly, the Nazis mastered technology while extolling the virtues of a simpler life, and Heidegger may have seen in them some way of mastering a relationship with technology that doesn't alienate people.

The point is, though, that Heidegger sees the Nazi movement from a bird's-eye, ivory-tower view. His biggest concern is not the Holocaust, but the philosophy of technology. At a human level, this is damning to Heidegger. But when you look at him as a philosopher, this info suggests two points:

> ✔ He took the most abstract portions of Nazi philosophy and ideals concerning how people would live in the new order very seriously — perhaps even more seriously than the Nazis took it themselves.

> ✔ Whatever connections there may be between Nazism and Heidegger's philosophy, they occur at an extremely abstract level. The level is so abstract that the connection between his philosophy and the day-to-day atrocities of the Nazis is tenuous at best.

These points don't defend Heidegger or his philosophy, but they do suggest that if his philosophy and Nazism have an insidious relationship, it is by no means clear and direct or one-to-one. In the end, critics generally agree upon the extent of Heidegger's involvement in the Nazi party, but they still hotly contest the final significance of that involvement for his philosophy. Now that you have some necessary context, we let you decide the taint it leaves on the man and on his brand of existentialism.

Viva la Revolution! The French Left

Of all the existentialists, the French were by far the most outspokenly political. If you were living in Paris in the 1930s and 1940s, it would've been hard not to be. Politics for the French wasn't merely something you got involved in; it was something of a blood sport. The leading existential thinkers — Jean-Paul Sartre, Simone de Beauvoir, Maurice Merleau-Ponty, and Albert Camus — were all involved in one way or another with the largely Leftist political scene of French intellectuals.

In this section, we focus on Sartre and Camus. Merleau-Ponty was an important figure at the time but is somewhat less influential to American thought. The best way to understand the politics of Sartre and Camus is first to review their place in the cultural and political world in Paris. Then we discuss the largely political feud that erupted between them and how it relates to both their divergent politics and philosophies.

The French political scene

Existentialism came of age in Paris in a cultural and political environment that most people can't quite imagine. The major French thinkers in the movement lived at a time and in a place where being a famous philosopher, novelist, or political thinker was like being a movie star or a rock star. Try to imagine if instead of covering Lindsay Lohan and Paris Hilton, *People* magazine covered people like John Irving, Toni Morrison, Henry Kissinger, and the authors of that important new philosophical work *Existentialism For Dummies.* Now imagine that instead of being judged on their weight or fashion sense, these celebrities were judged repeatedly, publicly, and ruthlessly (often by one another!) on things like originality of thought, use of irony, and their politics. Finally, imagine these big, deep, serious thinkers having skins as thin and egos as big as any Hollywood movie star. Britney and K-Fed have nothing on the battles these people could wage on one another.

Paris back in the day had something else in common with Hollywood: It was a relatively small space where all the big names regularly ran into one another, whether in person or in the major journals, magazines, and newspapers they all read, edited, or published articles in. The major French existentialists all knew one another. The superstars, in fact, were quite close. Simone de Beauvoir and Jean-Paul Sartre were lifelong companions, though in keeping with their beliefs about freedom, they never married or made any exclusive commitment to each other. Sartre, de Beauvoir, and Maurice Merleau-Ponty edited a political journal, *Les Temps Modernes* (literally, *Modern Times*), together for many years. Sartre and Albert Camus were close friends for years, having similar interests in philosophy, literature, the theater, and politics. Indeed, even before they met, they had read and written reviews of each other's work.

In fact, Sartre first became seriously interested in politics because of Camus. Sartre had always been vaguely Leftish in the way academics of his time were almost expected to be, but he wasn't seriously committed or involved. This is somewhat ironic and tragic, because Sartre would later accuse his friend Camus of, among other things, not being political enough.

As with today's American society, the Left in existential Paris wasn't completely unified. Certain issues, however, dominated everyone's thinking. These issues are referenced repeatedly in the writings of the existentialists at the time — usually in a way that assumes you know the context. Now you will!

- ✔ **Nazism and the French occupation:** The disturbing thing about both of these things, besides the obvious horrors they had inflicted, was that ordinary people had to one degree or another *accepted* them. The Germans elected the Nazis to power, and French collaborators aided and abetted the German occupation of France from 1940 to 1944. Some had certainly collaborated at gunpoint (which garnered little sympathy), but many had seemingly done so out of a desire for political or economic gain (which garnered even less sympathy). The middle class (or bourgeoisie, as the writings and translations of the French existentialists almost always refer to it) in particular was accused of rolling over very quickly, whether from a lack of backbone or more insidious motives. In either case, people on the Left widely believed that the middle class had abdicated any claim to leadership in the society because of these actions. Living through such times made it exceedingly clear to the existentialists that political choices have real and often severe consequences. This made political involvement seem all the more essential and immediate in its relevance to everyday life.

- ✔ **Support of the working class:** The (alleged) involvement of the middle class in the French occupation discredited its people and led to a fairly vibrant and radical Left that almost universally supported the interests and liberation of the working class instead. This support was also due in part to the immense impact at the time of Marxist philosophy on the intellectual community.

- ✔ **Marxism:** Today, Karl Marx is known mostly as the inspiration for a series of revolutions that led to brutal dictatorships all over the world. But Marx was also a philosopher who analyzed the effects of capitalism on human beings and has great influence on thinkers of all kinds to this day. Marx argued persuasively that the exploitation and oppression of the working class severely limit and threaten human freedom for *all* people. For the existentialists, particularly for the French and most particularly for Sartre, freedom is a critically important dimension of human life. So if Marx is correct, any philosophy concerned with human freedom, like Sartre's, must be highly suspicious of Capitalism and must support Communism. (For more on Sartre and freedom, see Chapter 8.)

✔ **The cold war:** The recognition of the cold war to come starts in French writing even before Hitler's defeat is finalized. For the Left, the United States is often seen as imperialistic, opportunistic, and threatening to French independence (which had already received a blow in the occupation). Stalin and the Russian Communists were a tough issue; they claimed to be Marxists and to support the workers (and human freedom), but Stalin gives Hitler a run for his money in the ol' "epitome of evil" contest.

✔ **The end of colonialism:** In the decades after World War II, nations that had traditionally been "possessions" of powerful European countries like Britain and France started declaring their independence. Not everyone was willing to accept this very quickly, however, and not every revolutionary was a pacifist like Gandhi. Many of the revolutions that followed were violent and often Communist in orientation. Before the U.S. Vietnam war, for example, came the French Vietnam War, which was similarly controversial and divisive, starting as a war to overthrow French colonial rule.

Which Left is right? Sartre chooses Communism

Politically and to a large extent philosophically, Sartre was first and foremost a devout Marxist. He fully believed that humanity's freedom rested upon the triumph of the working class. His love of freedom and hatred of all forms of oppression led him to be a virulent supporter of anticolonial movements across the globe but especially those movements that resisted French colonial occupations, such as those in Vietnam and Algeria. All these positions, along with the ascendancy of McCarthyism in the United States in the 1950s, led Sartre to be fairly consistently critical of, and even hostile to, the United States; its uncontrolled form of Capitalism; and, as he saw it, its imperialism.

His position toward Communism and the Soviet Union, however, was complex and stormy. Most Communist parties, and particularly France's, saw themselves as allied with the Soviet Union and — in his day — with Stalin. This alliance put Sartre in a bit of a quandary. Many Leftists, including Camus and eventually Merleau-Ponty, fled from any relationship with such an oppressive regime. But Sartre was certain that Communism was *the* party of the working class, which Sartre supported unconditionally, at least in theory. But in practice, the party of the working class was in league with the Devil. Further, in a cold-war environment, you had to take sides: Capitalist (imperialist) democracy or Communist dictatorship. What's a good Marxist to do?

Sartre's response was threefold:

✔ **Adopt a means-ends stance:** If the eventual triumph of the working class and the liberation of humanity depend upon a period of authoritarian and oppressive rule, well, so be it, as long as this is done in service of that eventual goal. History moves by violence. The only question is "On which side will you fight?"

✔ **Adjust the level of support as appropriate:** Sartre's relationship with the Communists was extremely stormy. He had a violently on-again, off-again relationship with various Communist parties, and he was never actually a member of France's Communist Party. He felt the party was too uncritically pro-Soviet. Philosophically, he was always with the party, but despite his means-ends stance, he had little real stomach for many of its concrete actions.

✔ **Work for change from the inside:** Although Sartre was never really an insider per se, he believed the only way to criticize the actions of the Soviet Union and the Communists was as a Communist sympathizer and as a supporter of their ultimate aims. And to his credit, he did criticize the actions of the Soviet Union and the Communists, vehemently at times, from within the family, so to speak. He was always an anti–anti-Communist, opposing anyone who would oppose the Communists on general principle rather than condemning the actions of particular Communists at particular times (as he himself did).

In the harsh social and political climate of Parisian intellectuals, this position was guaranteed to bring trouble. Sartre got it, from both sides. The Communists (never the most understanding of critics) accused him of everything from political quietism to being a Fascist puppet of the Americans, while those on the more moderate Left (including some of his closest friends) accused him of condoning atrocities. Because he wavered between attacking and praising the Communists and the Soviet Union, both sides had ample evidence on which to base their criticisms. With the best of humanitarian intentions, Sartre tried to walk a middle path — being pro-Communist but not uncritically so.

Camus rejects violence

> *It is better to be wrong by killing no one than to be right with mass graves.*
>
> —Albert Camus

Camus was, in many respects, the conscience of existentialism. Decent and deeply compassionate, he is rarely placed on the list of philosophers held up to discredit existentialism or tie it to political atrocities. Perhaps this is why his philosophy is not particularly well known. He edited a journal called *Combat* during World War II and was active in the French Resistance to German occupation. Later, he protested oppression as propagated by both the Right (such as the French treatment of the Algerians) and the Left (such as the Stalinist regime in Russia). Despite his involvement in such movements and his deep commitment to political action, Camus spent most of his life as a pacifist. Though he often sympathized with rebellions, particularly against Totalitarian regimes, he rejected violent means of attaining political ends.

The roots of his pacifism can be seen in his version of existential philosophy. It rested primarily on two points:

- **Death is the ultimate injustice.** Whatever evils the current political situation is guilty of, and whatever benefits are promised by revolt, to alter the situation through violence is to involve yourself in the greatest of injustices, and thereby you only increase the injustice in the world.

- **No ideal is worth fighting for.** To fight *against* one political situation is to fight *for* another and the ideals that underlie that system. But Camus rejects the absolute assurance in any set of values that advocates of rebellion say make the fighting defensible.

For Camus, the only way to defeat the absurd situation human beings find themselves in is to embrace it — to accept the fact that there is no meaning. You can assert individual values, but you must remember that any objective values are myths. The problem with revolutionary ideologies, according to Camus, is that they must start with presenting a set of values as somehow objectively more correct than those of the status quo. The result is the creation of a value that's not only worth dying for, but also worth *killing* for. Camus thinks that after you make this turn, the inevitable result is that the injustices you were fighting against become acceptable in defense of the new, supposedly more just and righteous regime. In reality, what all revolutions do is replace one absolute ideal with another. In the words of the British rock band The Who, "Meet the new boss, same as the old boss." The true absurdist refuses to endorse or fight for any absolute ideal.

Camus, then, used his political activism not to erect a vision of a more perfect world, but to eliminate injustice wherever he saw it in this one. He focused his energies on opposing both violent oppression and violent resistance. He advocated treating people with compassion and respect, which he saw as being at odds with oppressive occupations of both the colonial and Communist powers. This set him at odds with many on the Left, who tended to be more narrowly, and often violently, opposed to the colonial powers while often turning a blind eye to the oppression of the Communists. One of those he came into direct conflict with was Jean-Paul Sartre.

Politics of liberation versus politics of life

Sartre and Camus met at a dress rehearsal for one of Sartre's plays. They became fast friends, but fewer than ten years later, largely political tensions between them exploded into a rift that would last the rest of their days.

In 1951 Camus published his philosophical essay *The Rebel*. *The Rebel* was many things: a meditation on murder; an attempt to develop an ethics; and, most important, an indictment of violent revolutions like those being waged by Communists all over the globe at the time. Sartre's journal *Les Temps*

Modernes wrote a damning review, which led to a bitter exchange of letters, published in the journal, between Sartre and Camus. The flap over *The Rebel* brought out differences between the two men that had been bubbling for some time. Some of the chief issues:

✔ Camus believed Sartre blindly and uncritically followed both Marxism and the Communists.

✔ Camus thought Sartre condoned murder, terror, and Totalitarianism in the name of history.

✔ Sartre accused Camus of *quietism,* an unwillingness to engage in the battles for justice he saw being waged around the world. He accused Camus of retreating from a world that he saw as irredeemably absurd.

✔ Sartre accused Camus of not supporting anticolonial rebellions, such as those being waged in Vietnam and Algeria. Camus, he thought, was far too accepting of the status quo of traditional political oppression.

The impetus for these differences has many sources, including differences in the way the two think about Marxism. In this section, we stick to the way in which these positions stem from and illuminate differences in their existential positions.

One of the central differences between their versions of existentialism is in the emphasis each gives in explaining the source of absurdity in life. For Sartre, the meaninglessness of life comes from human origins (see Chapter 8 for more on this idea). People are born as nothing, with no purpose, and with no meaning to their existence; going forward, they must create meaning, and so create themselves. For Sartre, the tragedy of life starts at its inception. Only through action can you "redeem" your life. You must strive to overcome this nothingness through action, and that action must be directed at enhancing human freedom — your own and that of others.

For Camus, the great tragedy of life, what makes it truly absurd, is that it *ends.* What makes life meaningless is that human projects ultimately fail because people don't live to see and partake in what becomes of them. Death, then, is the great injustice of life, and Camus asserts that you can make no excuse for partaking in it — for partaking in murder. By committing murder, the Communists weren't freeing anyone; they were condemning people to death on the basis of an ideal that was as ultimately meaningless and absurd as any other. As an existentialist, Sartre should have known better.

Sartre wasn't buying this idea. He felt that Camus's excuses represented a foul form of cowardice and, worse, dishonesty. For him, violence and conflict are part of the human situation. They're the conditions in which you must make your choices. If that's the reality, the choice isn't to fight or not to fight, but to decide on which side you'll fight. Sartre was determined to fight on the side of the working class and on the side of human liberation; to him, the status quo threatened this side.

Each, then, thought the other guilty of "bad faith" — of denying his own freedom to choose another path by denying the reality of his situation.

  ✔ According to Camus, Sartre was erecting a false absolute (for existentialists, all absolutes are false) and using it to justify murder and oppression.

  ✔ According to Sartre, Camus was dishonestly denying the effectiveness of action and the reality that he already lived in a violent world of oppression. Hence, Camus accepted and refused to oppose the murder and oppression that were already present.

Each position has some truth as well as a lot of falsehood. The simple fact is that although neither was as unwavering as the other thought he should be, each struggled with the issues the other raised. As we discuss in the previous section, Sartre never fully joined the Communist movement, for all the reasons Camus criticized it. And although Camus refused to support violent insurrection, he was a tireless political activist. Appropriately enough, for one who thinks the injustice of life is grounded in the death sentence everyone faces, one of his chief activities was his opposition to the death penalty.

Chapter 13

Existentialism and Other Schools of Philosophical Thought

In This Chapter

▶ Understanding existentialism's relationship to modern philosophy

▶ Exploring the difference between existentialism and postmodernism

▶ Seeing how existentialism is still relevant today

*M*ost of the chapters in this book attempt to tell you who the existentialists were, what they believed, and what existentialism is. In this chapter and the next, we follow up with existentialists and answer the question, "Whatever happened to them?" Or, rather, whatever happened to their philosophy? In the next chapter, we discuss the huge and enduring impact existentialism has had on the study of psychology. In this chapter, we stay closer to its roots. Existentialism, as we present it, is first and foremost a philosophy. It's an important contribution to a discussion of the human condition that's been going on in Western society since Socrates and Plato started it in fifth- and fourth-century Athens.

In the sections that follow, we explain the state of modern philosophy and where existentialism fits in. We start by examining how it gets on with the dominant strains of today's mainstream philosophical thought (hint: not well). We follow by examining how existentialism has found new life in the philosophies that have sprung up to detail and take up arms against the plight of the oppressed.

Existentialism's Run in the 20th Century

When the works of Kierkegaard and Nietzsche gave birth to existentialism in the 19th century, existentialism was largely ignored and dismissed as the fringe writings of two men who weren't doing *real* philosophy. At best it seemed more literary than philosophical; at worst it seemed like the ravings of madmen. In the 20th century, existentialism became respectable, among academics at least, after thinkers like Heidegger and Sartre wrote nice, long, systematized works about the philosophy that aimed at discrediting all systems. After a brief, meteoric rise in popularity among professional eggheads, artists, and even the wider public, existentialism seemed to disappear from the face of the culture. Although few thinkers ever embraced the characterization of "existentialist" themselves, for a time, many of them were characterized that way with some justice by others, and existentialism, its impact, and its meaning were hot topics of conversation.

Around the 1960s, however, the movement (if it ever was one) started to wane. After writing his magnum opus of 1927, Heidegger continued to work quietly. Although *Being and Time* continued to be vastly influential, Heidegger's involvement with the Nazi party (see Chapter 12) marginalized him as a philosophical personality after World War II. Albert Camus died in 1960. Jean-Paul Sartre, while still immensely important and respected, had his best work behind him at this point. And Simone de Beauvoir became better known and more influential for writing *The Second Sex,* and as the grand dame of the growing feminist movement, than as an existentialist.

After the fanfare died down, existentialism seemed to go away as a significant philosophical movement. Although many of its thinkers remained important and were mined for various contributions to the movements that followed, existentialism became to some extent persona non grata, an unwelcome and occasionally embarrassing member of the philosophical family. Existentialism has returned to its outsider roots and is questioned repeatedly for its bona fides as a philosophy.

Existentialism and Modern Philosophy: A Strained Relationship

Philosophy itself took an interesting turn around the time the existentialists started making themselves known. In the section immediately following, we examine the split that occurred between, roughly speaking, British and American philosophy and the philosophy of the European continent and where existentialism fits in to that split. The philosophy that developed on the Continent is generally known as, appropriately enough, *Continental philosophy,* and the British-American version is generally called *analytic philosophy.* We examine existentialism's relation to each in turn following this section.

Two branches of modern philosophy: Analytic and Continental

Around the 19th century, the philosophies of the European continent veered off from the direction of that of British and American philosophy. Or they kept going and the Brits and Americans veered off course, depending on your point of view. Because this is a book on existentialism and not modern philosophy, we don't dwell on the host of reasons how or why this occurred. We just attempt to give you an understanding of how the two philosophies, as they were when existentialism came about, differ and where existentialism fits in.

When Sir Isaac Newton wrote *Mathematical Principles of Natural Philosophy* in the 17th century, it's no exaggeration to say everything changed. Newton showed that the entirety of the physical universe could be understood with precise and mathematical certainty by human reason. Thinkers like Copernicus and Galileo had been giants, but it was largely Newton and those inspired by him who started the scientific revolution and made it an unstoppable and undeniable force. The major philosophers of the 18th century tried to emulate his rigor and systematic style as they approached traditional questions of knowledge, ethics, and the nature of the universe.

This attempt to be more scientific in the pursuit of philosophy resulted in the following two basic reactions during the 19th century:

- ✔ **In Britain and America,** the scientific instinct was strong, and philosophers went farther and farther in their attempts to be as rigorous and objective as the hardest of hard scientists. Philosophy became more and more concerned with logic, which is basically the science of making rational arguments and the language they're couched in as precise and objective as mathematics. Many philosophers in this tradition, the analytic tradition, have seen philosophy as little more than a secondary subdivision of science, working on small problems on the fringes. Like the science it tries to emulate, it has become more and more technical, more and more specialized, and more and more removed from everyday experience. Even when it deals with more human topics, such as ethics or political science, it does so at a great distance, treating human beings as abstract rational agents rather than three-dimensional persons.

- ✔ **On the European continent,** there was a backlash against this type of thinking and against the pretensions of reason. Philosophy became more and more about unmasking these pretensions, about rejecting the scientific model as both false (because it fails to live up to its own standards of objectivity) and misleading (because the rational scientific method fails to enlighten people about philosophy's most important subjects: human beings). The reaction on the Continent was so strong that the Continentals abandoned the specifically scientific model and ultimately rejected the more generally rationalistic bias within philosophy that had held sway to a greater or lesser extent since the time of Plato. Continental philosophers adopted, instead, literature as their primary model. Just as you may interpret a text in high school or college English classes, the Continentals tend to see everything — from philosophical and scientific theories to gender, politics, and pop culture — as textual and open to interpretation.

These two basic reactions are to some extent generalizations. The exact nature of the differences is subject to dispute, and the two do overlap in some areas (or so we contend!). To get an overall sense of the difference, look at Table 13-1. As you do so, think about anything you may know about the existentialists from this book or elsewhere. Where do you think the existentialists fit in? Where does your own personal philosophy of life fit in?

Table 13-1	Comparing Analytic and Continental Philosophy	
	Analytic Philosophy	*Continental Philosophy*
Overall Approach	Analysis: Breaking problems down into small pieces. Doesn't deal with "the big questions"; everything is fine grained and technical.	Synthesis: Combines insights from many disciplines and perspectives to provide a holistic perspective.
Model	Science	Literature
Main Subjects	Knowledge, science, logic, mathematics, ontology (the study of what exists)	The human condition, art, literature, ethics, politics, history, anthropology
Type of Answers	Universal/objective	Contingent/political/historical
Main Tool	Logic	Interpretation

As it turns out, both camps are heading in the same direction more and more as time goes by. Both are increasingly focused on the importance of language as the medium in which the ideas of all their subjects are conveyed. This turn was itself presaged by the existentialists — particularly Nietzsche and Heidegger, who both dealt thoroughly with the issue of language and brought up many of the problems both camps deal with today.

Kant and the limits of reason

One of the 18th-century thinkers who tried to emulate Newton was Immanuel Kant, who tried to demarcate the line between religion and science. You can also call it the line between faith and the increasingly expansionist reason. (For more on Kant, see Chapter 3.) Kant was the last thinker embraced by both branches of philosophy, analytic and Continental. His philosophy is sometimes used, in both traditions, as an example of the limits of human reason. Perhaps that argument is made even better in a story from his own life. Kant fell in love only once. He pursued a lovely young woman who was evidently open to his courtship. Kant hesitated, however. Was this the right thing to do? Was this the best choice? For months Kant subjected the decision to reasoned analysis — weighing the pros and cons; doing the relationship calculus; and considering every financial, social, moral, and philosophical consequence. At last he happily announced that he had decided that the math favored the marriage, and he would propose. Unfortunately, by that time his love had accepted the proposal of another suitor, and Kant spent the rest of his life rationally calculating alone.

Where existentialism fits in

Where does existentialism fit into the two branches of modern philosophy? The short answer is simple: Existentialism is part of Continental philosophy. Many of its thinkers are considered giants within that tradition. But what's peculiarly existential about them has often been less influential. Existentialism is, in many respects, a return to the philosophy of the ancients, where philosophy started. We discuss this return in greater detail in Chapter 1. There, we discuss health, but here, we want to discuss poetry and its relationship to existentialism and philosophy as a whole. Poetry is surprisingly crucial to the history of philosophy.

When Plato creates his perfect society in *The Republic,* one of the first things he does is throw out the poets. The poets, he says, communicate their ideas on a level that's irrational. They move people to act on the basis of lovely speeches, stirring tales, and emotionally involving language. They do so without regard to truth and goodness, and so corrupt society. Reason should guide the perfect society, for it and it alone discovers what's true and can guide people to right living.

For 2,000 years, philosophy enforced Plato's ban, never seeming to recall that at the end of *The Republic,* Plato invites the poets back in — provided, of course, that they use their craft to communicate only what's righteous and true. Although Plato was fundamentally a rationalist, a proponent of the supremacy and primacy of reason, he was also, far more than most of those who followed him, a *complete* philosopher. He recognized, investigated, and addressed all aspects of humanity.

The existentialists tried to invite the poets back in. Like Plato himself, they often worked in literary forms, because they wanted to address human beings and human life in a *complete* way, which acknowledges that people are emotional, passionate creatures who desire meaning. Although often described as irrationalists, they, like Plato, saw the question of rationality as one of emphasis. What they objected to wasn't rationality, but the pretensions of rationality to solve or explain *everything.* They felt something was being left out.

If nature abhors a vacuum, what Western civilization abhors is a moderate. People in Western culture seem to need to see things as black or white. Like Plato, existentialism shares much with the more holistic philosophies of the East. One way of seeing the split between analytic and Continental philosophy is that the two traditions took opposing attitudes on the place of poetry in philosophy.

By not accepting existentialism's holistic view, the analytics enforced the ban in stricter and stricter terms, sticking to logic, science, and the pursuit of objective knowledge and truth. In the process, questions that involved humanity, emotions, or poetry in the largest sense got pushed to the side. Even quintessentially human topics like ethics and politics were tolerated only if done in the most abstract, logical, and scientific terms. The Continentals, on the other hand, went farther than most (not all) of the existentialists ever dreamed and rejected reason entirely. They didn't just let the poets back in; they put them in charge.

Although existentialism is part of Continental philosophy, in many respects it's a philosophy without a country. Distinguishing the existentialism from the existentialists is important. Thinkers such as Nietzsche, Kierkegaard, and Heidegger in particular remain influential, but not *as* existentialists. Whatever the influence of these thinkers, something unique and special was lost to philosophy when their followers ceased to be interested in specifically existential themes.

Postmodernism: Existentialism's bratty stepchild

The most obvious and most important descendent of existentialism in Continental philosophy is postmodernism. Like existentialism, postmodernism is notoriously difficult to define, but we're doing it anyway. *Postmodernism* starts with the rejection of reason and with the rejection of all supposedly objective systems of thought that claim to provide objective truths. The mission of postmodernism (if we can speak of the mission of a group that defies all singular description) includes showing up reason in all its facets, in all its pretensions. Postmodernism doesn't show up reason through rational counterarguments but through a process called *deconstruction,* which aims at exposing the pretensions of reason for what they are and revealing the arbitrariness of not only rational inquiry, but also all interpretations of human experience.

The second movement of postmodernism is to go about, tongue thoroughly in cheek, reassessing and reinterpreting all human experience, usually with the aid of methods taken from historical and anthropological studies and literary criticism. We say *tongue thoroughly in cheek* because the concept of play is very important to postmodernism. Because there's no ultimately right answer, philosophy is seen as a kind of game. Pursuit of the wisdom through knowledge of the true gives way to pursuit of cleverness through the development of the novel, the witty, and the innovative.

This reinterpretation, however, does have at least one serious goal, which is overthrowing oppressive systems of thought and the political systems they are said to support. Traditional interpretations were dominant, not only because they were accepted by the majority of people, but also because they were tied together with systems of oppression with which they were mutually reaffirming. Traditional rationalist narratives, it is argued, often share the qualities of the power structures they arose to support. They are, then, imperialistic, racist, Totalitarian, and oppressive.

This description of postmodernism may sound familiar, and it may sound a lot like existentialism (if it doesn't sound familiar, check out Chapter 3). Well, it is . . . and it isn't. There are certainly similarities, but there's also a deep divide. Read the following sections to get a more detailed understanding of their relationship.

Stepchild or stepbrother?

The relationship between existentialism and postmodernism goes to the heart of questions like "What is existentialism?" and "Who is an existentialist?" Nietzsche, Kierkegaard, and Heidegger all had a profound influence on both existentialism and postmodernism. Their literary method and their emphasis upon interpretation and the significance of language gave way very naturally to the postmodern movement. As for the tone of postmodernism, Nietzsche and Kierkegaard both wrote in playful, elusive styles, which challenged the reader and left much ambiguous or open to interpretation. Much of postmodern writing has stuck to this as the model — if coming up with ever new ways of being clever can be called a model, that is!

You could argue, then, that the existentialists and the postmodernists descend from the same stock. Both intellectual movements descend from the writings of three giants — Nietzsche, Kierkegaard, and Heidegger — who were bigger, collectively and individually, than either movement. Existentialists focused on certain themes in their writings, and the postmodernists developed others. Each movement took its set of themes and marched off in a different, but related, direction. You could say that, but we won't. When push comes to shove, when you examine how existentialism differs from postmodernism, these three thinkers were first and foremost *existentialists* because they had the same *fundamental* concerns as the later existentialists. They *all* believed that humanity is in crisis and that a way forward must be found that will make authentic, engaged, and fulfilling human life possible. The postmodernists developed ideas the other existentialists missed or left to the side, but they removed this crucially important context.

The brats' rebellion: How they differ

Both existentialism and postmodernism start by challenging reason and rational systems that claim to provide answers. The two systems differ markedly in two senses:

- ✔ **The extent and nature of the challenge:** Although you can find some exceptions (particularly Nietzsche, who was particularly radical in this area), the postmodernists generally went farther than the existentialists in challenging reason. The existentialists' primary objection was that reason is inadequate to provide for the full panorama of human needs. For the postmodernists, the cult of reason is simply false. They consider rational inquiry just another form of interpretation, no more valid than any other. Further, because reason is tied to dominant systems of oppression in postmodern thought, it's a particularly suspect form of interpretation.

- ✔ **Where they go from there:** For the existentialists, the death of God, reason, and absolute systems is the death of traditional systems of meaning. The project then becomes finding new meaning. The postmodernists are unconcerned with meaning, anguish, or forlornness. Human beings interpret; that's what they do. The project simply becomes finding the best, most useful, most interesting interpretations.

These are the two broad differences between the two movements, but there are many others. We summarize some of these differences in Table 13-2.

Table 13-2	Comparing Existentialism and Postmodernism	
	Existentialism	*Postmodernism*
The Challenge	Finding meaning and value in a world without God	Unmasking the pretensions of reason
The Method	Creation of meaning and value	Interpretation of the text of human experience
The Danger	Nihilism: The surrender to despair in the face of the meaninglessness of existence	Oppression: The continued belief in narratives whose purpose is to support the dominant power structure

	Existentialism	*Postmodernism*
The Self	A first-person perspective defined by its being situated in a world of objects and other people	Another fiction, as subject to interpretation as anything else; people are historically situated, but the truths and meaning of their histories are open to interpretation
The Goal	Authenticity: Developing a truly human way of relating to your existence	There is no truth, so one form of life is as authentic as another
The Attitude	A hard optimism in the face of an uncaring universe	Playfully rebellious

Postmodernists see something staid and pious about existentialism. They think it clings somewhat romantically to the interpretations of a bygone era, even while challenging them. This is certainly one reason why, although postmodernism pays homage to certain existential thinkers, interest in the philosophy declined precipitously after the postmodern revolution that started in the 1960s. Once again, existentialism became, even within its home countries, a philosophy spoken only on the fringes and in the shadows.

Existentialism and American philosophy

With its abstract talk of being and obsession over emotions like anguish and forlornness, existentialism is seen by many in the United States and Britain as the epitome of Continental excess. Conversely, every complaint that existentialism weighs against science (see Chapter 5) can be applied, almost without modification, to the modern analytic philosophy of the English-speaking countries. This has made for an interesting split:

- ✔ In American schools, existentialism is almost universally shunned by serious research universities. For philosophers, pursuing this nonsense is considered professional suicide. Remember, dear reader, this type of nonsense won't get you hired anywhere — except small teaching colleges, where it's wildly popular, which brings us to our next point.

- ✔ On the street, it's another story entirely. People feel as alienated in today's society as ever before. People increasingly sense that their systems have failed them and that science isn't helping. Oh, it can provide you medicines, and space stations, and iPods, and bullet trains, but all the things it shuns, all the things it considers irrational nonsense — that's the *good* stuff. That's the stuff people need, and that's the stuff the secular, scientific society seems ill equipped to provide. So walk into any bookstore, and you'll find books by and about Nietzsche, Sartre, Camus, and the whole gang.

Existentialism and Philosophies of the Oppressed

Although mainstream philosophy has largely relegated existentialism to the dustbin of history, existentialism has proved to be fertile ground for a new generation of philosophical and theological rebels. Philosophies such as feminism, liberation theology, and (most directly) black existential philosophy have mined existential ideas to create unique and powerful new ways of interpreting and confronting the world and the oppressive relationships that too often characterize it. Existentialism has proved to be relevant to these projects for many reasons. We feel the most significant reason, however, is that existentialism has always been about recognizing and asserting human dignity, especially when that dignity is under fire — when it's denied, ignored, or alienated by political, social, or intellectual systems. This is precisely the project of what we refer to collectively as the philosophies of the oppressed.

Different philosophies of oppression, even within the same broad tradition, have made use of different aspects of the broad spectrum of existential philosophy. As a whole, however, it's remarkable just how thoroughly these systems make use of existentialism, echoing themes such as freedom and responsibility; feelings of anguish and alienation; and the importance of the concrete, subjective point of view. At the center of all these philosophies are the rejection of systems of thought that alienate and objectify, and the reaffirmation of human dignity. Many have found within existentialism the tools to describe that alienation and to assert that dignity. In the following sections, we discuss just a couple of the aspects of existential philosophy that have found particular resonance and resurgence in modern philosophies of the oppressed.

Alienation and otherness

Racism, sexism, and other forms of cultural and economic oppression have often been given legitimacy through tying (either explicitly or covertly) that oppressive philosophy to notions of a timeless, objective truth that reinforces the notion that this oppression is natural, understandable, or necessary. These false systems of thought put the affected class in a position of being, at best, second-class citizens. They become what de Beauvoir has called "society's other" (see Chapter 16). Each person sees the world starting from his own perspective and sees any other person as an "other," outside and different from himself. Likewise, the oppressive societies see privileged classes — men, whites, the dominant culture — as the starting point, the norm. Theirs is the assumptive point of view, whereas the oppressed classes take the role of the alien *other*.

These systems of thought infect even the perspective of those seen by society, and ultimately themselves, as other. The result is a feeling of alienation imposed not only by the overt acts of oppression, but also by the mindset that the oppressive relationship assumes and asserts. Many modern philosophies examine what it means to be placed in this position, along with the psychological effects and the change in perspective it engenders. Moreover, working from the existentialists' first-person perspective, these philosophies reconstruct the perspective literally from those on the other side. These constructions aren't valuable just for understanding a point of view that may be alien to some; they also set up the terms and conditions of the problem, describing the oppression from the inside out. Thinkers in this tradition assert that only with this kind of understanding can progress be made toward conquering oppression in all its most subtle and insidious forms.

Racism as inauthenticity

In his classic essay "Portrait of an Anti-Semite," Jean-Paul Sartre argues that anti-Semitism (or any form of bigotry) is a form of inauthenticity, or a flight from freedom. The essay has proved to be of lasting importance for the analysis of oppression. According to Sartre, when someone embraces bigotry, fundamentally he's really embracing his prejudices rather than rejecting the object of his hatred. The word *prejudice* is appropriate here, because what the bigot is doing is reaffirming his own notions (prejudgments) of how things are and should be. By casting Jewish people as evil and focusing on their unfitness for this or that parcel of respect, what's good and what's fit are *assumed*. Because what's good is assumed, it's never put into question; it doesn't need to be chosen or created.

Bigotry, then, is inseparable from the absolute systems and meaning narratives people create to console themselves and distract them from the fact that the world is fundamentally meaningless, and that rather than being a given, the meaning of the world is their responsibility. The bigot evades questioning these systems of thought and is consoled by wallowing in his hatred. Sartre points out that the characteristics of the object of bigotry are irrelevant. The stereotype many have of the Jews, he points out, is that they are smarter and, in that sense, more qualified for many of the jobs they're accused of taking unjustly from "good Frenchmen." These details don't matter, though, because what the bigot is affirming isn't a rational principle of comparative qualifications. He's affirming an absolute system that puts everything in its proper place without regard to the concrete particulars of the situation.

With the aid of insights like Sartre's, much of modern philosophy starts from an understanding of bigotry as a holistic phenomenon. In this phenomenon, individual occurrences have a direct connection to the systematic values of the entire culture, even if these values aren't obviously racist. These ideas have influenced not only theoretical philosophy, but also civil-rights legislation. Legislation such as affirmative action, hate-crimes legislation, and workplace discrimination laws don't aim simply at eradicating specific impediments to equality, but also attempt to effect a systematic change in the way people *see* things. The goal is to sever the link and, hence, reinforcement between institutional systems of thought and individual acts and feelings of bigotry.

This is also why much of modern civil-rights rhetoric is aimed at getting people to question their assumptions and engage in soul-searching reflection of the nature of bigotry. It isn't simply in hopes that the bigots will realize the error of their ways by learning through these reflections that blacks, women, and so on are human beings too. If Sartre is right, the point of this soul searching is that it's antithetical to bigotry. If bigotry is a way of avoiding the need to questions your assumptions, if it's a way to run from free choice, by confronting people with their free choice and making them confront their most basic beliefs, you give them occasion not just to reject racism, but also to embrace a freely chosen belief system. They are, of course, always free to choose bigotry, but if Sartre is right, much of the impetus for doing so has been undermined.

Chapter 14

Doing Psychology the Existential Way

In This Chapter

▶ Surveying existential ideas that affected psychology

▶ Investigating some key existential-humanist psychologists

*I*f you've been reading this book from the start, the existential program should be clear by now. Humans are unique. They're individual. They're free, and they're responsible for their situations. They crave meaning and a sense of purpose. They fear death and suffer from anxiety.

Because these descriptions are about the nature of the human being, you may expect a possible impact on the field of psychology. After all, psychologists are scientists who strive to understand the motivations and behaviors of the human being. In fact, you may expect an influence on the way some psychologists understand living a healthy psychological life or even on understanding how people develop any number of unhealthy dysfunctions.

In this chapter we look at the influence existentialism has on psychology. Existentialism altered the way some psychologists understood the human being as an entity and how they thought others should understand and analyze the behavior of the human being.

First, we analyze a list of basic similarities between existentialism and what later became known as the humanistic or existential-humanist movement in psychology. From there, we survey three specific psychologists whose theories of human psychology embody in different ways key existential themes.

Points of Contact: Existentialism Meets Psychology

Existentialist thinking had an influence on the way some psychologists understood and saw the human being. Previously, psychology viewed the human being as an object that could be studied in the same way that science tends to study all its objects. Before the existentialist influence, most psychologists saw the study of the human as no different from the way the biologist studied the cow or the way the physicist studied the motion of inanimate objects. Psychologists believed they could explain human behavior in terms of natural laws.

This way of thinking about humans dominated what was known as the *first wave* (Freudianism and followers of Sigmund Freud) and the *second wave* (behaviorism, following B. F. Skinner and John B. Watson). In the first wave, psychologists always explain human behavior in terms of unconscious drives and instincts and the laws that govern them. In the second wave, psychologists always explain behavior by the laws governing conditioning and stimulus, the same way scientists study the behavior of mice in labs.

Existential-humanism, also known as the *third wave,* reacted strongly to these approaches. The existential-humanists saw humans as irreducibly unique and individual and, therefore, not fully understandable in terms of general laws. They saw the human as creative, possessing free will, striving for goals and the fulfillment of potential, and strongly craving meaning and significance.

Stressing the importance of human uniqueness

Existential-humanist psychologists often found themselves in conflict with natural science. If psychology was a natural science, they had to see the behavior of individual human beings as entirely explainable in terms of larger natural laws, the same way the behavior of other entities is explained by the laws of physics, biology, or chemistry. The existential-humanists rejected this approach, believing that individuals were too unique to be captured by general laws of any type.

Think of a ball falling to the ground. You can analyze this event by thinking about the properties of the ball at a given time — its weight, velocity, and so on. Each of these falls under general laws. Dense objects behave in such-and-such ways, as do objects with velocity. After you think of the individual this way, you eventually understand its behavior completely in terms of those laws. Nothing about the ball as a unique particular thing seems to matter. The existential-humanists rejected this approach to understanding human behavior. They said that you can't understand the behavior of Sally without understanding Sally as a unique individual.

Abraham Maslow knew this approach would clash with the methodology of science. In response, he suggested that "if the study of the uniqueness of the individual does not fit into what we know of science, then so much the worse for the conception of science. It, too, will have to endure re-creation." Instead of the existential-humanists changing their view of the human to fit science, he argued, science needed to change its method to fit what human beings actually are.

Putting the patient's world front and center

Existentialism places high importance on the *phenomenological* method. Yup — big jargon word (we talk about it more in Chapter 6). The phenomenologist thinks that to understand what's truly important about human beings, you have to pay close attention to how they actually experience things "from the inside." In other words, the world of the first-person point of view matters.

The existential-humanists agree that to understand a particular person or human beings in general, you have to get into the head and see how things look from the inside out. Only by seeing how a person experiences the world, or how that person responds to what she considers meaningful within her world, can you ever truly understand that person's behavior.

Today, this theory may seem obvious. If you want to know why a person is having problems in her marriage, it's important to find out not only the experiences she lives through, but also how those experiences are meaningful to her and, as a result, how she feels about them. After you get in the person's world, you can start to understand what motivates her.

Of course, you're probably used to living in a "How does that make you feel?" culture. So you expect psychologists to talk that way. But this talk-about-your-feelings approach wasn't *always* important. Earlier psychology saw human behavior as either driven by instincts and unconscious drives (Freudianism) or by learned reactions to stimuli in your environment (behaviorism). Neither approach took the conscious world seen from the inside very seriously at all.

Focusing on freedom and anxiety

Existential-humanists agree with existentialists that humans are free beings. As a result, understanding their behavior and living in a mentally healthy way means emphasizing the role of personal choice in life.

For the existential-humanists, freedom is obvious. Living a healthy life requires that a person embrace, psychologically, her own role as the person in direct control of her own life. Of course, most people can point to times when they've felt out of control or powerless. When that happens, you typically get depressed, or you enter some state of denial about what's going on. It's hard to deny that feeling effective in your own life leads to feeling psychologically whole.

Of course, living up to your freedom isn't easy. The existential-humanists agree that freedom leads to anxiety. Being free to choose your path in life means a great deal of unsettledness. But like the existentialists, they see unsettledness as perfectly natural. The perennial lack of certainty about which way to go is just what it means to be human; it's the human situation.

Your response to anxiety, they suggest, is *courage.* You must have, as Paul Tillich once put it, the "courage to be." That means emphasizing the importance of choice in the here and now. Avoiding choices by living in the past or by daydreaming about the future is of no use. To be psychologically healthy, you need to know not only what's fixed in your life, but also what's possible. From there, you can decide which alternative best suits who you are.

Programming the "perfect" world

Not all psychologists think human behavior is free. John B. Watson, an early behaviorist, felt very strongly that the behavior of human beings could be entirely explained in terms of the ways individuals are trained by their environments to respond to external stimuli. In a famous quote, Watson stresses the extremely "plastic" nature of human behavior, saying, "Give me a dozen healthy infants, well-formed, and my own specified world to bring them up in and I'll guarantee to take any one at random and train him to become any type of specialist I might select — doctor, lawyer, artist, merchant-chief and, yes, even beggar-man and thief, regardless of his talents, penchants, tendencies, abilities, vocations, and race of his ancestors."

Essentially, Watson's position is that the individuals in question have *no* free will of their own to determine their futures; they do what their training (or Watson's training, in this quote!) makes them do. Pretty bleak as a description of what people are! One of Watson's behaviorist colleagues, B. F. Skinner, felt similarly and wrote a book called *Walden Two,* in which he described a possible utopia that could be formed by training people through conditioning to perform certain tasks — tasks that they'd be trained to love and be happy with. Of course, you may wonder about the *human* element. What about reflecting on the possible options for your own future and making individual decisions? Behaviorism seems to discount all that.

Seeing the people as goal directed

The fact that existentialists and existential-humanists see the human being as free leads to another central issue: that the human being is essentially goal directed. You're always reaching out for some project or aim that you can accomplish. Moreover, the existential-humanists think that you're driven toward higher levels of functioning. You strive to reach your potential.

Unlike the behaviorists who came before them, the existential-humanists thought that humans, unlike dogs and other animals, had aspirations and dreams. Dogs don't pace around the house thinking, "So what kind of dog do I want to be, anyway?" On the other hand, it's pretty obvious that humans *do* have dreams and aspirations. As Heidegger put it, you're always living one step ahead of yourself in the future, thinking of what to do and who to be next. The existential-humanists agree, but they stress that you're always striving forward to make the most of your potential.

Given this positive dimension to human existence, the existential-humanists departed from traditional psychology, which had stressed mostly the existence of defects in the human being. Instead, the existential-humanists stressed that these positive capacities, and the psychological components that make them possible, should be studied and brought to center stage.

Finding meaning is central to your existence

According to the existentialists, you need to find meaning in things. You just can't help it. And when you can't find meaning, your life gets disrupted. People need meaning like they need air. Both the existentialists and the existential-humanists stress this central component of human existence.

People today have an especially hard time fitting life into a larger significant plan or purpose. (See Chapter 3 for more about existential crises in modern times.) You may have a hard time plugging into the world in a way that your ancestors were able to do more easily. As a result, patients in therapists' offices are talking more and more despairingly about their own failure to find a real sense of purpose in life. Are you surprised that the self-help section in the bookstore has so many bestsellers?

The existential-humanists felt strongly that to live in a mentally healthy way, a person (or a patient) needed to be guided back toward the difficult task of finding meaning in life.

Positive psychology: Stressing the good

As far as Abraham Maslow saw it, Freudianism presented the "sick half" of the human being (with its focus on neurosis). Now it was time for psychology to present the "healthy half." Although this way of thinking about the human being is typical to existential-humanism, it became formalized in the 1990s as a movement known as positive psychology. Martin Seligman — a recent pioneer in the field and author of books with titles such as *Authentic Happiness* — and other positive psychologists believe that psychology needs to turn its attention to the kinds of psychological phenomena that contribute to human well-being. Some examples may be the psychological studies of happiness, courage, hope, trust, and determination. In addition, positive emotions are emphasized. Sounds cool, doesn't it? As far as Maslow and Seligman see it, psychology isn't just about what goes wrong with humans, but also about what goes right with them!

The Existential Psychologists

The preceding section provides a general discussion of the similarities and shared concerns that bind the existentialists and the existential-humanists. Now we talk about some of the specific existential-humanist psychologists and what they said. What did they prescribe? How did they incorporate some of the insights we look at earlier in the chapter?

First up is Rollo May. May's theories stress the importance of understanding human existence as *being-in-the-world,* and healthy living means being integrated in-the-world in the specific ways that are natural for you. Second is theorist Carl Rogers, whose understanding of the self shows clear connections to existential themes of individuality and authenticity. Last is Viktor Frankl. According to Frankl, what defines you as human is your need for meaning and your need to take control over the direction of your life by giving it purpose.

Rollo May: Reconnecting with existence

Rollo May (1909–1994) was an American psychologist and perhaps the first to explicitly identify his own leanings as existential in orientation. May's thinking has many aspects, so in the upcoming sections, we present one theme: his view that human existence is a way of being connected to the world. May felt that actualizing all these ways of being connected to the world was essential to mentally healthy living.

May's notion of human existence: Everyone lives in three worlds

Martin Heidegger argued that human existence exemplified what he called *being-in-the-world* (see Chapter 6 for details). This phrase means that you aren't a separate thing from the world, so you don't exist *in* it the way that a pen can be in a room. Instead, Heidegger felt that worldliness was a part of the actual way that people exist. Due to this fact, when you live in a way that fails to embrace what you are, thus rejecting the ways in which you're worldly, you're inauthentic. When you succeed in embracing your nature, you're living authentically.

Adapting those points to psychology is straightforward. Living authentically means living in a psychologically healthy way, whereas inauthentic living is unhealthy. With these points in mind, May suggests that everyone lives in three worlds (or *Welt,* which is German for *world*). They are

- ✔ *Umwelt* (environment-world): You have natural urges and drives; you possess a body and an unconscious. You're subject to the natural world around you and the laws that govern it.
- ✔ *Mitwelt* (with-world): You exist in a meaningful social world. In addition, in the *Mitwelt* you forge meaningful relationships with others as *persons.*
- ✔ *Eigenwelt* (own-world): You have a self-reflective relationship with your-self. You're conscious of how things affect you and how you feel. You're in touch with yourself.

Keeping your worlds in balance

According to May, being psychologically healthy means living in all three worlds at once. You have to keep all in the correct balance. But what does it mean for the worlds to get out of balance?

First, look at the *Umwelt,* or the world in which you're a natural being. (Kierkegaard would have called the *Umwelt* your finitude; see Chapter 10.) To embrace the *Umwelt,* you must embrace your natural being. In part, that means accepting your own inevitable death. We don't know about you, but most people we know don't do this very well. As a matter of fact, the way society handles death allows most people to easily avoid the subject until it can't be put off any longer. Although death is always all around you, binding you, you don't talk much about it. In today's society, it's taboo.

Your need for *Mitwelt* existence relates to your need to connect with others as *persons.* You need to have healthy relationships in which both parties recognize, respect, honor, and trust the other. People often fail to do this. One of the most obvious ways people fail to recognize and honor others is through sex, which is one of the most intimate ways people can have meaningful rela-tionships with others. Many times, people fail to engage in sex as a way of exemplifying the meaningful dimension of a human relationship and instead treat it as a way to manipulate another person as an object (a nonperson).

May says, "Individuals need to find each other for the sheer necessity of meeting biological needs . . . [but in this case] we are not really dealing with *Mitwelt* at all but only another form of *Umwelt.*" When you treat the other person as an object during sex, you rob your existence of the *Mitwelt* and overemphasize the *Umwelt.*

The *Eigenwelt* is the world of the self-relationship. Clearly, everyone needs to have a healthy relationship with herself; you need to treat yourself as a person. You need to learn to respect yourself, listen to yourself, and be responsive to your own ways of reacting to things or thinking about your life situations. Unfortunately, people often don't do this particularly well. At times, you may drag the world of the *Eigenwelt* in the world of the *Mitwelt* or the *Umwelt.*

When you drag the *Eigenwelt* into the world of the *Mitwelt,* you seek to become a robotic conformist. When you drag *Eigenwelt* into *Umwelt,* you think of yourself as nothing more than a set of biological drives and urges and instincts. In both senses, you obscure the *Eigenwelt* by objectifying yourself and refusing to acknowledge your own unique personhood.

Helping people reconnect

The three worlds typically fall out of balance due to unhealthy ways of reacting to anxiety. May thinks that people feel anxiety when they detect threats to their existence or to their way of being. As May sees it, these threats are normal. It's life; you grow and you develop. Your relationships mature, and your ways of relating to yourself and to your own drives undergo change. So you have to learn to deal with normal anxiety and face the situations in ways that allow your ways of existing to develop. When people refuse to do this, they become *neurotic;* they create defense mechanisms that attempt to obscure the situations they're threatened by, and as a result, their worlds get out of balance.

With this in mind, May believed that the function of therapy was to help people who had become alienated from themselves (by being out of sync in any of those three worlds) to learn to confront their true nature with courage. Ideally, therapy would allow people to reconnect with their being-in-the-world in the right way so that they could eventually live in a way that embraced everything they were.

Carl Rogers: Fully functional individuals

Carl Rogers (1902–1987) was an American psychologist famous for client-centered (or person-centered) therapy. He felt that people were essentially good and that you could find the basic motivational structure of human psychology in the fundamental desire to strive for the development of the unique potential of the individual. Rogers's claim echoes the existentialists' emphasis on the cultivation of authentic individuality.

For Rogers, a basic fact about nature was that all organisms (not just humans) seek to *actualize* themselves, which means that they all strive for the fulfillment of their potential. Humans are always reaching out for the possibilities that can help them develop and cultivate the unique individuality that each possesses.

So how do you develop your potential? For Rogers, each person can tell what's right for her development in a given situation. So you have the ability to know best how to navigate the changing world of your experiences. What this means, for Rogers, is that you must learn to listen to the inner voice that represents the true individual you (Rogers calls this the *organismic* self).

The characteristics of fully functioning people

Rogers called people who listened to their organismic self and successfully developed their potential *fully functioning people.* These people have a unique relationship with the world around them; they have a childlike wonder and an openness to experience. If you're fully functioning, you're

- **Open:** When life changes unexpectedly, you're open to what's new. You desire to have a kind of dialogue with life. You seek to learn from the diversity and novelty of experience, as opposed to making demands on it. You welcome change.

- **Engaged in the here and now:** You're not trapped in the past. You don't force preconceived notions onto your present experience. You appreciate each moment as special and meaningful on its own terms.

- **Self-trusting:** You trust your own inner intuitions and voice. You listen to what they tell you about experience. You don't suppress your own inner feelings or seek out others to find out how best to understand your experiences.

- **Creative:** You accept that no external rules dictate how you should mechanically respond to or interpret experience. Instead, you creatively engage with life, seeking to adapt in an artistically appropriate way what you found in older experience to the new world in which you presently live. Living is an art form that only you can master by utilizing your own inner resources and intuitions.

That sounds pretty darn cool, huh? Who wouldn't want to be fully functioning? Unfortunately, some people aren't fully functioning. For Rogers, the capacity to be fully functioning needs to be developed in the right context and conditions. Some people lack those contexts. Specifically, Rogers feels that you need to be at the center of loving relationships that foster self-esteem and the ability to trust yourself and listen to your inner voice.

Maslow's hierarchy of needs

Carl Rogers claimed that reaching your full potential requires first satisfying other, more basic needs (such as being in loving, esteem-building relationships). You can see this claim in other existential-humanist psychologists, specifically in Abraham Maslow, who is typically regarded as one of the founders of the existential-humanist approach. From the bottom up, here's Maslow's hierarchy of needs:

- At the most basic, Maslow suggests, are physical needs. Here, you strive for physical survival and have needs for air, drink, food, and even sex.

- After you satisfy these needs, you strive for safety and protection.

- Once again, when these two needs are satisfied, you turn toward a need for love and belonging among others. At this higher level of human existence, you need respect, admiration, and friendship.

- After you satisfy relational needs, you develop a desire for self-esteem. You crave a kind of self-confidence about your own abilities and ways of engaging with the world on your own terms.

- The last level is the most famous and clearly the most existential. Maslow felt that barely 1 percent of the population typically reaches it. He called it *self-actualization*. At this level, you begin to partake in an almost spiritual dimension of existence through the fulfilling of your own potential (this is Maslow's version of Rogers's fully functioning person). Some who reach this level, he felt, may have what he called peak experiences in which the person experiences a mystical and spiritual connection to reality. These people develop a real sense of peace with themselves and with their world. Unfortunately, Maslow thought, most people can't reach this level because they find themselves (for various reasons) trapped at lower levels within the hierarchy, seeking to satisfy more basic needs.

You may ask, "If everyone is running around just listening to their own inner voice, how will society function? Won't things just reduce to chaos?" Fortunately, no. Rogers doesn't think that being an individual puts you at odds with society or with the various societal roles that you might play. Instead, Rogers wants us to see that we aren't defined by those roles in such a way that the degree to which we conform to what others want us to do and to be determines our own self-worth. A psychologically healthy person may well live comfortably in society but would always have a very strong sense of self-worth not dependent upon the values of the society around her. In fact, Rogers feels that fully functioning people likely wouldn't stand out at all!

It's also important to note that Rogers feels that fully functioning people are driven by a desire to help others reach their own potential. So whereas believing that following your inner voice might lead to a lot of self-centered and perhaps socially destructive behavior, it actually leads to caring benevolent dispositions toward others!

The authentic individual self versus conditional positive regard

Rogers says that the abilities of fully functioning people grow and develop in relationships in which unconditional regard is given. Most people tend to get acceptance from other people but only in conditional form. This type of acceptance is actually damaging to the development of fully functioning individuals.

Socialization, on the other hand, is more common. By its very nature, it tends not to give unconditional positive regard. Instead, it gives conditional positive regard, programming you to think that you're okay or valuable *if* you do this or that or *if* you act in certain ways. It tells you to trust your inner voice *only if* it says the right things (in other words, what society likes).

When you're exposed to socialization or relationships that foster conditional positive regard, you develop what Rogers calls *conditional positive self-regard*. When this happens, you discount your own inner voice when it conflicts with what you're taught matters or is of value to those around you.

Instead of responding to changing experiences on the basis of trusting your individual unique voice, you match your feelings and behavior to what you think you're *supposed* to do or to what the existentialists might call your *inauthentic self* (the self that mirrors society, or what Heidegger called "the They" or Kierkegaard called "the Public").

Rogers's method of therapy aimed at getting people to feel more comfortable with their authentic individual self by being a good empathetic listener and by giving the client unconditional positive regard. As Rogers puts it, the therapist should aim to get the client to develop a "friendly openness to what is going on within him — learning to listen sensitively to himself." Thus, the goal of therapy is to help the client overcome oppressive socialization or dysfunctional relationships that stand in the way of full functioning. At its core, it aims at helping to allow a person become an authentic individual.

Viktor Frankl: Embracing the need for meaning

Viktor Frankl (1905–1997) was an Austrian psychiatrist who developed a method of treating patients called *logotherapy*. At its core is a strong existential theme: that all people have within them a strong innate drive for finding meaning. Many neuroses, Frankl felt, could be traced back to disruptions in that need, to "holes" within a person's life in which nothing held any real significance. As a result, he says that psychotherapy needs to address the patient's need for meaning in life, seeking to fill in the holes that exist.

Apart from his theories, Viktor Frankl is himself a man worth studying. In his book *Man's Search for Meaning,* he describes not only his proposed psychological method of *logotherapy* (meaning therapy), but also the experience that led him to posit the theory: his experiences in a Nazi concentration camp during World War II. Frankl's description of his experiences and what he learned about human psychology is a must-read. Frankl says that his experiences in the camps led him to develop three theses about the human condition:

- **Meaning always exists:** Meaning can be found in *every* situation. Meaning is a feature of your life situations. If you're open to it, you'll come see it; if you close yourself off from it, you won't.

- **Uniqueness:** Frankl felt that every person was unique, and so needed to find the meaning in the situation that was appropriate to the uniqueness of her experiences and life. As a result, you can't turn to society or to the masses to explain the significance of a situation. You have to find the meaning yourself.

- **Finding meaning is up to you:** You're free, which implies that in every situation, finding the meaning within it is up to you. It's always there; Frankl says that you need to go find it!

Although Frankl believes that meaning is *always* present — even in the Nazi camps — it's not always easy to find. In fact, Frankl suggests that some fail to find meaning and experience what he called an *existential vacuum.* When this happens, life simply fails to have any significance at all, and the person loses her sense of purpose. She despairs and loses hope and her will to live. As far as Frankl could determine, in the death camps many people lost hope and their will to live not simply as a result of the externalities they had to endure, but because of their inability to discern meaning in those situations.

You too can succumb to the existential vacuum and the neuroses that follow from it. If you fail to find meaning, you typically become self-destructive and fall into depression or even into addictive behaviors (think of Kierkegaard's *rotation;* see Chapter 10 for more on this). People within the existential vacuum live what Frankl calls *provisional existence.* Without real-life goals anchored in a secure sense of purpose and meaning, you fail to live in a true sense.

The methods of logotherapy

Recognizing that life situations can dislodge a person from living with a sense of purpose, logotherapy aims to get the client to frame her life in terms of meanings. As with most existential-humanist psychology, it's crucial that the patient not see herself as a passive victim. The patient learns to take control. Although logotherapy is complicated, two of its methods are worth pointing out:

✔ **Paradoxical intention:** This method aims to cure phobias or neurotic anxiety. One of Frankl's actual cases may help explain. Imagine that you have a fear of sweating in social situations. Instead of waiting passively (like a victim) for the inevitable to occur, Frankl suggests taking the wind out of the anxiety by *commanding* yourself to sweat — more than you typically do! Say, "I'm going to sweat a good gallon today! That'll show 'em."

Paradoxical intention (paradoxical because you decide to actively do what you fear most) is interesting because it teaches the person to take control by assigning a significance to the situation. Frankl also suggests that paradoxical intention adds humor to your relationship to your own life.

✔ **De-reflection:** This second method goes right to the heart of logo-therapy. Imagine any situation in which you find yourself anxious about some kind of performance. Maybe you have to take a big exam, and you always get test anxiety, or maybe the situation is sexual in nature. In both situations you're anxious to participate in some activity because you fear being exposed as a failure.

If you've ever experienced this, you know that the worst thing is thinking more about the object of the anxiety. The more you think about it, the more likely you are to fail. In fact, there's a name for this: the self-fulfilling prophecy. Frankl sees the problem this way: Your *hyper-reflection* (intense concentration on what's causing you performance anxiety) has dislodged you from your normal, seamless way of existing in your life.

How does de-reflection help? Well, it aims to help you reintegrate into flow. It helps you ignore the anxiety and instead concentrate on something completely different, something that would make the activity meaningful in a way unrelated to the concerns of your anxiety. Again, and like paradoxical intention, the aim is to take control and to teach the person to give her activities meaning.

Finding meaning

The aim of logotherapy is to help a person find meaning in life. According to Frankl, you can find meaning in at least three central ways:

✔ **Task oriented:** This way of finding meaning is very common for people. Think of what people often say to someone who doesn't have a direction in her life, someone who seems to just drift aimlessly without purpose. People tell her, "You need to find something that's important to you" or "You need to find your calling."

Often, what they mean is that the person needs to find some kind of activity that she can throw herself into. Perhaps that activity is being a good parent. Or being a good teacher. In typical existential fashion, Frankl doesn't insist on this or that activity; what's important is that the patient connect to the world in a way that allows her to feel as though things matter.

✔ **Experience oriented:** Frankl also points out that humans often experience meaning passively. You're at a museum and see a painting that strikes you. Or perhaps you see meaning in the way that a bee flies around honey. Suddenly, you feel as though you're connected with life in a way that can be very overwhelming. Sometimes such experiences can actually be life-altering!

✔ **Attitude oriented:** The last way in which people typically find meaning, Frankl suggests, is in moments of intense suffering — moments in which you feel as though your existence may actually be seriously threatened. Sometimes something physical causes these experiences; some people are faced with terminal illness. At other times, something psychological causes these experiences; some people are faced with the death of a loved one. In either case, you're presented with a horrifying question: "What's the point of life now?"

Frankl thinks that at these moments, you have to find meaning once again, *in* those situations. Frankl says that choosing *what* your experiences are isn't always up to you (having a terminal illness; losing a loved one; or even, in his situation, winding up in a concentration camp). But you *do* have the capacity to decide what your attitude will be toward that situation.

In an actual case study, Frankl talks about a patient who lost his wife. The man was overwhelmed with grief and couldn't find a reason to live on. Frankl asked the patient what it would have been like if he had died first. The man suggested that it would have been worse, because his wife wouldn't have been able to bear it, because she was less able to endure being alone than he.

Frankl then wondered whether his grief was his way of acknowledging that he was giving his wife the last gift to her that he could — bearing the role of being the survivor for the other. According to Frankl, the man's life was changed immediately because he found a meaning to give to his suffering.

Part V
The Part of Tens

The 5th Wave   By Rich Tennant

"I'm tired of letting everyone pull my strings."

In this part . . .

*E*xistentialism has always had a close association with the arts, particularly the narrative arts. Existential philosophers have not only influenced but also produced many fine novels and plays. It's no surprise then that movies, which are the ultimate narrative art form of modern American culture, are replete with existential themes. In Part V we review some of the great books, plays, and movies that incorporate (intentionally or not!) existential themes. Use this section as a reference guide to expanding your knowledge of existentialism, as a study aid for some of the masterpieces of existential storytelling, or just as a guide to great books and movies to pick up. Read them, see them, enjoy them!

Chapter 15

Ten Great Existential Movies

In This Chapter

▶ Reviewing existential themes at the theater

▶ Perusing a list of movies to see

Art is a very immediate experience. Through pictures, stories, and words, it brings you in direct confrontation with its subject matter. Movies blend all three, making it a particularly visceral medium. Much like painting and sculpture, movies often seem to have a direct line to our emotions. Perhaps this is what makes them such a good way of conveying existential themes. Unlike most other philosophies, existentialism calls you to think and feel, and it reminds you that you always make your decisions and take actions within concrete situations. Movies can present your existential situation in concrete terms and make you feel it. And as anyone who's ever seen the right movie at just the right time in his life knows, movies don't simply make you feel, but also help you process and work through emotions you already possess.

The movies have a rich history of presenting existential material. American *film noir* of the 1930s and 1940s, although not directly affected by the existential furor happening in Europe at the same time, seemed to be coming to many of the same conclusions. Their characters were often thrown into a world where the old rules of morality seemed to have been suspended. Themes of loneliness and forlornness cloaked morally ambiguous characters as they tried to navigate their way through a barren landscape where moral compasses seemed to have gone haywire.

Although not always as dark, movies have continued to present characters dealing with existential issues to this day. But where to start choosing the ten best of these movies? We haven't even tried. Too many films are too good and too existential. Instead, we tried to pick ten great films with a variety of styles and takes on existential issues. We include movies that we think you should see or, if you've seen them before, movies we think you should see again while reflecting on the existential nature of the stories they present.

Despite its reputation as a downer philosophy, existentialism has an optimistic, even hopeful side. Indeed, this is at the core of the philosophy in many respects. As a whole, the mix of movies in this chapter not only presents a world gone mad and unhitched from meaning, but also brings you back and shows you the light these thinkers saw at the end of the tunnel.

Ikiru (1952)

If you enjoy great foreign films, *Ikiru* is a must-see that you should pencil into your list of what to rent. Like *The Seventh Seal* (see the next section), the film is enjoyable not only from a purely philosophical angle, but also from the standpoint of pure aesthetics. This fact shouldn't be surprising, because *Ikiru* is, for sure, a masterpiece created by one of the greatest Japanese directors of all time: Akira Kurosawa.

Ikiru begins its story with a man in his late 50s, Mr. Watanabe, at the doctor's office. He's had some stomach pains and has X-rays performed to discover what the medical problem actually is. Unfortunately, it's cancer; Watanabe has just a few months to live.

This abrupt face-to-face confrontation with his impending finitude or death has an immediate and monumental effect on Watanabe. For more than 20 years he had worked as a low-level functionary within civil-service management, with no outside life to speak of. Now he suddenly finds that his old tasks provide absolutely no meaning for him. The news of his cancer casts him into an entirely unfamiliar world and forces him to ask, "How do I live?" (Translated, the title of the movie means *To Live*.) Thus the movie unfolds, chronicling Watanabe's different ways of responding to that question in light of his death.

The existential overtones should be pretty clear already! Although the film has many existential themes, the following three stand out as particularly important:

✔ **Death individuates you.** Although this is a common existential theme, it's one that's particularly pronounced in Heidegger (see Chapter 9). As Heidegger argues, when you come face to face with death, you strongly experience the mood of anxiety (see Chapter 4 for more about anxiety). Anxiety and death together have a powerful effect on you: They *individuate* you. In other words, they force you to come to grips with the fact that the meaning of your existence isn't exhausted by the social roles and routines that the crowd demands that you perform. As a result, facing death forces you to feel separate from the way you're expected to live. In the face of death, your routines seem artificial.

- ✔ **People strive hard to avoid death.** Even though honestly facing up to death can be liberating, people tend not to think about death, and they don't bring up the subject. Watanabe's own doctors don't tell him the truth; they lie about his illness. The film makes clear that before the diagnosis, Watanabe himself hadn't been honest about his own mortality. He lived a dead life, one deeply immersed in what "one" was expected to do. His relationships were hollow. If death is faced at all, it's wrapped up in social rituals meant to distract people from the actual confrontation with death they need to have. In fact, in *Ikiru,* Watanabe suffers partly because he finds it almost impossible to actually find people who will honestly acknowledge his situation.

- ✔ **Death forces you to give your life individual meaning.** Because an honest confrontation with mortality is so jarring, people often tend to try to run away from it, either back into the life of the crowd or into various kinds of hedonistic distraction. But if you can't distract yourself, you must face death, existentialists suggest, by creating a meaning for your life that is *your own.* One person who particularly suggested this was Viktor Frankl (see Chapter 14 for details), an existential psychologist who felt strongly that living in a healthy way required finding ways to meaningfully integrate yourself into the world as a unique person. As you watch the movie, ask yourself whether Watanabe ever does this — whether he finds true meaning to life.

The Seventh Seal (1957)

The Seventh Seal is a classic existential film that's also a cinematic masterpiece. Directed by Ingmar Bergman, this subtitled Swedish film is enjoyable, and the pleasure of viewing it goes beyond its admittedly clear philosophical dimensions.

If you like grim movies, the setting of *The Seventh Seal* is perfect for you. The film is set at the end of the Crusades and chronicles the return home to Europe of one of the knights (Antonius Block) and his faithful squire. When Block and the squire arrive in their land at the beginning of the film, the knight is approached by Death himself, who has apparently come to take him. The knight protests and challenges Death to a game of chess. They reach an agreement: As long as the game proceeds, Block's life is spared, and if he wins, Death leaves. Thus, the film begins with the portrait of a man who's forced to face his own death — literally! — throughout the whole film, as Death returns every so often to continue the game and conversation.

As the knight and the squire make their way through the countryside on the way to Block's castle, they encounter a Europe ravaged by the curse of the Black Plague. The countryside itself appears to have descended into total chaos, and they encounter many people who deal with the constant specter of death and suffering in very different ways (including an odd band of actors and musicians who are central to the plot and who seem oddly unaffected).

More than perhaps any other film, *The Seventh Seal* is consciously existentialist straight through. Although the film deals with many, many themes, perhaps two questions are central:

- ✔ **Does God exist?** This, of course, is a defining question in existentialism, one that different authors deal with in different ways. One way to think about it is as a series of questions: Are there right ways to live or right answers to the questions about life? Or is part of life dealing with the difficulties, trials, and suffering of an ambiguous existence that comes with no assurance of clear answers?

- ✔ **Is life meaningless if there is no God?** If there are no God, no right or wrong, and no way to live that's objectively true, what's the overall point of life itself? If there is no God, would life collapse into meaninglessness as a result? Should you be forced to despair in such a bleak world? As Block puts it, without proof of God's existence, the idea of God is nothing more than suffering — a suffering that people would be better to do without. The idea of God, as Block sees it, is a reminder to you that you live in fear and despair before the nothingness of the world. As he puts it, "Why can't I kill God within me? Why does he live on in this painful and humiliating way even though I curse him and want to tear him out of my heart? I want knowledge, not faith. . . . I want God to stretch out his hand toward me, reveal himself to me." When you study Kierkegaard (see Chapter 10), Block's request may sound a bit odd!

These questions, and many other ones, are raised in *The Seventh Seal.* Enjoy!

Apocalypse Now (1979)

Like war movies? Well, this is certainly a great one by any standard, set during the Vietnam War in the 1970s. Like a few of the other films on this list, *Apocalypse Now* is worth viewing for more than just the philosophical lessons; it's a cinematic classic brought to you by one of America's most famous directors, Francis Ford Coppola.

In the film, Captain Willard (played by Martin Sheen) is an assassin for military intelligence. He's sent up a river in Vietnam and into Cambodia to find another officer, Colonel Kurtz (played by Marlon Brando). As Willard is told at the start of the film, Kurtz was an amazing soldier with a storied career, one whom most people expected to end up in a high position in government.

But now Kurtz has gone mad and has set himself up as a god in the jungles of Cambodia, acting with a small army of his own and taking orders from no one. Because Kurtz has gone insane, Willard is instructed to ride on a small Navy boat up the river to find him and eventually terminate his command. The movie follows the boat's journey up the river and the experiences of the soldiers on board along the way. Eventually, toward the end, they get to their destination, and if you're not already exhausted in the film, that's when the fun really begins, in the heart of the jungle itself.

Of all the films on our list, *Apocalypse Now* is perhaps the one that's least driven intentionally by a desire to represent existentialism. That said, the film clearly deals with lots of important existential questions. We highlight the central question here:

How far are you prepared to go to take on the challenge of self-creation?

When you read Nietzsche (see Chapter 11) and Kierkegaard (see Chapter 10), you're presented with a picture of authenticity that demands that you follow *who you are* in creating yourself. You're to follow your unique individuality to wherever the voice within you takes you. Many existentialists recognize that this journey may require a great deal of hardness, because you may not initially be prepared to go where that voice will take you. For Kierkegaard, following his path as an individual leads Abraham to obey God's command to kill his son Isaac. Just how far are you willing to go to be an individual? Or are your attempts at self-creation always going to be safely enclosed within the boundaries of what you're allowed to do by the masses and the crowd? If so, how self-created are you, really?

Existentialists try hard never to give the concept of authenticity a *moral* reading. Authors such as Heidegger and Nietzsche and Kierkegaard all argue that what you are as an individual transcends moral codes. That doesn't mean you can't be moral, but it does mean that being an individual goes beyond it. As Nietzsche puts it, you must learn to live in the cold space beyond good and evil. This, of course, leads not to a kind of relativism, but actually toward a more demanding form of ethics.

In *Apocalypse Now,* you're asked whether Colonel Kurtz (or Captain Willard, perhaps) is a potential specimen of authenticity. As Kurtz puts it in discussing his own life, he's "beyond their lying, timid morality." He knows what the crowd is (here represented by society and the military establishment), and he rejects it. He's beyond it. He's an individual. As you watch the film, pay close attention to how, as the soldiers progress up the river, all semblances of order and structure fall away. This is a clear existential reference to the fact that as you get closer and closer into the heart of what you are, you find chaos there — chaos that only you can organize on your own terms.

Blade Runner (1982)

Ridley Scott's sci-fi noir story of a dystopian world in which humans hunt and kill their greatest creation has recently been rereleased with a brand-new ending, producing a new wave of enthusiasm for the science fiction classic. No matter which ending you prefer, the movie is replete with philosophical musings on a range of topics, including the nature of consciousness and identity, the dangers of capitalism and corporate-political collusion, and bio- and scientific ethics. But above all, it presents a radically existential view of the world and of the future.

Deckard, played by Harrison Ford, is a retired blade runner — someone whose job it is to hunt down and kill artificial people called *replicants*. The replicants are genetically based androids who are used as slave labor and prostitutes on off-world colonies but are illegal on earth and are destroyed immediately if discovered. Decker is brought out of retirement because he's the best and because four particularly dangerous replicants have arrived in Los Angeles.

Replicants develop emotions, feelings, questions, and a desire to live. In a very real sense, then, Deckard is an assassin, and Harrison Ford plays him with the haunted, detached loneliness you may expect of one. But Deckard isn't alone. The futuristic world he lives in is one of flattened emotions and alienation. People walk like ghosts through a nightmarishly foreboding urban landscape where it's constantly dark and always raining (even though it's L.A. — go figure). The most vibrant images are those of the ever-present advertisements and the video spokesmodel on display on giant Times Square-esque video monitors throughout the city. The high-tech ads say it all. This is a world governed by two things: technology and commerce. People have no place.

The human beings seem tired and resigned to this fact. The replicants, however, are almost youthful in their passion and curiosity. They're designed to have only a four-year life span, so everything to them is new and strange, and their emotions are raw and intense. As Deckard hunts them, he slowly learns from them and begins to recapture his own humanity.

Blade Runner presents a bleak landscape devoid of color, meaning, and ethical touchstones. The God of Abraham has been replaced by the gods of science (in the guise of technology) and capitalism. The problem isn't simply that these gods aren't up to the task, but also that their whole orientation is confused. Both work in a mechanistic way to produce results, but the results aren't calibrated to genuine human needs. The replicants represent and give voice to these human needs. They seek their creator for answers and find none (even though they, unlike the humans, are at least granted an audience with their creator).

But God isn't the real enemy in *Blade Runner*. This is a world that lost faith in God long ago and has been lost in a nihilistic stupor ever since. Nietzsche warned that the era beginning with the death of God is a dangerous time. He and the rest of the existentialists warn against taking it too lightly and plunging heedlessly forth in hedonistic glee, and they warn against trusting science and rationalism to save us. Science won't save you. Technology won't save you. Reason won't save you. These things won't save you because they can't address your most basic human needs, for meaning, purpose, and a sense of self.

The emotions of the replicants, their yearning for purpose and for answers, aren't solutions to these problems. Rather, they point to the direction in which something was left behind. When the nightmare world the replicants and the human blade runners both live in was created, something was forgotten and not taken into account. It is, in many respects, the world that the existentialists predict will come if people allow their humanity to be taken out of the equation — if we allow the mechanizations of rationality, science, and technology to go unchecked, and undirected, by human ends and true human needs.

Crimes and Misdemeanors (1989)

> **Cliff:** A strange man . . . defecated on my sister.
>
> **Wendy:** Why?
>
> **Cliff:** I don't know. Is there . . . Is there any reason I could give you that would answer that satisfactorily?

Woody Allen's existential masterpiece of choices and consequences (or the lack thereof) in a godless world is like an old-time morality play, without the morality. It's an anguished cry against a universe without justice, a quiet expression of hope that somehow we can find a way to live in that universe, and the humble suggestion, brilliantly expressed, that the only way we can and do get through it is by loving one another.

The movie tells two distantly intertwined tales. In one, Woody Allen plays a riff on his usual neurotic intellectual. Cliff is a director who specializes in biographical documentaries that make no money and that no one is interested in. His wife persuades him to take a job working for her brother, Lester (played by Alan Alda), directing a biopic of his life. Lester is a TV producer and Cliff's polar opposite — shallow; arrogant; self-confident; and, of course, highly successful. Soon, Cliff finds himself competing with his nemesis, Lester, for the beautiful Halley Reed (played by Mia Farrow), all the while making a documentary in which he compares his brother-in-law with Mussolini.

Meanwhile, Martin Landau plays Judah, a respected ophthalmologist who's having mistress trouble. His mistress (played by Angelica Huston) insists that he leave his marriage. She calls his house, sends a letter to his wife, and even threatens to expose him as an embezzler. Judah goes to both his brother, who has Mafia connections, and a friend who's a rabbi for help. Fittingly enough, the rabbi is going blind. Suffice it to say that the Mafia brother has no such handicap. By the end of the movie, you finally see Cliff and Judah together, and their two stories have painted a picture of a strange, indifferent universe and a few of the people struggling to understand as they wander through it.

Crimes and Misdemeanors deals with the choices you freely make, how those choices determine who and what you are, and what your life will be. It's about making choices in a world in which the only consequences are human consequences and the only results are human results. In a world where God is absent, there's no guarantee of the results, no guarantee the wicked will be punished or the just rewarded. More than anything, though, it's a meditation on a fact that all the existentialists acknowledge and even stress: Life without God, without ultimate justice, is *hard.* The anguish and forlornness you feel when you face this fact is felt even by those who, being wicked or doing wicked things, benefit from the lack of any ultimate consequence.

But this is a comedy, and as Lester repeatedly reminds us, in a comedy things are funny as long as they bend but don't break. Just when it seems everything is hopelessly broken, Cliff reminds us, as the existentialists do, that in a lonely universe, you can still find meaning in the people, projects, and activities with which you engage yourself; in this, there is hope.

Leaving Las Vegas (1995)

> *The value of life cannot be measured.*
>
> —Friedrich Nietzsche

If the optimism presented in the movie *Pleasantville* (see the later section about that movie) is a tough optimism, the optimism of *Leaving Las Vegas* is downright brutal. In many ways, the two movies resonate with each other, though each certainly stands on its own. Director Mike Figgis presents two characters, Ben (played by Nicolas Cage) and Sera (played by Elisabeth Shue), who seemingly (and to a large degree, really) have no hope, no prospects, and no future. She's a prostitute with an abusive pimp, and he's an alcoholic intent on drinking himself to death. They fall in love, and nothing much changes besides the fact that they're living these lives side by side.

Leaving Las Vegas is a challenging movie. It challenges moviegoers to look at two stock, cliché-ridden characters as people. It challenges the assumptions you have about those people; their lives; and the value of those bleak, often despairing, lives. The movie meets you halfway by presenting characters and events that are more complex, specific, and three-dimensionally human than a superficial description would lead you to expect. Having done that, it makes the events that unfold all the harder to watch. After you recognize its characters as people, the movie challenges you to watch without flinching as they bleed, often from self-inflicted wounds. The result is something beautiful and transformative. Few films can reacquaint you with your own humanity and the humanity of those around you, but *Leaving Las Vegas* manages to do both.

Watching *Leaving Las Vegas* is like an exercise in what Nietzsche calls the reevaluation of all values. We have for a very long time seen the world through the glasses of a certain, specific morality. We see and judge the world through this lens and a hundred others we routinely adopt from various systems of thought. These systems of thought inform how we judge right and wrong, what is and is not of value, and the way we see how things *are* and the way things *should be*. For the existentialist, these notions must be reassessed at best and more likely abolished.

Nothing in *Leaving Las Vegas* is life as it should be, and nothing about it is the way you were told drunks, prostitutes, life, or love are. Certainly, this is Hollywood, and probably no story like this could ever really happen, but the concrete humanity of everything onscreen is so undeniable that it shatters the limited notions of what life is or should be. Seeing the beauty in the ugly landscapes traveled by this movie forces you to reassess, rediscover, and even re-create those most fundamental notions.

Pleasantville (1998)

> **David's mom:** When your father was here, I used to think, "This was it. This is the way it was always going to be. I had the right house. I had the right car. I had the right life."
>
> **David:** There is no right house. There is no right car.

Pleasantville is an existential fable, an eccentric fairy-tale journey that combines comedy, drama, and fantasy with deep passion and belief in its underlying themes. On one level, it's a metaphor for and commentary on the radical and jarring changes that swept society in the 1960s. The commentary may be summed up in the words of Billy Joel, "The good ole days weren't always good, and tomorrow ain't as bad as it seems." It shows a world in which things fall apart and some genuinely sad things occur. Who can see the lovable George Parker (portrayed by William H. Macy) lose his wife and not feel for him? In the end, however, it shows a world it believes you can be optimistic about — a world where, despite all your troubles, you'll be okay.

The movie stars Tobey Maguire as David, a high school loser obsessed with the TV show *Pleasantville,* a *Leave It to Beaver*–style TV show from the 1950s in which everything is just so. Dad goes off to work at a job where he's respected and valued, Mom keeps the house tidy and has dinner ready when he comes home, everybody knows everybody else, everybody knows what his role in the town is, and everything just makes sense. The town consists of Elm Street, Main Street, and Town Hall, and as the school's geography teacher points out, that's all you need to know.

One day, David and his sister Jennifer (played to perfection by Reese Witherspoon) find themselves magically transported into their TV set, into the world of *Pleasantville.* Their interactions with the townspeople slowly start to change everything. The once-idyllic little town, in which everything was once (literally) black and white, begins to change, and life begins to become more complicated and, at the same time, more interesting.

Pleasantville contains a host of scenes that give voice to existential themes. One of our favorites occurs when the townspeople gather to discuss what to do about all the disturbing changes happening in the town. Big Bob (the closest thing to a villain in the movie) gets up in front of the crowd and advises, "The first thing we have to do is to separate out the things that are pleasant from the things that are unpleasant."

This is what the old concept of the true world, which Nietzsche and the other existentialists rail against, tried to do (see Chapter 3). It's one of the principal things that the existentialists say you must learn can't be done. If there are no heaven and hell, all the good in universe and all the evil are both right here on earth together. If you're to accept life, it must be an acceptance of the imperfect world that is, not an idyllic world you wish for or that you imagine exists elsewhere or existed once upon a time. By the end of the movie, the people of Pleasantville slowly learn to accept this.

More than anything, however, the movie is existential because its narrative about the journey of a small town mirrors the narrative the existentialists tell about the journey of the human species. When Nietzsche first proclaims the death of God, he does so with a mix of sorrow for what had been lost and excitement about what could now be. The excitement is about the possibilities given life by the shattering of the old dogmatic ways of thinking and the potential for a new human flourishing out of the ashes of the beliefs that used to comfort us.

If you boil down the existential narrative, it goes something like this (many existentialists would reject the notion they have a narrative, but in one way or another, we all do): We used to believe in God, the church, human reason. We used to believe that there were answers to everything and that those answers could be provided from the outside. Life made sense, and we believed it had meaning. The stories presented by the church and other purveyors of truth were comforting, but they were false and limited in scope — much like *Pleasantville*'s geography or the black-and-white thinking of its residents. When we lose these traditional ways of thinking, we experience anguish and forlornness, but these feelings only call us to engage in the world and take responsibility for what it will be. When you cast off the old systems of thought, everything doesn't then become okay. You're never fully rid of anguish. Rather, you're able to face the fact that things were never really okay, and you start to create a new world and new values.

Pleasantville tells this story metaphorically and brings great questions of God, meaning, value, and the history of the human species down to a very intimate, concrete, and human level. This in itself is an existential approach to big issues. Most of all, it tells the story with the passionate but grounded optimism of the best existential writings. You won't find the right house, but that's okay, because there is no right house. You'll make a worthwhile life in the house you choose.

Fight Club (1999)

Fight Club has a great cast, starring Brad Pitt, Edward Norton, and Helena Bonham Carter. The film begins in a place that most people probably find eerily familiar; it tells the story of a person who's deeply lost or immersed within the life that society expects him to live. He works his job robotically, and it seems to hold no real meaning for him. When he gets home at night, he dedicates his time to decorating his house with new furniture in the hopes of getting it just right. Essentially, the film sets up the story of a man trying to do his best to be a vague abstraction, an everyman.

But then his apartment, which he sees as the embodiment of his very self, blows up while he's away on business. Forced to find a new place to live, he boards with Tyler Durden, who's portrayed as a bit of an oddball (to say the least). Very soon into the film, these two characters start a fight club, a basement club dedicated to just that — a place where men can come together with the object of beating the tar out of one another for enjoyment. Along the way, the members of the fight club begin to take on missions designed to disrupt the smooth operation of the conformist world that exists outside their hidden underground club.

The fact that the film deals with existential themes is clearly intentional; it drips with existential metaphors and has a lot of dialogue meant to highlight themes you see in this book. Here are a few questions to get you thinking about this interesting movie:

- **Does your existence demand struggle and confrontation?** The film clearly presents you with a portrait of modern life as one in which struggle and confrontation have been, for the most part, either done away with or channeled toward society-approved projects. Most people live safely immersed within their very set routines. Desires to creatively express yourself, or even to struggle with existence, are redirected toward an addiction (or distraction) with consumerism (hence, the obsession the main character has with fixing up his apartment). As Durden puts it, "The things you own end up owning you."

  If you listen to writers such as Nietzsche, however, this kind of life is missing an essential component that's needed for health (or authenticity). That component is self-definition, and it requires that you continually fight new battles in trying to further challenge what you take yourself to be at any given moment. As Carl Rogers puts it (in Chapter 14), you must strive to develop your potential. For Nietzsche, the authentic person is like a warrior, one who's constantly testing his mettle against perspectives that are contrary to his own and always striving to develop himself further. Due to this need, healthy living requires doing battle not just against society, but also against yourself — against your weak desires to flee the battle and rejoin the safety of the herd.

  Those people who interpret *Fight Club* as a movie about a strange club in which men beat one another up lose the main point. Instead, see the fight club as a metaphor for the need to engage with that primordial need for struggle. The fight club represents your need to be a warrior in life and to resist the goal of society to subdue you and make you tame.

- **Do you create yourself? Does existence precede essence?** Jean-Paul Sartre's main point about self-creation lies at the heart of the film. While society or the herd will have you believe that you're really just the roles that you play in the world, you can always change all that and define yourself in a way that suits who you are as an individual.

  Unfortunately, after too much time in society, people forget these things. They start working on the furniture in their apartment. In an interesting scene, Durden pulls a gun on a poor store owner and threatens to kill him, asking him what the man always wanted to be in life but gave up on. After the man tells him, Durden lets him go, telling Norton's character that the man will now see his life differently, having been freed to become himself through this deadly encounter. As Durden puts it, "It's only after we've lost everything that we're free to do anything."

Stranger Than Fiction (2006)

> *The moment I set eyes on him I instantly push him from me, I myself leap backwards, I clasp my hands and say half aloud, "Good Lord, is this the man? Is this really [personification of passion]? Why, he looks like a tax collector!"*
>
> —Søren Kierkegaard, *Fear and Trembling*

This movie is a strange delight. One part romantic comedy, one part absurdist fantasy, it's presented with the kind of care and passion rare in movies today. Its story resonates with existential concerns of passion, death, and meaning, but the movie never gets too deep and never allows itself to get pulled down under the weight of its underlying themes. Even at its most dramatic moments, it's too busy being funny. Very, very funny.

Will Ferrell plays Harold Crick, an IRS tax auditor who starts hearing a woman's voice inside his head. The voice follows him wherever he goes, narrating the events of his life. It isn't a very exciting life. As the movie opens, you hear, as does Harold, a thorough description of his very detailed and precise method of brushing his teeth. Of course, this is very disturbing for Harold because he's not used to hearing strange voices narrating his life. Things really take a turn, however, when the voice refers to Harold's imminent death. The rest of the movie finds Harold splitting his time between searching for the meaning and origin of this voice in a desperate attempt to save his own life, and pursuing Ana (played by Maggie Gyllenhaal).

We figure that if you're in a race to save your own life, pursuing Maggie Gyllenhaal is about as worthwhile a distraction as you can find.

In real life, people tend to avoid those they see as serious, boring, uptight, and disconnected from the rest of the world. In literature and the movies, however, these people are often heroes. We love characters like Harold Crick, because although we like to think we're more fun at parties, we feel just as alienated. Most people fear their own lives are as small, empty, and meaningless as the lives of characters like these, and they want to believe they can somehow come to live more full and rich lives, as the characters do by the end of their stories. It's an existential concern given voice by hundreds of Harold Cricks in hundreds of stories about learning to love life. But this movie is richer. Some things to notice:

- ✔ **Absurdity:** Every scene in this movie has a touch of absurdity, including the movie's premise; Harold's relationship with Ana; the fact that he's about to die; and most important, the decision he makes with regard to that fact. As Camus and Kierkegaard were especially adept at pointing out, that absurdity can be cruel and painful, but you must ultimately embrace it. This movie embraces that absurdity, and so does Harold, ultimately.

- ✔ **Death:** The whole movie is about facing the reality, inevitability, and absurdity of death. As Professor Hilbert (Dustin Hoffman's character) point's out, "You will die. You will absolutely die. Even if you avoid this death, another will find you." Only in facing this fact does Harold finally learn what it means to be alive.

- ✔ **Narratives:** Harold doesn't merely face death; he faces an omniscient narrator (played by Emma Thompson) who defines not only the action, but also the meaning of his life. When you watch Harold brush his teeth, it's interesting because the narrator describes it with so much wit and insight that it becomes meaningful. The way in which our lives have been defined by external, absolute systems (see Chapter 3) or narratives of meaning and how we must become the writers of our own narratives are central existential themes. Watch how Harold and, ironically enough, the narrator herself struggle with this narrative, what it means, and how it should be written.

- ✔ **Passion:** This is a movie about living with passion. For Kierkegaard, this was epitomized by the knight of faith, a figure who seems no different from an ordinary person but lives with total commitment, total involvement, and total passion (see Chapter 7 for details). By the end of the movie, we like to think Harold Crick has become something of a secular knight of faith. Even Harold's test at the end of the movie is reminiscent of Kierkegaard's favorite knight of faith, Abraham (see Chapter 10). Both are asked to do the unthinkable, and incomprehensibly, absurdly, both find the courage and passion to make an impossible choice.

But perhaps what's most existential about *Stranger Than Fiction* is its optimism — the optimism that life doesn't have to be rote drudgery and that the absurdity of life doesn't have to defeat you. By engaging in the world passionately and exercising his human dignity, Harold is able to save himself. The existentialists tell you that you can too.

Superbad (2007)

Superbad tells the story of three teenagers in search of sex, booze, and a good time. The plot is familiar, but the actors and the script have a warmth that transcends the typical teenage sex comedy. Seth and Evan (played by Jonah Hill and Michael Cera) are best friends and high-school losers who get invited to a party hosted by the beautiful and popular Jules (Emma Stone). The catch is, Seth has bragged about his ability to supply the party with alcoholic beverages, so the two can't show up empty-handed. To accomplish this task, they enlist their friend Fogell (Christopher Mintz-Plasse), who's recently obtained a fake ID that says that he's 25 and that his name is McLovin. Just

McLovin. Every good teenage sex comedy has one guy who even the geeks find embarrassing to hang around with — the loser among losers, the geek among geeks. In *Superbad,* it's Fogell, a.k.a. McLovin.

Naturally, everything that can go wrong does go wrong. The night turns into a string of surreal and sometimes dangerous encounters. All the while, Seth and Evan argue as only best friends who truly love each other can while Fogell is busy being Fogell. By the end, Seth and Evan have stopped arguing and learned a few things about love and friendship, and Fogell has become who he always was: McLovin.

Every high school movie is a little existential. The history of the human race repeats itself, after all, in every human life. You start enmeshed in and clinging to the narratives your parents have spun for you, and at some point, you break away. That time is filled with anguish, uncertainty, and alienation as you find yourself adrift from any fixed meaning while you try to find your own and, in true Sartrean fashion, create yourself. Seth and Evan certainly go through this. They're de-centered from their traditional sense of self-identity, primarily in the reevaluation they make of the nature of their own friendship.

Fogell, however, makes *Superbad* exquisitely existential. Nietzsche tells us we must become who we are. He says we must create ourselves, preferably with some style. He speaks of the coming of a new type of man, a bold new conqueror of himself and a free spirit. He speaks of the emergence of the Übermensch — the superman.

Behold the superman; behold McLovin.

What makes a character like Fogell a geek among geeks is that he's immune, utterly immune, to the opinions of others. He is who he is — as bizarre and unacceptable as that may be (especially in high school, where individuality is particularly frowned upon). Seth and Evan try and fail to fit in. They aren't seen as cool, but they aren't total train wrecks either. Much of their discussions have the form, "Okay, you gotta say this" and "You gotta do that." The goal is to be acceptable, to fit in, to get the girl. As interesting as you, as a viewer, may find them, they spend much of their time fleeing their individuality and trying to get into the high school herd.

More specifically, Seth works at joining the herd while Evan struggles to come to terms with his own individuality. Meanwhile, Fogell has created himself in an image that may not please anyone else, but it pleases him. By the end of the movie, his proud statement early on, "I *am* McLovin," has proved prophetic. His image is transformed by then, but he hasn't become anyone he wasn't from the start. In true Nietzschean fashion, his self-creation is a matter of sheer will, creativity, style, and self-acceptance.

Chapter 16

Ten Great Works of Existential Literature

In This Chapter

▶ Understanding why literature matters so much to the existentialists

▶ Discovering the classics and then some

▶ Creating a list of books to read

*E*xistentialism has been called as much a literary movement as a philo-sophical one, and this statement contains some truth. Many of the existentialists at least dabbled in novels, plays, or even poetry, and a few became quite proficient. In fact, it has been said of the two kings of French existentialism that Jean-Paul Sartre was a philosopher who dabbled in litera-ture and Albert Camus was a writer who dabbled in philosophy. We tend to think they were each pretty good at both, but such sentiments highlight the degree to which the movement was deeply involved in literary concerns.

Unlike our list of ten movies (see Chapter 15), our list of literary works is populated, in part at least, by full-blooded existentialists — philosophers straight in from the front lines. These works not only give voice to existential themes, but also represent a working-out and further development of the specific ideas these philosophers were dealing with in their more straightfor-wardly philosophical work.

Existentialism is also considered a literary movement because of several authors whose works are seen as not just borrowing existential themes, but also as being original and independent statements of the issues with which the existentialists dealt. Writers like Kafka, Dostoevsky, and Tolstoy are seen as precursors of, or even influences on, later existentialist thinking. We include some classics by them, move on to some great books by the heavy hitters of existentialism, and complete the chapter with some other terrific works that deal with similar themes.

Hamlet, by William Shakespeare

There's nothing new in the world. If there ever was room to do something new, it seems, Shakespeare did it. Shakespeare wrote more than 200 years before the existentialists, yet there's nary a theme anywhere that hasn't made at least a passing appearance in his work. This fact underscores the fundamental truths of the human condition with which both he and the existentialists were dealing. Existentialism is considered a modern philosophy, but it wrestles with age-old questions.

In *Hamlet,* the title character must come to terms with the death of his father. He sees the ghost of his father, who informs Hamlet that he was murdered by his brother Claudius. Claudius has since married Hamlet's mother and ascended to the throne of his murdered brother. In a traditional revenge tragedy, the rest of the play unfolds organically and inevitably. But *Hamlet* is anything but traditional, and nothing is quite as expected. Hamlet mopes, he questions, and he waxes . . . well, existential. Has there been a more existential line in the history of English literature than Hamlet's query "To be, or not to be; that is the question"?

Hamlet reflects upon this question, the question of suicide, and upon death and how it's the equal fate of kings and peasants alike. He reflects upon questions of action and certainty, justice and retribution. With his father dead, he finds himself in a bleak landscape where the moral order has been overturned and where he alone must decide what to do. Even seeing his father's ghost, who tells him of Claudius's betrayal, doesn't settle the question of what to do. He considers the possibility that he may be mad, that some demon may be deceiving him. Kierkegaard says Abraham must ask himself just these sorts of questions when God asks him to sacrifice Isaac. Hamlet doesn't make any kind of leap of faith, however. Rather, he devises a test to see what the truth is.

Hamlet is an existential hero, then, in part because he feels anguished and forlorn about making his decision. He can feel these feelings only because he doesn't succumb to seeing his life in terms of a traditional, prewritten narrative. He finally does make a choice, but like all choices, after he makes it, it's out there in the world, and he can have no control over it. Virtually all the characters experience the absurdity of this same phenomenon. Plot after plot is made only to backfire in unexpected ways. One character agrees to spy on Hamlet but is killed when Hamlet mistakes him for Claudius. Claudius poisons a goblet meant for Hamlet, but his wife (Hamlet's mother) drinks it instead. Finally, Hamlet does kill Claudius, dying himself in the process. Hamlet was the rightful king of Denmark and was to ascend to the throne upon killing his usurping uncle. Instead, Fortinbras, prince of rival Norway, appears intent on leading his army against Denmark. Finding the country headless already, he simply fills the vacuum and takes the throne.

Why existentialists love literature

Many philosophers outside existentialism wouldn't touch literature with a 10-foot pole. Indeed, Plato initially banished poets from his perfect city in *The Republic*. On the other hand, the existentialists were keen on literature for the following reasons:

✔ **Literature is concrete:** The existentialists believed that each of us lives her life embedded in concrete situations. Indeed, they railed against systems that attempted to gloss over the specific details of our lives and create universal, one-size-fits-all narratives to guide us. Literature afforded them the opportunity to reflect the reality that all choices are made by real people in the context of their situations.

✔ **Literature speaks to you on an emotional level:** Literature can be used to evoke emotions without even raising the question of truth. For the existentialists, emotions are deeply valuable guideposts. Evoking the right emotions from you, then, can do as much as or more than any argument could to make you understand the nature of your situation.

✔ **Literature is nondogmatic:** Most good literature raises issues, concerns, questions, and emotions, and it allows you to walk in the shoes of another person to understand and appreciate a different point of view. Existentialists were always quick to avoid even the appearance of dogmatism, and literature allowed them to do this while tweaking the perceptions and emotions of their audience and helping them see the world from the existentialists' perspective.

✔ **Existentialism is about creation:** When you recognize that there's nothing, you have to start making something. If God is no longer a viable, absolute source of meaning and purpose, it's up to you to create it, to remake yourself and the world through an act of will and creativity. What better way to communicate this fact, to illustrate it, and even undertake it than by engaging in the act of creation? Authors create worlds from nothing, and this is precisely what your task is as a human being: to narrate a meaningful story for your life and the world that makes sense and has emotional resonance.

Notes from the Underground, by Feodor Dostoevsky

> I am a sick man. . . . I am a spiteful man. I am an unattractive man. I believe my liver is diseased. However, I know nothing at all about my disease, and do not know for certain what ails me.

So begins Dostoevsky's masterpiece of the misanthropic. *Notes from the Underground* is the story, often told in rambling, even nonsensical terms, of this man, how he lives, how he sees the world. The novel is split into two parts. The first is basically him kvetching like this at length, taking on such topics as illness, spitefulness, rationalism, and utopianism. The point that comes up again and again is that rational and utopian systems have it fundamentally wrong because they assume human beings are basically rational, and we're not. In the second part of the novel, the underground man interacts with the outside world. He gets into a dispute with a police officer, falls in love with a prostitute, but is ultimately brought down by his own pettiness and self-loathing. In something like a self-fulfilling prophecy, he watches as things fall apart.

Plato once said that "to know the good is to do the good." When people act in ways that are harmful to themselves and society, it's because on one level or another, they believe the act is good — that it will bring them happiness or success, for example. The underground man (whom Dostoevsky never names) rejects this kind of thinking out of hand. He speaks of his own experience of doing wrong precisely at the moment he's most sure it's wrong and describes his delight in his own degradation. If logic and rationality (of the type that tell you that twice two is four) are a stone wall, the underground man is happy to bang his head against it, even if he'll never break through.

Although the underlying target of much of his ramblings is the utopian socialism that was to become so influential in the history of his native Russia, his irrationalism speaks to the larger urge of religious, scientific, philosophical, and political systems to try to provide neat, orderly answers to everything. What all these systems have at their center is an assumption that human beings, whom these systems supposedly serve, are fundamentally rational creatures. As such, their well-being can be served by rational calculations. But if human beings are irrational, we neither want, nor will be served by, nor will cooperate with such systems. One traditional existentialist complaint about these systems is that they dehumanize us. But Dostoevsky's underground man turns this on its head, stating that these systems will ultimately fall apart because even if they're good for us, we're too warped, stubborn, and irrational to cooperate.

The Death of Ivan Ilych, by Leo Tolstoy

The importance of death in existentialism is famous, but it's sometimes misinterpreted to suggest that existentialists are always depressed, walking around moping and muttering about their eventual, approaching, and dismal end. That reputation is only half true. On the one hand, existentialists do care about death and finitude, but they don't see anything ultimately depressing about facing up to it. If anything, they think the consequences of *not* facing death are depressing!

With that in mind, try to pick up this great Russian novel, *The Death of Ivan Ilych*. Clearly, Tolstoy, although not an existentialist himself, recognizes the importance of facing death if you want to live an authentic life. When you avoid death, Tolstoy clearly believes (in agreement with later thinkers such as Heidegger) that your life tends to fall apart and lose its focus. You drift. You're alive, but you're really like a zombie. You may as well be dead!

The book starts with the wake service for the main character, Ivan Ilych. It's an interesting start to the novel, because Tolstoy wants you to see that no one at the wake ceremony seems to be addressing the actual death of poor Ivan, the protagonist, and what death represents for each of the individuals in the room. Sure, they know he's dead, but death has significance to them only in ways that allow them to avoid the actual subject of dealing with what death means in each of their particular lives. Instead, death turns out to be something totally impersonal for them all. For Ivan's wife, his death means the possibility for her to receive his pension. For Ivan's colleagues, it means a possible promotion in the court system (he left a vacancy, after all). For still others in the room, it means having to perform the right rituals, such as kneeling before the body and making the sign of the cross.

After setting up this theme — that people avoid the realities of death — Tolstoy takes you back into time, back to just before the time when Ivan contracts the disease that eventually winds up killing him. As the story proceeds and Ivan contracts his illness, Tolstoy masterfully shows how Ivan is no different about the subject of his own death from the guests at his eventual wake at the start of the book. Instead of facing up to his own finitude, Ivan hides inside a whirlwind of distractions, all of which succeed in allowing him to concentrate on achieving worldly and community success. He redecorates his house, he plays cards with the right people, he networks. He's intimately concerned with assuring that *they* think he's living the right kind of life.

As the book progresses, Ivan begins to recognize what's happening to him. Tolstoy beautifully explains how this starts to change the ways Ivan sees his world; the social network that once meant so much to him begins to mean nothing. He begins to suffer from the recognition that no one around him sees him as a person or an individual, but simply as a social role. In avoiding the subject of his death, they avoid *him,* and he feels it. How does it end for Ivan? Well, you know he dies. But does he first completely face up to his mortality? Read this short masterpiece and find out!

The Trial, by Franz Kafka

If *The Trial* had been written after writers like Sartre and Camus, it would be tempting to read it as a relatively straightforward parable reflecting the way human beings are condemned to be free; condemned to try to make sense of a world that refuses to be sensible; and, of course, condemned to death. As it is, the book is wonderfully elusive and refuses any such simple, direct interpretation. Denying its existential themes — anguish; forlornness; death; the elusiveness of answers to your most basic questions; and, most important, the fundamental absurdity of life — is difficult, however.

The predicament of *The Trial*'s protagonist, Josef K., is certainly absurd. One day, he's abruptly arrested and told he's on trial. He's never told what he's being accused of. In fact, K. is shortly allowed to go home and, despite the title, doesn't really spend any time at trial. He spends much of the book in a fruitless attempt to understand and gain access to the mechanizations of the law. He tries to hire a lawyer, but the lawyer is as unhelpful as the men who arrest him. Whatever he does, it seems, a sentence is hanging over him, and he has no way to get answers as to why or what he can do about it.

In what many consider the centerpiece of the story, a priest discusses his case with him. The priest, whom K. seemingly meets by chance, knows about his case and tells him it isn't going well. In the course of the conversation, he tells K. that K. is deluded about the nature of the law, and he tells K. a parable to help him understand. In the parable, a man from the country tries to gain admittance to an entrance to the law. A doorkeeper repeatedly refuses to let him in. The man grows old and eventually dies trying to gain access. At the end of his life, the doorkeeper tells him that this entrance was meant only for him.

This, of course, is absurd. K. objects to what he sees as the dishonesty of the doorkeeper, to which the priest responds that what matters isn't the truth of things, but their necessity. This sums up K.'s situation in many ways. He's stuck in the inexorable movement of a machine. The truth of his innocence, as well as all human truth and humanity itself, is irrelevant. All that matters is the movement of the machine.

It's worth noting at this point that Kafka himself, like K. in the story, was a bureaucrat. The world of *The Trial* is filled with nameless, faceless functionaries carrying out the perceived necessity of the system of which they're merely parts. The absurdity K. faces, then, isn't just the absurdity of life, but also the absurdity of the impersonal and absolute systems that human beings create to manage their interactions with and understanding of that life. Like the man from the country in the parable, K. is kept at arm's length from the truth he seeks by all the mechanizations of the law and all its functionaries.

But ultimately, the joy of Kafka's *The Trial* is that, like K.'s situation, the book is so inscrutable. What matters isn't so much discovering a final, true, one-to-one correspondence between its events and themes and existential notions about the nature of life. What matters are the very direct and visceral emotions it conveys and the vague sense you get from reading it that there's a very deep truth here. That truth alters your perceptions of what it means to be alive and resonates powerfully with the works of the existentialists. Fittingly enough, Kafka left *The Trial* unfinished at his death. Although you know K.'s ultimate fate, you, like he, may never fully understand it.

The Stranger, by Albert Camus

Quite simply, *The Stranger* is *the* existential novel. The lead character, Meursault, goes through life with flattened emotions. He takes great joy in physicality, whether it's making love to his lover, Marie, or going for a swim. Mostly, however, he wanders, aimless and detached. He attends his mother's funeral but doesn't cry or become upset. When asked to involve himself in a cruel scheme of revenge by a neighbor upon his girlfriend, he agrees with a morally noncommittal shrug. In the central action of the book, he walks along a beach and sees an Arab. His friends recently had a fight with some Arabs, including this one, while he was present. He could walk away, but he continues forward in a detached haze. When the Arab pulls a knife, Meursault, without really thinking or deciding to do it, pulls out a gun and shoots the man.

The Stranger is a short but rich novel. Among other things, it's about alienation and about how most of the time people wander through life without really recognizing its meaninglessness or absurdity. As the deadpan Meursault illustrates, this isn't necessarily a good thing. Only when something dramatic happens do people start to reevaluate things and see them in a different way. Meursault's transformation after killing the Arab and being sentenced to death is largely one of perception. Being in prison, he doesn't have the freedom to change the way he *lives* his life. But the way he understands and interprets life does change, as does the way he interprets the death sentence to which he has been condemned.

Many existential works deal with death, but few do so as passionately and succinctly as *The Stranger*. As Meursault faces his own death, he finally starts to understand the meaninglessness and absurdity of life. At the same time, he gains a new appreciation for living. He says he finally understands, for example, why his mother got involved with a man and made plans for marriage in the nursing home just before death. He rejects the judgment of the court not because he embraces his crime, but because he considers the court unfit to judge him. In facing his own mortality, he understands what he took from the Arab in a way the court doesn't. Perhaps nowhere is the essence of existentialism more succinctly put than in Meursault's observation concerning the priest who comes to visit him as he waits for his execution. The priest, he says, didn't know he was alive because he didn't know he was going to die. The same could be said of the court that has sentenced him.

In the end, he faces his sentence hoping only to be greeted by the "cries of hate." It's a final act of rebellion reminiscent of Camus's hero Sisyphus (see Chapter 5 for more about Sisyphus). He embraces the absurdity of his situation and, much like Sisyphus, rejects the interpretation of his situation imposed by those who have foisted it upon him. By embracing life passionately at its end, he rejects the death sentence imposed by both the court and by the universe.

No Exit, by Jean-Paul Sartre

Sartre says again and again in all his works that your choices make you who you are. You're the product of your own self-creation. Your will and creativity unite to boldly make a being that starts as nothing into something. It's a macho story of action and lone wolf individuality. You rely on no one and make of the world what you will.

The nagging problem is that after you ascend the mountaintop to stand proud and majestic, surveying all you've accomplished and all you are, one of your friends can always walk up behind you and say, "Wow, dude, you really look kinda goofy in those shorts." You're constantly defining and interpreting the world before you, but for other people, you're not the center of the universe; you're just one more object in their universe to be interpreted and defined. Yet you live among them, you both need and want to interact with them, and you crave and desire their love and approval. But as soon as you seek them, you put yourself in jeopardy by making yourself (or allowing them to make you) into an object.

This is the existential dilemma posed by Sartre's play *No Exit.* The three characters, Garcin, Estelle, and Inez, are in hell. At the beginning of the play, Garcin is brought to a simple drawing room where all the action takes place. Inez and then Estelle soon follow, and the three characters engage in an extended conversation in which they fluctuate in their allegiances and affections, at turns seeking validation from one or the other companion, accepting and then rejecting each other's approaches. The recurring theme is that people need and want validation from one another but are fundamentally separated and incapable of getting it. As Garcin puts it in the play's most famous line:

> So this is hell. I'd never have believed it. You remember all we were told about the torture chambers, the fire and brimstone, the "burning marl." Old wives' tales! There's no need for red-hot pokers. Hell is other people!

What makes *No Exit* a masterpiece is the way it takes grand psychological and existential themes and has them play out in a way that, despite the eccentric storyline, is essentially familiar. The intimacy of the characters' conversations at times seems strange for characters who have just met, but the emotions they express are thoroughly familiar. You can feel for these characters because you understand their needs and disappointments. Sartre may be wrong, and there may indeed be a way to bridge the gap between two consciousnesses, each trying to define itself. But it's certainly not easy, and *No Exit* is a brilliant explication of the perils you face when trying.

The Blood of Others, by Simone de Beauvoir

The Blood of Others may be subtitled *Exit This Way*. Whereas Sartre is convinced that human relationships are inherently frustrated by needs that can't be met (see the section on his book *No Exit* earlier in this chapter), de Beauvoir is convinced that your relationships with others are essential to your freedom and its expression. She explains this philosophically in *The Ethics of Ambiguity* but illustrates and communicates it brilliantly in this masterpiece of fiction.

The story concerns two main characters, Jean and Helene. Jean is a young bourgeois who can't bear the weight of responsibility that all people bear for their actions. He runs from this responsibility, particularly in the realm of politics; after a friend dies in a police raid on their Communist meeting, he becomes neutral and apolitical. When the Germans invade Paris, however, he finds he can no longer run away, and he joins the French Resistance. Helene is a passionate free spirit. She considers herself to be someone who never thinks of others, but in reality, she finds herself living through her lovers. She is likewise shaken by the invasion and eventually gets involved in the Resistance.

On one level, the book is about how these two people learn to live authentic lives by taking full responsibility for their choices. But it's deeper than that, because it's also about how others must be involved in those choices. Sartre believed that people *always* experience one another as objects and that this is inherently destructive of their freedom. *The Blood of Others* reflects de Beauvoir's insight that although we can see one another as objects (and this is oppressive and destructive to each of us), it isn't the only possible way for us to interact.

Even de Beauvoir's use of pronouns heightens your awareness of the ambiguous nature of our relationships. The book itself vacillates between Jean's first-person voice and an impersonal third-person perspective. Within Jean's narration, he wavers between the pronoun *you* (as though he were speaking directly to Helene) and third-person pronouns such as *she*. This mimics elements of the action later in the story. When Jean chooses to engage in sabotage, he does so knowing the Germans will respond by killing innocent French prisoners. In this case, Jean is choosing death for these people, and their wishes or choices play no part. In that sense, he's objectifying them in his attempt to foil the Germans.

But as Jean finally learns to accept, his role as leader isn't *just* a matter of choosing by himself to risk and sacrifice others. When it comes to the lives of his comrades working in the Resistance, the situation is significantly different from the case of the innocent prisoners. Those people in the Resistance choose, for their own reasons, to align themselves with him and to make their sacrifices. Interacting with these people in a way that doesn't turn them into objects is not only possible, but also essential. They freely choose to join the Resistance and sacrifice their lives, which allows him to bring his own project to fruition. Likewise, his free choice to make use of them allows them to fulfill their convergent goals.

When presented like this, it all sounds very obvious. But the truth is, people often have trouble recognizing and affirming the free choices of others. We fall into treating people as objects out of selfishness, thoughtlessness, or even (as is the case with Jean) an overdeveloped sense of responsibility. Both Helene and Jean slowly develop a recognition of their need for others on multiple levels. In the end, this recognition frees them.

Waiting for Godot, by Samuel Beckett

Vladimir and Estragon, the main characters in Samuel Beckett's tragicomic play *Waiting for Godot,* do nothing. They sit. They talk. They wait. And while they wait, they try to pass the time. They're aided in this attempt by the passing Pozzo and his servant, Lucky. In the first act, Lucky entertains them by dancing and thinking. (Yes, thinking.) In the second act, Pozzo is blind and Lucky is dumb. They don't remember meeting Vladimir and Estragon the night before. At the end of each act, a boy appears and tells the characters that Godot won't be arriving today but will definitely be here tomorrow.

Much of the action of the play is repetitious and absurd. You never find out who Godot is or why they wait for him, but they seem unable to stop waiting even when they try. Indeed, they often decide upon a course of action only to remain immobile. They consider suicide to escape the emptiness of their endless wait but decide against it principally because they don't have effective rope. Estragon repeatedly suggests they leave but is reminded by Vladimir that they can't because they're waiting for Godot.

Waiting for Godot doesn't line up point for point with any existential philosophy, but it raises fundamental existential questions and problems that all the existential philosophies attempt to address. The play explicitly has the characters recognize that they represent all humanity. Godot is traditionally interpreted as being God, but even this is open to debate. Beyond that, the play is wonderfully open to interpretation and, at the same time, resistant to any single interpretation. Much of its significance lies in its evocative nature and ability to elicit a direct emotional recognition of desolation, anguish, and forlornness.

Still, a lot of what's going on is worth noticing. Here are some things to notice and questions to ask yourself while reading it or seeing it performed:

- ✔ Is meaningful action impossible in a world without God, or is meaningful action impossible only while you're waiting for God, while you continue to look to an absent God to supply your meaning?

- ✔ Why do Vladimir and Estragon decide that suicide is an appropriate response to their situation? Is it? In the end, of course, they don't go through with it. Why are they unable even to perform this act of surrender?

- ✔ Estragon identifies himself with Adam. Where's Eve, and would they be better off with her around to pick some apples?

- ✔ Who are Pozzo and Lucky, and why are they there?

- ✔ For all the absurdity of the play, do you see something familiar here? In what sense are you like Vladimir and Estragon?

Interview with the Vampire, by Anne Rice

When it came out in 1976, *Interview with the Vampire* redefined and reawakened the vampire subgenre. It tells the story of Louis, a 200-year-old vampire in search of meaning. The most groundbreaking thing about the book is the way it humanizes the vampire, making it psychologically and spiritually normal, rather than some bestial creature of pure desire or a half-alive shade of pure evil.

Transformed in this way, the vampire ceases to be a mere external threat or some powerful force of sexuality and violence that the human characters must survive. Rice's work allows you to step directly into the vampire world and develop the vampire story from the inside out. In *Interview,* she uses this device brilliantly to tell of an existential search for meaning.

The story begins and ends in New Orleans. Louis tells how he was turned into a vampire by the flamboyant, callous, and thoroughly amoral Lestat. Believing the tales he's always heard, he naturally assumes that he has become a creature of pure evil. He quickly finds, however, that he still has a conscience, and he can pick up crosses freely and take a bath in holy water if he wants.

This drives Louis crazy. He's a moral vampire, horrified by what he has become. Surely, he feels, something as traumatic and terrible as becoming a vampire must have an obvious meaning. Surely now that he has become a supernatural creature, he must have some kind of direct knowledge, or at least direct sense, of God and the Devil, good and evil.

But this isn't the case. As his "father" Lestat repeatedly tries to teach him, there is no meaning. Louis, Lestat believes, should learn to enjoy the power and decadence of vampirism with the same relish that he does. But this isn't an option for the pensive Louis. He resists Lestat's tutelage, tries to survive on the blood of animals, and continues to question. Eventually, after being subjected to many of Lestat's sadistic and manipulative schemes, Louis breaks from the man who made him a vampire and goes in search of answers. But of course, he never finds any. Everyone he meets is just trying to fill the huge void of eternity — with knowledge; with love; with destruction; or, in one of the book's most prevalent themes, with beauty. The book is beautifully sensuous and drips with eroticism and passion for the physicality of the characters and their surroundings.

Using vampires instead of humans to describe the human search for meaning allows Rice to shift perspective in two ways:

- ✔ **The vampire point of view:** Like the movie *Blade Runner* (see Chapter 15), *Interview* brilliantly uses nonhuman characters to help you take a fresh look at very human questions and problems. The vampires look at human beings from a vantage point you generally don't have access to and are able to see truths that people often miss when seeing things from the ground level, so to speak.

- ✔ **Awakening your inner vampire:** Vampires, when they're turned, wake to a new world. Their senses are heightened; they see things they never saw before. Similarly, when you look at the vampires struggling with very human issues, the drama and intensity of the vampire mythology color and heighten your perceptions. That drama awakens you to the powerful mystery and significance of existence, something you normally take for granted. Rice's powerfully provocative prose is particularly adept at doing this.

The book also includes a wonderful convergence of existential and vampiric themes. Take, for example the following:

- ✔ **Death becomes them:** Existentialists aren't concerned with just the meaning of life, but also with the meaning of life given the reality of death. Because death isn't inevitable for vampires, they're a perfect medium for exploring the significance death and how its presence or absence affects the value of a life. All vampire stories are about death. They kill others to stay alive, but more important, vampires are the *un*dead. They're defined by what they are *not*. By redefining and putting into question what it means to be *un*dead, Rice simultaneously raises the question of what it means to be alive.

✓ **Sensuality versus the eternal:** Traditional philosophic and religious systems sharply divide the realm of the eternal and the temporal. We here in the dirt on earth are separated in a fundamental way from the perfection of mathematics, God's heaven, and everything eternal. The existentialists try to refocus not just attention, but value, on earth. Nietzsche in particular is keen on instigating a wholesale transformation of values that would extol the natural world, as the only world available to extol. (Chapter 3 talks about this in more detail.) Louis's transformation is a wonderful allegory for this transformation of perspective. When he becomes a vampire, when he becomes eternal, he finds that it doesn't lead to any grand revelation of truth. He finds there's nothing more to existence than the world as he knows it. The eternal *is* the temporal, only longer. Yet his perception of that world is heightened, and he's able to see it more vividly and intensely than ever before. If he could embrace what he sees there, as Lestat does, his existential transformation would be complete.

Rice wasn't trying to write an existential novel. At the time she wrote *Interview,* she says, she *thought* she was an atheist, and those themes seeped into the novel. But like any good writer, she's able to find the universal in her personal concerns. The result is a brilliant explication, whether intentional or not, of central existential questions and themes.

Run with the Hunted, by Charles Bukowski

If one of the misanthropic characters from an existential novel got up and walked around in real life, he'd probably look a lot like Charles Bukowski. Bukowski was one of America's greatest and most controversial poets and novelists. Alienated, alcoholic, lonely, poor, and even homeless for long stretches of his life, he wrote semi-autobiographically about the world he lived in, a world of flophouses and bars, racetracks and menial jobs, prisons, hospitals, and graveyards. Oh, and libraries. Being homeless and/or unemployed much of his life, he spent vast quantities of time in them, reading voraciously without guidance or structure, bias or preconception.

A literary man without pedigree, Bukowski didn't write about an existential perspective; he lived it. He once said of Camus that he wrote about death like a man who had just had a fine steak dinner. In his late middle age, he became famous and successful, but for much of his life, there were few steak dinners for Charles Bukowski.

Run with the Hunted is a posthumous collection of his short stories, poems, and excerpts from his novels, arranged "chronologically" — not in the order he wrote them, but in the order of the period of his life from which they're taken. The result is a fictionalized biography, a literary portrait of the man as he re-created himself in his work. It's an act of self-creation, and in that there is, of course, some artifice. But what strikes the reader is the degree to which his writing is raw, unvarnished, and uncolored by romanticism or apology. In true existential fashion, he stubbornly refuses to look away from the world as it is. What emerges is a kind of existential saint, one who adheres to no moral code but who consistently acts in what Sartre calls "good faith," seeing the world and acting within it in a way that's totally honest and doesn't abdicate responsibility.

The world he presents isn't one you'd normally call pretty, but it's often beautiful despite Bukowski's refusal to doll it up. His characters and situations all have an immediacy and an intense humanity. Many of his poems read almost like personal letters, and you get the rare experience of feeling a direct, unadorned connection to the writer and, ironically, to all humanity and our shared human condition.

Bukowski certainly has his nihilistic tendencies, which would place him in direct opposition to the existentialists. Much of his work is deeply cynical, even resigned. But poems like "Nirvana" and "The World's Greatest Loser" help illuminate, in a way no philosophy (and perhaps no novel) could, the beauty and wonder that you can see in this imperfect world when you accept it as it is without falsifying it or romanticizing it, and without hiding its scars or justifying its ugliness in terms of some more perfect world of which it is a part.

Bukowski arranged for his tombstone to read simply, "Don't try." Acceptance or surrender? Maybe a bit of both.

Index

• *Numerics* •

10 existentialist movies, 325–339
10 existentialist themes, 12
10 existentialist works of literature, 341–354
17th Century, philosophy in, 299
18th Century
    origins of existentialism, 11–12
    origins of utilitarianism, 35
    philosophy in, 299
19th Century
    branches of philosophy in, 299–301
    development of existentialism, 9–12, 39
    dismissal of existentialism, 297–298
    as period of radical change, 15–16
20th Century, existentialism in, 11–12, 297–298
9/11 terrorist attacks, 28, 32

• *A* •

absolute paradox of faith, 229–230
absolute systems
    bigotry as, 307–308
    nature of, 27–29
    rationalism as, 30–36
    rejecting traditional answers to, 43–45
    religion as, 37–40
    science as, 40–43
    as theme in literature, 343–344
abstract thought, reason and, 31
absurdity
    Camus on, 20, 74, 102–104
    central truths of, 95–98
    conceptions of, 75–76
    defined, 74–75
    as existentialist theme, 12, 73–74
    irrationality in the world, 76–80
    as Kierkegaard theme, 16–17
    making sense of, 86
    as movie theme, 337–338
    religion and, 204
    of suicide, 100–102, 162
    as theme in literature, 342, 345–347, 350–351
    of trying to impose order, 80–85
active versus passive choices, 134–135
Adams, Douglas, 115

addiction/addictive behavior, 83–85, 154–158,
    201, 215, 320, 335–336
aesthetic stages of self (aestheticism), 210–216
affirmative action, 308
Alda, Alan, 331
alienation
    and anxiety toward life, 66
    as emotion, 53
    as existentialist theme, 12
    as movie theme, 330–331
    oppression and, 306–308
    science as source of, 43
    as theme in literature, 347
Allen, Woody, 331
American philosophy. *See* philosophy
analytical philosophy, 298–301
anecdotes
    about the icon for, 6
    on absurdity, 77–78
    on anxiety, 63–64, 70
    on finding meaning to life, 82
    on making choices, 39, 171–172
    on power and completeness, 253
    on reason and absolute systems, 31–32
    on resentment, 260–261
    on self-deception, 262
    on watching life go by, 138
anguish, 3, 16–17. *See also* anxiety/angst/dread
anonymity, 149
antipathetic sympathy, 70–71
anti-Semitism, 280–284, 307–308
anxiety quiz, 66
anxiety/angst/dread
    determining the meaning of, 63–65
    distinguishing fear from, 61–63
    as existentialist theme, 12, 47–48, 60–61
    in facing death, 185–186
    feelings of freedom, 68–70
    feelings of nothingness, 65–68
    Kierkegaard on, 72
    as love-hate relationship, 70–71
    as movie theme, 331–332
    psychology and, 312
    as theme in literature, 345–346, 350–351
Apocalypse Now (movie), 246
Apology (Plato), 150
approximation/appropriation, 147–148

Aristotle, 13, 78
art, existentialist themes in, 4, 12
assumptions, about existentialists, 3–4
atheist existentialism
 as dominant strain, 20
 at odds with the church, 44–45
 as rejection of religion, 1
 using reason in, 32
attachment versus detachment, 51–52
Authenitic Happiness (Seligman), 314
authenticity
 central truths of, 95–98
 connection to genuineness, 87–88
 conscience is a nag to, 186–191
 of death, 182
 desirability of, 88–89
 determining a template or standard for, 89–90
 essential authenticity, 94–95
 as existentialist theme, 12, 86–87, 179–180
 in facing death, 185–186
 Heidegger treatment of, 18–19, 125, 129–130
 importance of time, 191–201
 Kierkegaard on, 234
 as movie theme, 328–329
 rejecting, 93–94, 98–103
 Rogers' theories on, 316–319
 of the self, 204–210
 of suicide, 102
 as theme in literature, 344–345
 understanding, 90–93
avoiding confusion, warnings on
 on anxiety, 64–65
 being alert to icons to, 6
 on death, 182
 existentialism, 305
 on individuality, 245
 on living passionately, 134–135
 on nihilism, 45
 on Platoism and Christianity, 33
 on time, 199
 on truth, 147
awaiting versus anticipation, 196

Bartleby the Scrivener (Melville), 101
"be"/"being," 60. *See also* conscience/will; self
Beckett, Samuel, 350–351
"becoming" versus "being," 238
befindlichkeit, 56
behaviorism, 310, 312
Being and Nothingness (Satre), 18, 19
Being and Time (Heidegger), 18, 112, 298

"being-in-the-world," 116–124, 314–316
Bergman, Ingmar, 327
beyond good and evil. *See* good and evil
Beyond Good and Evil (Nietzsche), 32
bigotry, 307–308
black existential philosophy, 306–307
Blade Runner (1982), 330–331
The Blood of Others (de Beauvoir), 349–350
Brando, Marlon, 328
British philosophy. *See* philosophy
The Brothers Karamazov (Dostoyevsky), 233
Buber, Martin, 20
Bukowski, Charles, 353

• **C** •

Cage, Nicolas, 332
Camus, Albert, 292
 on absurdity, 74, 102
 death of, 298
 early life and background, 20
 literature of, 347
 on mystery and risk, 141
 politics of, 290–296
 on suicide, 1, 102
capitalism, 291–292
Carter, Helen Bonham, 335
Categorical Imperative, principle of, 176
Catholic Church, 27, 32
Cera, Michael, 338
choice. *See also* freedom (freedom of man)
 active versus passive, 134–135
 creates self-definition, 190
 freedom means having, 159–163
 "Is that worth dying for?" is a, 138–140
 as Kierkegaard theme, 16–17
 in light of death, 183–186
 as movie theme, 331–335
 mystery and risk of, 140–142
 as theme in literature, 342, 349–350
Christianity. *See also* religion
 in absolute systems, 27–29
 Kierkegaard and, 15–16, 145
 lack of faith, 231–234
 Nietzsche on, 32
 reconciling existentialism with, 20
 as religion of hate, 265
 role in the death of God, 40–43
 role of reason in, 32–35
 Satre and, 19
 in a slave life, 263–264
 stages of development, 37–39
Churchill, Winston, 172

circumspection, 123–124
civil rights, 308
Communism, 278, 291–296
completeness, 253
complexity, scientific method and, 41
Concept of Anxiety (Kierkegaard), 72
Confucianism, 21
conscience/will. *See also* the self
   choices and limitations, 189–191
   as existentialist theme, 180
   facing guilt, 188–189
   is you talking to you, 187–188
   to live authentically, 186–187
   reason and, 30
   religion and, 204
   as theme in literature, 351–353
consciousness, 169–172, 330–331
consequences, 175, 331–332
conspiracy theories, 83
consumerism, 268, 335–336
contemporary existentialism, 21
Continental philosophy, 298–301, 305
Copernicus, Nicolaus, 38, 299
Coppola, Francis Ford, 328
The Corsair (tabloid), 154
cowardice/courage
   individual responsibility and, 149–150
   as response to anxiety, 312
   Satre on, 160–162, 173
   of the self, 241–242
Crime and Punishment (Dostoyevsky), 246
Crimes and Misdemeanors (1989), 331–332
crowd conformity
   Kierkegaard on, 148–151
   living nobly versus, 245–246
   loss of self-control to, 258–259
   as movie theme, 335–336, 338–339
   Nietzsche on, 269–270
   rejecting individuality, 264–268
curiousity, 129, 173

Dante Alighieri, 265
Dasien, theory of, 11, 118–119
Dawkins, Richard, 40
de Beauvoir, Simone
   early life and background, 20
   feminism and, 298
   literature of, 349–350
   politics of, 273, 290

death. *See also* "God is Dead"
   Camus on, 20, 107, 294–296
   as existentialist theme, 3, 12, 179
   Heidegger on, 18–19
   is a choice, 162–163
   "Is that worth dying for?," 138–140
   as key to life, 180–186
   as movie theme, 326–328, 337–338
   as theme in literature, 342, 344–347, 349–353
The Death of Ivan Ilych (Tolstoy), 344–345
decision-making. *See* choice; freedom
definitions
   absurdity, 74–75
   existentialism, 1–2, 13
   representing authenticity, 92
   theory of the forms, 33–35
democracy, 28
demonic desire, 197
Der Spiegel, 289
Descartes, René, 124, 169
desires. *See also* individuality
   choice and change impacts, 239–244
   in an ethical life, 217–221
   in life of a noble, 245–254
   in life of a slave, 258
   Nietzsche on, 236–239
   objectivity does not reflect, 49
   sin is giving in to, 226
   tips to understanding, 213
   of worldly authenticity, 93–94, 100
despair, 204, 207–210
detached existence, 51–52
detachment versus attachment, 51–52
discrimination, 308
Divine Comedy (Dante), 265
dogma, 249–251, 343
Donald Trump Effect, 43
Dostoyevsky, Fyodor, 233, 246, 341, 343
dread. *See* anxiety/angst/dread
Dreyfus, Hubert, 155
dualism, 34
Dylan, Bob, 140

• E •

18th Century
   origins of existentialism in, 11–12
   origins of utilitarianism, 35
   philosophy in, 299
Either/Or (Kierkegaard), 214
emotions and feelings. *See also* moods
   in existentialism, 51–53
   hatred, 236, 257–264

emotions and feelings *(continued)*
  meaning of, 48
  as movie theme, 330–331
  in philosophy, 49–50
  rationalism and, 31
  as theme in literature, 347
engagement. *See* passion/engagement
epic of Gilgamesh, 11
Epicureanism, 13, 180–181
epistemology, 49
equality/equal treatment, 28, 267–268
Escher, M. C., 86
essential authenticity, 94–95
ethical stages of self (the Universal), 216–222
ethics
  in absolute systems, 28
  cultural and gender bias, 53
  in history of philosophy, 13
  as movie theme, 328–331
everyday time versus existential time, 191–194
evil
  as choice, 159, 233
  in conformity, 269–270
  existence of, 26–28
  existentialism and, 278–279
  Kierkegaard on, 214
  as movie theme, 329, 334
  in politics, 279–292
  see/hear/speak no, 43
  in slave mindset, 259–262
  in story of Abraham, 225–227
  in story of Adam, 72
  as theme in literature, 351–353
existentialism
  assumptions about, 3–4
  choosing how to start, 6
  conventions in this book, 2–3
  in literature, 341–354
  in the movies, 325–339
  organization of topics, 4–5
  philosophies of oppression, 306–308
  philosophy and, 9–12, 297–302
  postmodernism and, 302–305
  psychology and, 309–314
"Existentialism Is a Humanism" (Satre), 19, 157
existentialists
  assigning a label to, 2–3
  contemporary philosophers as, 21
  introduction to the early, 15–20
  literature and, 343
experimentation, scientific method and, 41
explanatory power, scientific method and, 41

• F •

facticity, 160–161
facts, existentialist interpretation of, 41–42
faith
  absolute paradox of, 229–230
  contemporary lack of, 231–234
  of the existential hero, 231
  Kant philosophy on, 36
  in Kierkegaard themes, 16–17
  as movie theme, 330–331
  theist existentialism and, 20
  "What is?," 223–229
falling, 127–130, 200–201
false absolutes, 296
false beliefs, 239–240
Farrow, Mia, 331
Fascism, 283–284
fatalism, 60, 78, 172–173
fate/destiny, 78–79
fear, distinguishing anxiety from, 61–63
Fear and Trembling (Kierkegaard), 94, 337
feminism, 20, 298, 306–307
Ferrell, Will, 337
Figgis, Mike, 332
Fight Club (1999), 335–336
finite self, 205–207
Ford, Harrison, 330
forgetting, 197–198
for-itself, 11
forlornness, 171–172
  as existentialist theme, 12
  as Kierkegaard theme, 16–17
  as movie theme, 331–332
  as theme in literature, 345–346, 350–351
forms, Plato's theory of the, 11, 33–35
Frankl, Victor, 314, 319–322
freedom (freedom of man)
  creates meaning and value, 172–178
  existence precedes essence, 164–167
  as existentialist theme, 157–158
  Kierkegaard on, 133–134
  psychology and, 312–313
  relationship of anxiety to, 68–70
  as theme in literature, 345–346
  what it means, 158–163
  whether you like it or not, 167–172
French existentialists
  on death of God, 43
  friendships among, 273
  names and main ideas of, 19–20
  politics of, 290–296
Freud, Sigmund, 310, 314

friends/friendship
  authenticity in, 93
  choosing to become, 219, 221–222
  creating superficial, 155–156
  in hierarchy of needs, 318
  losing self-control to, 265–266, 268
  as movie theme, 338–339
  of the noble person, 255–257
future time, existing in, 195–196

• G •

Galilei, Galileo, 38, 299
Gandhi, Mohandas, 106, 292
The Gay Science (Nietzsche), 17, 25
The Genealogy of Morals (Nietzsche), 253
genuineness, 87–88
Ghost Dog (movie), 39
Gilgamesh, epic of, 11
God, existence of
  atheist versus theist views on, 20
  Garden of Eden story, 72
  imposing order by belief in, 78–79
  as movie theme, 327–328
  Nietzsche on, 25–26
  notion of heaven and hell, 265
  Paley on, 166
  proving, 230
  reason and, 30–36
  religion and, 37–40
  Satre on, 165
  science and the, 40–43
  as theme in literature, 350–351
The God Delusion (Dawkins), 40
"God is Dead"
  how to find out if, 4–5
  as movie theme, 330–331
  Nietzsche declaration of, 17–18
  what have you lost if, 43–45
  what is the meaning of, 26–29
"God-given rights," 28
good and evil, 22, 72, 159, 233, 269–270, 283–284, 329
"The Grand Inquisitor" (Dostoyevsky), 233
grand unified theory, 41
guilt, 16–17, 188–189
Gyllenhaal, Maggie, 337

• H •

Hamlet (Shakespeare), 342
happiness
  in an ethical life, 217, 221
  as an everyday mood, 59–60
  in life of a noble, 250–252
  in life of a slave, 264
  meaning of, 35
  versus a meaningful life, 35
  Nietzsche on, 237
  in a religious life, 233
hatre-crimes, 308
hatred. *See* emotions and feelings
hedonism, 268, 344–345
Heidegger, Martin
  on authenticity, 129–130
  on "being-in-the-world," 124–129
  on death, 180–182
  early life and background, 18–19
  on living an existential life, 120–124
  on meaning of human existence, 112–116
  on moods, 55–60
  Nazism and, 286–289
  on relationships, 156
  Satre as pupil of, 15–16
  theory of *Dasien*, 11, 118–119
Heraclitus, 238
herd mentality. *See* crowd conformity
hierarchy of needs, Maslow's, 318
Hill, Jonah, 338
history of existentialism
  addressing past and present in, 3
  philosophy and the, 13–14
  secularization of society in, 9–10
The Hitchhiker's Guide to the Galaxy (Adams), 115
Hitler, Adolph, 280–281
honesty quiz, 139
"How is it going?," 55–56
"How *should* I live?," 1
human condition
  Camus on, 74
  emotions and feelings, 52–53
  Frankl on, 320
  Kierkegaard on, 16
  in literature, 342
  Satre on, 159, 163, 167
human existence
  analyzing life with science, 114–115
  analyzing the experience of life, 115–116
  embracing death, 180–186
  finding a cause worth living, 136–142
  finding meaning and value, 1–2, 9–12, 313
  Heidegger on, 19, 111
  investigating the meaning of, 112–113
  investigating your own, 113–114
  living as a basic choice of, 161–163
  as movie theme, 335–336
  in Nietzsche themes, 18
  role of conscience/willself, 186–191

human existence *(continued)*
Satre on, 164–167
as theme in literature, 347, 350–353
human nature, 84, 158–165, 172–173, 176
human perspective, 80–86, 171
humanism, 19, 29, 157
"The Humanism of Existentialism" (Satre), 157
humanistic movement in psychology, 309–314
Hume, David, 141, 238
Hurricane Katrina, 28, 32
Husserl, Edmund, 18, 115
Huston, Angelica, 331
Huston, Anglica, 331

• I •

"I think, therefore I am.," 124, 169
icons, use and meaning of, 5–6
identity. *See* individuality
idle talk, 129, 156
Ikiru (1952), 326–327
immediacy, 63–65
inauthenticity, 98–103, 210–222, 307–308. *See also* authenticity
individuality. *See also* spirit; the self
crowd conformity versus, 148–151
as existentialist theme, 3, 12, 235–236
identifying who you are, 236–241
living as a noble person, 245–248
living as a slave, 257–264
living through conformity, 264–270
making choices and changes, 249–252
as movie theme, 328–331, 338–339
pursuing power as a noble, 252–257
Rogers' theories on, 316–319
understanding who you are, 241–244
Industrial Revolution, 9–10, 15–16
Inferno (Dante), 265
infinite self, 205–207
inkblot test, 85
intelligent design, 230
the Internet, 155–156
interpretation, 18–19
Interview with the Vampire (Rice), 351–353
inwardness, 134–135
irrationalism
Camus on, 74
Heidegger treatment of, 18–19
human perspective as, 80–86
importance to existentialism, 11
theist existentialism and, 20
trying to make sense of, 76–80
"It's Alright Ma" (Dylan), 140

• K •

Kafka, Franz, 341, 345
Kant, Immanuel
Categorical Imperative, 176
on God and religion, 35–36
on morality, 53
on science and religion, 301
Kierkegaard, Michael, 16–17
Kierkegaard, Søren
on anxiety, 70–72
on Christianity, 231–234
early life and background, 16–17, 228
on passion and truth, 131–132, 142–153
relationship with media, 153–156
King, Martin Luther, 106
Kurosawa, Akira, 326

• L •

Landau, Martin, 331
Law of Universal Gravitation, 30–31
Leaving Las Vegas (1995), 332–333
Les Tempes Modernes, 290, 294–295
Lessing, Gotthold, 141
liberation theology, 306–307
literature
contemporary existentialism in, 21
existentialist themes in, 4, 12, 341
origins of existentialism in, 11–12, 20
literature, existentialist
The Blood of Others (de Beauvoir), 349–350
The Death of Ivan Ilych (Tolstoy), 344–345
Hamlet (Shakespeare), 342
Interview with the Vampire (Rice), 351–353
No Exit (Satre), 348
Notes from the Underground (Dostoyevsky), 343–344
The Rebel (Camus), 104, 294–295
Run with the Hunted (Bukowski), 353–354
The Stranger (Camus), 20, 347
The Trial (Kafka), 345–346
Waiting for Godot (Beckett), 350–351
logical fallacy, 149
logotherapy, 319–322

• M •

Macy, William, 33
Maguire, Toby, 33
Man's Search for Meaning (Frankl), 320
Marcel, Gabriel, 20, 141

Marxism, 19, 291–296
Maslow, Abraham, 311, 314, 318
Mathematical Principles of Natural Philosophy
    (Newton), 299
The Matrix (movie), 68
meaning of human life
  in absolute systems, 27–29
  Camus on, 20
  central component of, 313
  existence of God and, 25–29
  finding a how-to guide to, 5
  finding a passion for, 131–132
  finding answers to, 9–12
  Frankl's theories on, 319–322
  in Heidegger themes, 19
  Kant philosophy on, 35–36
  as movie theme, 335–336
  in Nietzsche themes, 18
  nihilism and, 45
  philosophy and the, 13–14
  Platoism on, 32–35
  pursuit of inner power for, 252–257
  rejecting traditional answers to, 1–2
  suicide and, 100–102
  as theme in literature, 351–353
  when God is dead, 43–45
meaning-giving narratives, 27–30
meaninglessness of life
  Camus on, 103–104, 107
  in literature, 347
  as movie theme, 328
  Nietzsche on, 26
  nihilism and, 304
  opening Pandora's Box to, 173–174
  Satre on, 295
media and technology, 153–156. *See also*
    literature; movies
mediocrity. *See* crowd conformity
Meditations (Descartes), 124, 169
Melville, Herman, 101
Merleau-Ponty, Maurice, 290, 292
Middle Ages, existentialism in, 11–12
Milton, John, 11
Mintz-Pease, Christopher, 338
monotheism, 27
moods
  anxiety/angst/dread as, 60–72
  basic types of, 54, 59–60
  disclosing how you exist, 54–56
  as insight into your life, 56–57
  as a way of existing, 58–59
moral conscience. *See* conscience/will; the self
morality
  of crowd conformity, 267–269
  existentialism and, 277

Kierkegaard on, 145
living as a noble, 246
living as a slave, 263
as movie theme, 325, 328–329, 329, 331, 333
Nietzsche on, 259–260
Satre on, 44
as theme in literature, 351–354
mortality, 161–163
movies
  existential 10, 325–326
  contemporary existentialism and, 21
  existentialist themes in, 4, 12
movies, existentialist themes in
  Blade Runner (1982), 330–331
  Crimes and Misdemeanors (1989), 331–332
  Fight Club (1999), 335–336
  Ghost Dog, 39
  Ikiru (1952), 326–327
  Leaving Las Vegas (1995), 332–333
  The Matrix, 68
  Pleasantville (1998), 333–334
  The Seventh Seal (1957), 327–328
  The Shawshank Redemption, 140
  Stranger Than Fiction (2006), 337–338
  Superbad (2007), 338–339
"The Myth of Sisyphus" (Camus), 74, 102–104

• *N* •

Nagel, Thomas, 116
narratives
  belief in God, 27, 32, 37–39, 43–44
  bigotry, 307–308
  in existentialism, 12
  explaining everything through, 27–30
  in literature, 342–343
  meaning-giving, 12, 44–45
  as movie theme, 337–339
  postmodernism, 302–305
  science skepticism of, 40
The National Enquirer (tabloid), 154
nationalism, 282–283
Nazism, 279–289
neighbor, love thy, 32, 37
neighbor-lovers, 255–256, 268
Newton, Isaac, 13, 30–31, 42, 299
Nietzsche, Elizabeth, 280–281
Nietzsche, Friedrich
  on dead of God, 25–26
  early life and background, 17–18
  as founder of existentialism, 297–298
  Nazism and, 279–286
  politics of, 273–274
  views of the self, 235–236

nihilism, 45, 304, 330–331, 353–354. *See also* surrender
9/11 terrorist attacks, 28, 32
19th Century
   branches of philosophy in, 299–301
   development of existentialism, 9–12, 39
   dismissal of existentialism, 297–298
   as period of radical change, 15–16
"Nirvana" (Bukowski), 354
No Exit (Satre), 348
noble friend, 256
noble person
   dealing with choices and change, 249–252
   defined, 245–246
   Nietzsche on, 235–236
   pursuit of inner power, 252–257
   view of self, 247
   view of slave life, 248
Norton, Edward, 335
"not be". *See* conscience/will; the self
Notes from the Underground (Dostoyevsky), 343–344
nothingness, 65–68
nullities (limitations), 189

• O •

object versus subject, living as, 134–135
objective rationality. *See* rationalism
objective truth, 143–147, 239, 302, 306
observation, scientific method and, 41
Olsen, Regina, 16, 228
oppression, 258–259, 306–308
optimism
   of existentialism, 43, 104, 305
   as movie theme, 326–327, 332–335, 337–338
   Nietzsche on, 17
   Satre on, 157–158, 167, 172, 174–175

• P •

paganism, 28, 37, 145
pain, 16–17, 205, 237, 242, 258–259, 263–264, 268
Paley, William, 166
Pandora's Box, 173
Parmenides, 238
participatory existence, 51–52
passion/engagement
   as existentialist theme, 3, 12, 131–132
   finding a cause for, 136–142
   Kierkegaard on, 16–17
   life as a killer of, 150–156
   as movie theme, 337–338

Plato's treatment of, 30
   qualities of life for, 132–136
   truth as a way of living, 142–150
past time, existing in, 196–199
Paul (Saint), 148
perspectivism, 239
pessimism, 172, 251
Phaedrus (Plato), 50
phenomenology, 115–116, 311
philosophical suicide, 102–104
philosophy
   American branch, 305
   of Aristotle, 78
   branches of modern, 298–301
   contemporary existentialists and, 21
   development in society, 11–14
   Epicureanism, 180–181
   existentialism as, 1–2, 9–12, 18–19
   Nietzsche on, 239
   of nihilism, 45
   relationship to existentialism, 298–305
Pink Floyd, 139, 184
Pitt, Brad, 4, 335
Plato
   on absolute systems, 27–28
   in history of philosophy, 13
   on reason, 50, 301–302
   theory of the forms, 11, 33–35
Pleasantville (1998), 333–334
poetry, 301–302, 343
points to ponder
   being alert to icons for, 6
   on circumspection, 123–124
   on crowd conformity, 151
   on *Dasien* (existing-there), 118–119
   on death, 181, 183–184
   detachment versus attachment, 51
   on freedom, 160
   on God, death of, 26
   on individuality, 246
   individuality versus conformity, 266
   on moods, 55–60
   on nothingness, 65–67
   on relationships, 156
   on science and religion, 42–43
   on time, 199
   on truth, 143, 148
   the Universal, 218–221
   "What does it all mean?," 115
   "What's the meaning of life?," 126–129
politics
   in absolute systems, 38–39
   existentialism and, 19, 273–278
   feminism and, 20

finding evil in, 278–279
French existentialists and, 290–296
Nazism, 279–289
"Portrait of an Anti-Semite" (Satre), 307–308
positive psychology movement, 314
postmodernism, 19, 302–305
power and militarism, 284
power in the noble life, 252–257
prejudice, 307–308
present time, existing in, 200–201
Protagoras, 29
psychology
    existentialism and, 309–313
    Frankl's theories on, 319–322
    Maslow's hierarchy of needs, 318
    May's theories on, 314–316
    positive psychology movement, 314
    Rogers' theories on, 316–319

• Q •

questions
    anxiety quiz, 66
    defining existentialism by, 1–2, 10
    honesty quiz, 139
    on making choices, 161
    for the reflective aesthete, 216
    on rotation method, 214
quietism, 295

• R •

racism, 282–283, 306–308
rationalism
    importance to existentialism, 11
    scientific method and, 41
    as theme in literature, 343–344
    in Western philosophy, 30
reason
    characteristics of, 30–31
    crowd conformity and, 148–151
    existentialism and, 11, 30
    finding the human element in, 31–32
    Kant philosophy on, 35–36
    in Kierkegaard themes, 16–17
    as movie theme, 330–331
    Nietzsche on, 239
    Plato on, 30, 32–35, 50, 301–302
    rejection of faith by, 229–230
    theist existentialism and, 20
    as theme in literature, 343–344
The Rebel (Camus), 104, 294–295
rebellion, 104–107

relationship
    de Beauvoir on, 349–350
    in existentialism, 49, 51, 274
    existentialism to Philosophy, 298–305
    Frankl on, 321
    with God, 20, 37, 144, 204, 221–233
    Heidegger on, 116–119
    Kierkegaard on, 145, 154
    living passionately as, 132
    May on, 314–315
    with others, 33, 155–156
    Rogers on, 317–319
    of science and religion, 40–43
    as theme in literature, 349–350
    with your own existence, 66, 124, 136–142
religion. See also Christianity
    death of God and, 37–40
    existentialism and, 15
    Kant philosophy on, 35–36
    in Kierkegaard themes, 16–17
    Nietzsche and, 17
    reason as source of, 32
    reconciling existentialism with, 20, 203–204
    rejection of traditional, 1
    science as a, 40–43
religious life
    absolute paradox of faith, 229–230
    finding inner power in, 254–255
    Kierkegaard on, 222–223
    story of Abraham, 223–229
    story of Abraham and Isaac, 231
remorse, 16–17
repetition, 198–199
representing/representation, 92, 142–144
The Republic (Plato), 301–302, 343
resentment, 257–264
responsibility
    in absolute systems, 39–40
    of being a self, 207–208
    as a burden, 175
    for choices made, 170–172
    as existentialist theme, 12
    for finding one's own answers, 43–45, 249–251
    freedom as a, 167–168
    guilt calls for, 189
    as theme in literature, 349–350, 353–354
revolutionary age, 151–153
Rice, Anne, 351
Roberson, Pat, 32
Rogers, Carl, 314, 316–319, 336
romantic relationships, 88, 140–141
romanticism, 285
rotation method, 129, 200–201
Run with the Hunted (Bukowski), 353–354

• S •

sacrifice
  meaning of, 35
  in story of Abraham, 223–234
  as theme in literature, 342
Satre, Jean-Paul
  on anti-Semitism, 307–308
  early life and background, 19–20
  existentialism defined by, 164–167
  existentialist themes of, 157–158
  freedom as condemnation, 167–172
  freedom of choice, 158–163
  importance of freedom, 172–178
  literature of, 348
  politics of, 290–296
  as pupil of Heidegger, 15–16
  theory of "for-itself," 11
school of thought, existentialism as, 2–3
science
  in absolute systems, 28
  finding truth in, 143
  as God/religion, 40–43
  Nietzsche on, 239
  scientific method, 41–43, 311
Scientific Revolution, 9–10, 15–16
Scott, Ridley, 330
The Second Sex (de Beauvoir), 20, 298
secularization of society
  Christianity and, 39–40
  existentialism and, 15–16
  19th Century, 15–16
  utilitarianism and, 35
the self. *See also* conscience/will; individuality
  aesthetic stage of, 210–216
  to be or not to be, 204–210
  ethical stage of, 216–222
  Heidegger on, 19
  Kierkegaard on, 222–223
  Nietzsche on, 235–236
  religious stage of, 222–234
self-actualization, 316–319
self-deception, 215, 236–241, 246–248, 251,
    256–264
Self-Deception For Dummies (Wiley), 182
self-love, 236, 247, 249–250, 259, 263
self-mastery, 243–244, 254–255
self-overcoming, need for, 249–251
Seligman, Martin, 314
selling out, 237
The Seventh Seal (1957), 327–328
17th Century, philosophy in, 299
sexism, 28, 157, 306–307
Shakespeare, William, 11, 342

The Shawshank Redemption (movie), 140
Sheen, Martin, 328
Shue, Elizabeth, 332
simplicity, 27, 41
Skinner, B. F., 310, 312
slave, living as a, 235–236, 248, 257–264
socialization, 319
society
  authenticity, 88–89
  crowd conformity and, 265–270
  development of philosophy in, 11–14
  ethics and cultural bias, 53, 218–221
  maintaining "the self" in, 127–129, 237–250
  Nietzsche as critic of, 17–18
  origins of feminism in, 20
  philosophies of oppression, 306–308
  religion in, 37–39, 232–233
  secularization of, 9–10, 35–36
Socrates, 13, 33, 150
sophistry, 29, 150
soul, 13–14, 34–35, 39, 50, 205–206, 253
"space" in existence and life, 118–119
spirit, 205–207, 210, 212–213, 216, 286. *See also*
    individuality
spiritual death, 9–10
Stalin, Joseph, 292
Star Magazine (tabloid), 154
Star Trek (TV series), 49, 152–153
stimmung (mood), 59
stoic philosophers, 21
Stone, Emma, 338
The Stranger (Camus), 20, 347
Stranger Than Fiction (2006), 337–338
subjective truth, 144
subjectivity, 134–135, 169–172
suffering
  coping with, 258–261
  finding significance in, 79
  meaning of, 35
suicide
  Camus on, 1
  facing absurdity by, 100–102
  Heidegger on, 182
  is a choice, 161–163
  loss of belief systems and, 9–10
  philosophical versus physical, 102–104
  as theme in literature, 342, 350–351
Superbad (2007), 338–339
superficiality, 153–156, 183
superstition, 35, 41–43
surrender, 10, 45, 105–106, 351, 354. *See also*
    nihilism
sympathetic antipathy, 70–71

• T •

technology and media, 153–156
theist existentialism
  embracing existence of God, 20
  rejection of religion and, 1
  tips to understanding, 159–161
  using reason in, 32
themes, existentialist
  addressing concerns and, 3
  in Kierkegaard, 16–17
  list of the "Top 10," 12
  in literature, 341–354
  in the movies, 325–339
  in Nietzsche, 17–18
theology. *See* Christianity; God, existence of;
    religion
third wave. *See* humanism
Thus Spoke Zarathustra (Nietzsche), 11, 85, 250,
    255–256
Tillich, Paul, 312
time
  different ways of looking at, 191–192
  everyday time, 192–193
  existential time, 193–194
  existing in future, 195–196
  existing in past, 196–199
  living in the present, 200–201
"Time" (Pink Floyd), 139, 184
tips to understanding
  about the icon for, 6
  absolute systems of thought, 29, 42
  absurdity, 75–76, 84, 102–104
  anxiety/angst/dread, 62–63
  authenticity, 87–88, 95, 130
  on "being-in-the-world," 127–129
  choice, 159–161, 171
  conscience/will/self, 187–188
  death, 181–182, 186
  existentialism as philosophy, 10
  fear, 71
  feelings and emotions, 48
  freedom, 69–70, 133–134, 159–161
  God, death of, 26–27
  human existence, 113–114
  individuality, 245
  kinds of existence, 51–52
  nihilism, 45
  the noble life, 250–252
  nothingness, 65–66
  origins of existentialism, 16–17
  participatory existence, 55

  passion/engagement, 136
  phenomenology, 115
  reason versus emotion, 52–53
  relationships, 140–141
  scientific method, 49
  time, 193, 196–197
  truth, 143, 146–150
Tolstoy, Leo, 341, 344
transcendance, 133–134
The Trial (Kafka), 345–346
truth
  in absolute systems, 28
  absurdity and, 96–98
  dealing with untruth, 148–150
  Kierkegaard on, 131–132, 138–140, 142
  Lessing on, 141
  paradox of living in, 145–148
  rejecting dogma as, 250–251
  science and the search for, 41–43
  as theme in literature, 351–353
  "What is?," 142–144
  when God is dead, 43–45
20th Century, existentialism in, 11–12, 297–298

• U •

Übermensch, 251, 283–284
understanding existentialism. *See* tips to
    understanding
the Universal, 216–222
universal truth, 30–31
untruth. *See* truth
utilitarianism, 35

• V •

value of human life
  in absolute systems, 27–29
  choices affect, 174–175
  death increases, 184–185
  finding a how-to guide to, 5
  finding answers to, 9–12
  freedom of choice and, 177–178
  in Heidegger themes, 19
  Kant philosophy on, 35–36
  as movie theme, 332–333, 333–335
  rebellion and, 105–106
  reductionist versus existentialist, 245–246
  rejecting traditional answers to, 1–2
  when God is dead, 43–45

• W •

Wagner, Richard, 283
Waiting for Godot (Beckett), 350–351
Walden Two (Skinner), 312
The Wall (Satre), 175
"Waterfall" (Escher), 86
Watson, John B., 310, 312
"What does it all mean?," 10, 115
"what" versus "how," living, 135–136
"What's the meaning of life?," 126–129
Whitaker, Forest, 39
"Who am I?," 92–98
"Why are we here?," 10
Wiley, *Self-Deception For Dummies*, 182
Witherspoon, Reese, 33
women
  feminism and, 20, 306
  sexism and, 28, 157, 306–307

the World
  choices affect, 176–177
  defined, 76–77
  everything has a function in, 78
  Heidegger on living in, 116–124
  from a human perspective, 80–86
  May's theories on, 315
  recognizing irrationality in, 79–80
  reinterpreting, 260–261
  seeing order in, 77–79
  as theme in literature, 353–354
  who you are in, 124–129
worldly authenticity. *See* authenticity
"The World's Greatest Loser" (Bukowski), 354

• Y •

"You know you're an existentialist if...," 3–4

USINESS, CAREERS & PERSONAL FINANCE

0-7645-9847-3

0-7645-2431-3

Also available:
- Business Plans Kit For Dummies
  0-7645-9794-9
- Economics For Dummies
  0-7645-5726-2
- Grant Writing For Dummies
  0-7645-8416-2
- Home Buying For Dummies
  0-7645-5331-3
- Managing For Dummies
  0-7645-1771-6
- Marketing For Dummies
  0-7645-5600-2

- Personal Finance For Dummies
  0-7645-2590-5*
- Resumes For Dummies
  0-7645-5471-9
- Selling For Dummies
  0-7645-5363-1
- Six Sigma For Dummies
  0-7645-6798-5
- Small Business Kit For Dummies
  0-7645-5984-2
- Starting an eBay Business For Dummies
  0-7645-6924-4
- Your Dream Career For Dummies
  0-7645-9795-7

HOME & BUSINESS COMPUTER BASICS

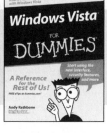

0-470-05432-8

0-471-75421-8

Also available:
- Cleaning Windows Vista For Dummies
  0-471-78293-9
- Excel 2007 For Dummies
  0-470-03737-7
- Mac OS X Tiger For Dummies
  0-7645-7675-5
- MacBook For Dummies
  0-470-04859-X
- Macs For Dummies
  0-470-04849-2
- Office 2007 For Dummies
  0-470-00923-3

- Outlook 2007 For Dummies
  0-470-03830-6
- PCs For Dummies
  0-7645-8958-X
- Salesforce.com For Dummies
  0-470-04893-X
- Upgrading & Fixing Laptops For Dummies
  0-7645-8959-8
- Word 2007 For Dummies
  0-470-03658-3
- Quicken 2007 For Dummies
  0-470-04600-7

FOOD, HOME, GARDEN, HOBBIES, MUSIC & PETS

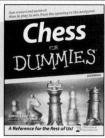

0-7645-8404-9

0-7645-9904-6

Also available:
- Candy Making For Dummies
  0-7645-9734-5
- Card Games For Dummies
  0-7645-9910-0
- Crocheting For Dummies
  0-7645-4151-X
- Dog Training For Dummies
  0-7645-8418-9
- Healthy Carb Cookbook For Dummies
  0-7645-8476-6
- Home Maintenance For Dummies
  0-7645-5215-5

- Horses For Dummies
  0-7645-9797-3
- Jewelry Making & Beading For Dummies
  0-7645-2571-9
- Orchids For Dummies
  0-7645-6759-4
- Puppies For Dummies
  0-7645-5255-4
- Rock Guitar For Dummies
  0-7645-5356-9
- Sewing For Dummies
  0-7645-6847-7
- Singing For Dummies
  0-7645-2475-5

INTERNET & DIGITAL MEDIA

0-470-04529-9

0-470-04894-8

Also available:
- Blogging For Dummies
  0-471-77084-1
- Digital Photography For Dummies
  0-7645-9802-3
- Digital Photography All-in-One Desk Reference For Dummies
  0-470-03743-1
- Digital SLR Cameras and Photography For Dummies
  0-7645-9803-1
- eBay Business All-in-One Desk Reference For Dummies
  0-7645-8438-3
- HDTV For Dummies
  0-470-09673-X

- Home Entertainment PCs For Dummies
  0-470-05523-5
- MySpace For Dummies
  0-470-09529-6
- Search Engine Optimization For Dummies
  0-471-97998-8
- Skype For Dummies
  0-470-04891-3
- The Internet For Dummies
  0-7645-8996-2
- Wiring Your Digital Home For Dummies
  0-471-91830-X

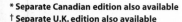
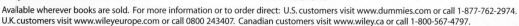
Available wherever books are sold. For more information or to order direct: U.S. customers visit www.dummies.com or call 1-877-762-2974.
U.K. customers visit www.wileyeurope.com or call 0800 243407. Canadian customers visit www.wiley.ca or call 1-800-567-4797.

WILEY

SPORTS, FITNESS, PARENTING, RELIGION & SPIRITUALITY

0-471-76871-5

0-7645-7841-3

Also available:

- Catholicism For Dummies
  0-7645-5391-7
- Exercise Balls For Dummies
  0-7645-5623-1
- Fitness For Dummies
  0-7645-7851-0
- Football For Dummies
  0-7645-3936-1
- Judaism For Dummies
  0-7645-5299-6
- Potty Training For Dummies
  0-7645-5417-4
- Buddhism For Dummies
  0-7645-5359-3

- Pregnancy For Dummies
  0-7645-4483-7 †
- Ten Minute Tone-Ups For Dummies
  0-7645-7207-5
- NASCAR For Dummies
  0-7645-7681-X
- Religion For Dummies
  0-7645-5264-3
- Soccer For Dummies
  0-7645-5229-5
- Women in the Bible For Dummies
  0-7645-8475-8

TRAVEL

0-7645-7749-2

0-7645-6945-7

Also available:

- Alaska For Dummies
  0-7645-7746-8
- Cruise Vacations For Dummies
  0-7645-6941-4
- England For Dummies
  0-7645-4276-1
- Europe For Dummies
  0-7645-7529-5
- Germany For Dummies
  0-7645-7823-5
- Hawaii For Dummies
  0-7645-7402-7

- Italy For Dummies
  0-7645-7386-1
- Las Vegas For Dummies
  0-7645-7382-9
- London For Dummies
  0-7645-4277-X
- Paris For Dummies
  0-7645-7630-5
- RV Vacations For Dummies
  0-7645-4442-X
- Walt Disney World & Orlando
  For Dummies
  0-7645-9660-8

GRAPHICS, DESIGN & WEB DEVELOPMENT

0-7645-8815-X

0-7645-9571-7

Also available:

- 3D Game Animation For Dummies
  0-7645-8789-7
- AutoCAD 2006 For Dummies
  0-7645-8925-3
- Building a Web Site For Dummies
  0-7645-7144-3
- Creating Web Pages For Dummies
  0-470-08030-2
- Creating Web Pages All-in-One Desk
  Reference For Dummies
  0-7645-4345-8
- Dreamweaver 8 For Dummies
  0-7645-9649-7

- InDesign CS2 For Dummies
  0-7645-9572-5
- Macromedia Flash 8 For Dummies
  0-7645-9691-8
- Photoshop CS2 and Digital
  Photography For Dummies
  0-7645-9580-6
- Photoshop Elements 4 For Dummies
  0-471-77483-9
- Syndicating Web Sites with RSS Feeds
  For Dummies
  0-7645-8848-6
- Yahoo! SiteBuilder For Dummies
  0-7645-9800-7

NETWORKING, SECURITY, PROGRAMMING & DATABASES

0-7645-7728-X

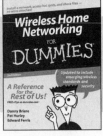
0-471-74940-0

Also available:

- Access 2007 For Dummies
  0-470-04612-0
- ASP.NET 2 For Dummies
  0-7645-7907-X
- C# 2005 For Dummies
  0-7645-9704-3
- Hacking For Dummies
  0-470-05235-X
- Hacking Wireless Networks
  For Dummies
  0-7645-9730-2
- Java For Dummies
  0-470-08716-1

- Microsoft SQL Server 2005 For Dummies
  0-7645-7755-7
- Networking All-in-One Desk Reference
  For Dummies
  0-7645-9939-9
- Preventing Identity Theft For Dummies
  0-7645-7336-5
- Telecom For Dummies
  0-471-77085-X
- Visual Studio 2005 All-in-One Desk
  Reference For Dummies
  0-7645-9775-2
- XML For Dummies
  0-7645-8845-1